Guide to American Literature from Emily Dickinson to the Present

the text of this book is printed
on 100% recycled paper

About the Authors

James T. Callow is Professor of American Literature at the University of Detroit, where he also directs the Computerized Folklore Archive. He holds a B.S.S. from John Carroll University, an M.A. from the University of Toledo, and a Ph.D. from Western Reserve University. His book *Kindred Spirits* (1967) treats the affinities between American writers and artists, as does his work on the (Old New York) Sketch Club, a project supported by the National Endowment for the Humanities. Since 1964 Dr. Callow has served on the American Literature Bibliography Committee of the Modern Language Association.

R. J. Reilly is Professor of American Literature and Literary Criticism at the University of Detroit. He holds the Ph.B. and M.A. degrees from the University of Detroit and the Ph.D. degree from Michigan State University. His essay "Henry James and the Morality of Fiction" won the Norman Foerster Award as the best essay to appear in *American Literature* in 1967, and his book *Romantic Religion* (1971) was selected by the Modern Language Association for inclusion in its Scholar's Library.

Guide to American Literature from Emily Dickinson to the Present

by

James T. Callow and Robert J. Reilly

BARNES & NOBLE BOOKS

A DIVISION OF HARPER & ROW, PUBLISHERS

New York, Hagerstown, San Francisco, London

To Lena Reilly, C. Carroll Hollis,
and Claude M. Newlin

First BARNES & NOBLE BOOKS edition published 1977

LIBRARY OF CONGRESS CATALOG CARD NUMBER: 75–39903
Hardcover edition ISBN: 0–06–480133–0
INTERNATIONAL STANDARD BOOK NUMBER: 0–06–460166–8

77 78 79 80 4 3 2 1

Contents

Abbreviations		vii
Introduction		xi
1.	Emily Dickinson	1
2.	American Humorists, 1850–1900	6
3.	Local Color	10
4.	Social Critics	22
5.	Literary Realists	27
6.	Naturalism	45
7.	Social Protest and Realism	55
8.	The Modern Temper	62
9.	Modern Poets	67
10.	Modern Novelists and Short-Story Writers	114
11.	Modern Dramatists	150
12.	Modern Literary Criticism	161
13.	Compiling and Updating Your Own Bibliography	169
General Bibliography		174
Chapter-by-Chapter Bibliographies		185
Index		261

Abbreviations

AACS	American Authors and Critics Series
AH	*American Heritage*
AI	*American Imago*
AL	*American Literature: A Journal of Literary History, Biography, Criticism, and Bibliography*
ALR	*American Literary Realism*
ALS	*American Literary Scholarship* (See chap. 13.)
AN&Q	*American Notes and Queries*
AQ	*American Quarterly*
AS	*American Speech*
ASch	*American Scholar*
Atl	*Atlantic Monthly*
ATQ	*American Transcendental Quarterly*
AWS	American Writers Series
BAL	Jacob Blanck, *Bibliography of American Literature* (See chap. 13.)
BB	*Bulletin of Bibliography*
BNYPL	*Bulletin of the New York Public Library*
BPLQ	*Boston Public Library Quarterly*
BuR	*Bucknell Review*
BUSE	*Boston University Studies in English*
CairoSE	*Cairo Studies in English*
CCC	*College Composition and Communication*
CE	*College English*
CEA	*CEA Critic*
CEAA	Center for Editions of American Authors
CHAL	*Cambridge History of American Literature*

CJF	*Chicago Jewish Forum*
CL	*Comparative Literature*
CLAJour	*College Language Association Journal*
CLQ	*Colby Library Quarterly*
CritQ	*Critical Quarterly*
DA	*Dissertation Abstracts*
DAB	*Dictionary of American Biography*
DAI	*Dissertation Abstracts International*
EAL	*Early American Literature*
EALN	*Early American Literature Newsletter* (original title of *EAL*)
EJ	*English Journal*
ELH	*Journal of English Literary History*
ELN	*English Language Notes*
ES	*English Studies*
ESQ	*Emerson Society Quarterly*
EUQ	*Emory University Quarterly*
Expl	*Explicator*
Expl Cyc	*The Explicator Cyclopedia,* ed. Charles C. Walcutt and J. Edwin Whitesell
GaR	*Georgia Review*
GB	General Bibliography (of this book)
HLB	*Harvard Library Bulletin*
HLQ	*Huntington Library Quarterly*
HudR	*Hudson Review*
JA	*Jahrbuch für Amerikastudien*
JAAC	*Journal of Aesthetics and Art Criticism*
JAF	*Journal of American Folklore*
JAH	*Journal of American History*
JAmS	*Journal of American Studies*
JEGP	*Journal of English and Germanic Philology*
JHI	*Journal of the History of Ideas*
JQ	*Journalism Quarterly*
JSH	*Journal of Southern History*
KFQ	*Keystone Folklore Quarterly*
KFR	*Kentucky Folklore Record*
KR	*Kenyon Review*
Leary	Lewis Leary, *Articles on American Literature* (See chap. 13.)
LHUS	Robert E. Spiller and others, *Literary History of the United States* (See chap. 13.)
Lud	Richard M. Ludwig, ed., *Literary History of the United States: Bibliography Supplement* (See chap. 13.)
MASJ	*Midcontinent American Studies Journal*
MFS	*Modern Fiction Studies*

MissQ	*Mississippi Quarterly*
MLN	*Modern Language Notes*
MLQ	*Modern Language Quarterly*
MLR	*Modern Language Review*
MP	*Modern Philology*
MR	*Massachusetts Review*
MS	manuscript
MTJ	*Mark Twain Journal*
MuK	*Maske und Kothurn* (Graz-Wien)
n.	note
N&Q	*Notes and Queries*
NCF	*Nineteenth-Century Fiction*
NEQ	*New England Quarterly*
NS	*Die Neueren Sprachen*
n.s.	new series
NYFQ	*New York Folklore Quarterly*
NYH	*New York History*
NYTBR	*New York Times Book Review*
PAPS	*Proceedings of the American Philosophical Society*
PBSA	*Papers of the Bibliographical Society of America*
Person	*The Personalist*
PLL	*Papers on Language and Literature*
PMASAL	*Papers of the Michigan Academy of Science, Arts, and Letters*
PMLA	*Publications of the Modern Language Association of America*
PN	*Poe Newsletter*
PNJHS	*Proceedings of the New Jersey Historical Society*
PQ	*Philological Quarterly*
PW	*Publishers' Weekly*
QJS	*Quarterly Journal of Speech*
QQ	*Queen's Quarterly*
RivEd	Riverside Editions
RLV	*Revue des Langues Vivantes* (Bruxelles)
RS	*Research Studies* (Washington State University)
SA	*Studi Americani*
SAQ	*South Atlantic Quarterly*
SB	*Studies in Bibliography*
SCB	*South Central Bulletin*
SDR	*South Dakota Review*
SFQ	*Southern Folklore Quarterly*
SIR	*Studies in Romanticism*
SLJ	*Southern Literary Journal*
SN	*Studia Neophilologica*

SNNTS	*Studies in the Novel* (North Texas State University)
SoCalQ	*Southern California Quarterly*
SoQ	*The Southern Quarterly*
SoR	*Southern Review*
SoWS	Southern Writers Series
SP	*Studies in Philology*
SR	*Sewanee Review*
SSF	*Studies in Short Fiction*
SUS	*Susquehanna University Studies*
SWR	*Southwest Review*
TCL	*Twentieth Century Literature*
TCV	Twentieth Century Views
TSE	*Tulane Studies in English*
TSL	*Tennessee Studies in Literature*
TSLL	*Texas Studies in Literature and Language*
TUSAS	Twayne's United States Authors Series
TWA	*Transactions of the Wisconsin Academy of Science, Arts, and Letters*
UKCR	*University of Kansas City Review*
UMPAW	University of Minnesota Pamphlets on American Writers
UMSE	*University of Mississippi Studies in English*
UR	*University Review*
UTQ	*University of Toronto Quarterly*
UTSE	*University of Texas Studies in English*
VMHB	*Virginia Magazine of History and Biography*
VQR	*Virginia Quarterly Review*
w.	written (Dates without w. are dates of first publication.)
WAL	*Western American Literature*
WF	*Western Folklore*
WHR	*Western Humanities Review*
WMQ	*William and Mary Quarterly*
WPHM	*Western Pennsylvania Historical Magazine*
WWR	*Walt Whitman Review*
XUS	*Xavier University Studies*
YR	*Yale Review*

Introduction

The time covered by this volume is approximately a century, from about the time of the beginning of the Civil War to the present. Our approach to the literature discussed is historical and traditional. We start with Emily Dickinson, who not only reflected her own age but also was an important forerunner of modern poetry. Next we move to the writers of the period of about 1870–1910: professional humorists such as Josh Billings and Artemus Ward; local-colorists such as Bret Harte, Sarah Orne Jewett, and Hamlin Garland; critics of the Gilded Age such as John De Forest and Henry Adams; such major realistic writers as William Dean Howells, Mark Twain, and Henry James; and such naturalistic writers as Stephen Crane, Frank Norris and Theodore Dreiser.

Next we see something of the panorama of twentieth-century literature, a body of writing truly amazing in its scope and quality. Every traditional genre is represented by writers who are unmistakably major figures and by other, later writers who seem destined for that same high praise. In drama Eugene O'Neill is, of course, preeminent, in a class by himself. In poetry, the "traditional" poetry of Robert Frost and the "new" poetry of Ezra Pound, T. S. Eliot, William Carlos Williams, and Wallace Stevens have already become classics. In fiction William Faulkner, Ernest Hemingway, and F. Scott Fitzgerald stand as the giants of the period between the two world wars, and the best works of later writers like Saul Bellow and Ralph Ellison have become contemporary classics. The broad area of literary criticism has produced such differing but excellent work as that of F. O. Matthiessen, Irving Babbitt, and John Crowe Ransom.

In all these literary areas the major intellectual currents of the time are evident, though in different forms and with different emphases: the current of naturalism or determinism (whether cultural or psychological, or both);

the current of Freudianism, or depth psychology in general; the current of existentialism, taken in its broadest sense as a rejection of traditionally accepted cultural and ethical norms. Twentieth-century American literature offers the reader God's plenty: the traditional vitality of writers such as O'Neill, Eliot, Faulkner, and Matthiessen, and the more contemporary verve of writers such as Albee, Sylvia Plath, Bellow, and Northrop Frye.

Guide to
American Literature
from Emily Dickinson
to the Present

*the text of this book is printed
on 100% recycled paper*

1
Emily Dickinson
(1830–1886)

Although scholars have found that she was influenced by the Bible, Shakespeare, Emerson, Isaac Watts's hymns, and several other sources, Emily Dickinson reigns as one of America's most original poets.

Life. Like Edward Taylor and Jonathan Edwards, Emily Dickinson belonged to the Connecticut Valley. Her birthplace and lifelong residence was Amherst, Massachusetts, where her father was a prominent lawyer. From 1847 to 1848 she attended Mount Holyoke Female Seminary at South Hadley, and though participating in a religious revival there, she managed (as in later life) to remain "unconverted." Her formal education over, she came under the informal tutelage of Benjamin F. Newton, a law clerk in her father's office. Newton helped her to widen her reading, introduced her to Emerson's poetry, and encouraged her to become a poet herself. Although her work soon reached print (the *Springfield Republican* published one of her poems as early as 1852), she was destined to become a semiprivate poet, writing for the enjoyment (and mystification) of her friends (to whom she enclosed poems in letters) and steadfastly refusing to publish a collection of her work. Only seven of her 1,775 poems were printed in her lifetime—all anonymously. While developing as a poet, Dickinson experienced several emotional crises and gradually began to withdraw from society. The causes of these crises are not clear, but certainly among them is the loss of various loved ones, including the Reverend Charles Wadsworth, Samuel Bowles (editor of the *Springfield Republican*), and Judge Otis Lord. Hyperemotional, she found the physical presence of friends such a drain that she usually kept in contact through letters. She is also said to have insisted on conversing with visitors from behind a partially closed door. Such eccentricities, coupled with her habit of dressing in white, earned her the title of the "New England nun."

Subjects and Themes.[1] Most of Dickinson's poems deal with nature, death, immortality, psychological processes (see poems J526, J701, J556, J1755, J1587, J126, J1304), love and friendship. Some of her works also qualify as definition poems (J435, J76, J650, J448), riddles (J287, J1068), and satires (J1207, J401). Her nature poetry encompasses the smallest subjects—for example, crickets and stones (J1068, J1510)—as well as the largest, including the progress of the sun and the seasons (J318, J1540, J130). While she could sometimes indulge in druidic moods (J324), at other times nature seemed alien to her (J348). Death, of course, she knew better than we who have delegated its handling to hospitals and mortuaries, and she made death the subject of more than 500 poems. Some of these contain death wishes (J160); others examine the act of dying (J1100, J547), imagine a funeral (J280), or envision existence in the casket and grave (J449, J187). She entertained marked ambivalence toward immortality throughout her life, alternating belief and doubt but achieving in her poetry an impressive sense of everlastingness if not a blessed assurance of heaven (J216).[2] Her love poems convey the most intense passions, even when dealing with the reading of a letter (J636) or the anticipation of meeting a friend (J1760). Sorrow comes from the thought of separation and bereavement (J511, J49, J640), but there is ecstasy in contemplating erotic delights (J249) or marriage to her earthly lover in heaven (J322, J664).

1. Numbers prefixed by *J* are those assigned to individual poems by editor Thomas H. Johnson in *The Complete Poems of Emily Dickinson*. Following are her best-known works exclusive of those to be analyzed separately below: J49 "I Never Lost as Much but Twice"; J76 "Exultation Is the Going"; J126 "To Fight Aloud, Is Very Brave"; J130 "These Are the Days When Birds Come Back"; J160 "Just Lost, When I Was Saved!" J187 "How Many Times These Low Feet Staggered"; J216 "Safe in Their Alabaster Chambers" (two versions); J249 "Wild Nights—Wild Nights!" J280 "I Felt a Funeral, in My Brain"; J287 "A Clock Stopped"; J288 "I'm Nobody! Who Are You?" J318 "I'll Tell You How the Sun Rose"; J322 "There Came a Day at Summer's Full"; J324 "Some Keep the Sabbath Going to Church"; J338 "I Know That He Exists"; J348 "I Dreaded That First Robin, So"; J401 "What Soft—Cherubic Creatures"; J435 "Much Madness Is Divinest Sense"; J448 "This Was a Poet"; J449 "I Died for Beauty—but Was Scarce"; J511 "If You Were Coming in the Fall"; J526 "To Hear an Oriole Sing"; J547 "I've Seen a Dying Eye"; J556 "The Brain, within It's Groove"; J636 "The Way I Read a Letter's—This"; J640 "I Cannot Live with You"; J650 "Pain—Has an Element of Blank"; J664 "Of All the Souls That Stand Create"; J701 "A Thought Went up My Mind Today"; J1068 "Further in Summer Than the Birds"; J1100 "The Last Night That She Lived"; J1207 "He Preached upon 'Breadth' Till It Argued Him Narrow"; J1304 "Not with a Club, the Heart Is Broken"; J1510 "How Happy Is the Little Stone"; J1540 "As Imperceptibly as Grief"; J1587 "He Ate and Drank the Precious Words"; J1755 "To Make a Prairie It Takes a Clover and One Bee"; J1760 "Elysium Is as Far as to."

2. Critics have often noted how aloof and inaccessible God appears to her in J338.

Techniques. In that totality we call style, Emily Dickinson's poems were unique. No doubt influenced by her Yankee heritage, she squeezed worlds of meaning into the smallest space. Her longest poem extends to only fifty lines. Such compression makes her work aphoristic like Emerson's but also results in occasional obscurity. The language of the poems is precise, instantly expressive, and richly connotative. Like the Elizabethans, Dickinson not only exhibited a lust for all kinds of words but also took noticeable liberties with grammar. She delighted in such indirections as ambiguities, incongruities, paradoxes, and puns—a method well described in her poem "Tell All the Truth but Tell It Slant" (J1129). Capitalization served her as a sort of underlining to emphasize any word she wished. For punctuation she used dashes with such abandon that her manuscripts have constantly frustrated their editors. Thomas H. Johnson and others even attribute a musical function to these dashes. Her prosody, at first sight, seems the most derivative of her techniques, for her meters are essentially those of English hymns. In fact, most of her poems employ probably the best-known of all meters, the so-called common meter, used traditionally in ballads as well as hymns. Yet Dickinson never felt bound to these forms but experimented with them, sometimes mixing several meters in a single poem. Rhyme in her hands proved equally flexible and functional. She frequently abandoned exact for approximate rhymes. These include (1) suspended rhymes (also called *near rhymes*): *Star-door, Rune-none-within;* (2) pararhymes: *Spar-Despair, endure-Door;* and (3) vowel rhymes: *away-me; glow-through.* Although this freedom with rhyme invites comparison with such poets as Vaughan and Emerson, it is safe to say that Dickinson went the furthest in it. More important, modern explicators have pointed to examples in her work of the use of approximate rhymes to reinforce ideas, shift moods, and vary sound patterns.

Representative Works

J67 "Success Is Counted Sweetest" (written ca. 1859; printed anonymously in *A Masque of Poems,* 1878). One of the few poems published in Dickinson's lifetime. The idea expressed in lines 3–4 of understanding growing out of privation resembles Emerson's doctrine of compensation. The gnomic style of the poem also sounds Emersonian, and it is not surprising to learn that her contemporaries attributed these verses to him.

J214 "I Taste a Liquor Never Brewed" (written ca. 1860; first printed 1861). Drunk with the beauty of nature, the poet carries her joie de vivre right into heaven, where (in the variant final line) the sun serves as her lamppost. In their daring hyperbole the cosmic images of this poem link Dickinson with the frontier humorists.

J241 "I Like a Look of Agony" (written ca. 1861). Typical in its concern with sensation. Begins with a shocking statement and develops it with unusual clarity.

J258 "There's a Certain Slant of Light" (written ca. 1861). A melancholy lyric in which nature depresses the poet with presentiments of death. Note the synesthesia in stanza 1, which translates light into weight and sound, both equally oppressive.

J303 "The Soul Selects Her Own Society" (written ca. 1862). Theme: the soul's single-mindedness. Whatever the object of her devotion, be it God, the muse, other humans, or herself, she excludes all rivals and distractions—a drive that the poet concretizes as the spurning of an imperial suitor. Lines 11 and 12 suggest the closing of eyelids, heart valves, mollusk shells, and double doors, as well as the final adamantine state.

J328 "A Bird Came Down the Walk" (written ca. 1862). Pictures the bird as representing an alien world the poet can observe but not share. Especially impressive are the images in stanza 3 and the image of air as water in the last two stanzas.

J341 "After Great Pain a Formal Feeling Comes" (written ca. 1862). Describes the aftereffects of pain with images of stiffness, heaviness, and numbness. The self has lost its hold on time and place, its parts have become dissociated, and its actions are automatic. The poem ends on a note of death and perhaps suggests the lowering of a corpse into a grave.

J441 "This Is My Letter to the World" (written ca. 1862). Shows that Dickinson wrote to be read by others.

J465 "I Heard a Fly Buzz When I Died" (written ca. 1862). A deathbed scene brought to anticlimax when the persona, about to greet her divine escort to the otherworld, is distracted by a common blue household fly, perhaps a symbol of doubt over the fate of her soul, but certainly a reminder that her body will soon become food for insects.

J585 "I Like to See It Lap the Miles" (written ca. 1862). A riddle-poem that gives life to the popular metaphor of the railroad engine as an iron horse. Dickinson described this iron horse with superb humor compounded of wild hyperbole, short breathless lines, surprise enjambment, and bizarre rhymes. She also cleverly achieved onomatopoeia by punctuating the entire poem with p's, which suggest the puffing noise of the train.

J712 "Because I Could Not Stop for Death" (written ca. 1863). Personifies death as an accommodating gentleman friend who takes the poet for a carriage ride. By uniting disparate symbols in the manner of metaphysical poetry, stanza 3 suggests the successive stages of human life. Of course, the carriage is the hearse, and the dwelling in the penultimate stanza is the tomb. The final stanza continues the quiet mood of the poem while boldly conveying a sense of time without end.

J986 "A Narrow Fellow in the Grass" (written ca. 1865; published 1866). A riddle-poem that concentrates on semblance and effect, presenting the snake (without naming him) as swift, elusive, and fearsome. This last aspect is heightened by the choice of a male persona (l. 11), who would be traditionally slow to take fright or feel revulsion. To Bible readers the snake may readily symbolize evil.

J1052 "I Never Saw a Moor" (written ca. 1865). Popularly taken as the poet's affirmation of faith, although such affirmation was not typical of her work. The final line, critics suggest, could refer to tickets for either a railroad train or a Presbyterian communion service.

J1078 "The Bustle in a House" (written ca. 1866). Domestic imagery describing psychological adjustment to the death of a loved one.

J1463 "A Route of Evanescence" (written ca. 1879). A riddle-poem that conveys the dazzling speed of the male hummingbird. (Note the male/mail pun.) With a few select images Dickinson hints that in the very act of flight the bird rapes the blossoms.

J1624 "Apparently with No Surprise" (written ca. 1884). Representation of the mysterious and seemingly indifferent destructiveness of nature.

J1732 "My Life Closed Twice before Its Close" (date uncertain). Probably refers to the traumas caused by the death of Newton and the departure of Wadsworth.

2
American Humorists
1850–1900

In the second half of the nineteenth century humor became more assured and mature than it had been in the first half. Although authors still used pseudonyms, readers easily learned that "John Phoenix" was George Horatio Derby (1823–1861), "Petroleum Vesuvius Nasby" was David Ross Locke (1833–1888), "Orpheus C. Kerr" (office-seeker) was Robert H. Newell (1836–1901), "Bill Arp" was Charles H. Smith (1826–1903), "Max Adeler" was Charles Heber Clark (1847–1915), "Bill Nye" was Edgar W. Nye (1850–1896), "Mr. Dooley" was Finley Peter Dunne (1867–1936), and, of course, "Mark Twain" was Samuel Clemens. Earlier humorists had hidden their identities for fear of damaging their careers as jurists, doctors, or educators; but they had enlarged the audience for humor. The new breed of humorists—now known as Literary Comedians—declared themselves professional wits devoted to entertaining an already receptive public. When the sales of humor books skyrocketed, the writers took to the lecture platform, thus anticipating the stand-up comedians of today.

The Literary Comedians tried to outdo their predecessors in getting laughs by using comic devices in clusters—a kind of shotgun approach that combined devices like malapropism, misquotation, tautology, incongruity, and anticlimax in a single sentence or paragraph. Especially prominent in their work was comic misspelling (cacography). Although some modern readers find it irritating, nineteenth-century readers may have relished this device as an irreverent questioning of educational values, while the humorists themselves used it to assume the role of the traditional American comic persona—the wise fool, weak in book learning but strong in common sense.

CHARLES FARRAR BROWNE (ARTEMUS WARD)
(1834–1867)

The pioneer of the Literary Comedians was Charles Farrar Browne (Artemus Ward), who was probably America's earliest syndicated humor columnist and professional funnyman. He influenced many aspiring humorists—Mark Twain among them.

Life. Born in Waterford, Maine, Browne worked as a printer in New England and Ohio, then as an editor of the *Toledo Commercial* and the *Cleveland Plain Dealer*. Success came swiftly after his first Artemus Ward letter appeared in the *Plain Dealer* for January 30, 1858, and during the 1860s Browne traveled throughout North America and England as a comic lecturer. London, in particular, lionized him, but tuberculosis, aggravated by a demanding schedule and a penchant for strong drink, cut his triumph short, and he died at the age of thirty-three.

Satire. Essentially a realist, Browne satirized many facets of society, including such groups as the Mormons, Shakers, spiritualists, free lovers, and feminists. For example, in recounting an interview with Brigham Young, he pointed out the inconveniences of polygamy from a practical standpoint. His realism also took the form of antisentimentalism, as in his Tower of London letter, and of antiprimitivism in his remarks about Indians.

The Character of Artemus. To perpetrate his satire, Browne invented a comic letter writer named Artemus Ward, a fascinatingly incongruous showman who goes from town to town exhibiting wax figures and live animals. Modeled upon P. T. Barnum, Ward is shrewd in his dealings with press and public and seldom stands upon principle; indeed, he denies having any principles. He advises prince and president; yet his grammar and spelling are patently low class. If on the one hand he qualifies as an illiterate picaro, on the other he is undeniably wise, moral, and gentle—a crackerbox philosopher, happily married, interested in his work, and proud of never consciously injuring anyone. We laugh at his foibles, but we are also expected to agree with his horse sense.

Artemus Ward: His Book (1862), *Artemus Ward: His Travels* (1865), *Artemus Ward in London* (1867), and *Artemus Ward's Panorama* (1869) constitute the bulk of Browne's work. Most often anthologized is the "Interview with President Lincoln," which recalls Jack Downing advising Andrew Jackson. "Artemus Ward among the Mormons," a burlesque lecture illustrated with panorama pictures, equally deserves to be remembered.

Browne's Techniques. The selective list below links Browne with the Down East humorists (his predecessors) and the Literary Comedians. Unlike the Old Southwest humorists, he put little stress on the interrelationships of character and setting.

1. Cacography. Not so frequent in Browne's later work. Includes digital spellings like "be4" and "a4sed." Sometimes used for word play; note, for example, the words we have italicized in this passage: "We belong to a Society *whitch* beleeves wimin has *rites*—whitch beleeves in *razin* her to her proper speer" (p. 77).[1] In words like *parsis* (passes) and *amarsed* (amassed) the *r* is silent but serves to indicate the Down East pronunciation of the *a*.

2. Nonstandard verb forms. "Slewd" for "slain" (p. 333), "istest" for "is" (p. 62).

3. Tautology. "More firmer" (p. 332), "female woman" (p. 78).

4. Understatement. To the ultrapolygamous Brigham Young: " 'You air a marrid man, Mister Yung, I bleeve?' sez I, preparin to rite him sum free parsis" (p. 64).

5. Irony and anticlimax. Of Chaucer: "Mr. C. had talent, but he couldn't spel" (p. 326).

6. Incongruity. "I've amarsed a handsum Pittance" (p. 55).

7. Misquotation. To a Mormoness who proposes marriage: "Awa . . . awa! Go & be a Nunnery!" (p. 67).

8. Aside. "This last remark is a sirkastic and witherin thrust" (p. 313).

HENRY WHEELER SHAW (1818–1885)

Although Henry Wheeler Shaw belonged with the Literary Comedians, he also harked back to the earlier humorists. A native of Massachusetts who had knocked about in the West, Shaw turned to writing as a career when he was in his forties. After Charles Farrar Browne found a publisher for his first book, Shaw, too, became a highly successful specialist in humor. His *Farmer's Allminax* (1869–1879) were annual best-sellers, and he was constantly in demand as a lecturer. Like the other Literary Comedians, he conveyed his humor through a pseudonymous alter ego—Josh Billings by name. Shaw also employed the favorite devices of the Literary Comedians. Note, for example, these excerpts from his most famous piece, "Essa on the Muel":

Tha [i.e., mules] weigh more, akordin tu their heft, than enny other kreetur, except a crowbar [surprise twist].

Tha haint got enny friends, and will live on huckle berry brush, with an ockasional chanse at Kanada thistels [incongruity: the two predicate clusters are unrelated].

Tha are a modern invenshun, i dont think the Bible deludes [malapropism] tu them at tall.

1. Quotations are from *The Complete Works of Charles F. Browne* (New York: G. W. Dillingham Co., 1898).

Tha never hav no dissease that a good club wont heal [euphemism].[2]

(pp. 163–164)

Shaw's link with an earlier tradition of American humor lay in his resemblance to Ben Franklin. Like Franklin he specialized in almanacs, and in his other books he employed the aphoristic style of the almanac makers, expressing his homespun wisdom with economy.

2. *Josh Billings: His Works, Complete* (New York: G. W. Dillingham, 1888).

3
Local Color

Stories that emphasize setting are often classified as local-color or regional fiction. If they were written during the second half of the nineteenth century, when this kind of writing enjoyed its greatest popularity, we tend to call them local-color stories. If they date from an earlier or later period, we tend to call them regional stories. In any case they display a careful fidelity to the landscape, customs, dialect, and thought of their chosen area. Often the life-style of this area appears to be vanishing, and the author sees himself as its first, last, or only recorder. With such emphasis on faithful depiction, these stories obviously belong to the realistic movement; yet many also contain such romantic ingredients as sentimentality and primitivism. Most local-colorists contented themselves with picturesque surface aspects, but a few found deep insights and universal meanings in the everyday life of common folk.

ANTECEDENTS OF THE LOCAL-COLOR PERIOD

Long before the 1860s, which mark the beginning of the local-color period in America, there had been a growing awareness of regional peculiarities and a resultant use of them in literature. Examples include the journals of Sarah Kemble Knight and William Byrd, the drama of Royall Tyler and Samuel Woodworth, the fiction of the Knickerbockers, and above all the poems and sketches of humorists from Down East and the Old Southwest. Local customs were treated seriously in the prose and poetry of Timothy Dwight, nostalgically in Joel Barlow's *Hasty Pudding,* whimsically in Francis Hopkinson's "On White-Washing," and irreverently in the Reverend Samuel Peters's *General History of Connecticut (1781).* Dialect was exploited as early as the late eighteenth century in Hugh Henry Brackenridge's *Modern Chivalry.*

And local-color writing had received a theoretical basis. St. John de Crèvecoeur's *Letters from an American Farmer* (1782), for example, was an eloquent testimonial to environmentalism, which emphasizes the close relationship between character and milieu. The contemporary nationalistic spirit also encouraged the growth of this literature, for in order to praise the entire nation (which was expanding under their very eyes) American writers found it necessary to celebrate its diverse regions.

LOCAL COLOR AT ITS HEIGHT

Several factors brought about the great vogue of local-color literature during the late nineteenth century. As place after place fell victim to changes wrought by industrialism and the Civil War, American authors hastened to record the old life before it vanished. Then, too, writers found that they could help reduce postbellum rancor by demonstrating to Yankees and Southerners that true virtue existed on both sides of the Mason-Dixon line. Perhaps the most important stimulus came from the phenomenal growth of magazines during this period. Just as the humorists had thronged to *The Spirit of the Times*, the regionalists found a ready outlet for their work in *The Atlantic Monthly, Harper's Magazine, Scribner's Monthly,* and *The Century Magazine*.

The short story proved the best medium for the local-colorists, but at times they could write impressively in other genres. The poems of Brèt Harte and James Whitcomb Riley, the *Pike County Ballads* of John Hay (1838–1905), "Christmas-Night in the Quarters" and other Negro dialect verses by Irwin Russell (1853–1879) all prove that local color could be achieved in poetry. And in the genre of the novel we find an undisputed masterpiece of local color, *The Adventures of Huckleberry Finn*.

During their vogue, which lasted approximately from 1870 to 1900, the local-colorists wrote about many regions and regional characters. The following list shows only a few of these areas, together with some authors who treated them. (Unless otherwise noted, all titles are collections of short stories or sketches.)

Massachusetts: Harriet Beecher Stowe (1811–1896), *The Minister's Wooing* (1859, novel), *The Pearl of Orr's Island* (1862, novel), *Oldtown Folks* (1869, novel), *Sam Lawson's Oldtown Fireside Stories* (1872), *Poganuc People* (1878, novel); Mary E. Wilkins Freeman

Maine: Sarah Orne Jewett

Vermont: Rowland E. Robinson (1833–1900)

New Hampshire: Alice Brown (1857–1948)

Connecticut: Rose Terry Cooke (1827–1892)

Pennsylvania: Margaret Deland (1857–1945), *Old Chester Tales* (1898), *Dr. Lavendar's People* (1903)

Indiana: Edward Eggleston (1837–1902), *The Hoosier Schoolmaster* (1871, novel), *Roxy* (1878, novel); James Whitcomb Riley (1849–1916), numerous poems in Hoosier dialect

Ohio, Michigan, and the Lake Superior area: Constance Fenimore Woolson (1840–1894), *Castle Nowhere: Lake-Country Sketches* (1875)

Kentucky: James Lane Allen (1849–1925); John Fox, Jr. (1863–1919)

Virginia: Thomas Nelson Page (1853–1922)

North Carolina: Charles W. Chesnutt (1858–1932), *The Conjure Woman* (1899), *The Wife of His Youth and Other Stories of the Color Line* (1899), and various novels

Florida, the Carolinas, Tennessee: Constance Fenimore Woolson, *Rodman the Keeper: Southern Sketches* (1880)

Tennessee: Mary N. Murfree (pseud. Charles Egbert Craddock, 1850–1922), *In the Tennessee Mountains* (1884), *The Prophet of the Great Smoky Mountains* (1885, novel)

Georgia: Joel C. Harris; Richard Malcolm Johnston (1822–1898); Harry Stillwell Edwards (1855–1938); Sidney Lanier (1842–1881), dialect poems

Louisiana: George W. Cable; Grace King (1851–1932); Kate Chopin (1851–1904), *Bayou Folk* (1894), containing "Desirée's Baby"

California: Bret Harte; Gertrude Atherton (1857–1948)

Wyoming: Owen Wister (1860–1938), *The Virginian* (1902, archetypal Western novel)

For other contributions to local-color literature, see Mark Twain (chapter 5) and Hamlin Garland (chapter 7).

BRET HARTE (1836–1902)

After Bret Harte achieved success in the 1860s with "The Luck of Roaring Camp" and other tales of the California gold rush days, he seldom varied the formula of his fiction. These stories do not qualify as the earliest local-color tales in America, but they were the first to capture such a large audience. Moreover, they added a new area—the Far West—to regional fiction. Harte resembled Washington Irving in dealing with a new region, but he went further than Irving, depicting gamblers, drunks, prostitutes, and outlaws with so little moralizing that he shocked his contemporaries. Like Dickens (his favorite author) and the frontier humorists, he created grotesque characters and mixed comedy with sentiment. His was a surface portrayal yet, at its best, a highly entertaining one.

Life. Harte was not a native of the West but did spend seventeen years there (1854–1871). He was born in Albany, and he lived in various other eastern cities, including New York and Brooklyn, before sailing to California, where he worked as a tutor, teacher, expressman, and clerk, and possibly also as a miner. After 1857 he made a career of writing. He worked for various California papers and became the first editor of the *Overland Monthly*. Collections of his verse and prose came out in 1867, but it was his humorous poem "The Heathen Chinee" (1870) and *The Luck of Roaring Camp and Other Sketches* (1870) that made him famous throughout the United States. Leaving California in 1871, Harte signed a contract with the *Atlantic Monthly* for the unprecedented sum of $10,000 a year. But this proved the end of his success, for his work failed to measure up to past performance, and he soon found himself in debt. The latter part of Harte's life was spent abroad in almost complete separation from his wife and four children. He held consular posts in Germany and Scotland, and from 1885 until his death he lived in London. During this English period Harte wrote with mechanical regularity, leaving the marketing of his work in the capable hands of A. P. Watt and Sons, a pioneering firm of literary agents.

Representative Works

"The Luck of Roaring Camp" (1868). Harte's best-known short story. It tells of a sinful, slovenly mining camp that is transformed by the presence of an infant born and nurtured in its midst. While critics have denounced various weaknesses in this tale, it is widely recognized as an important early document in the local-color movement, and it manages to entertain nicely. Especially fascinating are its numerous incongruities. Not only does it pair frontier crudities with religious imagery, the colloquialisms of the miners with the literary language of the narrator, and sentiment with humor, but the humor itself is composed largely of incongruity. For example, the newborn child is pronounced no "bigger nor a derringer" (7:6).[1] Other such devices include various euphemisms, catalogs, poetic interspersions, and mock-heroic elements.

"The Society upon the Stanislaus" (1868). Narrative verse-satire of local Darwinians trying to prove that a skull found in a Calaveras County mine shaft had belonged to a prehistoric man.

"The Outcasts of Poker Flat" (1869). A short story relating the fate in a snowstorm of two prostitutes (Mother Shipton and the Duchess), a professional gambler (John Oakhurst), and an innocent fifteen-year-old girl (Piney Woods). Mother Shipton and Oakhurst sacrifice themselves in a vain attempt to save the others.

"Tennessee's Partner" (1869). A short story. The hero seems incredibly faithful to Tennessee (who has even stolen his wife), but frontier mining conditions did link partners in an unusually strong bond. The bribery episode succeeds as humor and the graveside speech as dignified emotion, but the ending is maudlin.

---

1. Quotations are from *The Works of Bret Harte* (Argonaut Ed., New York: Collier, n.d.).

"Plain Language from Truthful James" (also known as "The Heathen Chinee") (1870). A humorous verse-narrative of a card game in which all the participants are cheaters.

GEORGE WASHINGTON CABLE (1844–1925)

The pioneer local-colorist of the New Orleans area and one of the earliest liberals among Southern regionalists was George Washington Cable. He is remembered chiefly for his stories of antebellum life among the Creoles (the French and Spanish whites of New Orleans and its environs), although some of his fiction also dealt with their country cousins, the Louisiana Cajuns.

Life. Cable was born in New Orleans, descended on his father's side from Virginia slaveholders and on his mother's from New England stock. During the Civil War he served in the Confederate cavalry; during Reconstruction, however, he became increasingly critical of the South. In these years he worked as a bookkeeper, cashier, and clerk and as columnist and reporter for the *New Orleans Picayune*. After his short stories had been collectecd as *Old Creole Days* (1879) and his first novel, *The Grandissimes* (1880), had proved successful, he was ready to make literature his principal occupation. Paradoxically, he found it impossible to remain in the region he wrote about. The Creoles resented his satirical treatment of them, and others took umbrage at his criticism of the penal system and the treatment of Negroes in the South. So Cable moved north and in 1885 settled permanently in Northampton, Massachusetts. Soon he and Mark Twain—"Twins of Genius"—toured the country giving readings from their works (1884–1885). Although the tour was otherwise successful, Cable piqued Twain with his religiosity, which proved especially inconvenient on the Sabbath, when Cable refused to travel. During the Northampton years, the second half of his long life, Cable founded the popular Home Culture Clubs, gave readings in England, and wrote on a variety of subjects, including gardening, Bible study, and the Negro problem. Twice a widower, he married for a third time not long before his death.

Creole Stories. Cable enthusiastically depicted the color, romance, and exotic quality of Creole life, which he also satirized. In "Parson Jone" he brought out the rather amusing differences between Creole culture and that of neighboring Protestant Anglo-Saxons. But in stories like "'Tite Poulette" he pictured the Creoles as ignorant, regressive, and sometimes decadent, their bloodlines confused by a system that allowed a man to take an octoroon for a mistress but not a wife. Although among themselves Creoles spoke French, often of the best kind, Cable of course could not cast his dialogue in French; he could merely interpolate an occasional French phrase or sentence. For the most part he rendered the Creoles' attempts to speak English in a dialect that tended to degrade them. The authorial voice of the stories presented no such problems; Cable's lush, whimsical style perfectly matched these Latin characters and their semitropical surroundings.

"Belles Demoiselles Plantation" (1874). A short story in which the Creole aristocrat Colonel De Charleu comes close to defrauding his half-breed relative Injun Charlie. A horror of betraying his own kindred prevents the colonel from taking Charlie's New Orleans' property in trade for his own plantation, which is doomed to sink into the river. Romanticism prevails in the improbable climax (the plantation sinks just as the colonel begins to stop the trade) and in the melodrama of the deathbed denouement. Yet there is realism, too, especially in the stark figure of Injun Charlie, living in squalor and laziness but proud to claim descent from the original Count De Charleu even though, ironically, the count had been a bigamist and a thief.

The Grandissimes (1879–1880). A complicated novel, with long, digressive episodes and a large number of characters, two of them further confusing matters by bearing the same name, Honoré Grandissime. Note the deft handling of dialect and setting, the well-realized characters, the gothic scenes (especially the torture of Bras Coupé and the shooting of Clemence the Negress), and the various folk elements, including love charms and voodoo. Like *The House of the Seven Gables,* this novel traces the working out of a curse.

JOEL CHANDLER HARRIS (1848–1908)

The local-colorist who most effectively popularized Negro folklore was Joel Chandler Harris. His portrayal of Negro character and of plantation life should not be considered definitive, but it contains more than enough truth and artistry to merit our admiration. In the Uncle Remus tales as well as in his lesser-known works, Harris demonstrated that humor could be achieved without disrespect and that local color could be used to reduce the bitter sectionalism that followed the Civil War.

Life. Harris spent his childhood in Eatonton, Georgia, and his teens on Turnwold, a plantation whose owner he worked for. His long and distinguished career as a journalist included years (1876–1900) on the *Atlanta Constitution,* writing liberal political essays as well as fiction. Notoriously shy, Harris refused to speak in public or even to read his stories to admiring children (see Twain's *Life on the Mississippi,* chapter 47). A week before he died, he became a Roman Catholic.

The Uncle Remus Tales. The most complex and most enduring of Harris's works are the Uncle Remus tales.[2] For even a rudimentary comprehension we must view them in several ways.

---

2. Among the collections are *Uncle Remus, His Songs and Sayings* (1880), *Nights with Uncle Remus* (1883), and *Uncle Remus and His Friends* (1892).

1. As frame stories. The inner narratives are folktales involving Brer Rabbit and the other "creeturs." The outer narratives show the elderly Uncle Remus, a plantation Negro, telling these stories to a little white boy. Like Chaucer, Boccaccio, and the humorists of the Old Southwest, Harris found this device an ideal one for mixing fantasy with realism.

2. As folktales. Although Harris claimed to be the editor rather than the author of the inner narratives, they were not verbatim texts but artful reconstructions. Many of the story outlines came to Harris directly from Negro raconteurs; others were sent by friends and correspondents. Apparently not until he had several versions of a given narrative did he consider it authentic and prepare it for print.

3. As animal tales. These books comprise one of the world's largest collections of this traditional genre, which has both folk and literary sources, including *Aesop's Fables* and *Le Roman de Renart*. Like the characters in most animal tales, Harris's animals act like humans, even to the point of smoking cigars and holding political assemblies; but here it is the wily rabbit who tricks a stupid fox in complete reversal of the European tradition.[3]

4. As trickster tales. Typical of this genre, the Uncle Remus stories depict a weak creature triumphing over a strong one, not by force, but by cunning. Rabbit uses simple reverse psychology, for example, when he escapes from Fox by begging not to be thrown into the briar patch, his native element. While many of the tricks in these stories may be called harmless mischief, there are also instances of lying, cheating, theft, murder, and cannibalism. Tabooed acts of this sort are typical of trickster tales, which allow listeners to enjoy bad deeds without feeling guilty.

5. As American Negro tales. Because the first book of Uncle Remus stories was a pioneer collection, it began the stereotype of a Negro repertoire limited to animal trickster tales. Today, as proven by such anthologies as Richard Dorson's *American Negro Folktales* (1967), we see that the repertoire of black raconteurs has embraced many more forms, including protest, wonder, preacher, horror, tall, and Old Marster tales. Unquestionably, however, the animal tale has been a favorite genre with blacks. The stories that Harris collected must have served as a subtle kind

---

3. To discover such parallels and variations see Stith Thompson's *Motif-Index of Folk-Literature* (GB) and the Aarne-Thompson *Types of the Folktale (GB)*, which analyze many collections, including the Uncle Remus books of 1880, 1883, and 1892. See type 175 for "The Wonderful Tar-Baby Story," type 1310A for "How Mr. Rabbit Was Too Sharp for Mr. Fox," type 66B for "Mr. Wolf Makes a Failure," type 291 for "Mr. Terrapin Shows His Strength," motif K404.1 for "How Mr. Rabbit Saved His Meat," motif J1791 for "The Moon in the Mill-Pond," motif A1016.1 for "The Story of the Deluge," and motif J217.0.1.1 (in Ernest W. Baughman's *Type and Motif-Index of the Folktales of England and North America* [Bloomington: Indiana University Press, 1966]) for "Death and the Negro Man."

of slave revenge against their masters, for in them the underdog wins. If Harris was true to the matter and function of Negro folktales, he was also true to the manner of the narrators. The stories sparkle with fancy words, onomatopoeia, and cante fable elements (interspersed chants or songs), all of which have been verified as characteristic of Negro delivery. "How duz yo' sym'tums seem ter segashuate?" says Brer Rabbit in greeting the Tar-Baby. Later in the same book Uncle Remus astonishes the little boy by imitating a turtle talking under water: "I-doom-er-ker-kum-mer-ker."[4] Unfortunately, the dialects of these stories (whether inland Georgian or Gullah) present difficulties to the reader unwilling to practice reading them aloud.

6. As part myths. By no means themselves pure myths, the Uncle Remus tales nevertheless contain mythical elements. Among these are the etiological or explanatory motifs in tales such as "The Story of the Deluge" and "Why the Alligator's Back Is Rough." Furthermore, the tales depict a world remote from our own—a world in which animals feel, think, and talk; mingle with an unidentified group called "Miss Meadows an' de gals"; and live by a morality based not on refined religion but on the instinctive tactics of survival.

7. As local-color stories in the plantation tradition. The picture of ante-bellum plantation life that Harris carefully developed in the outer narratives from his memories of Turnwold is thorough but essentially romantic. Here slaves and masters enjoy an unstrained paternalistic relationship. The little boy, sitting in Uncle Remus's cabin, symbolizes an easy communication between them, while Uncle Remus, even though Harris individualized him, may be said to represent the devoted black servant.

8. As humor. The local color, dialect, physical discomfort, and framework technique in the Uncle Remus stories place them squarely in the tradition of Old Southwest humor. Moreover, the inner narratives achieve a special humor through many shifts in character as the animals act like animals, like humans, and then like animals again. Indeed, the animals often function as parodists of human ideas and activities.

Other Work. In addition to the Uncle Remus tales, Harris wrote essays, poems, novels, and short stories; of these the short stories most deserve to be studied.[5] They deal semirealistically with Georgia Crackers and other local types before, during, and after the Civil War. Here, as elsewhere, Harris reproduced a variety of dialects with great accuracy and effect. Best known of these stories is "Free Joe and the Rest of the World," which traces the plight of a freed Negro separated from his wife by her spiteful master.

4. *Uncle Remus, His Songs and Sayings* (New York: McKinlay, Stone & Mackenzie, 1908), tales 2, 14.
5. The best are collected in *Mingo and Other Sketches in Black and White* (1884) and *Free Joe and Other Georgian Sketches* (1887).

SARAH ORNE JEWETT (1849–1909)

More than any of her contemporaries, Sarah Orne Jewett fulfilled the promise of local-color fiction. Her art appears artless, yet is eminently artful. She gained an impressive authenticity in her work by devoting a lifetime to studying a single region, and through localized stories, she achieved universal meanings. On page after page of her writing we find insights into humanity that generally go as deep as anything in American fiction, regional or otherwise.

Life. South Berwick, Maine, was Jewett's birthplace and lifetime home. Both parents had come from a long line of New Englanders. With her father, a respected doctor, she often went calling on rural patients, and on these trips he taught her to absorb the locale through careful observation of all details. Although her formal education ended with graduation from Berwick Academy, she had read widely in her father's well-stocked library and had done some writing of her own. Stirred by Harriet Beecher Stowe's *Pearl of Orr's Island* to become a local-colorist, she began the sketches of Maine life that were collected in *Deephaven* (1877). For twenty-five years thereafter she labored carefully and steadily at her chosen profession, turning out sketches, novels, juveniles, and a history of the Normans. She made several trips to Europe and spent part of each year in Boston and Manchester-by-the-Sea.

Stories. In subject and style the best of Jewett's stories[6] nicely develop her favorite theme—the grandeur of simplicity. Her characters are usually plain folk engaged in commonplace activities on inland farms and in coastal villages amid economic decay caused by Jefferson's embargo, industrialism, and the Civil War. Some of the most memorable are old, mateless, and eccentric (though seldom grotesque). A realist rather than a naturalist, Jewett thought of her characters as able to overcome the limitations of their environment even if they did not always avail themselves of the opportunity (see "The Hiltons' Holiday"). Sometimes the stories end with characters arriving at self-knowledge and clarification of values. Thus in "Miss Tempy's Watchers" Mrs. Crowe and Miss Binson reconcile their opposing temperaments as they discuss the virtues of their late friend. Here, as well as in such stories as "The Only Rose" and "The Passing of Sister Barsett," Jewett adroitly used conversation to portray the characters of those who are talked about as well as those who are talking.

While she frequently assumed a nostalgic tone—a primitivistic longing for the simple life of the past—Jewett could also display a fairly wide range of

6. Collected in such volumes as *A White Heron and Other Stories* (1886); *The King of Folly Island and Other People* (1888); *Tales of New England* (1890); *A Native of Winby and Other Tales* (1893); *The Life of Nancy* (1895); *The Queen's Twin and Other Stories* (1899).

humor, as witness the sustained irony in "The Dulham Ladies" or the examples of anticlimax and physical discomfort in "The Courting of Sister Wisby." Usually the plots of her stories are slight, but numerous symbols enrich the narrative. In "The White Heron," for instance, a giant pine tree functions as "a great main-mast to the voyaging earth" (p.17);[7] by climbing it, the young heroine reaches self-fulfillment. In keeping with these low-keyed narratives, Jewett's style is graceful, muted, clear, precise, and disciplined.

The Country of the Pointed Firs (1896). Jewett's masterpiece, *The Country of the Pointed Firs,* is a collection of first-person prose sketches set in Dunnet Landing, an imaginary Maine coastal town. The narrator, though only a summer visitor, grows increasingly close to the natives of this community and, in the climactic chapter on the Bowden family reunion, sees herself as one of them. Symbolism prevails throughout the book so that the characters are far more than mere regional stereotypes, and their actions take on a timeless significance. All the characters live close to nature, each in an individual way. Mrs. Todd, the herb-gatherer, performs woman's ancient role of interpreting nature's secrets. Mrs. Blackett, her eighty-six-year-old mother, represents the ideal blend of independence, youthfulness, and love. Although she lives with her son William in Edenic isolation on Green Island, she keeps close ties with clan and community. The reverse of this sense of community appears in the jilted Joanna Todd, who retires to a hermit's life. Other eccentrics are Abby Martin, who considers herself Queen Victoria's twin, and Captain Littlepage, who during his more than eighty years, has traveled to many parts of the globe and thus serves as a foil to his root-bound neighbors. Yet his mind has become addled, and he labors under the chimera of a world far to the north where "fog-shaped" souls wait at the threshold of eternity.[8]

MARY E. WILKINS FREEMAN (1852–1930)

Another author who specialized in New England local color but went beyond the merely picturesque was Mary E. Wilkins Freeman.

Life. Born into an old New England family, Mary E. Wilkins grew up in Massachusetts and Vermont. Although her formal education comprised only a year at Mount Holyoke and a few courses at a female seminary, she began writing seriously in her early twenties, at first for children and then for adults. In 1887 her first book, *A Humble Romance and Other Stories,* appeared, and after that others followed in a steady stream, winning her

---

7. *A White Heron and Other Stories* (Boston and New York: Houghton Mifflin, 1886).

8. *The Country of the Pointed Firs* (Boston and New York: Houghton Mifflin, 1897), p. 37.

such honors as the $5,000 prize in the *New York Herald*'s "Anglo American Competition" (1908) and the Gold Medal for Fiction from the American Academy of Letters (1926). Counterbalancing this literary success were a gradual loss of hearing and an unhappy marriage (1902) to Dr. Charles M. Freeman. The Freemans lived in Metuchen, New Jersey, where Mrs. Freeman died in 1930.

Stories. More than any other New England local-colorist, Mary Wilkins Freeman succeeded in portraying realistically the somber, stark, and even grim life of the Puritans' descendants. Despite frequent comic relief, her stories[9] carry the force of tragedies and are narrated in a spare style that matches the laconism of her rustic characters. Her most powerful work concentrates on the human will in dramatic revolt or, less often, in quiet atrophy. *Pembroke* (1894), her only novel of distinction, tells how Barney Thayer separates himself for years from his fiancée after quarreling with her father. Somewhat less grotesque are three women who rebel just once in their lives. Candace Whitcomb, eased out of her position as leading soprano in the church choir, drowns out her replacement during Sunday service, an outburst described as "more than tropical, for a New England nature has a floodgate, and the power which it releases is an accumulation."[10] The revolt of Aunt Rebecca, narrated in the frame story "On the Walpole Road," comes in the middle of her wedding when she tells the minister for all to hear that while she will marry the man beside her she actually loves another. Best known is "The Revolt of Mother," the tale of a woman who moves the family into the new barn when her husband refuses to house them better than the farm animals. Much different is the story of Louisa Ellis, the "New England Nun" who quietly drifts into such a deep state of spinsterhood that she gladly relinquishes her long-postponed marriage. In all these stories the author enriches the plot with symbols such as a photograph album, a forest fire, aprons, and a caged canary.

LOCAL COLOR AFTER 1900

At the turn of the century the local-color story lost its preeminent position, yet the regional impulse, though transformed, remained strong. New writers (like Willa Cather) who admired older ones (like Sarah Orne Jewett) continued to explore the relationships between characters and milieu, but they did so with greater realism. Nor did the end of the century bring a halt to the discovery of likely areas for the regionalist's pen. Jack London, for example, demonstrated the possibilities of Alaska. Equally interesting was

9. Collected in such books as *A Humble Romance and Other Stories* (1887), *A New England Nun and Other Stories* (1891), and *Edgewater People* (1918).

10. "A Village Singer," in *A New England Nun and Other Stories* (New York: Harper, 1891), p. 28.

the rediscovery of the city after more than a century during which local-color fiction had been dominated by agrarian ideals. It was William Sydney Porter (O. Henry [1862–1910]) who gave the city its rightful place in regional literature. True, such pieces as "The Cop and the Anthem," "The Gift of the Magi," and "An Unfinished Story," with their widely imitated trick endings, seem to stress plot more than place. Yet his work as a whole teems with characteristic urban settings and people. In fact, the same love of the common man that had prompted earlier local-colorists also moved him, so that, in answer to the term the Four Hundred, then used to denote New York society, he entitled one of his books *The Four Million* (1906).

4
Social Critics

As America emerged from the ashes of the Civil War the writers of the latter nineteenth century found the period ugly and often denounced it. The war itself, marked by corruption in both military and civilian life, had evoked vigorous satire. From the North came David Ross Locke's letters of "Petroleum V. Nasby" and the second series of James Russell Lowell's *Biglow Papers;* from the South came the voice of "Bill Arp" (Charles Henry Smith) and the harsher tones of George Washington Harris, who posed Sut Lovingood as Abe Lincoln's traveling companion. Reconstruction, an even worse period, was pictured in such novels as *Red Rock* (1898) by Thomas Nelson Page (1853–1922) and *A Fool's Errand, by One of the Fools* (1879) by Albion W. Tourgée (1838–1905), who had been a carpetbagger judge in North Carolina. As Reconstruction merged into the Gilded Age, corruption increased; and better talents than these came forward to expose the swindles and scandals perpetrated by such forces as the robber barons, the Tweed Ring, the Crédit Mobilier, and the U.S. Congress. Foremost among these writers stand John De Forest, Henry Adams, and Mark Twain.

As time went on, other evils and other critics emerged. Urban problems such as housing, labor unrest, and related offshoots of industrialism were bared if not solved in John Hay's (1838–1905) *The Breadwinners* (1883–1884), Howells's *A Hazard of New Fortunes* (1890), Crane's *Maggie* (1893), Henry Blake Fuller's (1857–1929) *The Cliff-Dwellers* (1893) and *With the Procession* (1895), Paul L. Ford's (1865–1902) *The Honorable Peter Stirling* (1894), Dreiser's *Sister Carrie* (1900) and *Jennie Gerhardt* (1911), Robert Herrick's (1868–1938) *The Common Lot* (1904), and Upton Sinclair's *The Jungle* (1906). Garland and Norris wrote movingly of the farmer's plight in *Main-Travelled Roads* (1891), *The Octopus* (1901), and *The Pit* (1903). Conflicting faiths, loss of orthodoxy, the impact of Darwinism, and other religious problems were discussed in such novels as Henry Adams's *Esther*

(1884), Margaret Deland's (1857–1945) *John Ward, Preacher* (1888), and Harold Frederic's (1856–1898) *The Damnation of Theron Ware* (1896).

A few of these writers suggested solutions to these problems, ranging from the simple love urged by Sidney Lanier in "The Symphony" to the elaborate social systems pictured in Howells's *Through the Eye of the Needle* (1907) and other utopian fiction that followed in the wake of Edward Bellamy's (1850–1898) influential *Looking Backward: 2000–1887* (1888). *In His Steps* (1896), a best-selling novel by Charles M. Sheldon (1857–1946), portrays a congregation guiding their behavior by attempting to answer the question "What would Jesus do?"

Some writers experienced difficulty integrating their proposed remedies into their works. Upton Sinclair, for example, devoted the final chapters of *The Jungle* (1906) to describing socialism, but few readers can tolerate this exposition after being whirled through the novel's fast-moving plot. However, this book, which depicted the meat-packing industry in Chicago, has enjoyed amazing popularity and is credited with hastening passage of a pure food and drug act.

Many of the above-mentioned social critics are treated more fully elsewhere in this book, for they belong among the humorists, naturalists, and other literary groups. Two writers, John De Forest and Henry Adams, seem to be, above all, social critics and will be discussed in this chapter.

JOHN WILLIAM DE FOREST (1826–1906)

In the best work of John W. De Forest, we find criticism combined with realism. His novel *Miss Ravenel's Conversion from Secession to Loyalty* (1867), which has become a minor classic, established him as one of America's pioneer realists. Drawing upon his experience in the Union Army, he wrote with honesty and conviction. Gore drips on many a page, brains bulge from bullet-torn heads, while severed hands, feet, and limbs lie underneath the operating tables in the field hospital. Yet all this is described with the calm, objective tone of a Hemingway. Equally realistic is De Forest's refusal to simplify, whether treating individual characters or society as a whole. His villains, Mrs. Larue and Colonel Carter, have their attractive qualities; and his heroes, Lillie Ravenel, Dr. Ravenel, and Edward Colburne, have their faults. Although the persona in this novel speaks as a Unionist, he criticizes New England for its social frigidity and praises the South for its warm manners. Throughout this book, De Forest engaged in substantial muckraking, particularly in exposing army corruption. Some of his subsequent novels have even more social criticism. *Honest John Vane* (1875), a satire on the Crédit Mobilier scandal, tells of a newly elected member of Congress whose wife's social climbing plunges him into a fraudulent scheme called the Great Subfluvial Tunnel. De Forest again took up the subject in *Playing the Mischief* (1875), the story of a female claimant who bilks Congress of $100,000 for a barn destroyed in the War of 1812.

HENRY ADAMS (1838–1918)

Although inferior to De Forest as a novelist, Henry Adams earned a greater reputation as social critic, historian, and litterateur. His attempt to interpret cultural development according to the laws of thermodynamics still compels admiration if not belief; his massive history of the Jeffersonian era remains standard; and his best-seller, *The Education of Henry Adams,* has become a classic. Even now, however, Adams is not fully appreciated for his style and humor, nor has enough attention been given to his *Mont-Saint-Michel and Chartres,* a remarkable re-creation of medievalism.

Life. By heritage, Adams belonged with the elite. One of his great-grandfathers was John Adams, second president of the United States; his paternal grandfather was John Quincy Adams, sixth president; and his maternal grandfather, Peter Chardon Brooks, was known as the wealthiest man in Boston. In "Quincy," the idyllic opening chapter of the *Education,* Adams charmingly describes his participation in this heritage.

After graduation from Harvard (1858), Adams served as private secretary to his father, Charles Francis Adams, American minister to Great Britain during the Civil War. At the end of the war, he wrote historical articles for the *North American Review,* including a vituperative and inaccurate essay on Captain John Smith. From 1868 to 1870 Adams worked in Washington as a free-lance journalist, exposing the scandals that sullied the Grant administration. In 1870 he became editor of the *North American Review* and assistant professor of history at Harvard. He served both posts with distinction, making the Boston magazine a vehicle for liberal thought, introducing the graduate seminar to Harvard, and training his students to work with primary sources.

In 1872 Adams married Marian Hooper, a Boston heiress. They moved to Washington in 1877, and soon their house in Lafayette Square became the gathering place for some of the city's leading intellectuals, including the diplomat John Hay, the geologist Clarence King, and the artist John La Farge. Adams now entered into an idyllic period of scholarship, writing the books that marked him as one of America's greatest historians. He also wrote two novels: *Democracy* (1880), which satirizes political and social life in Washington, and *Esther* (1884), which traces the moral development of a heroine obviously modeled on the author's wife. The idyll ended in 1885 with the tragic suicide of his wife, who was despondent over the death of her father. Somehow Adams managed to temper his grief with hard work, a passionate devotion to science and medievalism, and years of travel. He habitually attended world fairs, where he began to see the dynamo as a symbol of centrifugal force. Study of the Middle Ages, his other passion, also kept him abroad much of the time, especially in France.

Representative Works

History of the United States of America during the Administrations of Thomas Jefferson and James Madison (written 1879–1890). The classic treatment of its period; a detailed nine-volume study. As research alone, the work is amazing. Adams moved to Washington to be close to the bulk of his source material, but he also visited European archives. Moreover, he utilized all kinds of materials, ranging from official proclamations to topical poetry. As a work of art, the *History* is equally stunning. Adams not only synthesized and structured his materials but, like the romantic historians Motley, Prescott, and Parkman, he wrote sensuously and evoked moods. Yet here as elsewhere, he concerned himself with scientific interpretation.

"American Ideals," the most famous chapter of the *History*, serves as an excellent introduction to it and presents the standard against which the events that it depicts are measured. Here we find the characteristic sharp images, paradoxes, and scientific terminology. Europe, for example, is pictured on one page as alive with the energy of genius, on another as a "mass of inert matter" stifled by the incubus of its "social anomalies" (1:160–61).[1]

Mont-Saint-Michel and Chartres (1904). On the surface a guidebook to a Romanesque abbey and a Gothic cathedral; actually a poetic analysis of medieval culture. For Adams, who assumed the role of guiding his niece, this tour through time offered a chance not only to become "prematurely young"[2] by recovering his idealism and achieving a vision of unity but also to establish a starting point by which to measure the historical changes that he would chart in the *Education*.

The Education of Henry Adams (1907). An experimental autobiography narrated in the third person. Though roughly chronological, this book is far from complete; for its two parts, covering respectively the years 1838–1871 and 1892–1905, leave out the middle period of Adams's life, which included his marriage, his wife's suicide, his work on the *History of the United States,* and his trips to Japan and the South Seas. If Adams had been writing pure autobiography, such an omission would have been unthinkable; but he obviously was not. Autobiography gives way to national and world history throughout the book, and the final chapters are taken up with exposition of his various historical laws—the end product of his education. (To Adams

1. *History of the United States of America during the First Administration of Thomas Jefferson* (New York: Scribner, 1889).
2. *Mont-Saint-Michel and Chartres* (Boston and New York: Houghton Mifflin, 1905, 1933), p. 2.

education meant learning to use energy efficiently in order to adjust to environment.)

Cultural analysis was a dominant purpose of the *Education,* which Adams wrote as a sequel to *Mont-Saint-Michel and Chartres,* subtitling the earlier work "A Study of Thirteenth-Century Unity," the later "A Study of Twentieth-Century Multiplicity." Four especially important ideas emerge from this analysis: that the law of history, like the law of nature, is movement from order to chaos; that loss of feeling accompanies this movement; that a reassertion of feeling is needed to save mankind; and that man may still find unity in this chaos even though this unity is illusory. The persona who voices these ideas is indeed complex. Like William Bradford and Thomas Morton, he writes in the third person point of view, which helped make the work appear more objective. Then there is the notoriously pessimistic tone of the book. On nearly every page Adams calls himself a failure, noting that he was an anachronism, educated for the early nineteenth century.

The *Education* is a masterpiece of indirection. It contains, besides the authorial masks, numerous understatements, overstatements, ironies, paradoxes, and metaphors. For example, Chapter XXVI (and indeed much of the entire book) equates Adams's education with a journey, first in search of a career, then in search of meaning in a universe turned multiverse. Most memorable are the symbols of the dynamo and the Virgin, both representing force. Measuring this force in terms of its effect on man, Adams noted with regret that the Virgin, who in the Middle Ages had unified much of life, had been slowly losing her power. The modern world's own symbol of force, the dynamo, represented not unity but multiplicity—a chaotic universe that Adams could not understand, although he hoped that others, younger and more suitably educated, would be able to.

5
Literary Realists

We have already noted the drift toward realism in the work of the frontier humorists, the local-color writers, and De Forest. Where one finds carefully detailed settings, the effect of real speech, an attempt to depict a local and specific segment of human life, there is the raw material of realism. These elements may exist side by side with romantic elements, as in stories that have lifelike settings and speech but improbable or extraordinary actions. In humorous and satirical fiction we also find this coexistence, the realism appearing in the author's attitude, the romanticism in the material he laughs at.

It was not until the last quarter of the nineteenth century that realism as a serious literary theory began to be discussed in America, particularly by William Dean Howells and Henry James. However, the argument about realism in fiction (especially concerning the work of Balzac and Flaubert) had begun in France a generation before and had been continued heatedly in English literary journals. The student attempting to follow the fascinating debate will soon find what the disputants themselves eventually found: that they were arguing not merely a question of technique but the much more basic question of how fiction depicts human life.

Prose fiction is so much a part of our culture that we often forget how recently it came into being. For other categories of writing we have old precedents: Aristotle on drama; Homer, Virgil, and Milton on epic poetry; Pindar and Petrarch on lyric poetry, and so on. But we have no classic theory of fiction comparable to Aristotle's *Poetics,* nor any classic example of the novel comparable to Homer's epics. Thus those engaged in the great argument (which has not ended yet) had to begin from scratch; in both theory and practice they were formulating a new art form. Inevitably, they borrowed from other arts: James, for example, stressed the analogy between fiction and painting and between fiction and drama. The issue was further complicated by the introduction of science into the debate. The great French writer Émile Zola insisted that the novelist was comparable to the

27

sociologist, the physiologist, even the chemist; the novelist was less an artist than he was a scientist, dealing with men as natural phenomena subject to discernible (or discoverable) natural laws.

Perhaps the most basic argument that the realistic writer advances against the romantic writer is that the romantic does not depict human life as it really is; he sentimentalizes it or idealizes it, makes his people impossibly good or evil, puts them in situations unknown to ordinary life, and sends them to real or imagined exotic places. The implication is that romantic novels are meant to provide escape from reality; they do not deal seriously with the human situation. The realist, by contrast, stresses that the story should be contemporary in time, ordinary in setting, and faithful to the quality of most human existence. Some early French realists went so far as to insist that the realistic novel itself should be as dull as much of life is.

Neither James nor Howells subscribed to this extreme theory, but Howells did proclaim that common life accurately depicted is interesting. James argued that outward and obvious adventure is unnecessary, that the moral life of a child is as exciting as (and more important than) sea fights on the Spanish Main. The great body of James's own work is psychological realism, the portrayal less of outward happenings than of states of mind and feeling.

Neither Howells nor James sentimentalized or idealized their characters or situations, and if they and Mark Twain neglected or euphemized sexual love, it was mostly because the age demanded such decorum. All three writers, in fact, eagerly dealt in their work with the thorniest of moral and social problems. Although Howells spoke of "the smiling aspects of life," he carefully described the evil consequences of poverty, greed, and false patriotism. In James's novels there is so little idealizing of human life that the final effect of his work as a whole is tragic.

Twain represents a peculiar mixture of romantic and realistic elements. He attacked Scott and Cooper (two arch-romantics), and in such memorable passages as the Emmeline Grangerford section of *Huckleberry Finn* he satirized the excesses of romanticism. Yet his own work is anything but consistently realistic. In *Huckleberry Finn,* there is realism of speech, character, and setting, so that Twain seems not to be borrowing picturesque formulas from other books but to be going directly to life for his material. Equally important, the moral problem of slavery that confronts his characters is dealt with seriously and without sentimentality. But despite these realistic aspects, the novel is full of farfetched coincidences and improbable subplots. This unevenness is characteristic of much of Twain's serious fiction. Still, he was a realist by instinct and temperament, and he rarely sentimentalized. In fact, his later work (which was influenced by Zola and naturalism) is marked by a grimness and cynicism hardly equaled in American fiction.

Twain, James, and Howells were the chief American realists of the latter nineteenth century. Lesser realists of the period include the physician-novelist S. Weir Mitchell (1829–1914), who sometimes achieved psychological realism; Joseph Kirkland (1830–1894), author of *Zury, the Meanest Man in Spring County* (1887); the playwright James A. Herne (1839–1901); Ambrose Bierce (1842–1914?), best known for the short story "An Occurrence at Owl Creek Bridge"; James Lane Allen (1849–1925), a Kentucky local-colorist who shifted away from romanticism to realism; E. W. Howe (1853–1937), whose novel *The Story of a Country Town* (1883) relentlessly bares the small-town mentality; and Harold Frederic (1856–1898), who wrote *The Damnation of Theron Ware* (1896), a novel of religious disillusionment.

Realism steadily advanced during this period but did not take over the literary world. That readers continued to relish the literature of escape and entertainment can be seen in the vogue of Francis Marion Crawford (1854–1909) and Frank Stockton (1834–1902), still remembered for "The Lady or the Tiger?" An especially popular genre was the historical romance; memorable examples include *Ben-Hur* (1880) by Lew Wallace (1827–1905) and *When Knighthood Was in Flower* (1898) by Charles Major (1856–1913).

In his reaction to the optimism and sentimentality of romantic fiction, or at least bad romantic fiction, the realist turned more and more to the unpleasant aspects of existence: social injustice, personal fallibility, the quiet desperation of so much of human life. Near the end of the century this disposition to see life as essentially hard, if not tragic, was reinforced by the influence of Zola and other European naturalistic novelists. The effects of naturalism were far-reaching, and we shall examine the movement more closely in connection with such professed naturalistic writers as Stephen Crane and Theodore Dreiser.

SAMUEL LANGHORNE CLEMENS (MARK TWAIN) (1835–1910)

Surely the broadest achievement of all American realists was Mark Twain's. He wrote not one, but several classics. As a native humorist and local-colorist he stands supreme. He could use folklore not simply as picturesque trimming but as a means of developing plot and character. A one-time riverboat pilot (whence his pseudonym, meaning "two fathoms deep"), he knew the dangers that could lie under a beautiful surface and from this knowledge created settings that symbolized the coexistence of good and evil. For dialect he had the sharpest of ears. In character types he also excelled and displayed an unusual talent for describing crowds. What distinguished him most from his fellow local-colorists was his achievement as a psychological realist—his ability to go beyond the superficial aspects of a region to its very spirit and to give this spirit microcosmic significance.

Life. Twain was born in Florida, Missouri, and spent his boyhood in Hannibal, which in his fiction becomes St. Petersburg and Dawson's Landing. After working as a printer in Hannibal, St. Louis, New York, Philadelphia, Cincinnati, and some Iowa towns, he became a steamboat pilot on the Mississippi (1857–1861), served in the Missouri militia (1861), prospected in Nevada (1861–1862), and took up writing for various journals in Virginia City and San Francisco (1862–1866). Trips to Hawaii (1866), Europe, and Palestine (1867) furnished him with material for newspaper articles and lectures of increasing popularity, but not until publication of "The Jumping Frog" story (1865) and *The Innocents Abroad* (1869) did he receive national attention. In 1870 Twain married Olivia Langdon and settled in the East, living successively in Buffalo, Hartford, New York, and Stormfield, Connecticut. He soon achieved fame as a lecturer and writer. Unfortunately, however, his two chief investments (the Paige typesetting machine and the Charles L. Webster publishing company) drained his profits and then failed, forcing him to embark on a lecture tour around the world to pay off his debts. The somber cast of his later writing was caused partly by these events and partly by various family tragedies, including the death of his twenty-four-year-old daughter Susy.

Humor and Satire. Twain's humor combines several indigenous strains. The Down East strain reveals itself in his frequent understatements and political satire as well as in certain aspects of Tom Sawyer and Aunt Polly. The Old Southwest strain accounts for the ubiquity in his work of animal antics, frontier boasts, tall tales, and frame stories. A third strain, shared with the Literary Comedians, gave him the image and techniques of a professional. He could produce a laugh every sentence, for he knew all the tricks, including burlesque, malapropism, misquotation, euphemism, and anticlimax. On the platform he followed Artemus Ward's example of giving comic lectures in deadpan, with frequent digressions and perfectly timed pauses.

Throughout his career Twain employed satire. At first glance his targets seem completely disparate—melancholy, monarchy, reform movements, Gothic architecture, sentimental and flowery writing—but most have some connection with romanticism, which he hated with the passion of a confirmed realist.[1] During the two closing decades of his life Twain's satire became increasingly bitter and general. In his darkest musings he pondered over the source of evil, the meaning of determinism, and the nature of man's moral sense, only to conclude that of all the animals man must be the lowest. This satire, found at its harshest in such posthumously published works as "The Damned Human Race" and *Letters from the Earth,* comes close to the pessimism of Swift and Melville.

---

1. Twain himself sometimes resorted to the snapping twig and other devices used by such romantics as Cooper, whom he satirized in "Fenimore Cooper's Literary Offenses" and "Fenimore Cooper's Further Literary Offenses."

Representative Works[2]

"The Celebrated Jumping Frog of Calaveras County" (1865). Twain's version of a tale then being told in the mining camps and printed in the journals. Casting it as a frame story allowed him to create parallel hoaxes: one played on Jim Smiley by the stranger who fills Smiley's frog with quail shot, the other played on the "I" of the frame by his friend who sends him to Simon Wheeler, a storyteller certain to harangue him with an irrelevant yarn. The rambling speech of this inner narrator has the flavor of an oral tale; yet it reveals careful construction, progressing artfully through a series of anecdotes that not only establish Jim Smiley as a character dominated by a single trait but also prefigure the educated frog with two other unpromising heroes—a sickly looking horse and a bulldog named Andrew Jackson. Note the incongruities, the brief similes, the straight-faced narrator, the humanized animals, and the theme of appearance-versus-reality.

The Innocents Abroad (1869). A travel book reworked from letters Twain sent to American journals while touring Europe and the Holy Land in 1867. In this work Twain alternated sentiment with humor. More memorable than the reverent passages are his mock ecstasy over the "tomb of Adam," the deceptions that he practiced on guides, his refusal to praise the Old Masters, his jibes at travelers who put on airs, and the burlesque dramatic criticism he purportedly discovered in the ruins of the Colosseum.

Roughing It (1872). Combines fictionalized autobiography, travel, local color, and humor, especially the tall tale. Part 1 tells of Twain's journey westward and his life in Nevada, presenting him as a willing escapee from civilization, as a tenderfoot undergoing initiation, and as a veteran member of the new West. Part 2, reworked from his newspaper articles, takes him to San Francisco and Hawaii. *Roughing It* abounds in beautiful scenes, natural wonders, and animal curiosities—among them an alkali desert, the Washoe Zephyr, jackass rabbits, and Mexican plugs. Some of these (like Lake Tahoe) Twain described conventionally; on others he put his personal stamp. The lowly coyote, for example, he transformed into an unpromising hero, giving him the winner's role in that archetypal conflict between native and newcomer, a triumph repeated in the landslide case of Chapter 34. Local-color aspects include not only such characters as pocket miners, saloon keepers, Chinese, Mormons, nabobs, toughs, and outlaws but also the very spirit of these flush times—the optimism, the thrill seeking, and the lust for quick riches. The tone varies considerably. On the one hand, Twain idealized the pony express and the newspaper editor; on the other, he criticized the government, burlesqued sentimental literature, and displayed

2. Some of Twain's other works are *A Tramp Abroad* (1880), *The Prince and the Pauper* (1882), *The American Claimant* (1892), *Tom Sawyer Abroad* (1894), *Those Extraordinary Twins* (1894), *Personal Recollections of Joan of Arc* (1896), *Tom Sawyer, Detective* (1896), *Following the Equator* (1897), *What Is Man?* (1906).

a decidedly antiromantic attitude toward Indians. Humor, especially the tall tale, appears everywhere. A buffalo climbs a tree; a camel chokes to death on Twain's manuscripts. "Grandfather's Old Ram," the best of all these stretchers despite its crudities, also qualifies as a windy, a hoax, a frame story, and an unfinished tale (traditional counterparts are listed under types 2250–2280 in the Aarne-Thompson *Types of the Folktale* [GB]).

The Gilded Age (1873). Written, with Charles Dudley Warner (1829–1900), as a satire on the corruption and speculative fever of the Grant era. Much of the novel was based on actual events and people. Colonel Beriah Sellers, the story's most memorable character, is an irrepressible promoter reminiscent of Twain himself, some of his relatives, and an inventor-engineer named George Escol Sellers.

The Adventures of Tom Sawyer (1876). Probably Twain's most popular novel; combines initiation, local color, and humor. Its characters include Aunt Polly (who strikingly resembles Benjamin P. Shillaber's Mrs. Partington) and Huck Finn, here as in his own book enviably independent and resistant to civilization. Tom, unlike Huck, sees things in a literary context, strives for dramatic effects, and shows ingenious leadership ability. Like Huck, he speaks in a remarkably convincing vernacular, is highly superstitious, and belongs with the "bad boys" just then emerging in American literature. More mischievous than cruel, Twain's bad boys prove genuine innocents who are rewarded despite their breaches of convention. Tom, moreover, definitely matures as after a long struggle he overcomes his fears and testifies against Injun Joe. So thorough is Twain's development of the community—its setting, characters, and customs, its evil as well as its good—that the book qualifies as one of the few successful American local-color novels. The town has its graveyard, haunted house, nearby island and cave, each the stage for climactic scenes that sometimes verge on the mythic and legendary. Among its typical local characters are Muff Potter the town drunk, Judge Thatcher the bigwig, and Mr. Dobbin the schoolmaster. Also impressively integrated with the story are the customary activities of the town—Sunday school, the morning service, picnics—each the occasion for some of the book's richest humor or pathos. While this local color is obviously nostalgic, it is not overly sentimentalized. Indeed, Twain satirizes everything from detectives to female compositions and narrates the early chapters in a mock-heroic manner.

"Baker's Blue-Jay Yarn" (1880). A fable from *A Tramp Abroad* that depicts animals as having the same variety of powers, feelings, virtues, and shortcomings as humans. While the jays can see the quixotism of their attempt to fill an entire cabin with acorns, the owl lacks their sense of humor. Note the well-observed animal gestures, the telling similes, and the clever opening.

"Frescoes from the Past" (1883). Originally intended for *Huckleberry Finn* but instead published as Chapter 3 of *Life on the Mississippi*. One of

Twain's best frame stories. A magnificent simulation of a complete storytelling scene, supposedly overheard by Huck while hiding on a raft. First there are folksongs; then the raftsmen's frontier boasts lead to a fight won by an unpromising hero; next an interlude of tall talk about Mississippi water is followed by the ghost tale of Dick Allbright and the haunted barrel.

Life on the Mississippi (1883). A pioneer work on one of America's most romantic areas, the Big River. The book appeals as humor, autobiography, and social criticism, as background for *Huckleberry Finn,* and as local color with panoramic scope. Yet it can be tedious, for Twain included numerous statistics and quotations to get the work up to book size. The best section, originally printed in the *Atlantic Monthly* as "Old Times on the Mississippi," tells of Twain's experiences as a cub pilot. Here, in this microcosmic initiation story (Chapters 4–20) and in other chapters, we find many romantic elements: heroic pilots, exciting steamship races, a phantom boat, and tales of violence and horror. Yet the book also attacks romanticism, and more than one horror story ends in a laugh. Above all, Twain lashed out at the South for its aristocratic stance, its duels and feuds, anachronistic Gothic architecture, and fancy rhetoric—most of which he blamed on the influence of Walter Scott. The humor includes burlesques and tall tales: A lovers' leap story ends with the maiden falling on her parents, and one man tells a lie so big that his listener's left ear swells up. Also see "Frescoes from the Past" (above).

The Adventures of Huckleberry Finn (1885). Twain's masterpiece; regarded by many as the greatest American novel.

THEMES. Among those suggested by scholars are egalitarian comradeship (Hoffman), initiation accomplished through symbolic death and rebirth (Cox), the search for a substitute mother (Barchilon and Kovel) and a substitute father (Lynn), the acceptance of adult responsibilities (Adams), the pursuit of freedom (Marx), and the victory of innate humanity over an ill-educated conscience (Blair). Surely one of the most rewarding ways to view the story is as a conflict between self and society—between Huckleberry Finn as he wants to be and a society that would drag him down to its own level (H. N. Smith). Ironically, this slaveholding society has so twisted his conscience that when he decides to seek Jim's freedom, he thinks he has committed a sin that will send him to hell.

CHARACTERIZATION. From beginning to end, Huck never knows his own worth, which even in the early chapters shines through, as his Sancho-Panza-like realism shows the flaws in Tom Sawyer's quixotic fantasies (Moore). Later, away from this false romanticism, Huck leads a life of true adventure, each day bringing new opportunities for the development of his character. In situation after situation (the Grangerford-Shepherdson feud, the shooting of Boggs, the circus rider incident, and the Wilks affair, to cite but four examples), Huck's sympathies prove warm and wide. He meets knaves at every turn and is himself their victim; yet he can pity the trickster as well as the tricked. Even the King and the Duke arouse his sympathy when they are tarred and feathered.

Jim, like Huck, proves his worth as the novel progresses (Hoffman). Of course, we naturally feel for him. He is victimized from within and without: from within by an oversensitive conscience that recalls with anguish how he struck his deaf daughter for not shutting the door, from without by the King, the Duke, the Phelpses, and others intent on ending his freedom, and even by Tom and Huck (McIntyre). (That Tom does not repent his mistreatment of Jim indicates his static character here; that Huck does repent indicates his maturation.) Jim, moreover, not only serves as a companion on the river; he acts as Huck's teacher and father. Granted, what he teaches best is superstition, but these are functional superstitions useful for life on a primitive level. Jim's predictions, in fact, come true.[3]

STRUCTURE. Some scholars see this novel as having a structure of three (Adams, Doyno) or five parts (Gerber). Another way of analyzing its form is to identify rhythms in the many unconscious repetitions (Baldanza) and patterns in the larger prediction-fulfillment sequences. Still, we must not expect much unity here, for Twain wrote without a clear plan, improvising as he went along (H. N. Smith). In fact, after he composed the first sixteen chapters, which concentrate on Jim's escape, he laid the manuscript aside for two years or more. He then resumed with a new purpose in mind: to satirize all levels of antebellum Southern society by having Huck go from one class to another—the aristocratic Shepherdsons and Grangerfords, the low-class residents of Bricksville, the middle-class Phelps clan—only to find false values and cruelty everywhere. But Twain accomplished this at the cost of keeping Jim out of the plot for chapters at a time, changing Huck from actor-narrator to spectator-narrator, and sometimes having Huck report things that only a mature, well-read adult might notice (H. N. Smith, O'Connor). After the satirical section comes what is usually regarded as the story's climax, the passage in which Huck decides to risk hell to save Jim. Subsequent chapters (32–43) seem anticlimactic, not only because they follow this moral victory with a return to the situation in the early chapters (Tom again romanticizing, Jim again his victim, Huck again putting up with it), but also because Jim's escape has no purpose since he has already been freed in Miss Watson's will. For these and other reasons the ending has been attacked (Marx); but it has been defended, too (Eliot, Trilling), most convincingly perhaps as the proper culmination of the book's satire (Adams and *ALS* for 1967, pp. 69–70).

---

3. In "Jim's Magic: Black or White?" *AL* 32 (1960): 47–54, Daniel G. Hoffman relies primarily on Newbell Niles Puckett's *Folk Beliefs of the Southern Negro* (a standard work) to prove that most of Jim's superstitions are not derived from Africa. The societal function of superstition is discussed in J. G. Frazer's *Psyche's Task* (London: Macmillan, 1909).

A Connecticut Yankee in King Arthur's Court (1889). The story of Hank Morgan, an inventor and factory superintendent who suffers a head blow that sends him out of nineteenth-century America into sixth-century England. Here he becomes King Arthur's minister; modernizes this medieval civilization with Sunday schools, sewing machines, newspapers, telephones, bicycles, and gunpowder; proclaims a republic upon Arthur's death; is attacked by the established orders; blows up his improvements; and kills every knight in the realm.

At times the novel seems inconsistent. It begins as burlesque but ends as satire, and as the tone shifts the humor lessens. Although he harshly criticizes medieval slavery, the Church, and monarchy, Twain idealizes Arthur and at the end has Hank yearn for Camelot as his true home. The satire is sometimes aimed less at medieval English institutions than at modern American targets like the spoils system and the protective tariff. Equally complex is Hank himself—at best a high-minded demiurge, at worst a cheap, destructive trickster whose inventions are questionable symbols of progress. This complexity reflects Twain's ambivalent attitude toward the Middle Ages, his somewhat shaken faith in technology (Guttman) or his fear of the forces that threatened it (Andersen), and his growing pessimism.

Pudd'nhead Wilson (1893–1894). One of Twain's more powerful but less humorous novels. Set in Dawson's Landing in the antebellum period, it tells how a slave-woman named Roxy switches babies so that her child (the false Tom Driscoll) grows up free and rich while her master's child (the real Tom Driscoll) grows up a slave. When the lawyer "Pudd'nhead" Wilson discovers the fraud through fingerprints, the narrative qualifies as a detective story. Throughout, Twain achieves genuine realism by refusing to simplify. He gives Roxy the looks of a white woman, the speech of a black, noting that while she is actually fifteen-sixteenths white, she is black before the law. And while he motivates her with the highest maternal instincts, gives her all the courage that her son lacks, and shows her as the tragic victim of circumstances, he also makes her dishonest. Judge Driscoll (the false Tom's foster father) reveals similar complexities. He buys votes and avenges insults in blood; yet he has courage and admits his faults. This novel has been criticized for its foreign twins (who have little function), its lack of focus (who is the true hero?), and its confusing insistence on determinism. Yet its merits are many: tight structure, telling ironies, pioneer use of fingerprints, realistic treatment of slavery and miscegenation, and universality of characterization.

"How to Tell a Story" (1895). An essay showing Twain's preference for oral narration that meanders, makes effective use of pauses, and seems unconscious of its humor—qualities that describe his own comic pose. As an illustration of timing he tells "The Golden Arm," a traditional "jump story" (see Z13.1 in Stith Thompson's *Motif Index* [GB]).

"The Man That Corrupted Hadleyburg" (1899). A short story about a town put to the test by a character who embodies three of Twain's favorite types—the mysterious stranger, the sleuth, and the devil. Because Hadleyburg stressed a single virtue—honesty—and did not apply this virtue to concrete temptations, it succumbed to the stranger's hoax. Yet the story ends on a note of optimism, for the victims learn through experience and finally become truly honest. The story exhibits tight construction and fine irony.

The Mysterious Stranger (posthumously published 1916). The story of young Satan's visit to sixteenth-century Eseldorf (Ass Village) and its effect on the narrator, one of three favored boys. Unfortunately, this novelette is a bowdlerized composite assembled by Albert B. Paine (Twain's authorized biographer) and Frederick A. Duneka from two manuscripts that Twain never intended to go together. The much-discussed ending, actually written for a radically different story, dissolves the narrator into a thought, and everything else—including God, the universe, heaven, and hell—into a dream. Its solipsism has been regarded as Twain's way of achieving serenity in those dark final years of his life; but it may also be interpreted as a tribute to the transcendent power of the artistic imagination, which creates its own reality.

WILLIAM DEAN HOWELLS (1837–1920)

William Dean Howells was not only dean of American letters but also one of the most influential writers of the nineteenth century. He led the attack on contemporary romanticism and, more important, served as the chief spokesman for realism. Mark Twain and Henry James (who ironically had little use for each other's writings) both enjoyed his friendship and counsel. In various ways, chiefly as editor and reviewer, he also helped younger authors such as E. W. Howe, Hamlin Garland, Brand Whitlock (1869–1934), Harold Frederic, Stephen Crane, and Frank Norris, thus opening the door to later versions of realism and to its successor, naturalism. In practice as well as theory, Howells celebrated a new democratic art devoted to the commonplace. He was a prolific and impressive writer.

Life. Howells's early life was spent in various parts of Ohio, where he worked as compositor, reporter, and editor. *Poems of Two Friends,* which he coauthored with John James Piatt (1835–1917), was published in 1860; and in the same year Howells wrote the campaign biography of Lincoln for which he was rewarded with the American consulate in Venice (1861–1865). There he married Elinor Mead. At the end of his term they moved to Boston, where Howells worked on the *Atlantic Monthly,* serving as editor-in-chief from 1871 to 1881. In 1891 the Howellses moved to New York City, where Howells conducted two highly popular departments for *Harper's Magazine:* "The Editor's Study" and "The Editor's Easy Chair." In 1908 he was elected first president of the American Academy of Arts and Letters, which later (1915) awarded him a gold medal for his fiction.

Literary Creed. Howells believed that

1. Romanticism is pernicious. His contention that romantic novels gave readers a false view of life (and therefore ill prepared them for it) resembles arguments advanced against fiction in the eighteenth century.

2. Art and the artist must serve the masses in order to better their lot and enlarge their humanity. This belief, for which Howells was most indebted to Tolstoy, gives a high democratic purpose to the artist but at the same time robs him of the supreme individuality he enjoys under other theories.

3. The modern novelist should write about the commonplace, not about exotic settings, heroic characters, and unusual events. Realism of the commonplace is restrictive in the sense that it rules out the extraordinary, but broadening in the sense that it opens up the ordinary—a new, or at least neglected, area for literature.

4. The "more smiling aspects of life" (p. 128)[4] appeared in contemporary American novels because American life was less deeply tragic than life elsewhere. (By this Howells did not mean to advocate optimism in American literature. He was merely noting that literary realism varies from one culture to another.)

5. Decency rather than sordid and guilty sex is characteristic of the best Anglo-American novels because it is characteristic of Anglo-American society. Howells therefore traced this decorum to realism. If his attitude and his fiction nevertheless seem prudish, it is worth remembering that he championed some of the more daring writers of his day, and that even his own fiction sometimes shocked his contemporaries.

6. The novelist should not confine himself to the single emotion of love but should write about other states as well. This is a plea for psychological realism.

7. The novelist should subordinate plot to character, thus avoiding the contrived plots of the romantics.

Representative Works

A Modern Instance (1881–1882). Marcia Gaylord, of Equity, Maine, elopes with a newspaper editor, Bartley Hubbard; but their marriage proves discordant and ends in divorce. She returns to Equity, and he is killed in Arizona. Although this novel sounds conventional now, it created a stir in Howells's time, not just for the novelty of its divorce theme, but because of

---

4. *Criticism and Fiction* (New York: Harper, 1891). See Everett Carter (*Howells and the Age of Realism*, pp. 187–189) for Howells's earlier use of this phrase.

the author's refusal to simplify his characters or to rise above the common-place. Marcia is ruled by often unfounded jealousies and shows an almost unnatural affection for her father. Nor is she perfected by suffering, like typical romantic heroines. Bartley, less ill-tempered but cynical, has "no more moral nature than a base-ball" (p. 243),[5] a remark perhaps equally applicable to Marcia. Yet Howells ultimately places less blame on these individuals than on their society. The more commonplace his characters are, the better, for they represent millions of their contemporaries who have also been victimized by urbanization and other changes.

The Rise of Silas Lapham (1884–1885). Howells's best-known novel; a good example of his realistic theories in action. In the first place, the protagonist is not heroic by conventional standards. He is uneducated, uncouth, and boastful. He makes a fortune manufacturing paint and disfigures the landscape advertising it. At his first dinner party he sweats with apprehension and then gets drunk on the wine. Ultimately he fails in business, loses his new home in a fire, and instead of breaking into Boston's Back Bay society, returns with his family to rustic life in Vermont. He does rise morally by refusing to engage in a shady deal that would profit a few but harm many; yet Howells does not follow the romantic formula by rewarding this inner victory with external prosperity. Second, this plot contains no great climactic scenes. The fire is described with more irony than excitement, and Lapham's bankruptcy, instead of occurring with dramatic suddenness, is so gradual that his daughter Penelope pronounces it totally unheroic. (Despite this realistic appearance, the plot has a tight structure.) Third, in several passages but especially in the dinner scene, Howells denounces the romantic novel for its harmful effects. Even the most sensible characters fall victim to false romantic notions, and it takes an objective outsider, the Reverend Sewell, to restore them to their common sense. His solution to the love triangle in the novel's subplot is to observe an "economy of pain" (p. 338).[6] Penelope, by refusing to marry Tom Corey (who loves her and not her sister Irene), would cause three people to suffer; so the minister suggests that Pen marry Tom and leave the suffering to Irene, who would suffer anyway. With this practical advice (which is ultimately followed), Howells ridicules the stock ingredients of romantic novels that solve their plots with the "heroic" self-sacrifice of a character who then dies of a broken heart.

Indian Summer (1885–1886). An international novel about Americans in Florence. It celebrates maturity and common sense, exposes the follies of romanticism, and touches upon such subjects as expatriation and child-rearing. Yet all these ideas are presented in an unobtrusive manner. Delightful humor comes consistently from Theodore Colville (the protagonist) and in isolated instances from Mrs. Amsden, Reverend Waters, and the Inglehart

5. *A Modern Instance* (Boston: Houghton Mifflin, 1910).
6. *The Rise of Silas Lapham* (Boston: Ticknor, 1885).

boys (modeled on the students of Frank Duveneck, the American painter). *Indian Summer* is also noteworthy for its realism. Each of its major characters displays lifelike flaws, and none qualifies as a romantic hero or heroine. Colville, though eminently witty, is forty-one years old, graying, fat, rheumatic, and embarrassingly awkward on the dance floor. He succumbs to the romantic idea of regaining his youth by proposing to the twenty-year-old Imogene Graham. Imogene thinks she is curing Colville of melancholia, but he has already been cured by his own maturity, and Imogene's behavior must therefore be viewed as sentimental. Both she and Mrs. Bowen, the middle-aged widow whom Colville really loves and finally marries, labor under a false idea of self-sacrifice (akin to Penelope Lapham's). Once they and Colville modify their romantic illusions, the conflict is resolved.

Criticism and Fiction (1891). A collection of essays from "The Editor's Study" (1886–1891) that embody the ideas in Howells's literary creed.

A Traveler from Altruria (1892–1893). An outlander novel combining social criticism with utopian ideas. The outlander, Aristides Homos, learns by tactful but persistent questioning that America suffers from inequality and acquisitiveness. He in turn describes his homeland, where peace, brotherhood, altruism, and artistry prevail; where everyone works three hours a day; where there is no money or business, no poverty or luxury, no crime, no religious cultism, and no fear of death.

"Editha" (1905). A short story, powerful as an antiwar piece and as an exposé of the romantic heroine. Editha Balcom has little perception of reality and follows clichés furnished by art. She fancies herself worthy to be won by a knight of her own making, and when he dies she easily assumes the role of chief mourner. George Gearson's mother, on the other hand, sees through the rhetoric of war to the dead and bereaved on both sides and can even accept her son's death if it leaves him guiltless of killing. The perceptiveness of the Gearsons, mother and son, reveals itself in their fine ironies, which contrast neatly with the shallow speech of the Balcoms, father and daughter.

Through the Eye of the Needle (1907; belated sequel to *A Traveler from Altruria*). A utopian novel in epistolary form. Part 1 comprises outlander letters from Homos in America to his friend in Altruria. After Homos marries an American widow, he takes her to his native land; Part 2 consists of outlander letters in which she describes this marvelous place to her friend in America.

HENRY JAMES (1843–1916)

Although relatively close to us in time, James is one of our classical writers. We turn back to him not only as an innovator of psychological realism but also as one of the greatest American literary minds. He was an aesthete in the best sense of that term: a man whose fine mind saw art as the most interesting thing in the world.

Life. James was born into a brilliant and wealthy family in New York City. His father was an amateur philosopher and theologian who tended toward a mystical Swedenborgianism. Henry and his brother William (who was to become the renowned philosopher of pragmatism and one of the earliest American psychologists) were educated privately in the United States and Europe. Henry briefly studied painting and law but soon turned his attention to fiction and devoted his life to it with passionate intensity. In Europe he met the great novelists of the time, including Turgenev, Flaubert, and Zola. The last forty years of his life were spent abroad, and in 1915 he became a British subject, largely because of America's delay in entering World War I.

Critical Theories. It has been said that if James had never written a line of fiction he would still be known as one of its great theorists and critics. Many of his comments are scattered throughout letters, essays, and reviews, but the essence of his view is found in "The Art of Fiction," in his prefaces to the New York edition of his collected works, and in his notebook entries. Together they form what is surely the most distinguished body of theoretical and practical commentary on fiction in all of American literature.

"The Art of Fiction" (published 1884). James's best-known essay. James's basic assumption is that fiction is a serious art form—not a pastime nor a game in which the reader indulges his daydreams, as Stevenson thought—but an "imitation of life." James often seems to echo Aristotle's description of tragedy: Fiction is imitation (that is, a translation into a different medium) of life or a part of life. It deals with the larger truths of human existence that comprise the pattern behind the facts. But the novelist is not a philosopher; the patterns of life emerge in his work because he has succeeded in catching the "color" of life itself—a color that varies as it is perceived and felt by different artists. James anticipates such writers as Joyce and Lawrence in their arguments for the artist's complete freedom of choice in his subject matter. James's own tastes and temperament led him to deal largely with the moral and social problems of middle- and upper-class society, but his theoretical position demands only two qualities of fiction: that it be made of experience intensely perceived (either from life or from imagination) and that it be interesting.

Prefaces and Notebooks. These offer a wealth of technical information about the craft of fiction, with examples taken mostly from James's own work. He has much to say about the necessity of establishing "the sense of place," about the virtues of "dramatic" presentation of character (although he failed as a dramatist, he was much taken with the dramatist's methods), and about ways to foreshorten time. But his most famous comments concern "point of view," what he calls the "center of consciousness" (see especially his prefaces to *The American, The Princess Casamassima,* and

The Ambassadors and his notebook entries on *The Ambassadors*). He advocates the limited point of view, presenting the story through the filter of a single character or a succession of characters (as in *The Wings of the Dove* and *The Golden Bowl*). The first-person point of view is feasible in shorter works, but in full-length works it makes for looseness. James argues for characters of great sensitivity as his centers of consciousness, since the more they perceive of life the more the reader perceives. These "intense perceivers" may become too sensitive, too alert to the nuances of a given situation, but this is a gamble James is willing to take. Along with the increasing complexity of his style, his hypersensitive narrators, or protagonists, have alienated James from the common reader, as James himself realized.

Classification of James's Work. As is the case with many great writers, James's work is often divided into periods—early, middle, and late—usually on the basis of increasing subtlety of style and greater attention to the mental and emotional workings of his characters. Such an arrangement is useful because it allows one to follow the treatments of two of James's major themes: first, art and, second, the clash between the old European world and the new American world (the so-called international theme). One may trace James's progress as an artist by dealing with the fiction that takes art as its subject, beginning with *Roderick Hudson* (1876) and then turning to the most famous stories and novellas that deal with artists and various principles of art. Or one may assume the larger task of following James's use of the international theme from *The American* (1877) and *Daisy Miller* (1879) through *The Portrait of a Lady* (1881) to the novels of what Matthiessen called "the major phase": *The Wings of the Dove* (1902), *The Ambassadors* (1903), and *The Golden Bowl* (1904).

It is James's use of the international theme that makes up the bulk of his major work. The conflict of moral and cultural values between the Old and New Worlds was a milieu as endlessly interesting for James as the sea was for Melville—especially since it gave him an immense range of intense perceivers through whom this many-leveled conflict could be recorded. In general, the personal conflict in these works is between more or less ingenuous Americans and sophisticated Europeans. In the early work, the contrast is almost between American good and European evil. But the later work shows a greater awareness of complexities. Milly Theale (*The Wings of the Dove*) is still the American sacrificial lamb, morally superior to her European counterparts, as are Daisy Miller, Christopher Newman (*The American*), and Isabel Archer (*The Portrait of a Lady*). But Lambert Strether of *The Ambassadors* arrives at an awareness of the culpability of American moral simplicity, and Maggie Verver, the heroine of *The Golden Bowl*, achieves a moral triumph over her husband (a European prince) only at great cost both to herself and her father. Unlike Milly Theale, she does not literally die, but like Strether and many of James's other major figures, she faces a life in which moral righteousness has displaced the possibility of human happiness. Renunciations occur so often in James's work that many readers have concluded that for him sexual love was a tragic rather than romantic aspect of human life.

This classification of James's writing into such broad thematic categories, though necessary for an overall view, ignores some of his other works and even slights some of the work that is thus classified. The artist stories are not *merely* artist stories; the international works are not *merely* international conflicts. In both groups, in others such as the ghostly tales, and in still other stories not easily classified, one finds real people playing out real dramas of loneliness, suffering, and betrayal. Nearly all the major works, however classified, strike the reader primarily as dramas of individual humans, not as thesis stories.

Representative Works

Daisy Miller (published 1879). A novella that helped make James's reputation. One of his earlier treatments of the international theme, it depicts an ingenuous young American girl (fresh as a daisy, morally speaking) who is out of her element in cynical European society. Although her conduct is perfectly innocent by objective standards, she is ostracized not only by the European characters but also by a young American, Winterbourne, who has been in Europe too long to perceive her rightness. The novella ends with Daisy's death after exposing herself to Roman fever in the Colosseum. This scene at the foot of a great cross evokes the deaths of the Christian martyrs at the hands of the Romans, and Winterbourne is aptly named, for it is his moral coldness (his European view) that sends Daisy to her death.

"The Real Thing" (1893). One of James's most famous artist stories. The narrator, an artist, is trying to paint people of the upper class. When Major and Mrs. Monarch present themselves as models, he has a chance to paint from "the real thing," for they are upper-class people who have fallen on poor days but who still look their former parts. But their factual reality is not enough for the painter; he finds that he can paint upper-class people only by using professional models who in life are members of the lower class. Beneath the pathos of the Monarchs lies James's artistic point: Art in some way transmutes reality; it does not—cannot—reproduce it and should not try.

The Turn of the Screw (1898). A novella, and the most famous of James's horror tales, this has been dramatized in stage, television, and movie form in recent years. The story is told in the first person by a governess hired to care for two young children at a lonely English country house. She does battle (or thinks she does) with the ghosts of two former servants who have returned to corrupt the children. After several horrifying experiences, she believes she has saved the children, only to have one of them die in her arms, presumably from fear. The story has occasioned a great deal of commentary, most of it turning on the question of whether or not the governess really sees what she says she does. James has kept so carefully to her point of view and so artfully introduced her story that the controversy itself reads like a detective story.

"The Jolly Corner" (1908). A short ghostly tale that probably ranks second only to *The Turn of the Screw* in popularity. The hero, like James himself, is an American who has spent most of his life abroad; now he returns to the house on "the jolly corner" of his youth, wondering what he might have been if he had stayed in America and become a man of commercial affairs. Night after night he stalks a ghostly presence in the old house, somehow knowing that the presence is avoiding him. Finally, they confront each other, and the hero faints at the horror of his hypothetical double, who is hideously deformed and maimed. Like most of James's other ghostly tales, the story shows that, more than any other American writer since Poe, James could evoke and make believable strange and aberrant states of consciousness.

"The Beast in the Jungle" (1901). A short story sometimes placed with the ghostly tales and sometimes with the artist stories. It is an intense story in which almost nothing happens. John Marcher deliberately withholds himself from the joys and pains of ordinary life because he feels certain that he is somehow marked for a special (and terrible) experience. This belief he confides to May Bartram (who loves him), and for years they speculate about what form the experience will take. May finally dies, and at her grave, in a moment of profound revelation and despair, Marcher realizes the nature of the beast, the form of the experience. He was to be the one to whom nothing ever happened, whom life had entirely passed by.

"The Pupil" (1891). A short story that, like "The Beast in the Jungle" and many other of James's works, deals with the theme of the unlived life. Young Morgan Moreen, a brilliant boy with a congenitally weak heart, lives with his family, who are on the edge of poverty yet manage to racket about Europe, staying at inferior hotels and sometimes running out on their bills. He comes to know and love his young English tutor, Pemberton, and they have long talks about a larger and freer life. But when an opportunity for such a life presents itself, Pemberton (who is poor himself) cannot rise to the occasion, and Morgan dies—partly at the thrill of new possibilities, partly at the shock of his tutor's lack of enthusiasm, and partly at his parents' willingness to let him go with Pemberton. He has been betrayed from within and without.

The Ambassadors (1903). Probably James's most popular novel and the one he himself thought best. It is one of his last and finest treatments of the international theme. Lambert Strether, middle-aged and widowed, is sent to Paris by the wealthy Mrs. Newsome of Woollett, Massachusetts, whom he hopes to marry. His mission is to rescue Mrs. Newsome's son Chad, who is reportedly being corrupted by Parisian life. Beginning as a narrow moralist, Strether gradually awakens to an awareness of the beauty and the values in Paris. Chad seems to have become a better man through his affair with a lovely Frenchwoman, and Strether (like John Marcher in "The Beast in the Jungle") realizes that he has let most of his own life slip by. At the end, Chad and Strether reverse their positions. Chad, in whom the materialistic spirit of Woollett still lives, seems ready to abandon his mistress for the more "productive" life of Woollett business, and Strether begs him to stay with her. Strether finally renounces Paris and the possibility of the good life to return to Woollett.

It is the capacity for creating individual characters like Strether that makes James a great writer. We argue still about Strether's decision to return to America just as we argue about the characters of Hamlet and Raskolnikov. All of them remain in our memories and imaginations. They are all what James called "super-subtle fry," not much like us as we are, perhaps, but as we might be.

The reader coming to James looking for overt action and melodramatic thrills will find only opacity and dullness. But it is no accident that James's reputation is higher now than it has ever been. Freud, Jung, Joyce, and Proust have made the interior world at least as important and interesting as the exterior one. Like most great artists, James anticipated the truths of a later day.

6
Naturalism

In theory, naturalism is not necessarily either pessimistic or fatalistic, but in practice it deals with the evil aspects of human life and is in varying degrees deterministic, if not fatalistic. According to Zola, who coined the term, the naturalistic writer uses the knowledge and attitudes of current science in his depiction of human life. He does not try (as James said) merely to catch the color of life itself; he seeks to describe a segment of human existence according to the laws of scientific causality. This makes the writer, in Zola's definition, a "determinist"—one who believes in scientific causality—but it does not make him a fatalist. That is, the writer (aware of the work of Darwin, Marx, and later, Freud) analyzes his characters and their social situations as effects proceeding from various combinations of physical, emotional, and environmental causes. But like the scientist, he does not assume that these combinations must exist. In fact, as Zola said, the writer believes that when the causes operative in human life are better understood, human life itself will be improved, just as when the causes operative in the human body are understood, the body can be made healthier.

Zola allowed what may be called a "limited determinism"—a notion of causality drawn largely from the evolutionary biology of Darwin (interior causality) and the social thought of Marx and Auguste Comte (exterior causality). Man was a phenomenon caused by certain hereditary and environmental forces, but it might be possible by increased knowledge to understand these forces and, if they caused undesirable effects, to change them.

Other naturalists followed Zola in describing human life scientifically—analyzing the economic, social, and physiological forces they saw shaping that life—but carried Zola's limited determinism to its logical extreme, which is absolute fatalism. Once this concept of scientific causality is allowed, they said, there is no point at which it can be cut off. Howard Mumford Jones has divided American naturalism into the "hard" and the "soft." The hard naturalists (Ambrose Bierce, Crane, and Dreiser) accept complete determinism and see man as an effect produced by causes over which he has no control. The soft naturalists or "meliorists" (Hamlin Garland, Jack London, and Frank Norris) accept Zola's limited determinism but believe that the social situations they describe can be changed.[1]

Whether hard or soft, the naturalist concerned himself with the dark side of life, as a physician concerns himself with disease. A rigid determinist like Crane or Dreiser saw man as trapped and toyed with by the vast, indifferent forces of nature or of a cruel social system. Crane's "The Open Boat" is a classic image of this kind of fatalism, and Clyde Griffiths in Dreiser's *An American Tragedy* is a classic example of the victim of these forces. The limited determinist analyzed and exposed harmful social or political systems or the destitution of the small farmer or slum dweller in the hope that these causes of such evil and suffering might be removed.

Naturalism was and is a pervasive force in both fiction and drama. Once the concept of scientific causality had been introduced into imitative literature, no serious writer could ignore it. Much of the fiction and drama of the late nineteenth and early twentieth centuries is either consciously naturalistic or is at least touched by the concept of scientific causality. The student seeking a background for American turn-of-the-century writing need only glance at A. E. Housman's poetry, Hardy's novels, and such plays as Ibsen's *Hedda Gabler,* Strindberg's *Miss Julie,* and Chekhov's *The Cherry Orchard* to see, in varying degrees, the current of determinism and fatalism so common in American writing of the same period.

Crane, Norris, Dreiser, and London are sometimes called the "first generation" of American naturalists. The designation is primarily chronological, indicating that they were forerunners of the naturalistic writers of the late 1920s, 1930s, and later: Dos Passos, Farrell, Steinbeck, Sherwood Anderson, O'Neill, and others. But another way of distinguishing them from the later naturalists is to say that their scientific and philosophical point of view is pre-Freudian. Their outlook is based largely on the scientific work of Charles Darwin, T. H. Huxley, and Karl Marx, and on the philosophies of Herbert Spencer, Friedrich Nietzsche, and Arthur Schopenhauer. With the popularization of Freudian psychology in the 1920s, naturalism took on a new dimension, for Freud seemed to have shown scientifically that man is as predetermined in his inner mental and emotional life as he is in his outer social and economic life. Naturalism, especially in its Freudian bias, is by no means dead. Its scientific outlook has become more sophisticated than it was in the work of Dreiser and Anderson and the early plays of O'Neill. But in its haunting insistence on causality in human life—with the resulting curtailment of human freedom—

1. H. M. Jones, *Guide to American Literature and Its Backgrounds Since 1890* (Cambridge, Mass.: Harvard University Press, 1955), pp. 95–96.

it has helped shape the work of such writers as Hemingway and Faulkner, and it is still to be found as an active force in contemporary writers, including Norman Mailer, Ralph Ellison, William Styron, Edward Albee, and Tennessee Williams.

STEPHEN CRANE (1871–1900)

Often labeled America's first naturalistic writer, Crane was one of the most original writers of his time. All his best work—fiction, journalism, and poetry—is marked by a unique vividness of imagery, remarkable compression, and experimentation with techniques borrowed from music and painting.

Life. In the space of his twenty-nine years, Crane managed to live a Byronic kind of life beyond anything he depicted in his fiction. Born in New Jersey, the fourteenth child of a Methodist minister, Crane received an eccentric schooling and was, in effect, pushed into his literary career before he was twenty. His reputation came quickly but was tragically brief. In 1893 he paid for a private printing of *Maggie: A Girl of the Streets;* seven years later he was dead of tuberculosis. In the interim he published *The Red Badge of Courage* (1895), became well known as a short-story writer and experimental poet, and was involved in a series of escapades with women. He also became a war correspondent, covering the Cuban insurrection in 1896, the Greco-Turkish War in 1897, and the Spanish-American War in 1898. He lived his last two years in England with Cora Taylor, a divorcée who had run a house of prostitution. Incredibly, he managed, like Keats, to turn out some fine work in his last desperate days, including the volume of poems *War Is Kind.*

Naturalism. Assuming as the basic premise of naturalism the notion of determinism in human life, there seems reason to call Crane's major fiction naturalistic. What has confused an already not very clear literary argument is that some critics and readers have assumed that all naturalistic writing must be the same. And so it must be, of course, in its basic assumptions. But like any other kind of writer, the naturalistic writer must be allowed his unique quality of mind, his particular perception of the world he describes, and his private means of recording that perception. Crane was above all a stylist, a craftsman in the best sense, one in love with words as well as ideas. He did not write like Dreiser, either in the way he used words or the techniques by which he presented his fiction. Dreiser was a compiler, a detailer, who listed facts almost in the way that Joyce in *Ulysses* playfully listed the contents of a dresser drawer. By comparison, Crane needed only enough facts to present an impression. He loved the sharp, dramatic phrase; he loved the flat, laconic understatement that was to become a trademark of Hemingway's best prose; he loved to juxtapose motifs in almost a musical way; he loved to let a color work for him.

Economy by dramatic statement occurs everywhere in Crane's work; in Section III of "The Open Boat," for example, we read, "Shipwrecks are *apropos* of nothing." And in Section V, "The wind had a voice as it came over the waves, and it was sadder than the end." At the end of Chapter VI in *The Red Badge of Courage* a general is pleased that his command has fought off the Rebel attack, and Crane observes ironically: "In his eyes was a desire to chant a paean . . . . He held a little carnival of joy on horseback." "The Open Boat" ends with a masterpiece of brief understatement. The survivors stare out at the night sea, and Crane comments: "The white waves paced to and fro in the moonlight, and the wind brought the sound of the great sea's voice to the men on the shore, and they felt that they could then be interpreters."

Often, too, Crane juxtaposed certain scenes, almost musically, for thematic effect. Thus the novel *Maggie* opens with Maggie's brother Jimmie fighting with neighborhood boys, continues with his father kicking him and bringing him home, and then introduces Maggie. When Maggie upbraids Jimmie he hits her. When they enter the kitchen the mother attacks the boy, and then the mother and father quarrel violently. When Maggie drops a plate her drunken mother goes into such a frenzy that Jimmy flees the room, and the scene between Maggie and her mother is not shown—an offstage horror. What Crane has done is to build the violence in Maggie's life to an almost unbearable crescendo by juxtaposing the kinds and degrees of violence to which she is daily exposed. At the end of the novel, the tragedy of her death, after she has gone from man to man and finally to the river, where the waters are "lapping oilily against the timbers," is set against her mother's bizarre reaction on hearing the news; she first finishes her dinner, then transports herself into a ritualized frenzy of hypocritical grief.

Finally, Crane experimented with colors, in a way that caused Willa Cather to refer to him as a postimpressionist. Examples are everywhere at hand: the garishly blue hotel set against the white of the Nebraska blizzard; the famous image in *The Red Badge of Courage,* of the red sun pasted in the sky like a wafer; at the beginning of "George's Mother" the rainy street that "glistened with that deep bluish tint which is so widely condemned when it is put into pictures," and later in the same story George's drunken fall that is described without explanation as "yellow."

In brief, Crane's artistry sometimes seems to set him off from other naturalistic writers whose methods are more commonplace. Yet his assumptions are theirs. Maggie, who miraculously bloomed in a mud puddle, is ruined and killed by a milieu that is absolutely vicious. George Kelcey is destroyed by a combination of inner and outer forces over which he has no control. Henry Fleming is a hero or a coward depending almost completely on circumstances outside himself. And occasionally Crane, speaking in the authorial voice, underlines the naturalism of his work—in "The Open Boat," for example, and very specifically in "The Blue Hotel," where the world is described as "a whirling, fire-smitten, ice-locked, disease-stricken, space-lost bulb."

Representative Works

Maggie: A Girl of the Streets (1893). Crane's first novel. Maggie Johnson, brought up in the slums of lower Manhattan by drunken and hypocritical parents, pathetically seizes on a friend of her brother's as a knightly figure who will save her from her wasteland world. But this world itself has so shaped her view that she is unable to see that the worthless Pete is nothing more than a drunken lecher. He seduces her but refuses to marry her, and she ends as a girl of the streets, the very fate she has desperately tried to avert. She drowns herself, and her family and neighbors righteously lament her fall from virtue, ironically underlining the fact that this fall was inevitable.

The Red Badge of Courage (1895). Sometimes called the archetypal American war novel. Although it is much praised for its realism, Crane wrote it before he had ever witnessed any real war experience. Later, after covering the Greco-Turkish War, he commented that he found the book accurate. The story is primarily that of young Henry Fleming, who begins with youthful illusions about war and some doubts about his own courage; largely through circumstances, he discovers that the chaos and horror of battle make him practically mindless, so that he is alternately a coward and a hero. Ironic circumstances lead him into each role. Fleeing in panic before a Confederate attack, he comes on the corpse of a soldier sitting upright against a tree in a little chapellike copse of trees. The horror of seeing ants crawling on the corpse's lips sends the boy rushing back toward the lines. Later, an accidental blow to the head gives him his wound, his red badge of courage. In a later engagement, just as mindlessly as he had fled earlier, he acts heroically, even carrying the regimental flag. At the end of the novel he feels that he is a man, that he has faced death and can face it again. But this is his conclusion, as the conclusion by the survivors in "The Open Boat" is theirs, not necessarily either Crane's or the reader's.

"The Open Boat" (1898). Crane's most fatalistic story. Based on a real shipwreck that occurred while Crane was covering the Cuban insurrection, the story is a minor epic of four men's struggle to survive in a small lifeboat. Narrated partly by the correspondent character and partly by the omniscient author, the story implies that those who survive do so only by chance. There is no God to rail at, not even an evil God of the kind that Melville's Captain Ahab partly believes in. There is only the sea and luck—good or bad. The strongest of the four, Billie the oiler, drowns in the surf as they finally beach the boat. Although the survivors believe they can interpret the sea because they have lived with it, the larger implication of the story is that they do not know it, that if anyone can interpret the sea it is the dead man.

FRANK NORRIS (1870–1902)

Norris has sometimes been called America's most doctrinaire naturalist, often for reasons extraneous to his writing. Partly educated in France, he read Zola and occasionally referred to himself as a "young Zola." But compared to the work of Crane or Dreiser, his work is by no means consistently naturalistic. Much of his writing, in fact, is best described as romantic escapism (entertainment), and even his best work (by consensus, *McTeague* and *The Octopus*) is marked by romantic tendencies, in the worst sense of the term.

Life. Norris was born in Chicago to well-to-do parents who moved to San Francisco when he was in his early teens. Privately schooled, he spent more than a year in Paris as an impressionable eighteen-year-old, ostensibly studying painting but apparently writing romantic stories. He later attended the University of California at Berkeley, then Harvard, where he studied creative writing. Like Crane, he was briefly a war correspondent, first in Africa, then in Cuba. He wrote professionally for *McClure's Magazine* and also was a publisher's reader; and in the latter role he was largely responsible for the publication of Dreiser's *Sister Carrie*.

Occasional Naturalism. If Norris had written nothing but *Moran of the Lady Lettie* (1898) and *A Man's Woman* (1900) he could conveniently be classed with Kipling and lesser turn-of-the century romantic novelists. If he had written nothing but *McTeague* (1899) and his projected "wheat trilogy" (of which *The Octopus*, 1901, and *The Pit*, 1903, were completed), he could fairly be called a naturalist. But he wrote all these things and also some criticism. His best-known essay, "A Plea for Romantic Fiction," argues for a kind of fiction that is closer to Stevenson than Zola, or even Howells and James.

Norris is as hard to place as his contemporary Jack London. Both read the scientific, deterministic, naturalistic literature of their time, and both were no doubt influenced by it. But both retained elements of romanticism in their work. It may be argued that neither Norris nor London was an artist of the first rank; that neither saw completely the artistic possibilities of naturalism or of any other consistent artistic point of view. In any case, the parts of Norris's work that are still read with more than historical interest are those that seem most obviously naturalistic.

Representative Works

McTeague (1899). A naturalistic novel. McTeague, physically large but mentally small, is illegally practicing dentistry in San Francisco. He marries

Trina Sieppe, a cousin of his friend Marcus Schouler. Trina wins money in a lottery and by careful hoarding and investing increases it. But she will not share it with McTeague, whereupon McTeague begins to drink heavily and abuse her. Schouler exposes McTeague as a quack. McTeague steals part of the money, kills Trina, and tries to escape through Death Valley, pursued by Schouler. In an incredible fight McTeague kills Schouler, but not until Schouler has handcuffed them together, dooming McTeague to die of thirst in the desert. McTeague's decline from stupidity to bestiality is not ineffective, but what force the book has is dissipated by the nebulous characterization of Trina and Schouler and by the melodramatic ending.

The Octopus (1901). The first novel of Norris's projected Epic of the Wheat trilogy (*The Pit,* 1903, was also completed). In this novel Norris attempted naturalism on the panoramic scale popularized by Zola. The subject is the battle between the California wheat farmers and the economic monopolies of the railroads. As in Steinbeck's *Grapes of Wrath,* the novel depicts, in numerous subplots, the defeat of the farmers by what seem to be natural and inevitable social and economic forces. S. Behrman, representative of the monopoly, is ironically buried by wheat in the hold of a ship that is being loaded. But his death—nearly as melodramatic as that of McTeague—can do nothing to change the system.

THEODORE DREISER (1871–1945)

Dreiser was not only America's greatest pioneering naturalist but also, quite simply, one of its greatest writers. His writing has become a norm against which other naturalistic or seminaturalistic writing can be measured.

Life. Dreiser was born in Terre Haute, Indiana, one of eleven children. His father, a rigid and fiercely traditional Roman Catholic, fostered in the young Dreiser a hatred of all formal religion. The family was beset by economic misfortunes that on several occasions necessitated their splitting up. (One of Dreiser's brothers became Paul Dresser, of Tin Pan Alley fame.) Dreiser was brought up in the poverty and psychological insecurity that he was so often to depict. At eighteen he drifted to Chicago, where he worked at a number of menial chores before beginning a long series of newspaper jobs in St. Louis, Toledo, Pittsburgh, Cleveland, and finally, New York. His first novel, *Sister Carrie* (1900), was suppressed upon publication, necessitating his return to newspaper work. Beginning with *Jennie Gerhardt* (1909), his reputation grew slowly, until he could negotiate the movie rights to *An American Tragedy* (1925) for the then unheard of sum of $90,000. But he never achieved formal acclaim, being passed over for both the Pulitzer and the Nobel prizes.

Tragic Naturalism. Few critics seriously dispute Dreiser's position as America's premier naturalist, the American Zola. Both in theory and in practice he accepted the whole complex of ideas that seemed to form the basis of naturalistic thought. He knew Darwin, Huxley, Spencer, and, later, Freud; he admired the work of Flaubert and Zola; he encouraged the naturalistic bias of such younger writers as Sherwood Anderson and Sinclair Lewis. The characters of his novels are portrayed as the products of their heredity and environment. They are iron filings drawn to a magnet, or they are moved by subtle "chemisms" that are inevitable, if not completely understandable. As is often pointed out, there are no villains or heroes in Dreiser's work; there are only forces and the products, or victims, of these forces.

Primarily, the force driving a Dreiser character is that of illusion, the ingrained belief that money, property, and power constitute not only success but happiness. In fact, Dreiser's work as a whole is the most massive indictment of American materialism ever written. F. Scott Fitzgerald's Gatsby, for all his air of mystery and idealism, has as forebears Carrie Meeber, Frank Cowperwood, and Clyde Griffiths. Not only Fitzgerald but Anderson, Lewis, Dos Passos, and most of the other social-protest writers of the twenties and thirties owe a gigantic debt to Dreiser. Dreiser, however, was not primarily a social-protest writer. For all his famous clumsiness with words, his maddening prolixity, his often pointless accumulation of detail, he was above all an artist, an artist in the Jamesian sense of the term. Readers of James will recall his advice to young writers in "The Art of Fiction": not to think too much about optimism and pessimism but to try to catch the color of life itself. Dreiser obviously thought a great deal about optimism and pessimism, but he also succeeded in his own way in catching the color of life. An interesting comparison might be made between the pessimistic Dreiser and James, who found life ferocious and sinister. The typical action of each man's work is the bitter or tragic undoing of a character. The typical attitude implicit in the work of both is that the world is, after endless investigation, not really understandable but that it unquestionably tends toward human misery. It is the sense of dark forces shaping the lives of men that gives both men's work its tragic quality. For Lewis, Sinclair, Dos Passos, and others it is a particular system that is wrong; for Dreiser and James it is the world itself that is somehow wrong, but the wrongness remains shrouded in mystery.

One would not expect to find Dreiser testifying to the beauty of human life; yet he did. He clearly did not mean the happiness of life; he may well have meant the "beauty of tragedy." For Dreiser and James, each in his own way an intense perceiver of life, the sad drama of man's failure in his fight against forces he can never fully comprehend has a kind of beauty and dignity.

Representative Works

Sister Carrie (1900). Dreiser's first novel, suppressed upon publication and not republished until 1912. Young Carrie Meeber leaves her country home for the lure and excitement of Chicago. In search of the good life, which for her means clothes, money, and social position, she becomes the mistress of Charles Drouet, a salesman. Contented for a while, she then meets George Hurstwood, who is richer than Drouet and moves in better social circles. She leaves Drouet for Hurstwood, but through a series of unlucky circumstances Hurstwood loses his position and thus for her his charm. Then she goes on the stage and becomes a modest success on her own. She leaves Hurstwood, who has tragically declined and who, after being reduced to begging, kills himself. Carrie is left with her "success"—her money, her clothes, the assurance that there will be a new man soon—but also with a dim realization (of which the reader is keenly aware) that these things are not enough.

An American Tragedy (1925). Generally considered Dreiser's best novel. Like his trilogy (*The Financier,* 1912; *The Titan,* 1914; and *The Stoic,* 1947), the story is based on an actual case that was covered in great detail by the newspapers. Yet the work is by no means a nonfiction novel like Truman Capote's *In Cold Blood.* The first section, detailing Clyde Griffiths's boyhood, strongly recalls much of Dreiser's early life. Young Griffiths's character is slowly and meticulously established. One of its strongest elements is his assumption of the American dream: that happiness comes from money, success, and a kind of automatic romantic love. Griffiths has a rich uncle who employs him in his collar factory and thus allows him to live on the perimeter of wealth and success. He has an affair with one of the shop girls, Roberta Alden, who becomes pregnant; almost at the same time he becomes attracted to the rich and beautiful Sondra Finchley. Roberta demands marriage, and Griffiths is trapped. All his sense of values, built into him since childhood, tells him he must be free to marry Sondra, for that is the way to the dream. He plans to murder Roberta by drowning her in a lake, but in a scene replete with ambiguities he both does and does not kill her. (If ever Dreiser wrote a scene that shows the lurid intermixture of fate and seeming free will, this is surely it.) Whatever the cause, Roberta dies, and all circumstantial evidence is against Griffiths—as are the community, the wealthy Griffiths, and the public, inflamed by the newspaper coverage. He is judged guilty and sentenced to be electrocuted. Quite clearly, Dreiser means to suggest that Griffiths is not really to blame, and most readers assume that society is actually on trial. The further assumption is that this is a peculiarly American tragedy, that Dreiser is condemning American society for its hypocritical moral code, its corrupt political and legal methods, and the sensationalism that denies Griffiths any chance of acquittal. All this is quite true and was to be echoed in any number of other novels, including Richard Wright's *Native Son* (see p. 142). Yet when the book is read in the context of Dreiser's whole work, its anti-American bias seems much less important. Clyde Griffiths's story is a "concrete universal": Though local and American, it conveys the quality of life everywhere.

JACK LONDON (1876–1916)

To list the facts of London's life is to court incredulity. Born in San Francisco and largely self-educated, he became (among other things) a hobo, a seal fisherman, a war correspondent, a gold miner in the Klondike, a rich farmer, and a Socialist (of sorts). In odd ways he combined genuine narrative talent, a reporter's sense for important news, a professional traveler's ability to picture strange places, and a pseudo-philosophical turn of mind that allowed him to incorporate parts of the work of Darwin, Marx, Nietzsche, and others without any sense of contradiction. Some of his work is purely Marxian (*The People of the Abyss,* 1903; *The Iron Heel,* 1907); some is romantic agrarianism (*The Valley of the Moon,* 1913). But his best-known work—*The Call of the Wild* (1903); *The Sea-Wolf* (1904); and *White Fang* (1906)—is a strange blend of Darwinian natural selection and Nietzschean concepts of superman. It is in these stories that London comes closest to naturalistic writing; both his canine protagonists and Wolf Larsen seem to act according to traceable deterministic laws. A number of famous short stories, such as "To Build A Fire," are also naturalistic in the sense that they show man as subject to inexorable physical laws. But such stories are primarily local-color depictions of strange and harsh environments and do not seem to have any social implications. Like Norris, London was more concerned to tell a good story, to entertain, than to be a consistent naturalist, or indeed a consistent artist of any kind at all.

7
Social Protest and Realism

In the preceding chapter we examined some of the ambiguities and implications of the term *naturalism*. We saw that, despite Zola's argument to the contrary, the notion of determinism (the presence of a cause-effect relationship operating endlessly in human life) makes for tragic or pathetic literature.

None of the writers discussed in this chapter can be called naturalists in the sense that Dreiser, Crane, or Norris can. But the notion, introduced by Zola and his followers, of human life as in some sense determined by inner and outer forces was one that no serious writer could thereafter ignore. Looked at in one way, it induced pessimism, for the ultimate causes of current environment and behavior lie far in the past and are perhaps undiscoverable. Looked at in a different way, it induced optimism, for what was caused could perhaps be changed, while what simply happened could not. Most "social-protest" literature from about the turn of the century on worked from this double view (with varying degrees of emphasis): Social and human evil is determined by causality; yet it is also curable. This is a major motif in the work of such different writers as Hamlin Garland, Edith Wharton, Edgar Lee Masters, Upton Sinclair, Sinclair Lewis, James T. Farrell, John Dos Passos, and John Steinbeck, as well as many others. In short, there is hardly any serious fiction written since about 1890 that cannot with some reason be called naturalistic, and most of it has been so called.

HAMLIN GARLAND (1860–1940)

Most of Garland's early and most valuable work blends the kind of social-protest fiction discussed above with strong elements of local color and literary patriotism. His best work is in the form of the short story or the longish story that is practically a novella.

Life. Garland's early life was spent in the Middle Border region that was to be the setting of his most important work. Born on a Wisconsin farm, he was brought up in the rugged frontier country of Iowa and the Dakotas. At the age of twenty-four he took what little money he had, moved to Boston, and began seriously to educate himself. He haunted the Boston Public Library, reading Darwin, Spencer, Whitman, and Henry George as well as the realistic Russian, French, and English fiction then being published. His stories of the Middle Border, most collected in *Main-Travelled Roads* (1891) and *Prairie Folks* (1893), brought him a measure of reputation that was enhanced by his autobiographical books *A Son of the Middle Border* (1917) and *A Daughter of the Middle Border* (1922), which won a Pulitzer Prize. His later and less popular work, including fiction, poetry, reminiscences, biography, and studies of psychic phenomena, reflects a mellowing of his social consciousness and a diminishing of intensity.

Veritism. Garland coined the term *veritism* for what we call social-protest realism and local color combined. His depictions of the drab and demeaning farm life on the Middle Border are the best examples of what he meant by the term. They are written from the inside—not by tourists or visiting reporters, but by a native. It is this truth-by-experience that gives them their artistic merit. Like Whitman, Garland insisted that America could be portrayed only by Americans and that only inhabitants of a place could understand and depict its local elements. It was this nearness to the truth of a particular place, Garland thought, that would save the artist from preaching and sentimentality. Whatever the truth of this artistic dictum, Garland's early work at its best is direct, forceful, and unsentimental, at once evoking the feel of the country and the deadening poverty and labor of its inhabitants.

Representative Works

"Mrs. Ripley's Trip" (1891). One of the best-known stories from *Main-Travelled Roads*. Mrs. Ripley, aged and prematurely worn by poverty and labor, has dreamed for years of going back East for a visit. By dint of years of small economies, which make her life even harder, she finally manages the trip. But after twenty-three years on the farm the visit to an easier life can seem to her only a kind of spree. She returns to the farm with a mixture of loyalty and resignation, resolved never again to leave it.

"Under the Lion's Paw" (1891). Another of the veritistic stories from *Main-Travelled Roads,* a story that shows quite clearly Garland's early sympathy with Henry George's theory that only property should be taxed. A farmer named Haskins, driven out of Kansas by drought and a plague of grasshoppers, buys a farm in the Middle Border from a land speculator named Butler. But he buys it "on time," making only a small down payment and mortgaging the rest. After a year of slavish labor during which he and his family improve the farm, he discovers that Butler has raised the price of

the farm, precisely because it has been i
year for nothing—or rather for Butler—beca
Butler will foreclose his mortgage. As in Stein
real villain is not the individual speculator but the
him practice his jungle ethics.

EDITH WHARTON (1862–1937)

In her major works Edith Wharton combined some of the bes
the genteel tradition in fiction with the newer social-protest impe
fiction of the 1920s and 1930s. She was equally at home in the fields
short story and the novel, both short and long.

Life. Like Henry James, whom she greatly admired, Edith Jones wa
born into upper-level genteel New York society. She was brought up
within the graceful yet confining circle of that society, and although in her
work she was often critical of it, she never lost its imprint nor really wished
to. At twenty-three she married Edward Wharton of Boston, but the marriage soon dissolved in all but name. She suffered a nervous breakdown,
and her husband moved steadily into a mental state that ultimately led to his
confinement. Again like James, Wharton spent much of her life abroad,
especially in France.

Novels of Manners and Social Protest. Although Edith Wharton wrote
voluminously until her death, her best work (except for her volume of reminiscences, *A Backward Glance,* 1934) was done in the first two decades of
the twentieth century. It includes two collections of short stories, *The
Greater Inclination* (1899) and *Crucial Instances* (1901); three novellas,
Ethan Frome (1911), *Bunner Sisters* (1916) and *Summer* (1917); and two
novels, *The House of Mirth* (1905) and *The Age of Innocence* (1920).

A longtime friend of James, Wharton regarded him as the master contemporary novelist, and her work has marked resemblances to his, both in
theme and technique. No student of James can read of Lily Bart in *The
House of Mirth* without being reminded of Isabel Archer in *The Portrait of
a Lady,* or read *The Age of Innocence* without being reminded of *The Ambassadors,* or read stories such as "The Pelican" without recalling James's
"artist" stories. Even Wharton's style in these works seems to echo
James's endlessly subtle, elegant variation.

But whether or not Wharton tried to write like James, the best of her work
shows that she differs from him in important ways. She is much less subtle
in her character delineation, much less careful in her use of point of view,
and much more direct in her presentation of theme. Certainly, *The House of
Mirth* and *The Age of Innocence* are novels of manners like much of James's
major work, but they are novels of manners turning into the more obvious
kind of social criticism to be found in the work of writers like Sinclair
Lewis. In Wharton matters of social and class distinctions are much more

her characters are far less
ex than Lewis's. Her depic-
en the old aristocratic New
ng in from the West have a
iat point toward Lewis and

ers from James and allies
and 1930s. In novellas like
regional realist; she depicts
1 a way that James never
r closest approach to doc-
d intellectual and imagina-
only important difference
eiser's *American Tragedy*
n as inevitable, springing
_____ from fate or from a defective social system. Nonetheless, the defeat
happens.

n (1862–1937)

proved. Haskins has worked his
use if he refuses Butler's terms
beck's *Grapes of Wrath*, the
economic system that lets

57

t aspects of
s of the
of the

Representative Works

The House of Mirth (1905). One of Wharton's best novels. Lily Bart is
caught in the dilemma of whether to marry for love or for the considerations
deemed important by the New York society to which she partly belongs. Although the rendering of the social atmosphere recalls James, Lily's decline
in status and eventual suicide are much more melodramatic than are similar
depictions by James. The reader who can ignore the Jamesian quality of the
prose may well see strong resemblances between Lily Bart's tragedy and
that of Crane's Maggie Johnson.

Ethan Frome (1911). Wharton's best-known novella and an example of
her "regional" writing. Set in rural New England, the story is a grim depiction of the potential for horror in human relationships. It is almost a model
naturalistic story, a perfect example of what one of Sherwood Anderson's
characters called life—a trap. Ethan Frome, struggling for survival on a
poor New England farm, is married to a whining, neurotic woman. A young
cousin, Mattie Silver, comes to live with them, and she and Ethan fall in
love. When the wife, Zenobia, drives Mattie from the house, Ethan tries to
kill himself and Mattie by smashing their sled into a tree. But he succeeds
only in turning Mattie into a helpless cripple who becomes a ghastly echo of
Zenobia. He is left to live at the whim of these twin furies.

WILLIAM VAUGHN MOODY (1869–1910)

Born in Spencer, Indiana, Moody was brought up in the Ohio River town
of New Albany. Orphaned early, he still managed to attend Harvard (A.B.,
1893; M.A., 1894). Then he taught at the University of Chicago and in 1902

with Robert Morss Lovett wrote *A History of English Literature,* for many years a standard text. He had limited success in his poetic dramas but did write two prose plays, which were produced on Broadway. His poetry, like that of his friend Edwin Arlington Robinson, is often modern in theme but traditional in form. To the current reader, however, Robinson seems modern and Moody, Victorian. Although Moody admired Whitman, he seems to have learned nothing from him technically. His rhymes are all too often heavy and thumping and his metric rigid. The poems for which he is best remembered are "Gloucester Moors" (1901), which deals with evolution, and "An Ode in Time of Hesitation" (1901) and "On a Soldier Fallen in the Philippines" (1901), which treat American suppression of the Philippine liberation movement.

EDGAR LEE MASTERS (1869–1950)

Masters grew up in rural Illinois and became a lawyer in Chicago. A prolific author, he wrote a great deal of verse (most in traditional forms), novels, biographies, and a long autobiography. He is now known for one book of poems, *Spoon River Anthology* (1915), which was an enormous success on publication and for years afterwards. In retrospect, the critic can see it as one of the best examples of a literary subject then coming into popularity: the satire of small-town life, the indictment of the provincialism, bigotry, and stagnation often called "the revolt from the village." Sherwood Anderson's *Winesburg, Ohio* (1919) is a prose counterpart of the poem, as are some of the earlier works of Garland and the later works of Sinclair Lewis.

In form, the poem is a collection of "epitaphs," speeches given by the dead inhabitants of Spoon River. Usually in free verse, the epitaphs reveal the town's sordid community life. Among the best portraits are the corrupt newspaper editor ("Editor Whedon"), who is buried near the river where the garbage is dumped, and "Daisy Fraser," the town prostitute, who contributed ten dollars to the school fund each time she was arrested. Many of the portraits now seem too obvious and heavy-handed; yet the book remains at least a qualified success.

EDWIN ARLINGTON ROBINSON (1869–1935)

Robinson's work, like Frost's, is generally considered traditional when compared to the New Poetry of Pound, Eliot, and Williams.

Life. Robinson was brought up in Gardiner, Maine, the "Tilbury Town" of his poems. He managed two years at Harvard, then moved to New York where he wrote his early poems while living in poverty. Given a job in the New York Customs House by President Theodore Roosevelt (who had heard of Robinson's plight), Robinson managed to survive. His early and best work brought him little money and almost no recognition. His later and generally inferior work finally caught critical attention, and his *Collected Poems* (1921) received the first Pulitzer Prize for poetry.

"**Traditionalism.**" Like Frost, Robinson is content with the older forms: the sonnet, regular meter, blank verse and easily recognizable structure. Intellectually, too, he is more "late Victorian" than "early modern." The reader will find in his work echoes from Browning, Hardy, and Meredith in his use of the psychological vignette, and echoes of Tennyson and many of the late Victorian agnostics in his thought. But his best work is by no means dated. Though apparently without any real knowledge of Freud or Frazer, he nevertheless dealt with the same human situation as the more sophisticated Pound and Eliot. The world as wasteland, the alienation of the artist, the possibility that life is meaningless—these were as much preoccupations of the late Victorian writers as of modern ones. The New Poets did not invent new life situations; they talked of current versions of perennial situations in new terms and in new kinds of poetry. Robinson, again like Frost, chose to portray perennial things in old ways; it is a comment on his technical brilliance that he remains not only readable but relevant. Part of this relevance comes from his use of language. Though his work contains a good deal of diction reminiscent of Keats and other romantics, he was also capable of using the sharp, idiomatic language of common speech. And it is frequently this mixture of "literary" and common language that startles the reader and makes the poem both old and new.

Although Robinson was a real master of the sonnet and of even older lyric forms, he was basically a narrative poet. His long blank verse treatments of Arthurian material are not much read today, but his shorter poems retain their original freshness and power. Characters like Richard Cory, Miniver Cheevy, Mr. Flood, and the man and wife in "The Mill" are briefly and effectively set before us in narratives that are really short stories in verse (as Pound called Frost's narratives). Part of their strength lies in Robinson's attitude toward his characters, which combines irony with compassion. Robinson is weakest in his philosophical poems, perhaps because he had no firmly fixed religious or philosophical viewpoint. He could not project the flamboyant agnosticism of Housman or Hardy; yet, like Tennyson, he found little with which to replace it.

Representative Works

"Richard Cory" (1897). One of Robinson's best-known narratives. In four perfectly regular quatrains Robinson suggests the emptiness of Gilded Age values. Having all that age thought good, Cory "put a bullet through his head." The poem is a good example of traditional form made new by the use of precise and often colloquial language: Cory was "a gentleman from sole to crown" and "fluttered pulses" when he spoke.

"For A Dead Lady" (1910). An example of Robinson's lyric work at its most romantic pitch. In diction, syntax, and theme the poem is old-fashioned. Yet for most readers it is probably successful, if only by virtue of the remarkable last four lines, which suggest one of poetry's oldest themes: mutability and the transience of beauty.

"Eros Turannos" (1916). A short narrative that recalls Meredith's *Modern Love*. The narrator gives all that can be known of the necessary, yet destructive, love between a man and his wife. But he implies that the situation is ultimately understandable only to a god.

"The Man Against the Sky" (1916). A poetic statement of Robinson's philosophical and religious beliefs. It opens with a vivid image of a man going over a hill at sunset, an image that clearly suggests going to death and to whatever is beyond death. But the rest of the poem is often obscure. Robinson rehearses many of the arguments for belief and disbelief in an afterlife: the questioning of orthodox beliefs, the contentions of science that man is merely an animal, the logical argument for suicide. At the end he has reached no conclusion.

8

The Modern Temper

No brief discussion of modern American writing can explain its variety and frequent brilliance or tabulate the historical and cultural contexts that form it and give it its subject matter. The great clichés about all creative literature apply here. The most obvious is that creative literature deals with evil, that it is in fact a reaction to some kind of evil—moral, physical, social, psychological, metaphysical. The best of all conceivable worlds would produce no literature as we know it, hymnology excepted. Looked at this way, modern writing differs from older writing most importantly insofar as its perceptions of evil differ from earlier perceptions, insofar as the evils assume different faces, or both. This view is the theme of T. S. Eliot's famous essay "Tradition and the Individual Talent," which argues that literature is a continuum because human existence is a continuum. Neither human life nor the writing about that life is ever wholly new; yet neither life nor writing is ever exactly duplicated. The past persists in the present in the form of the invariables of the human condition—varieties of evil culminating in death—but the present modifies the past by its own cultural reactions to these invariables.

The twentieth century has not lacked for evils that evoke literature. War, depression, poverty, racial hatred, spiritual aimlessness have been the matter for such different writers as Eliot, Frost, O'Neill, Cummings, and Ralph Ellison. And as is always ironically the case, scientific progress has discovered new evil or sharpened the modern perception of older evil. Aside from the horror that we have imposed upon nuclear energy, the advances in depth psychology and anthropology have contributed greatly to the decline of orthodox religion and have forced many to look fearfully into what seems an abyss. But, again, the fear of the abyss, of oblivion after death, is as old as man's imaginings.

New reactions to perennial evil generally manifest themselves in literary techniques or forms, and literary history is really more an account of techniques than of subject matter, insofar as form and content can be separated. A brief examination of the major forms of modern American poetry, fiction, and drama may illustrate this ever-changing relationship between the old and the new.

POETRY

One of the most stirring literary movements in the early twentieth century was what was called the New Poetry, especially the poetry of Pound and Eliot. In its compression, its allusiveness, its pose of antiromantic objectivity, it was certainly different from the then prevalent Georgian or late Tennysonian verse. Yet both Pound and Eliot took pains to point out that it was not really new. Pound acknowledged his debt to Whitman, to Browning, to Chinese and Japanese verse, and to the marvelous directness of Greek and Latin, both to the languages themselves and to the great classical poets. Eliot's high praise of Dante, the English Metaphysical poets, and the French symbolists helped bring these bodies of writing back into popularity. Even the most difficult aspect of new poetry, its lack of logical or sequential structure, had its foreground not only in Oriental poetry and French symbolism but in earlier American writing, particularly such poems of Whitman's as "Song of Myself" and "The Sleepers." The question of Pound's and Eliot's influence on other poets is too tenuous to go into here except to note William Carlos Williams's obvious debt to Pound and the echoes of Eliot to be found in MacLeish, Crane, Ransom, and Lowell. But, direct influences aside, their experiments with free verse, irregular rhyme, and even the mixture of prose with verse opened a doorway through which many very different kinds of poets passed. As Pound himself said, modern poetry is possible largely because Whitman chose to write in free verse. After that, anything was possible: Cummings's splintered syntax and typographical puns, Marianne Moore's syllabic verse, Williams's attempts to write quantitative verse, Stevens's incredibly beautiful use of words as color and sound as well as units of meaning.

One thing seems clear about modern American poetry: it is certainly not impersonal and antiromantic in the sense that Pound and Eliot used these terms. In fact, it is very doubtful if even their own poetry was in any important sense impersonal. From the perspective of half a century we can see that Eliot's talk of an objective correlative and Pound's description of poetry as a kind of equation for emotion perhaps illustrate something of the way a poem does its work but do not imply anything one way or the other about the poet's personal feelings. The poem works—evokes intellectual and emotional reaction—by virtue of its parts, perhaps most often its imagery. But the poem also "says," if only by indirection. And the poet says the poem. The later poetry of both Eliot and Pound is intensely personal, though it retains the preciseness of techniques that both writers earlier associated with impersonal poetry. Stevens is perhaps the closest to a pure aesthete in American poetry, one who frequently seemed to write a poem simply for the words' sake. But he is the exception. For the rest, the factor of impersonality simply does not exist. Even experimental poets like Cummings and Marianne Moore speak clearly from personal points of view. The work of Crane, Roethke, Shapiro, and Lowell is so personal that it is occasionally painful. The black poets (Langston Hughes, Gwendolyn Brooks, Robert Hayden, James Wright, LeRoi Jones, and others) are passionate and personal in much of their work. The poetry stemming from the beat movement of the late 1950s (mainly the work of Ginsberg, Corso, Snyder, Brother Antoninus, and the later work of Shapiro) made almost a fetish of revealing one's personal feelings. And the work of such younger poets as W. D. Snodgrass and Sylvia Plath tends to be almost completely autobiographical.

T. E. Hulme and Pound predicted that the verse of the future would be "classic": hard, dry, precise, unsentimental. Their prophecy has turned out to be partly true, partly false. The language of modern poetry is certainly less literary than that of the turn of the century, and verse techniques have often moved toward precision, if only the precision of prose. But most modern poetry is just as "damp" and personal as that of Keats, Rossetti, or Owen.

FICTION

The continuity of American fiction from about 1890 to the present is probably more obvious than that of American poetry. It is true that the works of Henry James and Norman Mailer seem remarkably different; yet the canons of the early realistic novel, probability and serious attention to character, are the most obvious characteristics of modern fiction. No one can say of modern American fiction what Stevenson said of fiction in general: that it is to the grown man what the toy is to the child. Modern fiction writers take themselves seriously, even when they are comic writers like Philip Roth or Kurt Vonnegut, because there is general agreement that modern fiction is exactly what James claimed it was, a serious imitation of life, and always, at least by implication, a comment on life.

Perhaps it is this sense of the seriousness of fiction that has limited experimentation. What may be called the standard or normative fiction of the twentieth century is that of Katherine Anne Porter, Hemingway, Fitzgerald, Robert Penn Warren, Saul Bellow, and others: fiction that is relatively straightforward in its methods, using occasional flashbacks, keeping tight control over the stream of consciousness of its characters, distinguishing itself mainly by the writer's individual choice of theme, symbolism, and style. Faulkner and Dos Passos are probably the major experimenters (their work is discussed in detail later). Faulkner's experiments with time, point of view, and narrative strategies (some of them clearly echoing Joyce) are generally viewed as attempts to present something closer to the fullness and complexity of reality than the standard novel does. Like most experimenters, Faulkner sometimes succeeded and sometimes failed. The violent dislocation of time and the at first bewildering variety of point of view in *The Sound and the Fury, As I Lay Dying,* and a few other works seem generally acceptable now; they have endured as Joyce's *Ulysses* has endured. Whether the tortuous narrative method of *Absalom! Absalom!* is in the long run anything more than interesting is perhaps questionable, as is the famous Part IV of "The Bear." In any case, the great bulk of Faulkner's more traditional work is undeniably successful, and there is enough of that to make him one of our most important writers. Dos Passos's experiments, especially in *U.S.A.,* differ from Faulkner's in being less modifications than additions to stories told in the traditional way. The montage effect of the sections called "The Camera Eye," the brief biographies of noted figures, even the impressionistic prose-poetry sections in which the author presumably speaks for himself—all these devices are in a sense interruptions of, comments on, or adjuncts to these stories. That is why they can be (and are) anthologized as set pieces without regard for their position in the structure of the trilogy.

One other kind of experimentation should be mentioned, that found in varying degrees in the work of such writers as Nathanael West, Flannery O'Connor, Ralph Ellison, Eudora Welty, and Joseph Heller. It may be described as basically traditional work in which surrealistic or grotesque or gothic elements appear. In this work the norm of probability is set aside, usually in order to dramatize symbolically a significant event or experience. But generally these elements derive much of their effectiveness from occurring within the framework of a traditionally told story, where the other great norm of the realistic novel (attention to character) is still observed. Examples include the bizarre opening and closing chapters of Ellison's *Invisible Man,* the grotesque but pathetic letters to the agony column editor in West's *Miss Lonelyhearts,* the murder-baptism by the young prophet in O'Connor's *The Violent Bear It Away.* Like the castration and murder of Joe Christmas in Faulkner's *Light in August,* these incidents acquire added horror by violent contrast with the more probable events that surround them.

Two trends bearing on literary history should be noted. The first is that regional writing has practically disappeared from modern fiction, with the exception of Southern writing. While the bulk of modern writing is culturally homogeneous, Southern writing maintains a distinctive identity in the work of Faulkner, Carson McCullers, Robert Penn Warren, Eudora Welty, Flannery O'Connor, William Styron, and others. The other development is the emergence of black literature or, rather, its advance to a place of some prominence. Not to know the work of, for example, Langston Hughes, Gwendolyn Brooks, Richard Wright, James Baldwin, and Ralph Ellison, is to be ignorant of some of the finest and most exciting specimens of modern American writing.

DRAMA

Although most serious twentieth-century American drama is realistic in the sense of criticizing American life, it is by no means realistic in the sense of being uniformly illusionistic in presentation. As early as the 1920s, for example, both O'Neill and Rice were experimenting with expressionistic techniques that foreshadowed a great deal of experimental drama by many playwrights, including Williams, Miller, and Albee. Expressionism is usually defined as the attempt of the playwright to project his own subjective attitudes onto the characters, action, dialogue, and scenery of the play. This projection generally distorts traditional stage realism. Thus in O'Neill's *The Hairy Ape* (1922) and Rice's *The Adding Machine* (1923) characters often talk as they never would in real life; they live in places that only vaguely resemble real places; in short, they are meant to be taken not as individual human beings but as symbolic projections of the dramatist's imagination. Historically, expressionism, which is German in origin, was associated with social-protest plays, like those of O'Neill and Rice, in which a single nonrealistic figure could stand for the masses of the exploited. The experimental anti-illusionistic work of Williams, Miller, and Albee and a good deal of work by both O'Neill and Rice is not really expressionistic, but rather a personal attempt to enhance the traditional illusionism of the theater. Much of the best work of all these playwrights, in fact, is a combination of traditional "illusionistic" methods of dramatic presentation with varied symbolic experiments not only in lighting and staging but in such things as synchronic action, time distortion, and variations of older devices such as the soliloquy and the aside. In brief, modern American drama, like modern American fiction, has grown in sophistication and in a modest urge to experiment. It is however interesting to note that O'Neill, the most inveterate of the experimenters, began and ended his career with the relatively straightforward illusionistic form.

9
Modern Poets

AMY LOWELL (1874–1925)

Amy Lowell was born in Brookline, Massachusetts, of distinguished New England ancestry. A flamboyant and aggressive woman, she turned her attention to poetry when she was in her late thirties. She was romantic by temperament, as her early verse and her work on Keats show, but the poetry of Pound and the imagists soon caught her interest. She became the American champion of the imagist movement, by argument and example emphasizing free verse, cadenced prose, precise imagery, and irregular rhyme. But temperamental differences and a strong strain of nativism soon led her to dismiss Pound and Eliot as erudite "European" poets. She preferred American poets of less talent, anthologizing them as imagists (an association that led Pound to remark that imagism had become "Amygism").

Lowell's greatest contribution to American poetry is probably that of publicist, publisher, and entrepreneur (her *Tendencies in Modern American Poetry,* 1917, is still valuable). In this respect she is much like Pound, although she generally lacked Pound's discernment. Ironically, the best of her own work closely resembles Pound's early imagist poetry—both her original poems like "Meeting-House Hill" and "Wind and Silver," and her re-creations of Japanese poetry such as "Free Fantasia on Japanese Themes." Much of her other work, like the well-known "Patterns," is perhaps best described as inferior Keats.

ROBERT FROST (1874–1963)

More than any other modern American poet, Frost managed to achieve both critical acclaim and a remarkable popular reputation until in his later years he became a kind of folk hero. Most of Frost's best work falls into one of three classes: the short lyric, the longer meditative lyric, and the narrative. (Most of the narratives are really short stories in verse, as Pound pointed out in a review of one of Frost's early collections.)

Life. Though usually associated with New England, Frost was born in San Francisco and lived there until he was eleven. After the death of Frost's father, the family moved to Massachusetts, and it was there that Frost grew up, went to school, married, farmed, taught, and picked up what higher education he could in brief periods at Harvard and Dartmouth. In 1912 he took his wife and four children to England and there repeated his American experience of farming for a living and writing poetry on the side. His first work, published in England, was reviewed enthusiastically by Pound. In 1915 he returned to New England as a known poet, and thereafter his reputation grew steadily. The decades of the 1920s and 1930s established him as America's best-loved contemporary poet. He held distinguished positions at Dartmouth, Michigan, and Harvard, was four times winner of the Pulitzer Prize for poetry, and as a final tribute to his fame, read one of his poems at President John F. Kennedy's inauguration.

Traditionalism. Although Pound helped Frost publish his early work, Frost always objected to the technical innovations of the New Poetry of Pound, Eliot, and Williams. Like Robinson, whose work he admired, he was fond of "the old way of being new." He chose to work within traditional formal limitations: the sonnet, the iambic line, blank verse. His famous remark that free verse is like playing tennis with the net down indicates his preference for older forms.

But it is not only in his use of traditional forms that Frost differs from Pound and Eliot. Much of his verse is didactic, more like the poetry of Pope and Samuel Johnson than that of most of his contemporaries. He was a poet who intended to say something in verse; at his best he spoke directly but in a highly metaphorical poetry of statement. His work is saved from homily by the charm of his metaphor, his technical skill, and his ability to use the language of common speech. A lesser poet attempting this might have written like Edgar Guest. But Frost was not a lesser poet, and though many of his lyrics make flat comments on the human situation, he managed to be not simply a verse philosopher but a poet whose poems (as he said of other poetry) remain always new, whose meanings are always being rediscovered.

Themes and Imagery. Much of Frost's best poetry, and certainly most of his best-known poetry, is nature or pastoral poetry. It is worth noting that in a country where the majority of the population is urban and involved in one way or another with technology, the most popular poetry should be rural in imagery and deliberately "rustic" in tone. But on reading Frost, one soon discovers that the pastoral form conveys a variety of ideas and attitudes and that many of the poems are complex, disquieting, and "dark." Most of

Frost's famous images are of natural objects or processes—woods, snow, ice, orchards, birds, flowers, rivers and pools, farmhouses, stars, apples— and much of his work involves man's relationship to these things. But the relationship is not a constant one. Man by no means lives idyllically amid the beauties of the New England countryside. Many of both the lyrics and the narratives show him alienated from his rural surroundings, or doing battle with them, even in some cases driven mad or killed by them.

Frost rarely romanticized nature in the way that Hemingway and Faulkner did; he rarely suggested the therapeutic value of nature. Characteristically he used natural scenes as the backdrop against which the human drama is played out. Frost's most incisive comments on the human situation suggest classical writers like Aeschylus and Sophocles. They show that man is often cruel to man, that man often misunderstands man, that man is a creature concerned with moral choice, that man lives in a world he only partly understands, and that thus his life is to be seen as tragic or at least ironic. "An Old Man's Winter Night" might well stand for the grimness and pathos that pervade so much of Frost's work. The old man, alone in an isolated farmhouse, is benumbed by the natural process of aging; outside the house the snow, the dark woods, and the night sky go on in their own way, having no relation at all to him.

Representative Works

"Mending Wall" (1914). One of Frost's most famous and most discussed meditative lyrics. An ironic poem, it suggests on one level that only meaningful separations should exist among men. On a less obvious level it indicates the processes of nature that do not take into account men's beliefs; "something" does not like walls and other man-made things.

"The Death of the Hired Man" (1914). Perhaps Frost's most famous verse narrative. In unobtrusive blank verse it sketches out the life and death of an itinerant farmhand seeking a "home" to die in. In the poem, the old man, Silas, is shown only in the discussion about him between a husband and wife. The husband's view of Silas (and life) is relatively harsh and "realistic"; the wife's view is much more sympathetic. The poem's tone suggests Frost's agreement with the wife's feelings, but the objectivity of the conversational structure saves the poem from sentimentality.

"After Apple-Picking" (1914). A meditative lyric that, like "Mending Wall," is not easily explicated. It is clear enough that the poem moves from a literal physical act (apple picking) to a symbolic meaning. There is an intermediate step between the literal and symbolic, when the speaker looks at nature through a sheet of ice and sees it transfigured. But the next step— the coming on of sleep and the expected dream—involves both the apple picking itself and the intermediate step of seeing nature as not quite usual. The picking and sorting of apples seem to assume for the speaker a kind of moral responsibility. The cryptic comparison of the speaker's sleep to the groundhog's winter sleep suggests the mystery of human nature itself.

"The Road Not Taken" (1916). A lyric that seems to pose the problem of human freedom. The ambiguity of the poem suggests that the question of choice is subjective.

"Birches" (1916). A meditative lyric suggesting Frost's philosophy. The boy climbs the birches toward heaven but swings back down to earth. Frost implies that one may speculate about a transcendental heaven, but all he really knows are the certain joys of earth. The poem may usefully be compared to Stevens's "Sunday Morning" (see p. 74).

"Stopping by Woods on a Snowy Evening" (1923). Frost's most famous lyric. In carefully rhymed quatrains it shows his respect for the traditional forms, and in content it shows his ambiguous use of nature. The coldness and stillness of the snowy woods appeal to something in man that desires sleep, oblivion, or even death. The speaker toys with the notion of oblivion, but other, human qualities drive him to home and duties. The poem is often read as an optimistic comment on human nature. But the last quatrain may be read to imply that after the duties are performed, the quiet coldness of winter sleep will be the ultimate end.

"The Figure a Poem Makes" (1939). Frost's best-known essay about poetry. Like most poets' statements, it applies to his own work. (It is complemented by another well-known essay, "The Constant Symbol.") Frost argues for the necessity of traditional form in poetry and also for "meaning," that is, a decipherable theme in lyric poetry. But he asserts that the true poem is not one that states an idea but rather one that begins in a certain mood and forms the idea or meaning as it progresses. It is this sense of a poet's arriving at a meaning as he writes that gives the poem its perennial freshness.

CARL SANDBURG (1878–1967)

Of all modern American poets Sandburg worked most consciously in the Whitman tradition, both in form and content.

Life. Born in Galesburg, Illinois, Sandburg repeated many of the characteristics of Whitman's life, as later he was consciously to imitate many of Whitman's literary and emotional traits. He worked at odd jobs, received little formal education, and early turned to poetry as a way of life, although for a while he earned his living as a newspaperman. His reputation grew slowly as a poet, collector of folk songs, biographer of Lincoln, and finally as a novelist. He received the Pulitzer history prize for the second part of his six-volume biography of Lincoln (1939). In his later years he became a kind of folk hero, second only to Frost in popular esteem, and his *Complete Poems* (1950) won him a second Pulitzer Prize.

Poetry. Some of Sandburg's early lyrics, such as the famous "Fog" and "Nocturne in a Deserted Brickyard," resemble imagist poetry in their compressed free verse and precise imagery. But the Whitman strain in Sandburg was too strong for him to stay within the rather strict limitations imposed by Pound's imagist credo. Like Whitman, he was by temperament given to expansion, not compression. He moved inevitably to a loose, free verse (far looser than Whitman's), which often is indistinguishable from heavily rhetorical cadenced prose. Poems like "A. E. F.," "Prayers of Steel," and the famous "Chicago" may fairly be called free verse in their rhythmic repetitions and their relative compression, which gives the reader a sense of return. But in works like *The People, Yes,* even though Sandburg employs some of Whitman's devices (such as beginning consecutive lines with the same grammatical and syntactical structure), there is much less sense of any repeated movement in the work as a whole and thus less of the effect of verse.

In content, much of Sandburg's work portrays what Whitman called the "mystical divine average." It is the Whitman of the 1850s and 1860s revived in America of the 1920s and 1930s, when Whitman's transcendental individualism was no longer realistically possible. Sandburg spoke in terms of masses, of brotherhood, or the "solidarity" of the common man—all terms implying movements and organizations. Still, there is something of Whitman's effectiveness in Sandburg's sheer descriptions of the energy and vitality of American life—in the way he could idealize even the building of skyscrapers, the brutality of large cities, and most important, the vast western land. It was perhaps this basically romantic notion of the free West that led Sandburg to collect and sing the folk music and stories of an older time and in his last years to retreat to the "older" country of the Great Smoky Mountains.

Representative Works

"Chicago" (1916). One of Sandburg's earliest and best-known lyrics. In loose free verse that often borders on prose, it celebrates the "youth," raw strength, and vitality of the burgeoning city. Chicago's evil—its amorality and exploitation of the poor—is dismissed as an inevitable aspect of its youth and strength. This bland praise foreshadows much of Sandburg's later poetry, which exalts "the people" as enthusiastically and indiscriminately.

"Cool Tombs" (1918). A prose-poem elegy suggesting that death means oblivion and forgetfulness—for Lincoln, Grant, Pocahontas, and the common man.

The People, Yes (1936). A long, loosely structured, and vaguely socialistic prose poem. Its main theme is a kind of Whitmanesque eulogy of the masses: their folk wisdom and endurance, despite their inability to combat the forces that shape their lives. The work is best seen as an example of the "protest" literature of the Great Depression years.

VACHEL LINDSAY (1879–1931)

Lindsay was born in Springfield, Illinois, a symbolic birthplace; like Whitman, he was a great admirer of Lincoln. Like Whitman, too, he saw himself as the American bard singing the beauty and vitality of the country. More literally than Whitman, he tried to become this bard, walking through large areas of the country, reciting his poetry to whoever would listen. He celebrated in his verse the great American folk heroes, both historical and mythical—Lincoln, Daniel Boone, Andrew Jackson, Johnny Appleseed, General William Booth (of the Salvation Army).

He was one of the first American poets to try to bring the rhythm and syncopation of jazz into poetry. He was not often successful; the rhythms, rhymes, and themes of his best-known verse (for example, "The Congo" and "General William Booth Enters into Heaven") seem too obvious to be really effective. But technically his verse is still of interest. Much of it is intentionally oral, meant to be chanted, as he himself chanted it on innumerable reading tours.

WALLACE STEVENS (1879–1955)

One of the most difficult modern writers, Stevens has grown in critical estimation until he is now regarded as one of the major twentieth-century poets.

Life. Born in Reading, Pennsylvania, Stevens was graduated from Harvard, then studied law and was admitted to the bar in 1904. While practicing law, he published his early poems in the little magazines of the day and established friendships with other struggling young poets such as William Carlos Williams and Marianne Moore. In 1916 he joined a Hartford, Connecticut, insurance firm and thereafter combined the writing of poetry with a business career. His success in these disparate parts of his life may be measured by the fact that he was made a vice-president of his company in 1934, was awarded the Bollingen Prize in poetry in 1949, and in 1955, the year of his death, received both the Pulitzer Prize for poetry and the National Book Award.

"Obscurity" of Stevens's Poetry. The difficulties of Stevens's poetry are of several kinds. Following the French symbolist tradition, he sometimes uses words more for their sound and suggestiveness than for their literal meaning. In many of his poems (especially the early ones collected in *Harmonium,* 1923) the sense is subservient to the technique. It is not that these poems have no meaning; it is that it may be their colors or sounds that dominate the reader's attention. In other poems Stevens's verbal skill allows an approach to what Poe called the condition of music, in which the sense is an "undercurrent," no more isolated than the rhythms, the verbal melody, and the rhyme; in short, these are poems in which the meaning seems part of the technique. Other poems seem to invite the kind of appraisal one makes of a painting, sometimes "abstract," sometimes "impressionistic" or even "surrealistic." Finally, there are poems in which the symbolism seems simply arbitrary, poems about whose meanings there is no general agreement among critics.

Stevens's View of the Imagination. The greatest obstacle to an appreciation of Stevens's poetry is more basic than any matter of technique. What one must understand is his estimate of the human situation and the part poetry plays in it. Most of his major poems dramatize this philosophy, and many try to state it openly.

If we allow for certain important differences, we may say that Stevens's philosophy is "romantic" in the sense that we apply that term to Emerson and Coleridge. For both these older writers the imagination was man's most important faculty, allowing him to see beyond the commonsense world, the world of perception, to an ideal world; it was, as Coleridge said, a kind of spiritual seeing. It arrived at truths knowable in no other way; it "saw" a goodness beyond this world of here and now, and what it saw was the basis of the famous Emersonian optimism. For Stevens, too, the imagination is man's most important capacity, but for different reasons. Stevens is a prime example of the modern man for whom all the old gods are dead and the old orthodoxies false. When we have put away the myths and religions of the past, we perceive that the world is vacuous, empty, as white as Melville's Ishmael feared. The only order or pattern discernible in the outer world is that projected upon it by the imagination, and this projection is usually accomplished through art. The imagination is the "Blue Guitar" (one of Stevens's favorite symbols for the imagination, taken from a Picasso painting), which "plays" for us not things as they are but things as we must have them in order to survive.

The great difference between Stevens's imagination and that of earlier romantics is that for them the imagination transcended this world, saw a world above or beyond this one. For Stevens the imagination merely changes the appearance of this world temporarily, as Wordsworth's Westminster Bridge sonnet depicts London only as it exists briefly on a quiet, clear morning. Stevens's imagination transcends nothing, for to him there is no realm beyond the here and now. The most that he can say of divinity is that, however we define it, it exists within us now as a purely human quality.

Stevens said that it is the function of poetry to help people live their lives. In general, the easy hedonistic assurances of the early poetry disappear in the later. The insistence that art orders reality and thus comforts us is balanced in the later poetry by a counterinsistence on the transience of this ordering. The older romantics believed that imagination actually ordered nature, gave it form. But as Hyatt Waggoner has so well said, Stevens's imagination orders reality only within the poem itself.[1]

Representative Works

"Sunday Morning" (1915). A blank verse lyric, one of Stevens's earliest and most moving portrayals of man as a transient being who must find what glory and happiness he can in this state.

"Peter Quince at the Clavier" (1915). A lyric depicting the imagination in musical terms. It introduces one of Stevens's favorite themes: Beauty exists only in the concrete, the here and now; it must pass away, but it may be immortalized in art.

"Thirteen Ways of Looking at a Blackbird" (1917). A cryptic lyric, something like a sequence of haiku poems. It argues for the ordering power of the imagination in poetry while implying that the objective universe of the blackbird exists on its own before and after the imagination has dealt with it.

"A High-Toned Old Christian Woman" (1922). An ironic argument that the imagination may construct a "heaven" as true as that of traditional Christianity.

"The Emperor of Ice-Cream" (1922). One of Stevens's most debated lyrics. There is no general agreement about the imagery, but the tone seems to suggest the naturalness and inevitability of death.

"The Idea of Order at Key West" (1935). One of Stevens's lyrics that most clearly suggest the ordering power of the imagination (the girl's song) and the essential vacuity of nature (the sea) as it exists outside the song.

"Of Modern Poetry" (1942). Stevens's sharpest poetic statement of the function of modern poetry: the absolutely subjective satisfaction it gives in a world unexplainable by either philosophy or religion.

The Necessary Angel (1951). Essays that give the clearest explanation of Stevens's views of imagination and its relation to the objective world. Best-known and most helpful is "The Noble Rider and the Sound of Words."

Opus Posthumous (1957). Miscellania, including the important and cryptic aphorisms in the section called "Adagia."

WILLIAM CARLOS WILLIAMS (1883–1963)

A practicing physician in Rutherford, New Jersey, Williams, like Robert Frost, went no farther for his poetic material than the region in which he lived.

Life. Williams was born in Rutherford of an English father and a Puerto Rican mother. He practiced medicine for some forty-five years, at the same

1. Hyatt Waggoner, ed., *American Poets from the Puritans to the Present* (Boston: Houghton Mifflin, 1968), p. 434.

time experimenting tirelessly with new poetic forms. He met Ezra Pound while both were studying at the University of Pennsylvania, and Pound's theories and practice were a lifelong influence on his work. Williams's body of writing includes short stories, novels, plays, a collection of historical sketches, an autobiography, and numerous essays and letters dealing with poetic theory and practice. He received the 1963 Pulitzer Prize for poetry for his last volume, *Pictures from Brueghel*.

Poetic Theory. The general reader is likely to find Williams's scattered comments on poetry more interesting in themselves than for the light they throw on his poetry. However, certain broad areas of poetic belief are evident in both his critical comments and his verse. He has said that it was Pound who wooed him away from Keatsian romanticism, and certainly Pound's imagistic principles are evident throughout Williams's poetry. From the simplest lyric such as "The Red Wheelbarrow" to the complex poetry of *Paterson*, Williams is concerned with presenting the object of the poem as precisely and economically as possible, not in metrical verse, but in what Pound called the musical phrase. Pound is echoed, too, in Williams's distrust of abstractions. "No ideas but in things," he says in *Paterson*; and like Joyce, Eliot, and Pound, he avoids direct statement, letting his mythical "vehicle" carry his meaning. In many of his finest short lyrics, too, he simply presents as sharply as possible a limited segment of reality and allows the reader to infer a general truth that is expressed only in concrete terms in the poem.

Like Pound, Williams wrote much about language itself and the poet's need to keep it clear and meaningful (this is a major theme of *Paterson*). But like Whitman and unlike Pound, he believed that the American poet should work with the language peculiar to America, and most of his poetry is consciously American in tone and diction. One may find echoes of Whitman in his strictures against Pound and Eliot and their abandonment of the American scene for the eclectic tradition of European poetry. In fact, as Wallace Stevens and Yvor Winters pointed out long ago, Williams is in many ways a romantic poet. In arguments that recall both Whitman and Wordsworth, he demanded for American poetry a clean break, not only with the traditional forms of diction, stanza, and meter, but also with the whole "literary" quality of the tradition itself: its stories, myths, structures, attitudes. Like Whitman, he wanted a poetry that would deal with the unpoetic aspects of American life. And, however inconsistently Williams argues in prose, his poetry illustrates this desire.

In prosody, again like Whitman, he spent a lifetime searching for a poetic form that would somehow both echo and accommodate the basic character of American speech. He spoke in his later years of "the variable foot" and of "the triadic line," though there is no general agreement about what he meant by these terms. But what is clear about all his best poetry is that he was a master of free verse, not the long rolling lines of Whitman, but the more compressed and tightly organized lines that so often really echo the rhythms of common American speech.

Representative Works

"Tract" (1920). A lyric diatribe against the formality of American funerals. Williams would have a simple, natural funeral that would emphasize, rather than hide, sincere grief. The poem is sometimes read as a symbolic argument for simple and natural language in poetry.

"Queen-Ann's-Lace" (1921). One of many lyrics in which Williams stresses the familiar homely imagery in contrast to the traditional literary kind. Thus his loved one's body is white, not like anemone, but like the flowers of the common wild carrot.

"Spring and All" (1923). One of Williams's best-known lyrics and one that shows his concision, his accuracy of description, and his aversion to general statement. Death, implicit in the passing allusion to the contagious hospital, is sharply juxtaposed against the new life of trees and shrubs struggling into being in the cold spring wind.

"The Yachts" (1935). A lyric often read as a "depression" poem depicting the oppression of the poor by the rich. It is certainly this, but it also suggests the larger world of peril and death by the symbolism of the "safe" harbor in which the yachts move. Not even the yachts are safe in the open sea.

Paterson (1946–1958). A long poem originally in four parts, published separately in 1946, 1948, 1949, and 1951 (although sections of them had existed in various forms in earlier works). Williams added a fifth part in 1958 and was projecting a sixth part at his death. Although there are echoes of both Pound and Eliot, the poem's basic technique is that of Joyce's *Finnegans Wake*. Williams took certain historical places and events (the town of Paterson, the Passaic River, events recorded in early local histories) and from them forged a myth. The poem's general theme is the decay of life in a small eastern town meant to mirror American society. The falls above the town suggest both the possibility of good and healthy life and the correlative health of native speech. But, true to both history and myth, the river below the falls becomes polluted by industry, and the people's language and the people themselves take on a parallel dirtiness and loss of purpose. The process of decay, however, is not irreversible, as Williams indicates late in the poem when he insists that the sea (into which the river issues) is not man's true home.

Like most long modern poems that abandon traditional forms, *Paterson* is not easy to follow. One must first understand its basic and arbitrary symbols (Paterson as city, man, and poet; the land as not only that waiting to be civilized but also the poet's raw material; the river as language and the natural movement of historical life). The poem, like Pound's *Cantos*, mixes prose documents with verse and, again like Pound's poem, is not an unqualified success. But parts of it show Williams at his best.

EZRA POUND (1885–1972)

Now almost a legendary figure, Ezra Pound was one of the most influential forces in poetry and criticism for more than fifty years.

Life. Born in Hailey, Idaho, Pound attended Hamilton College and the University of Pennsylvania, where he began a lifelong friendship with William Carlos Williams. He taught briefly at Wabash College in Indiana but was dismissed for bohemian behavior. He became one of the earliest modern expatriates, moving to London in 1908, then to Paris, and finally to Rapallo, Italy. From about 1910 through the 1920s he was involved in most of the new movements in poetry, painting, music, and sculpture. As both poet and theorist he not only helped popularize such innovations as the imagistic techniques but also pioneered in the revival and "making new" of such poetry as Anglo-Saxon, Provençal, Chinese, Japanese, and Latin. Much of his best work, in fact, is translation or "re-creation" of poems in these older traditions. In addition to his own work (which included the beginnings of *The Cantos*), he served as foreign editor for such American little magazines as *Poetry* and *The Little Review*. He worked unselfishly to bring the work of unknown young writers into print; in one way or other he helped such writers as Joyce, Eliot, Frost, Williams, Hemingway, and Marianne Moore.

In the decade preceding World War II, Pound became increasingly obsessed with economic theory and concluded that a great part of the world's ills could be traced to capitalistic monetary policies, which he categorized as "usury." This theory led him to support Mussolini's regime. He made several radio broadcasts before and during World War II attacking Churchill, Roosevelt, and "the international Jewish conspiracy" for fomenting the war. In 1945 he was arrested by American forces and imprisoned near Pisa. He was returned to the United States for trial on treason charges but in 1946 was judged insane and committed to a mental hospital in Washington, D. C., where he remained until 1958, when he was released. In 1949 he was awarded the Bollingen Prize for poetry for *The Pisan Cantos*. The award touched off one of the most interesting literary-political controversies of the century. After his discharge he spent the remainder of his life at Rapallo, where he composed several more segments of *The Cantos*.

Poetic Theory and Practice. The core of Pound's theories and practice of poetry may be oversimply stated as condensation and compression, best illustrated by his enunciation of the principles of imagism and his interest in the Chinese ideogram. *"Dichten=condensare,"* he said: To make poetry is to condense.[2] In 1912 he, H. D. (Hilda Doolittle), and Richard Aldington agreed on the following principles, which are the basis of imagism: "(1) direct treatment of the 'thing' whether subjective or objective, (2) to use absolutely no word that does not contribute to the presentation, (3) as regarding rhythm: to compose in the sequence of the musical phrase, not in sequence of a metronome."[3] The first two statements suggest the paring away of all but essential words. The third statement suggests the movement toward free verse, which is the form of most imagist poetry, but does not rule out rhymed verse. What the three principles argue against is the misuse of traditional poetic forms and meters by padding out or filling in a given verse form simply for the sake of the form. The principles (which echo the views of T. E. Hulme) say in effect that the poet must sharply visualize his subject, present it concisely in images (visual, aural, tactile), and utilize the rhythm that seems naturally to fit it.

Pound's interest in the Chinese ideogram is a correlative of this passion for conciseness. Pound assumed (wrongly, according to many linguists) that the Chinese written character lends itself to concision and particularity because each character is a stylized picture of the meaning it conveys. For example, one reading the ideogram for "dawn" would see something like the sun behind tree branches. This seeing of the concrete thing precisely pictured would (Pound thought) prevent both writer and reader from drifting off into the abstractions that Pound abhorred. Thus Pound advocated poetry that was rooted in images rather than ideas. He recommended this kind of poetry to Yeats, Eliot, and Williams, all of whom were variously affected by his advice. Yeats noted that he became terribly conscious of abstractions in his work after listening to Pound; Eliot gave the manuscript of *The Waste Land* to Pound, who, Eliot said later, cut it in half; Williams in *Paterson* was still repeating Pound's early advice: no ideas but in things.

Pound's desire for compression, for the precise image, and for the idea in concrete form is evident in his major poetry. It often leads to erudite and sometimes private allusions, as does Eliot's similar doctrine of the "objective correlative." In the later *Cantos* Pound increasingly used a kind of poetic shorthand, citing lines of poems, old conversations, scraps of history, and odd bits of knowledge as the quickest way of expressing complexes of ideas and emotions.

It seems likely that time will sift out the best of Pound's work, as it has with other prolific poets. Such sifting will probably leave many of his early lyrics, some of his translations, *Mauberley,* and parts of *The Cantos*. It will probably also bear out the contention that his technical skill often overshadowed his thought. Chesterton once remarked that Tennyson could

2. *ABC of Reading* (New York: New Directions, 1960), p. 36.

3. Ezra Pound, "A Retrospect," in *Literary Essays of Ezra Pound,* ed. T. S. Eliot (New York: New Directions, 1954), p. 3.

not always think up to the height of his style. Ironically, because Tennyson stood for so much that Pound despised, the same comment may be the final judgment on Pound's work.

Representative Works

"Portrait d'une Femme" (1913). A satirical picture of a society lady as spiritually empty as the world she inhabits. The poem reminds the reader of many of Henry James's ladies, of Eliot's "Portrait of a Lady," and of the women in Eliot's "The Love Song of J. Alfred Prufrock."

"The River-Merchant's Wife: A Letter" (1915). One of Pound's most famous "re-creations." A translation from an eighth-century Chinese poet, it is a moving, low-keyed love poem.

"In a Station of the Metro" (1916). Probably the most famous of all imagist poems. In two lines it combines a sharp visual image with an implied meaning. The faces in the subway station suggest both the impersonality and haste of city life and the greater transience of human life itself.

Hugh Selwyn Mauberley (1919, 1920). A relatively long sequence of short poems that add up to an ironic defense of Pound's own poetic beliefs and a satiric attack on the society that denies a hearing to serious artists. Mauberley, like Pound, admires the ancient classics and the nearer classics such as Flaubert. The flabby materialistic society in which he lives drives him to a symbolic death, paralleled by the terrible waste of World War I, which buried so many promising youths. The later sections of the 1919 poem and most of the 1920 poem are erudite and private, requiring a knowledge of the literary and social climate of opinion of the turn of the century.

The Cantos (1925–1972). Pound's long, controversial, unfinished poem (109 cantos exist in collected form). It has been the object of intense and varied study (see Bibliography). Pound himself described the poem as "ideogrammic," and in many cantos he used actual Chinese ideograms. Even more than other long modern poems (such as those of Eliot, Williams, and Hart Crane), the poem puts the general reader off by its lack of traditional structure. Yeats, who read the early cantos, found them puzzling though full of beautiful isolated passages. His reaction has been generally repeated over the years and about the later cantos as well. Pound's original intention seems to have been comparable to Eliot's in *The Waste Land:* to condemn modern society by juxtaposing certain pictures of modern life against certain pictures of past cultures. For example, Confucius and Jefferson in characteristic speech or action, were to be ideograms for past nonusurious cultures; Odysseus was to be an ideogram for the search for social stability. But to the general reader only a few of the cantos (and parts of others) stand as representative of Pound's great mastery of rhythm, imagery, and diction. Canto I, which recreates part of *The Odyssey* in Anglo-Saxon verse form, is perhaps best known; Canto II, which "makes new" a part of Ovid's *Metamorphoses,* shows Pound's talent for enlarging on his original; Canto XLV is a marvelously rhetorical diatribe against usury; and parts of *The Pisan Cantos* are as fine as anything Pound ever wrote, depicting in unforgettable imagery and rhythms his physical and spiritual torment in the army detention camp.

ROBINSON JEFFERS (1887–1962)

Jeffers was what Melville called an isolato. He physically removed himself from the mainstream of American life by building a stone house overlooking the Pacific near Carmel, California. There he wrote narrative and meditative poetry which differs in important ways from the other poetry of his time.

Life. Jeffers was born in Pittsburgh, the first child of very religious parents. His father was a Presbyterian minister and professor of Old Testament literature. As a child, Jeffers traveled in Europe and was tutored by his father. At sixteen, he moved with his family to California. He was graduated from Occidental College and later studied medicine at the University of Southern California and forestry at the University of Washington. This peculiar mixture of academic disciplines was to be reflected in his poetry. Jeffers fell in love with a married woman and, after an eight-year wait for her divorce, finally married her. It was an enormously successful marriage; she became his inspiration, his critic, and in many ways his link with the outside world. Though he went east to read his poetry and traveled abroad, his spiritual home was the California coast. His best poetry uses that locale not only as the boundary of a continent but, symbolically, as the boundary of a spiritual world.

Evolution of Jeffers's Poetry. Most of Jeffers's early poetry is conventional in form, using the fairly regular iambic line, rhyme, and even the sonnet structure. *Tamar and Other Poems* (1924) marked his first sustained use of free verse. Thereafter, both in short lyrics and in the long narrative poems for which he became famous, his free verse was distinctive. In its subtlety of cadence and diction it differs from and surpasses the verse of Sandburg, and in its rhetorical expansiveness it is worlds apart from the compression and allusiveness of Pound and Eliot. In his narrative and dramatic poems Jeffers was often colloquial and prosaic, but in his lyrics and in parts of the longer poems, his work will remind the reader of both Whitman and Emerson and of their common ancestor, the King James Bible. The resemblances are not merely matters of technique (of certain kinds of repetition, for example) but also of tone. Jeffers's best work is prophetic and even apocalyptic, producing an effect that is not only literary but also religious.

Jeffers's Inhumanism. Jeffers's view of life was never consistent. Like

Melville, he said no much more cogently than he said yes. He certainly rejected any version of orthodox religion; and just as certainly he was drawn to the naturalistic scientific view of man begun by Darwin and culminating (for Jeffers) in Freud. He has often been classified as a verse-naturalist, comparable to Hardy, Dreiser, and Sherwood Anderson. But such a classification is too simple. He clearly damned man and most human institutions, and like older romantics, he contrasted man with the purity of nature. But his poetry often suggests the existence of a superhuman force or level of being with which man may (or can) identify. Unlike Emerson and Whitman, though, Jeffers rarely asserted that this union is a happy and conscious one; more often he implied that it will be unexpected and ironic. Nor did he ever really specify the nature of the being or process beyond man. When man's humanity is burnt away, like the energy dissipated in a fading star, man, like the star, may simply return to the cosmic processes of nature. At his bitterest, Jeffers suggested this possibility as an improvement over the present human condition. In rare moments of hopefulness he implied that this process may be analogous to what the orthodox religions see as a mystical union with a personal God.

Representative Works

"Roan Stallion" (1925). Jeffers's most famous narrative poem and one of his most sensational. As with many of his other narratives, the erotic realism of the story masks a symbolic argument. The simple Indian woman, California, mistreated for years by a drunken and bestial husband, falls in love with a magnificent roan stallion. In a lurid night scene in the mountains she imagines that she has intercourse with the beast. The next night, as her husband drunkenly pursues her into the corral, she allows the stallion to kill him; only then, and reluctantly, she kills the horse. Jeffers blends early Freudian interpretations of religion with classical mythology to suggest that California's experience with the stallion is not only sexual but religious. She kneels to adore his strength and purity and prostrates herself beneath his hooves while the archetypal myths of the union of the gods with women pass through her mind. Thus Jeffers reduces religion to mere subjective longing, to mythmaking. But he also implies (as he does in other poems) that love for the inhuman in nature is saner and cleaner than most human love. In a famous passage (ll. 153 ff.) he suggests that man's destiny is to be scoured of his humanity and somehow made one with nature.

"Shine, Perishing Republic" (1925). Jeffers's most famous lyric and a characteristic condemnation of man and civilization. Its prophetic tone and exhortation to man to flee to the mountains recall Christian apocalyptic writings. The distinctive oratorical quality of Jeffers's free verse is evident throughout the poem.

MARIANNE MOORE (1887–1972)

Along with Ezra Pound, William Carlos Williams, and E. E. Cummings, Marianne Moore was one of the important experimental poets of the twentieth century.

Life. Marianne Moore was born in St. Louis, received her college education at Bryn Mawr, and then held such disparate positions as teacher in a U.S. Indian school, librarian in New York, and editor of *The Dial,* one of the best-known of the 1920s little magazines. Her early work was praised by Pound, Eliot, and Williams, though her more general acclaim was slower in coming. Among many awards and prizes, she received the Pulitzer Prize, the Bollingen Prize, and the National Book Award, all in 1952, for her *Collected Poems.*

Experimental Poetry. Like William Carlos Williams, Moore began writing poetry just before World War I, when the greatest single influence on young poets was that of Ezra Pound. Though she was never an imagist poet even to the extent that Williams was, the imagists' insistence on "the direct treatment of the thing," their economy of wording, and their bias against traditional metrical forms are evident in all her work. Some of her poems are in free verse, some in rhyme, but all of them (in form at least) are clearly and consciously a departure from traditional nineteenth-century lyric poetry.

Moore's major technical innovation is the use of the syllable rather than the traditional poetic foot as the basis of her poetry. In an early poem, "The Past Is the Present" (1915), she described Hebrew poetry as "prose with a sort of heightened consciousness," and this comment may be said to apply to her own work. Her poetry differs from prose also in her careful syllabic arrangements and occasional, usually subtle, use of rhyme. "Poetry," a typical example, has five stanzas of six lines each. The first line of each stanza has nineteen syllables and the last line thirteen. The four intermediate lines vary in syllabic count but are visually similar: The second lines are about the same length as the first; the third, fourth, and fifth lines are all short. The rhyme is irregular, some of it obvious but much of it light (for example, what-bat, statistician-and). Most of the rhymes occur in run-on lines, making them even less obvious.

Marianne Moore has sometimes been compared to Emily Dickinson, but the differences are more apparent than the similarities. Dickinson at her best wrote poetry so impassioned, so moving, so jarring in its effect that hardly any critic has discussed her work without using the word *intensity.* But Moore is rarely intense. She is witty, intellectual, perceptive, and occasionally emotional. But her emotional pitch is much lower than Dickinson's. Both poets frequently use understatement, but with different results. Dickinson's understatement usually adds to the intensity of the poem. Dickinson turns emotion loose; Moore (comparatively at least) holds it back.

Themes. Moore's themes are much more traditional than her techniques. Although she was fond of bizarre imagery (for instance, meticulous description of little-known animals), what her poems say will remind the reader more of Frost than of Williams or Pound. She satirizes critics, praises poetry, comments on poetic style, appraises the limits of the human mind, eulogizes courage, and suggests the latent horror of human life. Once accustomed to the oddity of Moore's syllabic verse and the literary borrowings she usually encloses in quotation marks, the reader going through her work will find a disciplined craftsman who prefers to speak in a low and unromantic key. Within the limits she set for herself, she presents a fine and civilized mind commenting in a lucid and often ironic way on the human situation.

Representative Works

"Poetry" (1921). Probably Moore's most famous lyric. It is an ironic defense of poetry on the grounds that real poetry re-creates the real experience of life.

"A Grave" (1924). A lyric in which Moore departs from her usual syllabic technique to use long lines of free verse reminiscent of Whitman and Jeffers. The symbolism (the sea as rapacious death) is obvious but effective.

"The Steeple-Jack" (1935). An ironic lyric suggesting the ever-present peril of human life. The superficial order of a seaside town is set against the vast destructive power suggested by the stranded whales and the Danger sign marking a church as the steeple-jack symbolically climbs up to repair the star atop the steeple.

"What Are Years?" (1941). A straightforward lyric which praises the courage that enables man to live while knowing both his limitations and his mortality.

"The Mind Is an Enchanting Thing" (1944). A lyric in praise of the human mind. Paradoxically, the mind is buoyed by its sense that it can arrive at truth while at the same time aware that it must have the flexibility to allow for error.

"In Distrust of Merits" (1944). Written during World War II, this lyric is more impassioned than most of Moore's poetry. It proclaims that the hatred in the human heart is the root cause of war and pleads for its conquest by love.

T. S. ELIOT (1888–1965)

During the period from about 1920 to 1950 Eliot, like Samuel Johnson before him, was very nearly the literary dictator of poetry and criticism. His name, the titles of some of his works, and even some of his critical terms have become part of the literary vocabulary of our time.

Life. Thomas Stearns Eliot was born in St. Louis, Missouri, although his family roots were in New England. He studied philosophy and literature at Harvard, the Sorbonne, and Oxford under such distinguished professors as Irving Babbitt and George Santayana. By 1915 he was a struggling young expatriate poet in London, where he made his living first as a teacher, later as a bank clerk. Ezra Pound helped publish his early poetry. His fame began with his first book, *Prufrock and Other Observations* (1917), and was solidified by *The Waste Land* (1922). During these years Eliot also published his early, influential essays, including "Tradition and the Individual Talent" (1919), "Hamlet and His Problems" (1919), and "The Metaphysical Poets" (1921). In 1927 he became a British subject and joined the Church of England, proclaiming himself an Anglo-Catholic, a Royalist, and a classicist. His work after this is increasingly Christian in outlook, especially his verse play *Murder in the Cathedral* (1935), *Four Quartets* (1943), and his later plays. Eliot was awarded many honors, including the Nobel Prize for literature in 1948.

Criticism and Poetic Theory. Eliot produced a considerable body of literary criticism, of which the best (and the best-known) is what may be called *workshop* criticism: comments on areas of literature that bear on what interested him as a practicing poet and playwright. Like Pound, he rediscovered and made new certain older poets and kinds of writing. He wrote perceptively about Dante, the Metaphysical poets, French symbolist poetry, the seventeenth-century English dramatists, Shakespeare, and the importance of a literary tradition. All these subjects are connected in one way or another with Eliot's own poetry, and his comments on them give us insights into his poetry that can be had in no other way.

Like Pound and T. E. Hulme (and his teachers Babbitt and Santayana), Eliot often spoke of himself as an antiromantic. He disliked the "autobiographical" poetry of Byron and Shelley, and he often argued for an impersonal poetry, the emotional content of which is not obviously related to biographical data in the poet's life. *Obviously* is the key word, for certainly the emotional content must be related to the poet in some way or other or it would not appear in the poem. Eliot dealt with this problem in two ways. In "Tradition and the Individual Talent," he spoke of the poetic process as analogous to a chemical process by which two elements fuse into a compound. The poet is a catalyst, bringing a poem into being, but is not himself *in* the poem. In "Hamlet and His Problems," Eliot advanced the famous notion of the objective correlative, which also has scientific overtones. Wishing to evoke a certain reaction in a reader's mind, the poet searches until he finds the right situation or plot or image that will automatically call up that emotion. In this way, too, the poet is not *in* the poem but is rather a presenter of an object.

Eliot's comments on impersonality in poetry have been much discussed, and it is questionable whether this doctrine agrees with Eliot's own comments on the metaphysical poets, whom he praised highly (especially Donne) for their "unified sensibility." By this Eliot meant that their intellectual and emotional life was a single entity so that they reacted emotionally to ideas and intellectually to emotions. It was after their work, he thought, that a dissociation of sensibility set in, brought on largely by Milton and Dryden, whose brilliant language helped hide the fact that their ideas and emotions did not exist on the same plane. But Donne and Herbert are certainly *in* their poems as much as Shelley and Keats are, and though their thoughts and feelings may be fused, the poets themselves are not in any sense detached from what they feel. In Eliot's own poetry, the speakers in such early poems as "Prufrock" and *The Waste Land* may be personas or masks, but it is certainly Eliot's own voice that we hear in the later poetry such as *Four Quartets*.

Dante appears by direct quotation, by allusion, and by echo in many of Eliot's most important poems. He seems for Eliot to have been the perfect poet: a master craftsman working within an intellectual and religious framework in which he sincerely believed. Eliot's final religious commitment to a semimystical Anglo-Catholicism placed him in a similar position. The French symbolist poets (especially Jules Laforgue) represented for Eliot the return to the tradition lost with the eclipse of the metaphysical poets. They presented once again a unified sensibility; they were neither simply discursive nor simply emotional. Their ideas and intellectual attitudes were buried in their imagery, in their objective correlatives. They also embodied a significant addition to the great literary tradition, which for Eliot was the great current of literature from Homer's time to our own, a current inevitably changing but remaining essentially the same. Narrative and logical structure had spent themselves, and now the tradition produced something new (though not entirely different) to replace it. The new symbolist form was the associational structure, the association of ideas and images as they existed in the poet's mind and imagination. It was a structure that Eliot seized on eagerly in his earliest work and never completely abandoned. He took, too, for his earlier poetry, some of the poses he found in French poetry: the first-person narrator suffering from the ennui of life, usually symbolized by the great city; the bizarre imagery that mixed sounds and sights and colors; the ironic tone that suggested alternately absurdity and despair.

Representative Works

"The Love Song of J. Alfred Prufrock" (1915). The most famous of Eliot's early lyrics, and one that shows clearly his use of French symbolist techniques and attitudes. The pathetic narrator, afraid of both real and imagined horrors, is a common figure in Laforgue's poetry. The seeming incoherence of Prufrock's interior meanderings and personal associations, which form the structure of the poem, conceals the fact that the poem is in form a dramatic monologue. Prufrock is generally assumed to symbolize modern man—lost, aimless, fearful, inarticulate. The motif of being locked within one's own hellish subjectivity recurs in most of Eliot's important works. It is a major theme of *The Waste Land* and appears in a specifically religious context in such late plays as *The Cocktail Party* (1949) and *The Elder Statesman* (1958).

"Sweeney Among the Nightingales" (1918). Probably Eliot's most famous short lyric. It is a miniature of the general techniques of his early poetry, asserting nothing but implying much. Sweeney appears in other Eliot poems as the prototype of debased modern man, deaf and blind to the spiritual values of past cultures and religions. Here he is apparently about to be attacked, perhaps murdered, in the sordid setting of a cheap saloon. The vignette is juxtaposed against the enormously significant murder of Agamemnon, a heroic figure out of a heroic past. Although set against a cosmic backdrop (gloomy Orion and the Dog) the scene suggests that Sweeney dead will be neither resurrected nor metamorphosed.

The Waste Land (1922). Probably the most famous, and most explicated, poem of the century. It is Eliot's great extended picture of the spiritual sterility of modern civilization following World War I. As such it may be compared with Pound's *Mauberley* and Hemingway's *The Sun Also Rises*. The general sense of the poem comes through on a careful reading; a more informed appreciation will (for most readers) involve a knowledge of some of the commentaries on the poem. The characters (with the exception of the speaker) are spiritually dead, like the people in "Prufrock," "Sweeney Among the Nightingales," and *Murder in the Cathedral*. In various ways the poem suggests the religious adage that he who would save his life must lose it, that death is the only way to resurrection. Much of this imagery is taken from the ancient Grail legends as Eliot knew them from the books of Jessie Weston and Sir James Frazer. Other of Eliot's many sources include the Bible, Dante, Shakespeare, and Baudelaire. Water is Eliot's major symbol for death and consequent new life (baptism); fire is his major symbol for the meaningless lust that replaces love in the wasteland world. The commentaries are helpful in pointing out how Eliot manipulates his symbols, and occasionally the knowledge of the source Eliot is quoting or paraphrasing is useful. But the danger for the average reader is that he will become bogged down in exegesis and may thus miss the relatively "happy ending" suggested by Parts IV and V. The speaker has won through to the Chapel Perilous; he knows he is dead and he wants life. And that is the step that leads through symbolic death to final peace.

Four Quartets (1943). Eliot's most extensive and most difficult religious poem, and one that repays careful study. The title suggests musical quartets or chamber music, and the poem has often been studied as structurally analogous to music. The titles of the individual sections are all names of places important in Eliot's life. "Burnt Norton" is a Gloucestershire country house that Eliot visited in 1934; "East Coker" is the Eliot family's ancestral home in Somerset; "The Dry Salvages" are a group of rocks off Cape Ann, Massachusetts, a scene familiar to Eliot as a boy; and "Little Gidding" is the first Anglican retreat house, a haven for high churchmen (including poet George Herbert) during the seventeenth-century civil wars. "Burnt Norton," the most difficult section, introduces the poem's major themes: time, eternity, the transcending of time, the Christian belief that time may be "redeemed"—that what has happened is not necessarily fixed permanently, that there is the hope of a "might have been." The poem thus contemplates the intersection of time and eternity from a semimystical point of view (as do some of Eliot's later plays). In so meditating, Eliot arrives at the mystery of the Incarnation, which offers the possibility that the time-bound human being may be assumed into timelessness as the temporal fire and the eternal rose become one.

JOHN CROWE RANSOM (1888–1974)

Ransom was one of the best and earliest examples of an important phenomenon in modern American literature: the writer who is also a critic and a professor. In recent years both poets and fiction writers have gravitated toward the universities, accepting teaching positions as artists in residence. As such, their influence has tended to be "academic" in the sense that their ideas are transmitted to university students, some of whom become artists in their own right. The larger cultural fact is evident: Recent American creative writing (and criticism), for good or bad, proceeds from an academic source. The "antiacademic" work of Pound, Eliot, Faulkner, Hemingway, Mencken, and other great names of the 1920s and 1930s has been largely succeeded by the work of writers who have learned from poets, critics, and novelists who are formal teachers. Ransom's importance lies in the fact that he was not only a poet and critic but also a man peculiarly fitted by position to influence younger writers.

Life. Ransom was born in Pulaski, Tennessee, and educated at Vanderbilt University and Oxford (as a Rhodes scholar). He taught at Vanderbilt from 1914 to 1937 and from 1922 to 1925 edited *The Fugitive,* a little magazine. Most of his important poetry appeared first in this journal. In 1930 he contributed an essay to *I'll Take My Stand,* a collection by twelve southern writers (including Allen Tate and Robert Penn Warren) which defended the southern agrarian way of life against that of the industrialized north. In 1937 he moved to Kenyon College in Ohio and became editor of *The Kenyon Review,* still a major American literary journal. Always concerned with poetic theory, Ransom grew increasingly interested in literary criticism and became in effect a critic rather than a practicing poet. His name has become synonymous with the movement known as New Criticism, and his critical reputation has become at least as important as his poetic one.

Poetic Theory and Practice. Ransom said that for many years he was preoccupied with the ancient critical problem of how a poem might be both universal and particular, how it might be said to be a concrete universal. He finally arrived at a partial solution by concluding that a poem is made up of "structure" and "texture" (terms used by many New Critics). The poem's structure is a core of meaning that can be said in prose. Its texture to Ransom means particularity of situation or scene, sometimes simply the concrete details. The job of the critic is to establish the structure of the poem and then to examine the texture in order to show how the poet has particularized his meaning. This argument for close reading of the entire poem and the examination of all its parts places Ransom alongside such other New Critics as Cleanth Brooks and Robert Penn Warren. Ransom's own poetry generally requires such close reading because, although not new in its techniques, it is carefully wrought. It has been called metaphysical for its use of irony, paradox, elegant erudition, and especially its occasional bizarre imagery and understatement. Although his critical views are modern, his verse echoes such seventeenth-century poets as Marvell and Donne. His poems frequently deal with such themes as love, death, and transience, usually in twentieth-century language, but with attitudes that Donne and Marvell and (to leap two centuries) Emily Dickinson would have understood and approved. His best work has been exclusively in the form of the relatively short lyric.

Representative Works

"Bells for John Whiteside's Daughter" (1924). A lyric in five quatrains that uses slant rhyme and understatement in ways reminiscent of Emily Dickinson. A small girl has died, a lively child who cared for the geese in this rural setting. The "we" of the poem are shown to be mourning, but in a low emotional key: They are "vexed" that she seems to be so lost in a "brown study."

"Blue Girls" (1927). A lyric mourning the transience of feminine beauty. Like Herrick and Marvell, the speaker tells the young girls to ignore their teachers and "practise" their beauty, for he could tell them a story of a woman once lovelier than they who now has fallen to age and bad temper. The ancient theme is enhanced by the "texture" of the poem. The setting seems to be a girls' school at which the girls wear blue skirts as uniforms and are taught many things, but not the impermanence of their youth and beauty.

"The Equilibrists" (1927). One of Ransom's most metaphysical lyrics. Although there are echoes of Dante, the poem will likely remind the reader more of Donne's "The Ecstasy." Like Donne, Ransom deals with the theme of love, both spiritual and sexual; and like Donne he uses imagery that startles the reader. Unlike Donne, however, he does not resolve the problem by asserting that spiritual and sexual love are parts of a single entity. Rather he places his lovers in a kind of Dantean inferno. Never having consummated their love because of a sense of honor, they now spin eternally in different orbits. The speaker fashions their ironic epitaph: They are "equilibrists" whose moral dexterity has condemned them.

ARCHIBALD MACLEISH (b. 1892)

MacLeish is one of the most gifted and versatile of modern poets. In the half century that he has been writing poetry he has worked with distinction in the forms of the short lyric, the long narrative, and the poetic drama.

Life. MacLeish was born in Glencoe, Illinois. He received his A. B. at Yale (1915) and his law degree at Harvard (1919) and then served with the U.S. Army in France in World War I, rising from private to captain. After the war he practiced law in Boston. In 1923 he took his family to France to devote his time to poetry, and his five-year stay there produced much of his early work. By 1928 he was an established poet, and he also became widely known for work outside of poetry. In addition to various teaching positions in the 1930s and 1940s, he was an editor of *Fortune* magazine for eight years, Librarian of Congress for five years, assistant secretary of state for two years, and chairman of the American delegation to UNESCO in 1946. He has received numerous honorary degrees and awards, including three Pulitzer prizes.

Poetry. MacLeish is a skilled craftsman who has written many different kinds of poetry. His early work reflects the influence of both Pound and Eliot not only in many verbal echoes of their work (especially Eliot's) but also in its use of the past. Like Pound's early *Cantos* and Eliot's *The Waste Land,* MacLeish's *The Pot of Earth* (1925) employs ancient myth as a vehicle for presenting new meaning. (MacLeish's version of the mythical gardens of Adonis is taken from Frazer's *The Golden Bough,* one of Eliot's favorite early sources.) Again like Pound and Eliot, MacLeish early learned ways of integrating the literature of the past into his own work: Thus *The Hamlet of A. MacLeish* (1928) uses Shakespeare's play as a frame for a new poem and the character Hamlet as a persona for the later poet. In other ways, too, much of the early poetry is literary: There are poems in the seventeenth-century metaphysical manner, poems in the nineteenth-century French symbolist manner, even poems about poetry. But this early poetry, although it shows various influences, is not apprentice work. Most of MacLeish's best lyrics, which are among the finest in modern poetry, date from this time (about 1925 to 1935).

MacLeish has often insisted on the distinction between private poetry and public poetry: between poetry written to please the poet and the discerning reader and poetry written for a wider public. Private poetry (like much of MacLeish's early work) may be intense and difficult; public poetry must be looser, more obvious, easier to assimilate. Much of the poetry and poetic drama MacLeish wrote in the late 1930s and 1940s is public poetry, a complement to the considerable body of social and political prose that he was writing at this time. Both the poetry and prose reflect what MacLeish has always taken to be the essential American political tradition: a blend of genuine patriotism and a democratic liberal philosophy.

After MacLeish became less of a public figure, he went back to his private and probably more important work both in the form of the lyric and the poetic drama. Many of the poems in later collections (*Songs for Eve*, 1954; *The Wild Old Wicked Man & Other Poems*, 1968) and the verse play *J.B.* (which received the 1959 Pulitzer Prize for drama) return to a theme of his early work: the vexing question of the essential meaning of man and his place in the universe.

Representative Works

"*Ars Poetica*" (1926). Perhaps the most famous poetic argument that poetry is not discursive but presents its meanings in concretes, in experiences. It is a poetic version of Eliot's famous doctrine of the objective correlative (see p. 84) and has been much used by the New Critics who have argued that the poem is a self-contained organic unity.

"You, Andrew Marvell" (1930). A lyric that uses the symbolism of place names to evoke a disturbing awareness of the oncoming dark. Here "darkness" suggests the disappearance of ancient eastern kingdoms into the shadow of the past. The title is a reminder of Marvell's famous lines from "To His Coy Mistress": "But at my back I always hear / Time's wing'd chariot hurrying near." Thus the speaker (presumably an American) feels the warm sun on his back but dreads the coming darkness, the ultimate and seemingly inevitable historical extinction.

"Immortal Autumn" (1930). A lyric on one of MacLeish's recurring themes: man's essential aloneness in the world. MacLeish's handling of the hexameter quatrains is a measure of his technical competence.

EDNA ST. VINCENT MILLAY (1892–1950)

Born in Rockland, Maine, Millay was educated at Barnard and Vassar colleges. Much of her early and still most popular poetry was written while she lived in the vibrant atmosphere of Greenwich Village in the 1920s. After her marriage, she lived on a farm in the Berkshire Hills near Austerlitz, New York, until her death. Although in her Village years she seemed the very type of the new emancipated woman, her work is now most accurately seen as traditional, in theme and form closer to the nineteenth-century romantics than to the new poetry of Pound, Eliot, and Williams. She translated parts of Baudelaire's *Les Fleurs du Mal,* tried her hand at poetic drama, and wrote poems of social protest (for example, "Justice Denied in Massachusetts," which deals with the Sacco-Vanzetti case). But her best work is in the form of the short lyric, especially the sonnet. She was in fact a remarkable sonneteer, among the finest in all American poetry. She has sometimes been compared to Keats; many of her best sonnets (like his) deal with such timeless themes as death, love, art, and the transience of beauty. Representative Millay sonnets are "Euclid Alone Has Looked on Beauty Bare," "On Hearing A Symphony of Beethoven," and "Oh, Sleep Forever in the Latmian Cave."

E. E. CUMMINGS (1894–1962)

For some forty years Cummings was known as the most famous experimental poet in modern American poetry. His most successful work is in the form of the relatively short lyric.

Life. Cummings was born and brought up in Cambridge, Massachusetts. The son of a Congregational minister who had taught English at Harvard, Cummings was educated at Harvard, receiving his B. A. in 1915 and his M. A. in 1916. Like many others of his literary generation, he joined the Allied forces in World War I before the United States entered the war. He was mistakenly imprisoned in a French prison camp for several months, an experience he used in his novel *The Enormous Room* (1922). After the war, again like many of his literary contemporaries, he went to Paris, where he studied both writing and painting. He returned to America, to the congenial atmosphere of Greenwich Village in the 1920s and 1930s, and soon acquired the reputation of an avant-garde experimental poet, a reputation that he managed to maintain through four decades of writing.

Romanticism. Emerson and Thoreau would have endorsed the spirit of Cummings's poetry, if not its form. From his earliest collection in 1923, Cummings wrote consistently from a viewpoint best described as romantic individualism. Pervasive in his work is a hatred of the large and impersonal forces in modern life: government, political parties, churches, big business, society in general—what a later generation was to call the Establishment. Against them Cummings projected the power of the personal, the private, the individual. Some of his best poetry is a direct satirical attack on war, politics, and social conformity. But a greater part of his work celebrates human love, and it is in this portrayal of private relationships that Cummings most memorably opposed the gray impersonality of modern life.

Experimentalism. Cummings was as rebellious in his poetic techniques as he was in his social, political, and religious opinions. Critics agree that he wrote some of the finest lyrics in modern poetry, but there the agreement ends and the arguments about experimental techniques begin. The lack of consensus is understandable, since Cummings defied tradition in many ways, most obviously in breaking rules of punctuation, capitalization, and word spacing. He even lowercased his name—e. e. cummings. He often used capital letters within words instead of at the beginning; he refused to space in the usual way and often put punctuation within words; he often broke words into pieces with no regard for syllabification and used these pieces as actual lines in a poem. This effect has been called visual experimentation or typographical poetry. Less apparent to the common reader, because it is not simply visual, is Cummings's seemingly bizarre vocabulary. Somewhat like Pound, he went in fear of abstractions. He used concrete words or images to signify abstract ideas, but he also used abstract words to signify particular experiences. In addition, he frequently interchanged the usual functions of nouns, adjectives, and adverbs. Yet, for all his experiments, Cummings by no means abandoned traditional poetic forms. Beneath the oddity of punctuation, spacing, syntax, and vocabulary, the reader often finds to his surprise a poem in the old form of a series of rhymed quatrains, or even a sonnet.

Representative Works

"Buffalo Bill's defunct" (1923). One of Cummings's most famous lyrics. It relies heavily on visual effects: There is no punctuation, and the spacing of words and lines is unconventional. On rereading the poem, one realizes that the joining of words with no spacing between suggests the awe of a child viewing Buffalo Bill's performance. The boyish admiration is taken up into the last lines, which are a kind of challenge to death in their rhetorical questioning of death's capacity to absorb the vitality of Buffalo Bill.

"In Just-" (1923). A famous short lyric in which the unconventional spacing, lack of punctuation, and telescoped words form not only a visual but also an aural pattern. The balloon-man, suggestive of Pan and of the spring season, whistles the children to him in a kind of spring ritual. The description of the ritual must be read according to Cummings's musical notations. Quick movement is suggested by both tone and spacing; the fairy quality of the balloon-man's whistle is suggested by the spaced adjectives that describe it: it is somehow far-off and only half understood. Thus he whistles, not far and wide, but "far/and/wee."

"somewhere i have never travelled" (1931). A celebrated love lyric. The form is not obviously bizarre; except for peculiarities of punctuation and capitalization, it is in a conventional form of five quatrains, although the only rhyme occurs in the final quatrain. The theme is as old as romantic love itself: the lover's praise of his mistress and his awareness of her power over him. The poem's oddity consists largely in its imagery, which is not simply paradoxical and unphraseable but also without rational justification. The loved one's hands, for example, are praised in the comment that not even rain has hands as small. The imagery is surrealistic rather than realistic; but the celebration of the beauty, fragility, and power of the mistress is apparent.

"anyone lived in a pretty how town" (1940). A relatively conventional poem in its form, nine four-line stanzas with rhyme and slant rhyme and a basically iambic meter. The poem's strangeness lies in its vocabulary and syntax. The poem tells the story of two lovers (anyone and noone) who are perfectly in love and whose love is thus in rhythm with the seasonal beauties of nature. They are contrasted with the "someones" and "everyones" who simply exist.

HART CRANE (1899–1932)

Influenced by such diverse poets as Whitman, Rimbaud, Pound, and Eliot, Crane is one of the most difficult of modern poets, but one of the most interesting, too.

Life. Like Keats, Crane led a brief life and one marked by pain (although in Crane's case the pain was mostly psychological). Born in northern Ohio and brought up in Cleveland, from childhood he was torn by a particularly vicious relationship between his parents that ended in divorce. Most critics have concluded that his later homosexuality stemmed from this early experience. Largely self-educated and never emotionally stable, Crane turned to poetry not as a craft but as a kind of religion, a personal as well as aesthetic tool. Most of his poetry, both good and bad, reflects this sense of strain. When even his work failed to give Crane the personal justification he needed, he drowned himself in the Caribbean Sea.

Difficulty of Crane's Poetry. The difficulty of much of Crane's poetry is readily apparent, although it is difficult to describe. One can assign certain probable causes, however (literary causes, as distinct from personal and temperamental ones). Crane was fascinated by analogics between poetry and both music and painting, for example, and he often used words less for their sense than for their sound or, as he would say, their "color" or "composition." In this respect, of course, he resembles French symbolist poets such as Rimbaud or Laforgue. But other, sometimes conflicting, tendencies were also at work in his poetry. He was an avowed disciple of Pound and Eliot, whose rhythms, imagery, and allusiveness he greatly admired. Yet relatively little of his work is in free verse, the form that Eliot used in "Prufrock" and *The Waste Land* and Pound in the early *Cantos*. Even when his poetry echoes Eliot (as parts of *The Bridge* do), it is likely to be in fairly regular blank verse. Crane apparently never really felt at ease with free verse, just as he never felt at ease with Pound's or Eliot's philosophy. Again, Crane felt himself to be in the Whitman tradition, which he saw as affirmation, and thus opposed to the negation and asceticism of Eliot's work. But here, too, a conflict arose, for most writers who have felt themselves heirs of Whitman (Sandburg, Shapiro, Ginsberg) have more or less followed his form of expansive free verse. Perhaps most important, Crane apparently did not experience this sense of affirmation in any deep personal way. When he echoes Emerson or Whitman or (as some have thought) certain German romantic philosophers, he seems simply to be echoing, not really restating, or stating anew. Thus in reading his work one is aware of strain, between form and idea, in what is said but apparently not felt.

The mixture of these unassimilated influences at least partly accounts for the peculiar density of Crane's verse. Syntactically (as in *Proem: To Brooklyn Bridge,* for example) it is often bewildering, as if Crane could not quite decide whether to write in sentences or fragments, or in free or metrical verse. And frequently his imagery, though intensely personal (like Eliot's and Pound's), is difficult not for this reason but because he has tried (like Donne) to "yoke together" disparate levels of experience and has not succeeded (see "Voyages II," for example). In Eliot's terms, this imagery has not "fused" in the poet's imagination and thus does not fuse in the reader's, no matter how much explication is given by Crane himself or others. And there are numerous places in *The Bridge* where the idea and the form are at odds. In the section called "The Dance," for instance, what Crane apparently intended as a wild and primitive kind of poetry comes out impossibly literary, not Whitman's "barbaric yawp," but Longfellow's parlor poetry.

Yet, in spite of the difficulties, unevenness, and incoherence of much of Crane's work, he is not a minor poet. Critics who know his work best (including Tate, Winters, and Spears) have generally agreed that parts of *The Bridge,* parts of "Voyages," and several lyrics (both early and late) are not only successful but of the highest quality, worthy of comparison with any other American poetry.

Representative Works

The Bridge (1930). Crane's most ambitious work, intended as an epic of modern American life in the Whitman tradition of optimism and the Eliot manner of *The Waste Land.* The poem is made up of eight major sections and a variety of subsections. (An instructive statement of Crane's intentions in the poem is his letter of September 12, 1927, to Otto Kahn; see Weber's edition of the letters or Horton, pp. 335–340, both listed in the Bibliography.) Briefly, the poem begins with a depiction of the Brooklyn Bridge as symbolizing the relationship between man and God (as does Whitman's "Brooklyn Ferry"). It then moves into a semihistorical, semimythical rendering of America's past, with Pocahontas symbolizing the great natural body of the country. Returning to the present, it dwells on the vastness and variety of modern America ("The River") and also the "wasteland" aspects of modern life ("The Tunnel"). It concludes ("Atlantis") with an optimistic prophecy of man's ultimate union with God.

"The Broken Tower" (published 1933). One of Crane's last lyrics. Dense and difficult, it nevertheless sums up his poetic aspirations and his sense of personal failure. Arising from a real incident (his ringing of the morning bells in a Mexican church tower), the poem suggests his own poetic attempts, which have "broken" him by their intensity, and contrasts them with the ideal poetry of the sun that in a natural and effortless way "unseals" the beauty of earth.

LANGSTON HUGHES (1902–1967)

As poet, fiction writer, playwright, editor, compiler, and columnist, Hughes probably did more than any other writer to advance the cause of black literature.

Life. Born in Joplin, Missouri, Hughes was erratically schooled in Kansas, Illinois, Ohio, and Mexico, with one year at Columbia University. He had been down-and-out in many European settings and had become a relatively well-known poet before he finally took a degree at Lincoln University, Pennsylvania, in 1929. One of the best-known figures of the 1920s Harlem Renaissance, he worked tirelessly at poetry, fiction, drama, musical comedy, and any other kind of writing, including a newspaper column, that could depict the black's position in America. (His column introduced Jesse B. Simple, a kind of black counterpart to Finley Peter Dunne's Mr. Dooley; both characters were fountains of folk wisdom and common sense.) Hughes helped put into print books on black poetry, music, and folklore; founded black theater groups; and edited several anthologies of black writing (both American and African). He managed the remarkable feat of keeping abreast of the rapid advancement of black writing. His own late work is perfectly contemporary in tone, and three years before his death he edited an anthology of new black poetry. Hughes was all things to black literature: creator, critic, editor, explainer, defender, and prophet.

Poetry. As Eliot said of Pound, Hughes's contribution to American poetry should be judged not only on his own poetry but on his total contribution to poetry. The number of wholly successful Hughes poems is not great, considering the size of his output. But his persistence in writing black poetry, from an American Negro's point of view, broke ground for later poets such as Mari Evans, Gwendolyn Brooks, James Wright, and LeRoi Jones. His early models were the dialect poems of Paul Laurence Dunbar and the free verse of Sandburg and Masters. Later he tried with some success to capture the haunting quality of Negro blues music and (like Sandburg) some of the rhythms of jazz. But like many poets he discovered that it is possible to set poetry to music but nearly impossible to turn music into poetry, or at least into poetry as it appears in print. Very few of Hughes's poems are in the standard blues form because in poetry that form is too restrictive. His experimenting led him to a hybrid form of lyric poetry: some of the characteristic themes and feeling of blues music written either in free verse or in variations of rhyming verse that could easily be set to music. His best lyrics project the usually sad, often absurd life of the contemporary American Negro. Sometimes this theme is poignantly presented in basic free verse, as in "Daybreak in Alabama" and "Theme for English B." But more often it is depicted in some variety of rhymed lyric, some in dialect with a folk flavor, others in conventional English.

Representative Works

"Dream Variations" (1924). One of Hughes's best-known poems. A beautifully cadenced seventeen-line rhyming lyric, it epitomizes a black's dream of belonging. A carefree dance in the sunlight is complemented by the coming on of the tender and gentle night, which, like the speaker, is black.

"Weary Blues" (1925). An irregularly rhymed lyric describing a black piano player playing blues in a Harlem bar. Most of the lyric is a depiction of the man and his song, but the song the man sings is in standard blues form and in dialect. The combination of description and presentation is very effective.

"Song for a Dark Girl" (1927). A ballad in which a black girl laments that the white Jesus was of no help when a young black was lynched. The ironic first line of each of the three quatrains is "Way Down South in Dixie."

"Daybreak in Alabama" (1940). A free-verse lyric, somewhat reminiscent of Sandburg. The beauty of an Alabama dawn suggests to the speaker a kind of natural and mutual acceptance of all people—a vision that must be deferred until he becomes a composer and can write music about it.

RICHARD EBERHART (b. 1904)

Born midway between the generation of Pound and Eliot and that of Robert Lowell, Eberhart is one of the elder statesmen of contemporary American poetry. Although he has written long poems and plays, he is best known for his short lyrics.

Life. Born in Austin, Minnesota, Eberhart was educated at the University of Minnesota, Dartmouth, and Cambridge. He taught at an eastern prep school, then served as a naval gunnery instructor in World War II. After six years spent in business he returned to teaching and lecturing. He has taught at several universities, most recently at Dartmouth. Among other honors, he was awarded the Bollingen Prize in 1962 and the Pulitzer Prize in 1966.

Poetry. Readers of Eberhart's poetry will find many affinities with other poetry, both past and present, but Eberhart is much more than the sum of these influences. Both in theory and practice, for example, he is avowedly romantic—in the obvious sense that he believes a poet works best by means of inspiration or illumination, and in the less obvious sense that he presents no mask or persona but generally speaks as himself in the poem. Thus critics have compared him with romantics like Blake and Wordsworth, and one could as easily compare his war poetry with Wilfred Owen's. But Eberhart's technique is often metaphysical in its compression and startling imagery. This combination of a sensitive man's direct reaction to experience with an intellectual questioning of that experience gives his best work an intensity of impression that is matched only rarely by contemporary poets.

Representative Works

"For a Lamb" (1936). A lyric, reminiscent of Blake, that asks a question recurrent in Eberhart's poetry: What is death? The poem contrasts the obvious signs of death (the rotting body) with the question of where the "essence" of the lamb has gone.

"The Groundhog" (1936). One of Eberhart's most famous lyrics. The poet returns season after season to the disintegrating corpse of the groundhog, wondering at the mystery of death, angrily (and symbolically) even probing the corpse with a stick. In the "wisdom" of his last visit, when the corpse has vanished, he cuts a stick for walking, not probing, and is suddenly aware of the transience of all things. The groundhog not only symbolizes but is a part of the same process that has subsumed ancient China and Greece, Alexander, Montaigne, and St. Theresa and will take the poet as well.

"The Fury of Aerial Bombardment" (1944). A lyric that angrily questions the nature of a God who permits war. Like Hardy, the poet wonders if this God is simply indifferent. But the poem's effectiveness lies in the particulars of the last stanza, which lists men now dead whom Eberhart had instructed in machine gunnery.

THEODORE ROETHKE (1908–1963)

Roethke's relatively early death removed from the American literary scene a poet who had reached what seemed the height of his powers. Highly esteemed by critics and other poets, he also achieved a considerable popular reputation.

Life. Born in Saginaw, Michigan, Roethke spent a good part of his formative years playing and working in a large greenhouse run by his family. (These early days he recalled vividly both for their literal and symbolic value in what are called his *greenhouse* poems.) He took a B. A. and M. A. at the University of Michigan and taught at Lafayette College, Pennsylvania State College, Bennington College, and the University of Washington. Among many honors he received for his poetry were the Pultizer Prize (1954), the Bollingen Prize (1958), and the National Book Award (1965) for his posthumous collection, *The Far Field*.

Poetry. Critics have found many influences and even specific echoes of other poets in Roethke's work. Some of his poems echo the metaphysical techniques and tone of Donne; some are cryptic and aphoristic after the manner of Blake; a few deliberately imitate the later terse style of Yeats; and there are innumerable reminders of such diverse modern poets as Dylan Thomas and Eliot. In the less successful poems the reader is likely to be uncomfortably aware of voices other than Roethke's. In the better ones, however, the influences have been assimilated.

What is most apparent about Roethke's poetry is its intense subjectivity. As Roethke himself said, his life was an "open house," and his poetry often utilizes even the most personal and private aspects of that life. But his subjectivity, somewhat like Kafka's, is microcosmic, emblematic of the experiences not only of the individual but of the race. Influenced by Freud and Jung, Roethke believed that in speaking of himself he spoke of mankind. The great recurrent theme of his work is the struggle of the individual to achieve an identity and after that to determine his destiny. His later work blends psychological insights of Freud and Jung with the teachings of various mystical writers.

What gives Roethke's best poetry its undeniable power and distinction is that he does not meditate on theological matters as Eliot does but gives something nearer experience itself: the sense of struggle, of advance and retreat, of moments of spiritual vision ended abruptly by an awareness of the somber actualities of human body and mind. Like Whitman and Wordsworth, Roethke was at his best in portraying correspondences between his psychic and spiritual states and certain natural phenomena—stones, water, flowers—when (as Emerson said) he could make us feel that nature wears the colors of the spirit.

Many of Roethke's best lyrics are parts of sequences and are best read in those contexts. Some, like "Elegy for Jane" and "In A Dark Time," stand well by themselves, but Roethke's talent is best shown by connected lyrics such as the greenhouse poems or "Four for Sir John Davies."

Representative Works

"Four for Sir John Davies" (1954). A sequence of four lyrics that shows Roethke's poetic debts to Yeats and Donne in addition to his obvious borrowing from "Orchestra," a sixteenth-century poem by Sir John Davies. The cadence and rhyme echo Yeats, the subject matter and its treatment echo Donne, and the basic image of the world as harmonious motion is taken from Davies. More important than the poetic influences, though, is the argument of the sequence and the blending of some of Roethke's important themes. The older world view of universal harmony is diminished to the dance, the more particular harmony of sexual love between two lovers. But this, in turn, is seen as somehow not ultimate, not enough. Sexual love, if it is to be a formula for life, must be like Dante's love for Beatrice, a means to beatitude. The closing lines are typically ambiguous—hopeful rather than conclusive.

KARL SHAPIRO (b. 1913)

Both in his poetry and criticism, Shapiro was an important force in shaping the reaction to such older poets as Eliot and Pound and to the poets of his own generation and later. He has worked with great success in the short lyric form and in longer forms of varying complexity.

Life. Shapiro was born in Baltimore and educated at the University of Virginia and Johns Hopkins University. His collection *V-Letter and Other Poems* won the Pulitzer Prize for 1945, and in 1946 he was made Consultant in Poetry at the Library of Congress. He has edited two influential literary journals, *Poetry* and *Prairie Schooner,* and has taught at Johns Hopkins, the University of Nebraska, the University of Illinois (Chicago Circle Campus), and the University of California at Davis.

Poetic Theory and Poetry. Early in his career (1945) Shapiro published a verse study of modern prosody, *Essay on Rime,* in which he expressed his dissatisfaction with the technical aspects of much modern poetry. In his later critical work he condemned as intellectual and pretentious some of the classic poetry of the 1930s and 1940s, especially that of Pound and Eliot. Whitman, he felt, was the watershed of modern American verse, and he praised poets like Randall Jarrell who could be lucid and commonplace and yet poetic.

Shapiro's poetry reflects his critical views, but at its best (like all good poetry) it succeeds not because of its theme but because of its intrinsic merits. His early poetry (for example, the war poetry of *V-Letter*) is quite conventional in technique, employing with remarkable skill the sonnet, metrically regular blank verse, and various combinations of rhyme. The language of this poetry, while generally colloquial, is literary compared to that of his later work. As his rebellion against the Pound-Eliot poetry intensified, Shapiro began to change both the form and language of his work. In *The Bourgeois Poet* (1958) he moved to a free-verse form that sometimes echoes Whitman and to cadenced (and sometimes not even cadenced) prose resembling the prose poetry of the "beat" writers, especially Kerouac and Ginsberg. His language, like that of the beats, became violently colloquial and vulgar: the language of the bar, the school corridor, the army camp. In his collection *White Haired Lover* (1968), a series of intensely personal love poems, Shapiro returned to traditional metrics and forms, although his language remained absolutely frank.

Representative Works

"Elegy for a Dead Soldier" (1944). One of Shapiro's most famous poems, it is both a bitter comment on war (recalling Wilfred Owen's poems in World

War I) and an ironic statement about the limited social and moral views of both the soldier and America. So far as the soldier was fighting for anything intelligible, it was a richer, more comfortable life for himself; and he and his country had "winked" at each other, agreeing that this is what life is all about. The form of the poem illustrates Shapiro's technical talent. On first reading, it seems to be irregularly rhymed except for the epitaph; but examination shows a careful rhyme scheme. In each of the twelve-line stanzas the rhymes occur in the second and third lines, the fifth and eighth, and the ninth and eleventh.

"The Conscientious Objector" (1947). A poem praising the conscientious objector for refusing to bow before the terrible forces of public opinion during wartime. This conscience is what we all come back to at armistice time. The four eight-line stanzas are irregularly rhymed and the metric is less regular than in much of the early poetry.

RANDALL JARRELL (1914–1965)

Randall Jarrell was one of the many contemporary poets who combined the writing of poetry with literary criticism and university teaching. He handled equally well the very short lyric and the longer meditative or narrative form.

Life. Jarrell was born in Nashville, Tennessee, and received his B. A. from Vanderbilt University. He taught at several colleges both before and after World War II, in which he served as an air force navigator. He was Consultant in Poetry for two years at the Library of Congress and in 1961 received the National Book Award for his collection of poems *The Woman at the Washington Zoo*. His book *Poetry and the Age* (1953) is a standard work.

Poetry. Jarrell's most popular work is still his war poetry, though many critics believe that his later poetry is more significant. Certainly poems like "Next Day" and "In Montecito" from *The Lost World* (1965) are memorable comments on life and death, as direct as the war poems and perhaps more terrifying because they depict the horror of ordinary life and death. Whatever Jarrell's subject matter, however, his work reveals that, like Frost, he was a remarkable craftsman who could manage the conversational tone for purposes of pathos, dignity, or irony in whatever verse form he chose.

Representative Works

"The Death of the Ball Turret Gunner" (1945). In the view of many critics the best short war poem in the language. The ironic imagery of birth (or birth and miscarriage) forms the whole poem. It suggests the youth of the gunner and his essential ignorance about his life and death. Mindless, he left his mother's womb; mindless and bodiless, he leaves the artificial womb (the ball turret) of the state.

"The Woman at the Washington Zoo" (1960). One of several poems in which the speaker probes life and finds no meaning. Here an aging government worker sees in the caged animals an image of her own life. In panic, she pleads for something—a man, a vulture, death—to take her and make her over into what she used to be. Her desperate prayer is perhaps sexual on one level, but certainly religious on another.

ROBERT LOWELL (b. 1917)

Lowell is generally acclaimed as one of the finest of a group of American poets born roughly a generation after Eliot and Pound—a group that includes Karl Shapiro, Randall Jarrell, and Richard Wilbur.

Life. Lowell is a descendant of two old and distinguished New England families, the Lowells and the Winslows. He went to Harvard but left after a year to work under John Crowe Ransom at Kenyon College. In 1940 he married novelist Jean Stafford and was converted to Roman Catholicism, although neither the marriage nor the conversion was permanent. Early in World War II Lowell tried to enlist in the navy but was rejected. Later he tried to claim status as a conscientious objector, citing the American and English saturation bombing of Germany as inhumane and immoral. This claim was also rejected, and he served five months in federal prison. *Lord Weary's Castle* (1946), his second collection of poems, brought him wide acclaim and the Pulitzer Prize for poetry. Later, among many other honors, he won the National Book Award for his collection *Life Studies* (1959) and the Bollingen translation prize for his *Imitations* (1961). In 1949 he married novelist Elizabeth Hardwick.

Poetic Development. Much of Lowell's early poetry is Metaphysical in its deliberate harshness of rhythm and diction and its violent and often strained imagery. It is also openly Roman Catholic in viewpoint. Technically, it utilizes traditional stanza patterns and meters. The later poetry is markedly different—more relaxed in form, more modern. As fine as much of the early poetry is, there is a kind of hyperliterary quality to it. But the later poetry seems much more candid, less committed to literary devices and traditions or to any formal religious point of view. In brief, Lowell has moved away from traditional literary forms and a traditional religious outlook. But his poetry throughout is the work of a sensitive and religious man, poetry that probes at the evil and smallness of man whether in the aggregate of a war or in the privacy of his own soul.

Representative Works

"Mr. Edwards and the Spider" (1946). A lyric of five semi-Spenserian stanzas in which Lowell re-creates the moral consciousness of the great eighteenth-century Calvinist preacher Jonathan Edwards. Lowell does this by closely paraphrasing passages from Edwards's early tract on insects and two of his famous hellfire and damnation sermons, "Sinners in the Hands of an Angry God" and "The Punishment of the Wicked." Apparently not satirical, the poem is as frightening in its moral outlook as the work of Edwards himself.

"Colloquy in Black Rock" (1946). A meditative lyric of alternating six-line and four-line stanzas, both sets of stanzas having a consistent rhyme scheme. Setting the poem in a Bridgeport war plant, Lowell juxtaposes the "earthiness" of the human condition against Christ's Incarnation. In literal mud the factory workers build helicopters that, in their capacity for flight and descent, remind the poet of Christ, who may dive like a blue kingfisher into the mud of the human heart.

"The Quaker Graveyard in Nantucket" (1946). An elegy for Lowell's cousin, lost at sea during the war. As Hugh B. Staples has pointed out, the poem has marked resemblances to Milton's *Lycidas*. In both poems the body is not recovered but is left to the depths and mysteries of the sea. Also like Milton, Lowell uses irregular rhyme, alludes to the pagan sea god, and "digresses" (from the corruption of the clergy to the corruption of man, as shown by the war and by the cruelty of the early Quaker whalers). As in all classical elegies, there is a movement from intense grief and questioning to a kind of acceptance of death as part of some divine plan. Lowell's acceptance occurs in Part VI, when the scene shifts from the sea to the shrine of the Virgin in Walsingham, England, and Lowell suggests that the horror of the human situation is lost in the infinite mystery of God. The poem impressively echoes imagery from Thoreau (in the opening lines) and from Melville's *Moby-Dick*.

"For the Union Dead" (1959). A series of short, unrhymed stanzas, in which Lowell uses Eliot's and Pound's technique of setting a meaningful past against a vacuous present. Here the past is particularized by the South Boston Aquarium and the monument to Colonel Shaw, who led a Negro regiment in the Civil War. The aquarium is boarded up and abandoned, and the monument is propped up to protect it from steam shovels excavating for an underground parking lot. No World War II monuments stand here, only an advertising photograph of a safe that survived the Hiroshima bombing.

"Skunk Hour" (1959). One of the most personal of Lowell's lyrics, it manages (like Eliot's "Prufrock") to capture the qualities of a culture as they exist in miniature in the mind of the poet-narrator. In eight intricately rhymed but perfectly colloquial stanzas, Lowell suggests the decay of New England civilization as it is reflected in the poet's own sense of despair and isolation. Only the skunks, the healthy animals of the poem, can live naturally, passing the "chalk-dry" church to fearlessly feed upon garbage in the moonlight.

GWENDOLYN BROOKS (b. 1917)

Not so well known a name in black poetry as Langston Hughes or LeRoi Jones, Gwendolyn Brooks emulated both men. Like Hughes, she has done much to advance the cause of black literature, and especially in her later poetry she has kept abreast of the increasingly militant strain in black writing.

Life. Brooks was born in Topeka, Kansas, and brought up in Chicago, where she attended school and junior college. She began writing poetry as a child; her first poem was published when she was thirteen, and throughout high school and college her work attracted the attention of teachers and editors of little magazines. She won several prizes in creative writing conferences sponsored by Northwestern University in the 1940s. Her first collection, *A Street in Bronzeville* (1945), was highly praised, and her second, *Annie Allen* (1949), won the Pulitzer Prize for poetry. Since then she has published a novel, *Maud Martha* (1953), and four more collections of poetry. She has taught and lectured at several universities, encouraging young would-be poets by sponsoring poetry competitions and donating money for prizes.

Artistry. The dominant subject throughout Brooks's poetry is the tragedy of black life in America, and her latest poetry became increasingly militant. But though black American poetry surely has every reason to be "thesis" or social-protest poetry, Brooks managed the feat of writing black poetry that is primarily art, whatever its social effect may be. In the old phrase, she mastered the art of speaking in verse. If racial strife should miraculously disappear tomorrow, one would still read her work with sheer delight, marveling at her way of bending language to her will.

Brooks's skill and versatility are evident in her earliest collection, *A Street in Bronzeville,* and she has rarely descended from that high level. She has written sonnets, ballads, metrical lyrics with both regular and irregular rhyme, and free verse in both long and short forms. She has composed formal tributes to such public figures as Malcolm X, Medgar Evers, and Emmett Till, and she has created numerous vignettes of anonymous blacks. Among the most moving are one of a woman mourning her children lost by abortion and one of a dead "Madame" (both from *A Street in Bronzeville*) and "The Ballad of Rudolph Reed" from *The Bean Eaters*. A long free-verse poem, "In the Mecca," from the 1968 volume of the same name, is a vivid and incisive depiction of black slum life in Chicago.

Representative Works

"The Bean Eaters" (1960). A short irregularly rhymed lyric on the old age of a poor black man and his wife. The pathos of their life is quietly suggested by the simple enumeration of details: beans as a steady diet, a rented room, receipts, doll clothes from the past, tobacco crumbs from the present. Beyond suggesting one aspect of the racial problem, the poem evokes a sense of the sadness that attends the terminal days of all human life.

"The *Chicago Defender* Sends a Man to Little Rock" (1960). A long lyric dealing with the government-enforced integration of the Little Rock public schools in 1957. The speaker of the poem, sent to report the particular racial hatred of the city's people, ironically defends them by finding them normal and ordinary—like the people who crucified Christ. The alternation between long and short lines and the rhyming, mostly regular but sometimes delayed, serve admirably to form the vehicle of the irony.

"Malcolm X" (1968). A short free-verse lyric that depicts by explicitly sexual terms Malcolm X's function in the racial situation. He was the male hardness that penetrated the "female" passiveness of the American black and brought to birth a new sense of identity and purpose. The poem's sexual imagery—Malcolm X fathering a new and frightening black strength—suggests his unsettling effect on white America.

RICHARD WILBUR (b. 1921)

The technical brilliance of Wilbur's poetry is so apparent that he has sometimes been accused of elegance, of writing poetry that is more an exercise in virtuosity than a product of strong feeling and serious ideas. His best-known poetry is in the form of the relatively short reflective lyric.

Life. A native of New York City, Wilbur received his B. A. from Amherst College and was an infantryman in World War II. After the war he resumed his education, receiving his M. A. from Harvard in 1947. He has taught English at Harvard, Wellesley College, and Wesleyan University. The merits of his work have brought him many awards, among them the Pulitzer Prize and the National Book Award in 1957 for his collection *Things of This World*.

Poetry. Although critics generally agree that Wilbur is among the most gifted and brilliant contemporary poets, he has not achieved the popular reputation of poets like Roethke and Lowell. One critic has described him as an "occasional" poet,[4] a rarity in our time. An occasional poet need not speak passionately and consistently from a particular and describable point of view, like Pound and Williams; nor need he, like Lowell and Roethke, make poetry out of intense personal problems. Thus Wilbur's work is difficult to categorize. He has said that he agrees with Eliot that a poem is a relatively impersonal construct, detached from the poet's life. And critics have agreed that his poetry lacks the overt intensity and passion of more romantic poets such as Lowell, Roethke, or Dylan Thomas.

4. Ralph J. Mills, Jr., *Contemporary American Poetry* (New York: Random House, 1965), p. 172.

Like Frost and Robinson, Wilbur has chosen to use traditional verse forms and to work within strict metrical and stanzaic limitations. In defense of this style, he has said that the genie's power comes from being imprisoned in the bottle, and he might well have echoed Chesterton's remark that the essence of a picture is its frame.

Wilbur has written a considerable amount of satirical and even comic verse, for example, his translation of Molière's *The Misanthrope* and his lyrics for a comic opera version of Voltaire's *Candide*. In either a serious or a comic mode his technical skill makes him successful; he has mastered the art of "saying" in verse. His translations are of the highest order and his comic verse really witty. His original serious poetry reveals a sensitive and questioning mind as modern in its attitudes as his verse is traditional in the strictness of its form.

Representative Works

"The Death of a Toad" (1950). A lyric of three strictly rhymed stanzas that illustrates the almost Elizabethan richness of Wilbur's diction. The narrator's power mower has crippled a toad, and the beast has "sanctuaried" itself in the shade to die. The narrator sees the toad as returning to the prehuman world of "lost Amphibia's emperies" and imagines that the toad's eyes watch the daylight across the mown "castrate" lawn. The final image is usually taken to mean the sterility of modern life, symbolized by the mower, the neat lawn, and the ironically heart-shaped leaves.

"Still, Citizen Sparrow" (1950). A lyric of six four-line stanzas with strong and obvious rhyme. The speaker is replying to "citizen sparrow," who has condemned the vulture and, by implication, all highly placed leaders and officials. Defending the vulture as a necessary part of the order of nature, the speaker suggests that "heroes" are equally necessary in the social order. Like Noah, they endure trials beyond the comprehension of their smaller brethren; if their sins seem greater than ours, we must nevertheless forgive them.

"Love Calls Us to the Things of This World" (1956). One of Wilbur's best-known lyrics, unrhymed but metrically regular. Wilbur has said that the title and the Christian-Platonic point of view of the poem come from St. Augustine. Asleep, the soul dissociates itself from the evils of the material world, then on waking, forces itself to accept them. Desiring to live in the realm of pure spirit, it accommodates itself by a "bitter love" to God's world of matter.

JAMES DICKEY (b. 1923)

Among the large group of contemporary poets, Dickey, by the quality and quantity of his work, is easily one of the most distinguished. He is equally at home with the short or moderate-length lyric or narrative form.

Life. Dickey was born in Atlanta, Georgia, received his B. A. and M. A. degrees from Vanderbilt University, and served as a pilot in both World War II and the Korean War. Among many honors were his appointment as Consultant in Poetry to the Library of Congress and the National Book Award for his collection *Buckdancer's Choice* (1965). He has been poet-in-residence and visiting lecturer at several universities, has published three books on contemporary poetry, and reached the best-seller list with a novel, *Deliverance* (1970).

Poetic Development. Dickey assessed his own poetic development accurately in an essay called "The Poet Turns on Himself" in his book *Babel to Byzantium* (1968). As a young poet looking for a form, he decided to try to write verse in short lines, each of which really "said something," and to work in basically anapestic meter, a meter that from Chaucer to the present has been regarded as going against the "natural" iambic grain of English. His first two volumes of verse are in this form, and several of his early poems are remarkably successful. But then he found this rhythm too restricting and began to experiment. As might be expected, the experiments led him to a basically iambic line, though in both the earlier and later poetry he avoids rhyme of any kind. The later poetry is often quite traditional in form. But often also it is in a quite open form, utilizing long free-verse lines that in their typographical spacing and lack of punctuation recall both Whitman and Pound.

For Dickey, theme is more important than technique. Like Frost, he is determined to say something, even at the risk of being discursive. And, like Roethke, Jarrell, Shapiro, and many other contemporary poets, he draws his truths from the private experiences of his own life. Yet, as in all good romantic poetry, these experiences become concrete universals that the reader can relate to his own, and all, life.

Representative Works

"The Performance" (1960). A war lyric from Dickey's first collection. Written in basically anapestic meter, it portrays a comrade who was beheaded by the Japanese. The man's feat of being able to walk on his hands (which Dickey imagines him doing before his enemies) ironically underlines the viciousness of war that exalts nonhuman capacities.

"The Firebombing" (1965). A narrative from *Buckdancer's Choice*. In it the persona in his comfortable suburban home meditates on the firebombing raids he carried out against Japan during World War II. He tries to translate the burned homes and people into the people and homes of his neighborhood but finally concludes that the experiences have become a part of him that is past rational judgment. The form is idiomatic free verse, with a remarkable variation of rhythms.

"For the Last Wolverine" (1967). A long free-verse lyric calling for a new wildness and passion in poetry—Dickey's own, poetry in general, or both.

In a kind of apocalyptic vision, the persona sees the last wolverine climbing a burning spruce to mate with the last eagle and spawn a new creature that will scourge the world of evil. The passion and purpose of the poem are reminiscent of William Blake.

ALLEN GINSBERG (b. 1926)

Ginsberg's work illustrates three important strains of thought, or attitudes, in modern American poetry: A general social and political radicalism, an interest in oriental religion, and a penchant for unplanned or spontaneous poetry. Like Whitman, he has worked with some success in both the fairly short and quite long forms of intensely subjective lyric.

Life. Ginsberg was born in Newark, New Jersey; attended high school in Paterson; and was graduated from Columbia University. He read deeply in Blake and other mystical and romantic writing, particularly Whitman. While living in Harlem in 1948 he had, or claimed to have had, a series of visions in which Blake's voice spoke to him. This experience was followed by an eight-month stay in a mental hospital. In the next few years he traveled a great deal, finally gravitating to San Francisco and the group of writers dubbed the beats, who included Jack Kerouac, Gregory Corso, and Lawrence Ferlinghetti. In 1956 he published *Howl and Other Poems,* which was found obscene with an enormous amount of ensuing publicity. In 1957 a court decision held that the book was not obscene; Ginsberg's reputation was made; and he again began to travel, giving frequent readings of his work. In 1961 he published *Kaddish and Other Poems 1958–1960*. He has since published five more collections of verse and meditations and a correspondence with William Burroughs about the use of drugs, *The Yage Letters* (1963).

Poetry and Popularity. No doubt a good deal of Ginsberg's reputation among college-age readers stems from his espousal of many of their causes, both in his public life and in his work. There is hardly an aspect of youthful radicalism that he has not championed: He has condemned American Asian policy, defended drug taking, advocated absolute freedom of dress and behavior, and been harshly critical of established social structures, including that of universities. He is hairy, bearded, blithely vulgar in his speech and verse, and willing to disrobe at such occasions as poetry readings. That he is partly a poseur is very probable; that he is wholly aware of what the younger reading public wants is most likely. Yet it is only fair to say that Ginsberg has been defending youthful radicalism since the days when he himself was a youthful radical. Long before it became commonplace to condemn the Vietnam War, Ginsberg was attacking not only that but American conduct in World War II as well. Perhaps Ginsberg is not really keeping up with youthful causes; it may be that youthful causes are finally catching up with Ginsberg. *Howl* (1956) is still a kind of underground classic, and *Kaddish* (1960) is still not often surpassed in its contemporary concerns.

A more difficult question than the subject matter of Ginsberg's work is its quality as poetry. Like the poems of his spiritual godfathers, Whitman and Blake, his poetry is very uneven. The shaping spirit of much of his work, like that of Whitman's, is Eastern, specifically Zen Buddhism, which Ginsberg and Kerouac made almost a fad in the 1950s. Since true Zen is essentially subjective and contemplative, it does not easily lend itself to expression of any sort. The Zen master hardly speaks or writes at all; he quietly desires an ineffable experience, not poetry. Both Kerouac and Ginsberg tried to resolve this difficulty by writing "spontaneously," trying to dissolve the conscious mind in a flow of words produced by a kind of free association. Their intention was to produce something like the Zen experience, though by definition this experience is too fine to be caught in any net of words. The results in Ginsberg's work are mixed. Many parts of the longer poems seem to be nearly gibberish—long rolling Whitmanesque lines of free verse that often dissolve into the dullest kind of prose. But when Ginsberg is Western enough to impose a kind of order, something of the Eastern flavor often comes through.

Ginsberg's work has another quality, one he shares with both Whitman and Blake. That is the element of the "prophetic," the stance taken by the poet as the seer and announcer of great truths, the element often called "apocalyptic." Thus the characteristic Ginsberg verse is a strange and often startling mixture of Eastern attitudes filtered through a Western consciousness and frenetically uttered in American English that often seems to go out of its way to shock. When the mixture works it is very, very good; when it fails it is awful.

Representative Works

"Sunflower Sutra" (1955). An often anthologized but not very good extended lyric. In headlong prose-poetry Ginsberg describes Kerouac and himself sitting in the shade of a locomotive and gloomily watching the sunset. Kerouac points out a grimy, dusty sunflower, and Ginsberg suddenly sees in it something of the true "inside" of man, which can survive the hideous mechanical civilization in which he lives. For all the sense of Eastern vision that Ginsberg tries to evoke, the poem beneath the welter of seemingly spontaneous language is absolutely discursive. It seems not only a failure but nearly a hoax.

Kaddish (1960). A long lament for the poet's mother, who for years had been paranoid and who finally died of a stroke. The first two sections, called "Proem" and "Narrative," tell in loose free-verse form the poet's experiences with his mother, from the first time he took her to a mental hospital, when he was twelve, to her death. The nightmare of her life comes to an end when, two days after her death, he receives a peculiarly moving letter from her that tells him that the key (to something) lies in the sunlight shining through the window. The section "Hymn" is a formal lament, Whitmanesque in its use of initial rhyme: "Blessed be . . . ," and so on. The "lament" briefly recapitulates the material of the first two parts. The "litany" is a horrendous cataloging, in actual litany form, of the horrors of her life and death. The "fugue" is a final lament at her graveside, with crows cawing overhead. The poem, or at least the first two-thirds of it, is almost completely formless—great gobbets of Ginsberg's personal life in what even Whitman would have called "barbaric yawp." Yet the overall effect is undeniable. The poet's anguish, as in a formal elegy, is brought into focus and allayed by the final sections, which strangely recall both Whitman and certain phrases from the Old Testament.

SYLVIA PLATH (1932–1963)

Both critics and general readers have found qualities of greatness in Sylvia Plath's intense poetry. Critics have found reasons to compare her work to that of Keats, Dickinson, Lowell, and Roethke; readers have tended to romanticize her as an archetypal poetic figure who lived and wrote briefly and intensely, then chose to die young. Both views seem understandable and at least partly true. Plath worked almost exclusively in the field of the short and moderate-length lyric poem.

Life. Born in Boston, Sylvia Plath lived in the seacoast town of Winthrop, Massachusetts, until the age of nine when her father died and the family moved back to suburban Boston. Her father's death and the move back inland were events that were to reverberate with increasing intensity in her poetry. She attended Smith College on a scholarship, and her early writings won her a magazine award that sent her to New York City as a kind of student editor—events that she recorded in her novel *The Bell Jar* as a prelude to her mental breakdown. She went to England to attend Cambridge University on a Fulbright Scholarship, and there she met and married Ted Hughes, who, like her, was soon to become an outstanding poet. Most of Plath's best work was done in the last three years of her life, after her two children were born. A month after the publication of *The Bell Jar* she committed suicide. Her major collection of poems, *Ariel,* was published posthumously in 1965.

Poetic Development. Critical comparisons of Plath's work with that of Keats, Dickinson, Lowell, and Roethke are apt and fruitful. Like Keats and Dickinson, she was preoccupied with and perhaps even half in love with death; and like Dickinson, Lowell, and Roethke she wrote poetry that is autobiographical and even "confessional." Having undergone the nightmare of a nervous breakdown, she must have seen the work of Lowell and

Roethke as peculiarly sympathetic, since both of them (particularly Lowell) had recorded in verse something of their ordeals. There are obvious echoes of both these poets in her poetry, although she chose to tell of her own breakdown most explicitly in the prose of *The Bell Jar*. But like all fine poets Plath is more than the sum of the influences on her; if she reminds us of Lowell and Roethke, later readers of Lowell and Roethke may well be reminded of her.

The terms *early* and *late* in connection with her poetry may seem odd, since the early poetry is that of the collection of 1960 *(The Colossus)* and the late, that written in the next three years. But there is generally such a marked progression from the poetry of 1960 to the later poetry that some such terms must be used. The progression is of two kinds, which may be roughly termed technical and psychological. There is, on the one hand, a progression, or a movement, from relatively conventional rhyme, meter, and general poetic presentation to a less obviously literary way of saying—a lessening of rhyme, meter, and literary formality for the illusion of direct, idiomatic speech that William Carlos Williams thought should be the poetic presentation of the future. On the other hand, there is what a critic might call a sharpening of sensibility and what a psychiatrist might call a pathological growth of self-consciousness or self-preoccupation, to the extent that things external to Sylvia Plath's mind—external things as unlike as bees, her children, and her long dead father—became meaningful only as projections of that mind. It is in this psychological aspect of her poetry that she is most reminiscent of Emily Dickinson. Neutral outer things become vehicles of an inner anguish; for example, in "Daddy" her father becomes a Nazi, and in "The Moon and the Yew Tree" the moon becomes a cold and lifeless surrogate of the Blessed Virgin Mary. It is this late "poetry of anguish," supported by the revelations of *The Bell Jar,* that has made Sylvia Plath the mythical figure she has become. Later critics and readers will doubtless demythologize her to find what is left when the current cult of the neurotic has passed. When they do, it seems likely that they will see her, as they will still see Keats and Dickinson, as a poet whose verbal skills make her tortured mind meaningful.

Representative Works

"The Moon and the Yew Tree" (1965). A poem composed of four stanzas of seven free-verse lines each. The simple and idiomatic diction and sentence structures of the speaking voice serve to set off the startling symbolism of the natural objects presented. The poet associates her mind with "planetary" things—the dark earth, the yew tree, the black ocean. The moon (with its associations of lunacy) is her mother, wholly unlike the tender Virgin Mary whose image is in the nearby churches. A frightening polarity is suggested between the cold whiteness of the moon and the silent blackness of the earth, a mother-child polarity that calls the poet to oblivion.

"Daddy" (1965). Probably Plath's best-known lyric. She once said of it that it presented the classical Electra complex of Freudian psychology, and readers who know something of her life cannot fail to see in it a tortured depiction of her relationship with her own father. The poem consists of sixteen irregularly rhymed five-line stanzas, and the rhythm and occasional verbal repetition ironically recall a nursery rhyme, rather like Auden's "September 1, 1939." The imagery is direct and startling: The father (long dead) is a brutal Nazi; the speaker is a Jew tortured and violated by him. But the speaker's feelings are ambivalent; she hates the Fascist father but at the same time asserts that every woman "adores" Fascist brutality. The poem closes with the furious imagery of the father as vampire, killed in the classical way by a stake through his heart, but the end of the poem does not resolve the psychological problem, unless the resolution is the death of the poet herself.

"The Arrival of the Bee Box" (1965). One of several lyrics dealing with bees and bee raising, a hobby Plath learned as a child from her father. In seven irregularly rhymed five-line stanzas plus a single closing line, the poet records her reaction to a large wooden box of bees that she has ordered. The interior darkness of the box and the angry noise of the bees frighten but fascinate her. She wishes them dead or sent back, then wishes them set free, but only if they will not harm her. It is almost impossible not to read the poem as a parable of the speaker peering into the angry darkness of her own being and finding herself appalled at what she sees.

LE ROI JONES (IMAMU AMIRI BARAKA) (b. 1934)

Jones is one of the best and also one of the most militant of contemporary black poets. His best work is in the short and moderate-length free-verse lyric.

Life. Jones was born and brought up in Newark, New Jersey; received his B. A. from Howard University; did graduate work at Columbia University; and served two years in the U. S. Air Force. Though he is primarily a poet and playwright, he has done serious social criticism, written extensively on black music, and published two books of fiction. His one-act play *Dutchman,* a shocking racial play somewhat reminiscent of Albee's *The Zoo Story,* won an Obie Award in 1964. In recent years he has worked with black theater groups in Harlem and Newark and has devoted much time to political activism.

Militant Poetry. Although much of Jones's recent work has been in the form of drama (probably because drama is a better vehicle for his militant racial views), he is unmistakably a poet. He is a master of the short free-verse lyric, and one who has read his "For a lady i know" or "Preface to a Twenty Volume Suicide Note" may regret that such poems of quiet beauty make up so small a part of his poetry. But as Jones has himself said, in an introduction to an anthology called *The Moderns* (1963), he is concerned less with the form of writing than with significant content. And the significant content of most of Jones's poetry is passionate racism: praise of blackness, damning of racial moderation (Roy Wilkins and the NAACP), and a mighty curse laid on the white race in general.

Jones is most effective when he has taken some care with form, not necessarily traditional form, but form as a means of containing and thus conveying the turbulent emotions of "black rage." Sometimes this form comes closer to prose than to poetry, but the same may be said of many other poets working in free forms (such as Whitman, Ginsberg, and Shapiro). The length of the poem is not necessarily a determining factor. A little poem like "Civil Rights" (an attack on Roy Wilkins) is a failure in the use of language; better insults are spoken every night in most bars. On the other hand, a poem like "Blank," which at first glance seems not only long but formless, on careful reading reveals itself as a "wild" but effectively phrased question: What do time and man mean in a Godless world? The fact that both poems employ what used to be called gutter language is simply another aspect of Jones's poetry that the reader must get used to; most of his poetry, even his love poetry, uses this kind of language. It is presumably part of Jones's studied contempt for traditional American poetry, which, of course, is predominantly white and ordinarily uses standard English.

Few would deny that Jones's poetry at its best has enormous power. As to its permanence, the most obvious conclusion is that it will remain vital as long as racial hatred exists in America, and that statement seems a sad guarantee that his poetry will survive him indefinitely. Beyond that, it may be said that language well used always survives, even when concentrated on a historical situation that may in time disappear. Every particular historical situation mirrors in some way the larger human situation. Jones hates white men, with good reason; but ultimately his best work, sifted by time, will be read by those who love poetry, regardless of their race, simply because they are human beings.

Representative Works

"A Poem for Black Hearts" (1965). A free-verse elegy for Malcolm X. In form it recalls both Whitman and the Christian litany. Each of the rhythmic units begins with *For,* though the word is not placed at the beginning of the line, as in Whitman's poetry. The praises of Malcolm X are thus separated syntactically and resemble the "names" given to Mary or to Christ in the formal litany. Even the conclusion, which is a demand that black people act as Malcolm X did, echoes the intent of the litany—be as these holy ones were—except that Jones calls for vengeance as well as holiness. From the very first image the poem builds in intensity to the remarkable racial anathema in the conclusion.

"The Test" (1966). A free-verse condemnation of white treatment of blacks, rising to its highest pitch of rhetoric with a condemnation of the white God who keeps the black man in a special hell. The potential spiritual development of the black man, Jones says in heavy, pounding rhetoric, is stunted by the white man's image of him.

"The Black Man Is Making New Gods" (1966). A free-verse diatribe against whites, and particularly Jews, that presents one of Jones's recurring themes: Much of so-called white culture was "stolen" by Jews from black Arabian sources. Even the white God of both Christians and Jews, Jones implies, is a distorted version of a true black God. But Jones prophesies that the blacks will win the coming war and then freeze into impotency the dangerous germ of whiteness.

10
Modern Novelists and Short-Story Writers

WILLA CATHER (1873–1947)

The generally high quality of Cather's style and her insistence on traditional values have kept her work popular and readable for more than sixty years.

Life. Although Cather was born in Virginia, she was essentially a midwesterner. She grew up in rural Nebraska and was graduated from the University of Nebraska in 1895. Slowly gravitating eastward to the centers of writing and publishing, she worked for a Pittsburgh newspaper, taught high school in Pittsburgh, then moved to New York and became an editor of *McClure's Magazine* from 1906 until 1912. The success of her early work allowed her to travel extensively in Europe and in the southwestern states, especially Arizona and New Mexico, regions that provided material for her deeply felt sense of origins and foundations in human culture. Her novel *One of Ours* (1922), though not generally regarded as one of her best works, won the Pulitzer Prize for fiction.

Traditionalism. Cather is sometimes considered in the James tradition. Like James, she loved verbal precision, and like him she was at her best in character analysis, although neither her style nor her characters are of the famous Jamesian complexity. His influence is strongest in her early stories such as "Paul's Case" and "The Sculptor's Funeral" (both published in her first collection, *The Troll Garden,* 1905). In these stories and others, she dramatized one of James's favorite themes, the beauty and vitality of art contrasted with the drabness of everyday life. Some of Cather's critical writing also seems to echo James, particularly her essay "The Novel Démeublé" (1922), which argues against the cataloging of physical details and sensations that she found obnoxious in Lawrence.

Although critical estimates of Cather vary, she will probably be remembered best for the work in which she evoked the time, the atmosphere, the sense of place, of her girlhood—the rugged Nebraska farm life about the turn of the century. In the novels *O Pioneers!* (1913) and *My Ántonia* (1918) and in stories like "Neighbor Rosicky" (1932), she brought to life the rough beauty of the plains and, more important, the human beauty to be found in the struggles of Czech and Swedish immigrants to the American West.

Representative Works

"The Sculptor's Funeral" (1905). A short story that is almost a parable of the struggle between the artist and a materialistic society that misunderstands and despises him. With perhaps too obvious symbolism, Cather contrasts the bleakness of the Kansas town and the hypocrisy of its inhabitants with the short artistic life of the sculptor. The coffin lies in the family parlor, surrounded by the cheap and ugly trivia that pass for art among the townspeople.

My Ántonia (1918). Cather's best-known novel. The story is told in the first person by Jim Burden and is primarily based on his recollections of Ántonia Shimerda, a Bohemian immigrant girl whom he first meets when both are children on the Nebraska frontier. Ántonia's early years on a farm are ones of poverty and hardship that cause the suicide of her genteel, ineffectual father. Later she becomes a hired girl for various townspeople, a position aspired to by most of the immigrant farm girls. She is seduced by a railroad conductor, gives birth to a daughter, and returns to the farm in disgrace. But with her great gift for life, she survives, marries a recent Bohemian immigrant, and together they raise a large family and become successful farmers.

"Neighbor Rosicky" (1932). A long short story that utilizes the Nebraska farmland background of *My Ántonia*. The title is apt: The Bohemian farmer Anton Rosicky is everyone's neighbor. A simple, hardworking man who has made a success of his farm, his family, and his life, he is told at the age of sixty-five that he has a bad heart. He tries to follow the doctor's instructions to slow down but feels compelled to do some work for his son Rudolph, whose wife Polly is an "American" town girl and not completely happy on the farm. He is stricken at his son's farm, and as Polly helps him she senses his special goodness and is strengthened by it. He dies the next day and is buried in the graveyard next to his own field. Cather suggests that his goodness is as close to his survivors as his grave is to his land.

SHERWOOD ANDERSON (1876–1941)

Anderson's best work dramatizes American life as it is localized in small towns and rural areas.

Life. Born in Camden, Ohio, Anderson grew up in a relatively poor family. After army service in Cuba during the Spanish-American War, he was graduated from Wittenberg Academy in Springfield, Ohio, in 1900. Then he worked as an advertising writer in Chicago and became president of his own paint factory in Elyria, Ohio. But increasingly dissatisfied with business, he began to think seriously of writing for a living. He returned to Chicago (during what has been called the Chicago Renaissance), where he continued to write advertising but now also worked on his own fiction. His first two novels were not well received, but *Winesburg, Ohio* (1919) was an immediate success, as were two collections of stories, *The Triumph of the Egg* (1921) and *Horses and Men* (1923). After two relatively successful autobiographical works, *A Story Teller's Story* (1924) and *Tar: A Midwest Childhood* (1926), Anderson's reputation declined. He moved to a Virginia farm, bought and edited two Marion, Virginia, newspapers, and became involved in various labor movements in the South. He was four times married and three times divorced. On a trip to South America he died of peritonitis in Panama.

Themes and Characteristics of Anderson's Fiction. There is general agreement that Anderson was at his best in the shorter forms of fiction. Although he began with the novel form (*Windy McPherson's Son,* 1916) and often returned to it, he lacked the sense of structure and the interest in character that the longer narrative requires. He is best represented by *Winesburg, Ohio* (1919), which is a collection of related short tales, and by several short stories that have been acclaimed as among the finest in American literature: among them, "I Want to Know Why," "I'm a Fool," and "Death in the Woods."

Anderson had a strong sense, based on his own experiences, of the evils of industrialism and the essential loneliness of all human beings; these ideas permeate his work. But unlike the doctrinaire naturalists or "thesis" novelists such as Dreiser, Farrell, and Steinbeck, he did not attempt to bring the two ideas together in a cause and effect relationship.

Anderson's real talent lay in brief depictions of people in what he saw as their natural state: isolated from each other and usually unable even to articulate this isolation. This sense of the quiet desperation of much of human life is what makes *Winesburg, Ohio* and some of the short stories so moving. Much of his work is marked by a kind of literary simplicity (learned partly from Gertrude Stein), by obvious repetitions, and by a deliberately archaic syntax that (often unfortunately) reminds the reader of certain stylistic qualities of Old Testament writing. Such bad writing, in which the style does not match the content, often conflicts with the easy, idiomatic prose that Anderson was also capable of writing. In *Winesburg, Ohio* this stylistic conflict is minimal, and in the best of the short stories it does not occur at all.

Representative Works

"I Want to Know Why" (1918). One of Anderson's earliest and best-known short stories. In theme it is an initiation story of a certain kind. Like many of Hemingway's early stories, it dramatizes a boy's idealism, an idealism that is incapable of understanding the equivocations of adult life. The boy who tells the story is not really initiated; he does not come to terms with the problem. But the reader is in a sense initiated, or reminded of the blandness with which adults accept moral evils that the young find inexplicable.

Winesburg, Ohio (1919). Anderson's best work, a collection of twenty-three stories related by a common setting, a common theme, and recurring characters (notably George Willard, who appears in several stories as actor and listener). Thus the book has something of the effect of a novel (like Faulkner's *The Unvanquished* and *The Hamlet*). There are other reminders of Faulkner, such as the four-part story "Godliness," which in theme and gothic sensationalism reminds one of *Absalom! Absalom!* But the best and most characteristic stories are those in which young George Willard figures. As town newspaper reporter, George learns much about life, and most of what he learns is that the lives of the townspeople are warped and lonely. Some try to love and fail; others have given up even the attempt. Wing Biddlebaum cannot communicate with others because in order to do so he must touch them, and such physical contact is forbidden. George's mother cannot tell him what she wants for him or of her love for him. The schoolteacher Kate Swift tries to tell him something about life and writing but gives up in despair. Dr. Parcival can tell him only that all men are Christ and that they are all crucified. Ray Pearson can only conclude that life is a trap. There are brief moments of unspoken communion between George and Helen White—these moments, indeed, are set up as the goal of all human striving—but they are passing, and there is no indication of why they come or whether or not they will ever come again. In the end, George, full of a Wolfe-like, inarticulate wish to experience more of life, leaves Winesburg for the big city.

None of the characters in the story is revealed in depth; certain aspects of their lives are shown quickly, a technique much like Joyce's "epiphanies." But when the mosaic pieces are put together, the pattern emerges, and it is a tragic one. Anderson has often been called a naturalist because his people seem driven and unfree. But the book does not argue for determinism, as Dreiser's work often does, nor does it argue for fatalism, as Stephen Crane's work often does. In James's terms it presents a deeply felt, direct impression of life.

SINCLAIR LEWIS (1885–1951)

In the decade of the 1920s Sinclair Lewis was generally recognized as America's foremost fictional satirist.

Life. Lewis was born in the small Minnesota town of Sauk Centre, which he was to immortalize as Gopher Prairie. From boyhood an inveterate roamer and observer, he spiced and delayed his education at Yale with hobo trips to England and the Canal Zone. After graduating in 1908 he worked tirelessly on the outskirts of serious creative literature as manuscript reader, reporter, advertising writer, reviewer, and free-lance writer; it has even been said that he sold plots to Jack London. But until the publication of *Main Street* (1920) he was relatively unknown. After *Main Street* he was a celebrity, both at home and abroad. He refused the Pulitzer Prize for *Arrowsmith* in 1926 because he felt that his earler satirical work, *Main Street* and *Babbitt* (1922), had been unfairly ignored. But he accepted the Nobel Prize in 1930. His work after 1930, although it often made the best-seller lists, is generally inferior to his earlier novels. The primary reason for this decline in his writing seems to be that he had discovered, exploited, and exhausted the material that he handled best, the spiritual aridity of the American middle class in the 1920s.

Social Satire. Lewis's reputation today rests almost entirely on his novels of the 1920s: *Main Street* (1920), *Babbitt* (1922), *Arrowsmith* (1925), *The Man Who Knew Coolidge* (1928), and *Dodsworth* (1929). As many critics have pointed out, there is a certain sameness to these works, the repetition of a basic motif or pattern. (This observation is not necessarily a condemnation; much the same thing has been said of writers as different as James, Marquand, and Hemingway.) Lewis's basic pattern was to set a major character in a certain American background, then to describe in great detail the cultural and moral shallowness, the ugly materialistic life-style of the inhabitants of this background. Often the background was a small midwestern town—Gopher Prairie or Zenith—and Lewis is frequently bracketed with Sherwood Anderson, Edgar Lee Masters, and others who wrote antiromantically of American small-town life. Lewis's major characters then were given varying degrees of insight into the arid bourgeois values of the place. Occasionally they attempted to escape, but with the exceptions of Arrowsmith and Dodsworth, they came back because they really belonged there.

In *Main Street* Carol Kennicott tries to bring culture to Gopher Prairie, fails, leaves, then returns. In *Babbitt* George Babbitt flirts with art and radical politics before coming home again. Even Lowell Schmaltz of *The Man Who Knew Coolidge*, perhaps the dullest of Lewis's protagonists, has occasional moments of awareness of his own and his society's limitations. Lewis varies the pattern by allowing Martin Arrowsmith and Sam Dodsworth to leave their materialistic and provincial milieus, but at the cost of probability.

Technically, Lewis's special talent lay in his ability to present realistically the society he was satirizing. His style has justly been called phonographic. By patient research and careful looking and listening he was able to make his people seem real, if not especially individualistic. Even for readers a generation or more removed from his novels, the dialogue rings true. The persistent idiomatic quality of American speech survives the dated phrases and contemporary allusions. By this speech Lewis evoked the spirit of the Rotary Club, the small-town ladies' literary society, ultraconservative Republican politics, the superficialities and bigotries of atrophied formal Protestantism, and other aspects of provincial midwestern life. In short, at his best he depicted the hollowness of the American dream of material success that Arthur Miller was later to dramatize in *Death of A Salesman*. Babbitt, in fact, may well be the prototype of Willy Loman.

Representative Works

Main Street (1920). Lewis's first successful satirical novel. Carol Kennicott marries a midwestern doctor and takes on the task of rescuing Gopher Prairie, Minnesota, from ugliness and provincialism. But Gopher Prairie is not interested in civic beauty and theater groups, and actively resists her efforts. She leaves both the town and her husband but later responds to her husband's kindness and returns with him, defeated.

Dodsworth (1929). Perhaps Lewis's best novel. Sam Dodsworth is usually considered Lewis's best-developed character. Somewhat reminiscent of Lambert Strether in James's *Ambassadors*, Dodsworth in middle age becomes aware of the provinciality of Zenith and the larger and more humane world of Europe. After a long struggle with his middle-class midwestern conscience, Dodsworth finally decides to leave his shallow and unfaithful wife for Edith Cortright and the obviously good life she represents. But Dodsworth is not thumbing his nose at middle-class values. He has been so clearly wronged that his decision seems not only sensible but wholly moral.

KATHERINE ANNE PORTER (b. 1890)

For many years known as a writer's writer, Porter finally achieved popular recognition with the publication of her only novel, *Ship of Fools,* in 1962.

Life. Porter was born in Indian Creek, Texas, and received her early education in convent schools in Louisiana. Twice married and divorced, she has lived in various parts of the South, in Mexico, Paris, and New York. She received two Guggenheim Fellowships for creative writing in 1931 and 1938, and the Pulitzer Prize and the National Book Award for her *Collected Stories* (1965). In the years following World War II she emerged from privacy as a popular university lecturer and won fame and fortune with the publication of *Ship of Fools* and the subsequent movie version of the book (on which she worked for some twenty years).

Art. Porter is primarily a short-story writer. A scrupulous and subtle craftsman, she has published relatively little; like James she is a "passionate corrector." In addition to *Ship of Fools,* her reputation rests on perhaps a dozen stories and novellas (or long stories; she dislikes the term *novella*) that seem likely to become classics of symbolic and psychological realism.

Of all Porter's work *Ship of Fools* comes closest to pure allegory, a form that she avoided in her earlier and more characteristic work. Though distinctions between symbolism and allegory are difficult to make and often arbitrary, one need only look carefully at the work preceding *Ship of Fools* to realize that its symbolic quality adds meaning to the stories but not the precise and easily described meaning of allegory. Stories like "Flowering Judas" and *Noon Wine* are realistic in the sense that they are rooted in a certain time and place and in the sense that the action evolves through a careful, almost Jamesian analysis of character. They are also symbolic in the way that Faulkner's, Hemingway's, and Fitzgerald's best work is symbolic: The stories take on meaning for the reader after he has assimilated their absolutely local and personal levels. Said differently, in psychological and symbolic realism the reader induces the meaning (or meanings) by immersing himself in the work, while in allegory he is to some degree *given* a meaning. Most critics have concluded that Porter was at her best in realistic-symbolic fiction, not in *Ship of Fools,* although such a judgment says nothing about the absolute values of symbolism and allegory as such.

Many of Porter's finest stories deal with a character named Miranda. They somewhat resemble Hemingway's Nick Adams stories in their portrayal of a recurring character seen variously as a child, then as a young adult. Like the Hemingway stories, they are best read as a loose unit; also like the Hemingway stories, they are apparently highly autobiographical and could presumably have been worked into a single novel. This group includes seven short stories collected in *The Leaning Tower* under the general heading "The Old Order." They are "The Source," "The Journey," "The Witness," "The Circus," "The Last Leaf," "The Fig Tree," and "The Grave." The group also includes two of Porter's finest longer stories, "Old Mortality" and *Pale Horse, Pale Rider.* The short stories dramatize Miranda's Southern childhood and family background; the longer stories picture her life as an unhappy young woman. In "Old Mortality" her family rejects her because she has run away at seventeen to be married. In *Pale Horse, Pale Rider* she loses her lover to the 1918 influenza epidemic. Although they lack the coherence of a novel, the Miranda stories represent Porter's best attempt to depict and fathom a single character at some length and with attention to familial and historical background.

Representative Works

"Flowering Judas" (1930). One of Porter's best-known stories. The title and theme, as Ray B. West pointed out,[1] very likely derive from Eliot's poem "Gerontion." But certainly an analogue, if not a source, is James's "The Beast in the Jungle" and other James stories that deal with the theme

---

1. Ray B. West, "Katherine Anne Porter: Symbol and Theme in 'Flowering Judas,' " *Accent,* 7 (1947): 182–187.

of the unlived life. The story is a subtle character analysis of a young American woman who is unable to give herself wholly to anything—to love, to religion, to the revolutionary movement that is the immediate action of the story. At the end of the story she is granted a moment of insight in a dream, in which she discovers the particular person she is; this is the meaning of the story.

"The Jilting of Granny Weatherall" (1935). A story of the dying moments of an old woman who strongly resembles the grandmother in the Miranda stories. Granny has weathered all, or most, that life can give. Her incoherent dying reveries indicate the full life she has led, the dominating role she has played in the lives of her children and grandchildren. But her last thoughts are not of her family but of her experience of being jilted half a century before. The technique of the story is what may be called controlled stream of consciousness, a technique Porter used' to perfection in *Pale Horse, Pale Rider*. The reader is not left on his own, as he frequently is in Joyce and Faulkner; he knows that he is dealing with the rambling thoughts of a sharply delineated character, and he knows why.

Noon Wine (1939). Probably the best known of Porter's longer stories. Haunting in its symbolic evocation of paradisiacal life blasted by evil from the outside, it is nevertheless a careful and skillful analysis of a certain man (Mr. Thompson) whose character dooms him to live by appearances. He must see all the actions of his life as morally and socially acceptable, and it' is this trait of character that leads to both his murder of the intruder and to his own suicide. As in most of Porter's work, one may infer larger symbolic meanings, but these meanings are rooted in the person and actual situation of Mr. Thompson. An example of Porter's narrative skill and economy is the character of Mr. Homer T. Hatch, the intruder. Although he appears only briefly, the reader will probably remember him as one of the most malignant and repulsive characters in American fiction.

F. SCOTT FITZGERALD (1896–1940)

Fitzgerald is usually ranked with Hemingway and Faulkner as one of the classic fiction writers of twentieth-century American literature. He worked best in the short-story form or in that of the relatively short novel.

Life. A summary of Fitzgerald's life reads like a plot outline made from parts of his stories and novels; from the outside, at least, it was dazzling, romantic, short, and tragic. He was born in St. Paul, Minnesota; attended prep school in the East; then went to Princeton. He left college to join the army in 1917, became a dashing lieutenant (although he was not sent overseas), and met and fell in love with a beautiful Southern girl, Zelda Sayre. In 1920, after the publication of his first novel, *This Side of Paradise* (an instant success), he married Zelda; for the next ten years their lives seemed to symbolize the abandon and excitement of the Roaring Twenties.

He wrote an enormous amount of fiction, much of it "magazine fiction," but some of it his very best (*The Great Gatsby*, 1925, and several stories). His work was relevant and contemporary: It dealt with the times he was living in, and it brought him a great amount of money. But by the time of the 1929 stock market crash he and Zelda had wasted most of it, and worse, Zelda had a mental breakdown in 1930. Fitzgerald's reputation declined during the depression years; his later serious work, including *Tender Is the Night* (1934), was badly received; his health failed, and he was heavily in debt. He spent his last few years in Hollywood, writing scenarios and some last serious fiction, such as the unfinished *The Last Tycoon*, which was posthumously published in 1941.

Emergence as an Artist. During Fitzgerald's lifetime and for several years after his death, his reputation as an artist suffered from two stereotypes, both having an element of truth and thus hard to eradicate. First, critics and readers tended to see him as a 1920s' figure whose career paralleled those turbulent years and ended with them. Second, because he had published so much magazine fiction, it was generally assumed that he was only a slick writer. The beliefs are not only partly true but also related: Most of Fitzgerald's work *does* depict life in the 1920s, and his style *is* slick in the sense that it is immensely readable. But the whole truth is that Fitzgerald's best work is a highly symbolic rendering of the reality of his time, and his prose style at its best (whether in magazine stories or novels) is of a very high quality, Twain-like in its easy and idiomatic tone and brilliant in its imagery.

The realistic writer, James argued long before Fitzgerald began his work, writes his own impressions of his own time. If he goes back beyond a generation before his own he risks losing the direct impression of life that James considered vital to realism and thus risks becoming a historical novelist. The past may impinge upon the present in fiction as it does in real life, but the realist depicts this impingement, not the past itself. By this standard Fitzgerald was a realistic writer. In his work the past exists only as an influence on the present that he intensely felt. Jay Gatsby's past, for example, lives on in his present life and is part of his present character.

Yet Fitzgerald has often been called a romantic, and many of his characters are romantics in the sense that they abide by traditional concepts of sexual love and are attracted to wealth. Jay Gatsby believes that to be once in love is to be always in love, and he and innumerable other Fitzgerald characters believe in the glamour and natural goodness of money. But Fitzgerald, in his best work, depicts these people ironically or pityingly. Gatsby, Dick Diver (*Tender Is the Night*), and Dexter Green ("Winter Dreams") are essentially pathetic characters because they hold a view of life that will not bear up when put to the test of reality. Such characters are always distinguished from those like the Buchanans (*The Great Gatsby*) and Anson Hunter ("The Rich Boy") who live an unexamined and amoral life of material success. And both these groups are distinguished from the relatively small number of Fitzgerald characters who go through romantic illusions about love and money and come out the other side to a kind of sanity and balance. Nick Carraway *(The Great Gatsby)* is the prime example, although Charlie Wales ("Babylon Revisited"), Joel Coles ("Crazy Sunday"), and a few others achieve partial awareness. Briefly, then, in one way or another, Fitzgerald's best work is realistic about romantic attitudes toward life. It is largely because he depicted these attitudes in all their attractiveness that he sometimes seemed to be endorsing them.

If Fitzgerald's subject matter seems limited, it is well to remember Freud's comment that man's basic drives are for love and recognition. Fitzgerald's special luck was that he was able to see these basic impulses in a historical time when they were so obvious as to be a certain country's way of life, and his special triumph was that his art could depict them. In *The Great Gatsby* he came closest to suggesting that his stories were partial projections of America—its historical roots, its national aspirations, and its probably inevitable failure. But on reviewing Fitzgerald's serious work as a whole, one discovers that *The Great Gatsby* is special only in being Fitzgerald's best novel; in its depiction of one man's failure to distinguish appearance from reality it only dramatizes brilliantly what most of Fitzgerald's other work implies. The dream of love and recognition, even when seemingly fulfilled, is still only a dream. If Gatsby is emblematic of America, America is emblematic of the human condition.

Not an intellectual writer, and not usually termed a naturalist, Fitzgerald nevertheless suggested in his work as a whole a sense of human incapacity for greatness, a sense of what Marquand was later to call the sadness of predestined human failure. Catching what James called "the color of life," Fitzgerald also caught in his flappers and sad young men a quality of human life that is less tragic than it is vacuous. Hemingway was discursive enough to name this quality *nada* (nothing). Fitzgerald, in the tradition of James, merely dramatized it. Gatsby and Dick Diver are Fitzgerald's best-known examples of individuals whose ideals are proved wrong; Nick Carraway is the best known example of one who sees through others' illusions. But though Fitzgerald sometimes allowed his characters to tear away the veil of illusion, he never depicted a positive reality behind it. Nick Carraway, sickened at the moral decadence of the East, goes back to the West, which, ironically, has produced not only Gatsby's false idealism but also the more obvious evil of Daisy and Tom Buchanan. Although he depicted specific times and places, Fitzgerald knew that evil (or the absence of good) was not to be localized geographically or temporally. It was a condition of human existence.

Representative Works

"Winter Dreams" (1922). One of Fitzgerald's many early stories that foreshadow *The Great Gatsby*. Dexter Green dreams of being rich enough to marry the wealthy and lovely Judy Jones. Dismissed by her, he marries another girl, becomes rich, and then finds that Judy Jones has also been married—to a man who now finds her unattractive. Worse, he learns that she seems content to stay at home with her children and simply grow old. Because she represents for Green his past and his romantic illusions, this discovery drives him to tears of self-pity and some dim sense of the cruelty of passing time. He thus falls somewhere between Gatsby, who never loses his faith in his early dreams, and Nick Carraway, who sees them for what they are.

The Great Gatsby (1925). Fitzgerald's most famous novel and generally considered his best. With a high degree of artistry, the novel sums up and clarifies much of Fitzgerald's other work. Brilliantly written, it depicts both the glamour and the sordidness of America in the post-World War I decade. Through the eyes of the narrator, Nick Carraway, the reader sees the brutality and amoral insularity of the very rich (Tom and Daisy Buchanan); the lesser and frivolous immorality of Jordan Baker and all the parasitic hangers-on who attend Gatsby's parties; and the hopeless dreams of the poor in Myrtle Wilson and her husband, who operate a gas station outside the golden city of New York. Gatsby himself is an amalgam of the good and the evil in America. He follows the Ben Franklin rules designed to make one good, popular, and rich, but they lead him to become a semicriminal who works with real criminals like Meyer Wolfsheim. Gatsby is "great," Fitzgerald implies, in the sense of the old American dream of wealth and goodness—great in conception, tragic in its failure.

The famous closing section suggests America's moral decay (Fitzgerald had been reading Spengler), symbolically contrasting the first American settlements with the decadence of the 1920s. Gatsby symbolically lives through those 300 years, trying to fulfill his early ideals by criminal methods, and failing. The end of the novel, implying the inevitable failure of both Gatsby and America, gains force from Gatsby's earlier assertion that one can change the past. He thinks that the romantic love he and Daisy had felt for each other erases her marriage to Buchanan. (Symbolically, he remarks of her love for Buchanan that it was "just personal.") But both Gatsby and America are shown to have left an earlier age of innocence for a world of evil.

"Babylon Revisited" (1931). Among the best of Fitzgerald's late stories. Charlie Wales is depicted "after the fall." He and his wife had lived wildly and mindlessly through the 1920s, much of the time in Paris, the capital of pleasure. Partly through a drunken quarrel, his wife became ill and died. Now, after being ruined in the stock market crash, Charlie has returned to Paris, sober, penitent, full of self-pity, trying to regain custody of his daughter (ironically named Honoria). He fails because his wife's sister and her husband, who have been caring for the child, cannot be convinced that Charlie has changed—partly because of his old drunken friends who appear inopportunely, like memories of unforgiven sins.

JOHN DOS PASSOS (1896–1970)

One of the most interesting experimental writers in modern American fiction, Dos Passos did his best work while writing from a generally liberal or leftist viewpoint.

Life. Born in Chicago to a wealthy family of Portuguese-American descent, Dos Passos was educated in private schools in the United States and abroad and graduated from Harvard in 1916. He served in an Allied ambulance corps in World War I and later was a member of the U. S. Army Medical Corps. Private funds allowed him to stay abroad after the war, and it was in Spain that he did his first important work, which, not surprisingly, was war fiction: *One Man's Initiation—1917* (1920) and *Three Soldiers* (1921). Through the 1920s and 1930s he supported many liberal and radical causes, including the widespread condemnation of the Sacco-Vanzetti trial. It was during these years that he published his best fiction: *Manhattan Transfer* (1925) and the novels that make up the trilogy *U.S.A.* —*The 42nd Parallel* (1930), *1919* (1932), and *The Big Money* (1936). The trilogy was published in its complete form in 1937. It was followed by more fiction, including another trilogy, *District of Columbia* (1952), and a great deal of journalistic writing, much of it distinctively conservative in nature. His last novel of any significance was *The Great Days* (1958), apparently autobiographical and marred by sentimentality, an almost hysterical anti-leftism, and a complete lack of any of the experimental methods that give interest to his earlier work.

Experimental Fiction. Dos Passos made the most serious attempts in modern American writing, Faulkner excepted, to create "panoramic" fiction, the purpose of which is to depict, in as great depth and variety as possible, a range of national life. There are literary hazards involved in this kind of fiction, as Tolstoy and Zola could have attested. Stevenson's metaphor of the novelist as juggler is apt. The panoramic novelist must keep two balls simultaneously in the air: characters and setting (in the broadest sense of this term). Further, from the very outset the panoramic novelist discards the unity that James considered an advantage of the limited point of view, that is, the concentrated view of reality achieved by dealing in depth with a small and select group of characters. By this standard the panoramic novel is doomed to diffusion of effect. This is particularly so when instead of letting a few characters stand for a larger group, the novelist portrays a succession of individual characters. Faulkner was content to use a relatively small number of recurring characters to represent the various levels of Southern society. But Dos Passos generally refused to "reduce"; with boundless energy he presented a seemingly endless parade of particular people.

As early as *Three Soldiers,* Dos Passos showed his predilection for telling multiple stories as a means of depicting reality, in this case, the brutalizing effect of war on three different types of American soldiers. *Manhattan Transfer* and *U.S.A.* are his most ambitious and most successful works in what is perhaps the most difficult of all fictional forms. In both works Dos Passos's strategy for uniting character and milieu consists mainly in the insertion of various kinds of "fillers" or additions to his stories. In *Manhattan Transfer* short prose poems introduce some sections of the novel, providing a kind of mood music for the action to come. In *U.S.A.* these additions, or "frames," are used more consistently and formalized as "The Camera Eye" and the "Newsreel."

The critical question that must be asked, of course, is whether Dos Passos kept the two balls of character and milieu simultaneously in the air. But the answer cannot be simple and categorical. Considering their inherent difficulties, *Manhattan Transfer* and *U.S.A.* are remarkable achievements of a writer who tried to do what James called "the major thing." Yet it must be said that, though the environment is not allowed to dwarf the characters, the characters nonetheless tend to emerge as types. This is especially true in *U.S.A.* In *Manhattan Transfer* a few characters stand out, and one, Jimmy Herf, becomes something like the novel's hero. But in *U.S.A.,* perhaps partly because of its tremendous length, the characters resemble illustrated figures in a tapestry. We are told much about them; they are in fact "documented" like many of Dreiser's people. Yet none of them remains in the memory beyond the book's end. What does remain is the evocation of the milieu—certain "Camera Eye" sections and some of the biographies.

But the books' defects do not mean that the books are dull. On the contrary, in spite of the minimal characterization, they are consistently interesting because they are passionately written books, burning with sympathy for the poor and luckless and with hatred for the system, or the fate, that breaks so many of them. The works are not formally Marxist; but like the best work of Dreiser, Steinbeck, and Sandburg, they find their poetry in their compassion for the oppressed. It is this generally "leftist" humanitarianism that disappears from Dos Passos's later work, to be replaced by a kind of querulous patriotism that often amounts to jingoism.

Representative Works

Manhattan Transfer (1925). An experimental panoramic novel that depicts the lives and milieu of people in New York City from about 1900 to World War I. The stories of several major and dozens of minor characters are presented, some interweaving, some isolated. The time and place are evoked by atmospheric prose-poetic descriptions, lines from current songs, newspaper headlines, and advertising jargon. The most important character, Jimmy Hert (who reminds the reader of the young Dos Passos), finally decides to leave Manhattan and the interwoven evil he has lived through there. Somewhat like Nick Carraway in *The Great Gatsby* (published the same year), he decides that Manhattan is only a transfer point and heads vaguely toward the heartland of America.

U.S.A. (1938). Dos Passos's most ambitious panoramic novel, an elaboration and formalizaton of what he had done in *Manhattan Transfer*. A trilogy, it tries (in Whitman's term) to "tally" America from about 1900 to the stock market crash of 1929. It recounts the individual stories of several major characters, ranging from homeless roustabout to millionaire, and frames these stories in various ways. In the sections called "The Camera Eye" the narrator writes impressionistically of the very feel of the time and place. In the sections called "Newsreel" the stories are set in their milieu by a deliberately jumbled montage of news scraps, lines from popular songs, newspaper headlines, and other bits of flotsam that mark a time as unique. In addition to these devices are the biographies of certain pivotal figures of the time, including Woodrow Wilson, J. P. Morgan, and Frank Lloyd Wright. As an example of the way the sections interact, note the famous ending of the second novel, *1919*. There one of the major characters, Richard Savage, attends a news conference shortly after the war. The millionaires are there with serious talk of oil and hypocritical talk of the League of Nations. This conference is followed by a newsreel that gives a blurred impression of the aftermath of the war in the United States: radicals beaten by ex-soldiers; Wall Street closing weak; lines from "America, I Love You" interspersed with reports of mobs gunned down in Knoxville and of radicals repressed. This newsreel is followed by a section called "The Body of an American," an imaginative and deeply moving story of the Unknown Soldier. Probably no more effective denunciation of war and expression of pity for its victims exists in all American writing.

WILLIAM FAULKNER (1897–1962)

The quantity and quality of Faulkner's work rank him as one of the great figures of twentieth-century literature. His status is not merely American but international. His Nobel Prize for literature suggests this, but his popular and critical acceptance in England and on the Continent is even stronger evidence. Faulkner is famous both as a short-story writer and as a novelist. But even his best novels are generally novella length stories thematically connected.

Life. Faulkner grew up in Oxford, Mississippi, which becomes the Jefferson of many of his stories and novels, as Lafayette County was to be his Yoknapatawpha County and his family the model for the Sartoris clan. In 1918 he joined the Royal Canadian Air Force, but the war ended before he had finished his training. Back at Oxford, he attended the University of Mississippi for two years, then did odd jobs for several years while he worked on his early poems and stories. A visit to New Orleans introduced him to Sherwood Anderson, who encouraged him to devote himself to writing. His reputation grew slowly through the 1930s and early 1940s, the years of his major work. Malcolm Cowley, when he edited *The Viking Portable*

Faulkner in 1946, remarked that none of Faulkner's books was then in print. However, Faulkner's reputation grew rapidly in the late 1940s, and in 1950 he received the Nobel Prize for literature. Among later honors he received Pulitzer prizes for *A Fable* and (posthumously) for his last novel, *The Reivers.*

Vision of Reality. It has become a commonplace of criticism that the best realistic fiction, though local and particular in its setting and time, implies the greater reality of the general human condition. In short, good realism is symbolic in Coleridge's sense: The particular symbol participates in the larger reality it represents. This critical truth has preserved the great American realism of the past—the work, for example, of Twain, James, and Crane—and preserves the work of later American realists, such as Hemingway, Fitzgerald, and Faulkner. It has often been said that Faulkner's work as a whole is a semihistorical depiction of the South from its early days through the Civil War to the present. It is certainly this. But it is the sense of something larger than Southern history that makes Faulkner's work endure.

Malcolm Cowley was probably most responsible for depicting Faulkner as the creator of the "myth of the South." In his *Portable Faulkner* he arranged many of Faulkner's stories and selections from the novels according to the historical time they depicted. He emphasized the interlocking quality of Faulkner's work—the recurring characters, the allusions to other stories and novels, even the occasional errors in chronology, characters' ages, and other minor inconsistencies—in order to bolster his contention that Faulkner had created a world that was organically unified within a semihistorical framework. That Cowley did a real service to Faulkner cannot be denied, and a great deal of Faulkner criticism has since taken this direction.

But one need not be a New Critic to hold that most of Faulkner's best works stand on their own merits, just as each member of a family has a value of his own, though he is related to the other members. And one need not deny the reality of Faulkner's "history" to maintain that there is another figure in the Faulkner carpet which has no special relation to that history: It is that sense of something larger than history mentioned above. Faulkner came close to saying it discursively in his Nobel Prize address. The view of man he gave in that address seems oddly old-fashioned to many readers. Man is a spiritual being, he insisted, a being capable of love and pity and courage and endurance. These are the positive verities of human nature, and these are the only things worth writing about. Man will endure and also prevail because he is not merely a creature of glands but a creature of soul.

Faulkner remarked of Dilsey and the other blacks in *The Sound and the Fury* that they endured; he might have added that they gave witness to the possibility of human heroism in contrast with many of the white characters who are weak, cruel, or mad. The point is that Faulkner wrote about exactly what he said was important in the Nobel Prize speech. He wrote about the battle between good and evil in the human heart, and his view of this battle is traditional and even old-fashioned. The view is also basically religious and, though not wholly Christian, can be articulated in Christian terms, as Faulkner himself showed in *A Fable*.

Fictional Experiments. It is difficult to discuss briefly Faulkner's experiments with language, structure, and point of view. With rare exceptions ("A Rose for Emily," "That Evening Sun," and a few others), Faulkner's way of telling a story is as far as possible from Hemingway's. The terse, direct, straightforward approach was simply not Faulkner's style. Furthermore, his linguistic and structural innovations often accompany and overlap each other (as in the famous Part 4 of "The Bear"). However, some generalizations are possible. There is first the aspect of his work that may be called simply *authorial rhetoric*. Like Melville, Faulkner was a kind of prose poet, given to high-pitched, sometimes purple, writing. This kind of writing is usually marked by long sentences, complex syntax, vague reference pronouns, and sonorous Latinate adjectives. It is sometimes effective (as in the opening pages of "The Bear") but sometimes dull and distracting, as in many parts of *Sartoris* and *A Fable,* where the intensity it aims at is not achieved.

Faulkner combines language and structure in what may be called the "headlong" technique of narration. Characteristically, he pitches the reader into a story or novel without preliminary exposition ("The Bear," *The Sound and the Fury, As I Lay Dying*) and leaves him to put together the chronology and characters on his own. Even relatively simple stories like "Red Leaves" and "Was" deny the reader certain basic information that would allow easy reading. In many of the novels this difficulty is intensified, as in *The Sound and the Fury, Light in August,* and *A Fable*.

Like many other modern writers, Faulkner was intrigued by the possibilities of the limited point of view. He told stories from the limited juvenile point of view (for example, "That Evening Sun" and parts of *As I Lay Dying*), as Twain, Hemingway, Anderson, and Fitzgerald did, but he went a step further when he told the first part of *The Sound and the Fury* from the point of view of an idiot. He also used the old device of telling the same story from several different points of view, as in *Absalom, Absalom!* and *As I Lay Dying* (a technique that Browning had used in poetry and James in fiction), but with Faulkner's usual elliptical and headlong methods, the works are remarkably difficult to read.

One of Faulkner's most obvious structural experiments is his handling of time. In this respect (as critics have pointed out) he was probably influenced by Joyce and Proust in fiction and Eliot and Pound in poetry. Generally his stories (when put together by the reader) are on the level of sequential time. But many of them blur past and present, suggesting that the real meaning of an event lies in an assimilation of the two tenses. This is certainly true in actual human life; what one recalls is part of his present existence, and this common yet strange aspect of our psyches is the quality that marks a great many of Faulkner's works. It is as if he were less creating than remembering the stories he tells; thus, though difficult to read, they are as realistic as our own psychic life.

Faulkner has sometimes been accused of intentional obscurity because of his rhetoric and experiments. But it seems much more sensible to say that, like James, he saw in his stories innumerable ramifications of meaning, saw (as Melville said) that all subjects are infinite. The rhetoric and experiments (whether successful or not artistically) would better be called attempts to project a reality that to the human mind is endlessly intricate.

Representative Works

The Sound and the Fury (1929). One of Faulkner's best-known novels and one of the best examples of his experimentation with fictional point of view. The theme of the novel is the decline of one of Faulkner's famous aristocratic families—the Compsons—and it is told from four different points of view. Maurice (Benjy) Compson, a thirty-three-year-old idiot, tells the first part; Quentin Compson, Benjy's idealistic brother who is attending Harvard, tells the second; Jason Compson, another brother who keeps the family home intact by sharp commercial dealings, tells the third; and Faulkner tells the last, concentrating on the thoughts and actions of Dilsey, the Compson's old black servant. Much of the first three parts is presented by the stream-of-consciousness technique, and the overall effect of the novel is nightmarish. Symbolic of the deterioration of the Compsons (and the South) are Benjy's castration, Quentin's incestuous feelings toward his sister Caddy and finally his suicide, and Jason's adopting the commercial ways of the North in order to survive. Only Dilsey and the other blacks give any evidence of mental health and vitality, and Faulkner emphasizes Dilsey's simple but strong religious feelings. An appendix discussing the various characters clarifies the events of the novel, performing a function similar to that of Eliot's footnotes to "The Waste Land."

Absalom, Absalom! (1936). One of Faulkner's most difficult novels, usually read as a parable of the founding, glory, and decay of the South. Told partly from memory by Quentin Compson to his Harvard roommate and partly by persons involved in the actual events, the novel circles round the story of a man named Sutpen who came out of a vague background to brutally build a great plantation. Ruthless with his slaves, his wife, and his neighbors, he is finally destroyed, partly by the Civil War, which wrecks his plantation, but more so by his past. Once married to a mulatto, he has fathered both white and part-Negro offspring. When an incredible (though symbolic) turn of events leads to a love affair between a mulatto son and a white daughter, his sin is completed. His white son kills his black son,

Sutpen himself is killed, and the only real survivor is Sutpen's black grandson—homeless, savage, and mysterious. As with *The Sound and the Fury,* Faulkner "explains" his mixing of past and present and his elliptical way of presenting the story in a "chronology" and a "genealogy" at the end of the novel.

"The Bear" (1942). Usually printed as a long short story in five parts, this is a section of *Go Down, Moses,* which Faulkner apparently intended as a novel made up of long, more or less connected parts, something like *The Unvanquished.* In its earliest version it was primarily a hunting story in which young Ike McCaslin was initiated into adult life by Sam Fathers, his Negro-Indian mentor. In the final version the theme of initiation—a boy's discovering the meaning of bravery and honor—remains, but other elements have been added. Old Ben and the wilderness he lives in become the relative nobility and dignity of the past, the good, natural life once available to man. Change—a kind of Fall—occurs with the deaths of Old Ben, Sam Fathers, and the hunting dog Lion. Part 4, which Faulkner added in the final version, has been much discussed. An incoherent depiction of the old slave days and a long argument between young Ike and his cousin underline the moral thesis that the South has been cursed for its sin of slavery. Part 5 shows Ike returning to the wilderness, which is now only material for a lumber company, and visiting the graves of the past: Sam Fathers's, Old Ben's, and Lion's. The elegiac tone of his visit is broken by the appearance of Boon Hogganbeck, who previously had many of the old "natural" qualities of Sam Fathers, now senselessly claiming that the squirrels he has treed are his alone. Faulkner's jumbling of time throughout the work suggests the perennial as well as the historical nature of the decline and fall.

ERNEST HEMINGWAY (1899–1961)

To use a cliché that Hemingway would have hated, he and his work became a legend in his own time. His popular reputation and his influence in fiction were so great that his suicide received the kind of publicity usually reserved for the deaths of great political figures or movie idols. Critics have generally agreed that Hemingway's best work is in the form of the relatively short novel and the short story.

Life. Hemingway was born and brought up in Oak Park, Illinois, and spent most of his boyhood summers in northern Michigan, the scene of some of his finest stories. He served in the Red Cross on the Italian front in World War I (an experience fictionalized in *A Farewell to Arms,* 1929), was wounded and invalided home. He became Paris correspondent for the *Toronto Star* in 1921 (an experience used in *The Sun Also Rises,* 1926) and shortly thereafter began to publish his early stories. As his fame grew, he began to travel extensively and to use his life in his fiction. His stay in Africa provided material for *Green Hills of Africa* (1935) and stories such as

"The Short Happy Life of Francis Macomber" and "The Snows of Kilimanjaro." His newspaper coverage of the Spanish civil war provided material for *For Whom the Bell Tolls* (1940), and his role as correspondent in World War II gave him material for *Across the River and into the Trees* (1950). He lived most of his later years in Cuba, where he married his fourth wife and where he acquired the atmosphere used so well in *The Old Man and the Sea* (1952). He received the Pulitzer Prize in 1953 for *The Old Man and the Sea* and the Nobel Prize in 1954 for his work as a whole. Seriously depressed in his last few years, he shot himself to death in 1961, thus ending a career that in both life and art had concerned itself with violence.

Philosophy and Techniques. Perhaps the shortest way to account for Hemingway's eminence in fiction is to say that he portrayed not only the appearance but also the reality of his time. Above all a literary realist, he was passionately concerned to render accurately what he described: war, hunting, fishing, bullfighting, drinking, lovemaking. His best work is graphic in the best sense of the term: One *sees* men shot, fish caught, coffee made. He gave what James called "the sense of place" so completely that many of his works have been made into films with a minimum of change; no other American writer has given more realistic depictions of Paris saloons, artillery barrages, the look of hills and valleys and streams in Michigan or Italy or Africa. In short, he depicted appearance as well as any other American has ever done. This was for him an immensely important aspect of his art and one in which he took great pride, the pride of a great photographer or of a great representational painter like Goya. But his famous dictum that the good artist pictures things as they really are implies more than accurate depiction of things. The great writer, Eliot said, reflects his time—not only the appearances of his time, but also the spiritual meaning of the events he renders. And when one examines Hemingway's work from about 1920 to 1960, one finds that Hemingway has told the real story of his time, the biography of the human spirit. The best of his work deals with violence: war, murder, mutilation, and suffering. And although most of his work is local and particular (wartime incidents, safaris, fishing trips), when one regards his work as a whole, the figure in the carpet clearly emerges as a symbolic rendering of human spiritual experience in the twentieth century. Emerson and other romantics said that spiritual truths appear in physical phenomena, and in this sense Hemingway's preoccupation with war, violence, death, and the apparent lack of pattern in these events suggests strongly the modern temper—the psychic chaos and disorientation of our time.

Hemingway's vision of the ultimate harshness of life was leavened by a belief in certain "naturally" good things. In war there is the possibility of love, however brief; in times of personal torment there is the therapy of nature; when all else fails there is a purely human sense of man's dignity evidenced in the heights of stoic courage and endurance to which he may rise.

Much has been said of the Hemingway code, the values that his characters set for themselves. The best of his heroes value courage, endurance, and personal integrity; they ally themselves rarely with large causes or movements, usually with other people. Such an attitude also seems to suggest the spirit of our time. Without Eliot's intellectualism, Hemingway depicted the world of Eliot's early poetry—"The Waste Land" world—but did not offer the religious consolation of Eliot's later poetry. Instead he offered not ideas so much as a kind of primitive will to endure, given dignity by an unorthodox version of the Golden Rule. There is perhaps little logic to Hemingway's philosophy, but there is no logic at all to the world as he saw it.

Hemingway had two distinct ways of presenting his material. The first, and more often imitated, is a flat, understated newspaper style in which he gave realistic description, usually in short simple sentences. The second is impressionistic in viewpoint and rhythmic in sentence structure, often echoing the repetitions and seeming simplicity of Gertrude Stein. The newspaper style is evident in stories like "The Killers" and "The Undefeated" and parts of nonfiction works like *Death in the Afternoon*. The rhythmic impressionistic style may be seen in stories like "The Snows of Kilimanjaro" and in many of the novels, especially *A Farewell to Arms, For Whom the Bell Tolls,* and *The Old Man and the Sea*. No matter which style Hemingway was using, his dialogue generally remains constant, giving as nearly as possible the illusion of real speech, often to the point of dullness. Usually the two styles complement each other in the same work. The aim of both is generally compression and an attempt to create a distinct impression or mood. The short simple sentences describing Nick Adams pitching his tent in "Big Two-Hearted River" serve the same artistic purpose as do the longer cadenced sentences describing the war in the opening pages of *A Farewell to Arms*. Both evoke a psychological impression and meaning beyond the physical facts described. In brief, Hemingway's styles and techniques at their best convey spiritual as well as material effects. In this respect his work is in the tradition of symbolic realism that includes Twain, James, Faulkner, Fitzgerald, and Katherine Anne Porter. Although the actions and speech of Hemingway's people may be more sensational than James's, for example, and although he presents a stronger photographic or realistic surface, his work is not less symbolic than that of James. The grotesque death of the young boy in "The Capital of the World" and the suffering and defeat of Santiago in *The Old Man and the Sea* are not merely realistic depictions of physical events; they are symbolic renderings of that quality of human life James called "ferocious and sinister."

Representative Works

"Big Two-Hearted River" (1925). One of the many stories in which a boy or young man, often called Nick Adams, is the protagonist. The stories are loosely connected and appear in different collections. But when put together they reveal a boy (much like the young Hemingway) who grows up in northern Michigan, first encounters death there ("Indian Camp," 1925), and who later is initiated into various kinds of evil, culminating with his experiences in World War I. "Big Two-Hearted River" shows Nick Adams back from the war, shattered and in desperate need of help to regain his balance. Ritually, like so many other Hemingway characters, he goes back to simple physical processes—making camp, catching grasshoppers for bait, and finally fishing. Symbolically, he does all this in a countryside that has been ravaged by fire and is only slowly recovering its natural form; even the grasshoppers are seared and changed, as Nick himself has been by the war. The trout fishing is a step toward the old prewar life, but even this has its perils. Nick, like the countryside, must go slowly and not yet fish in the swamp, where casting is difficult.

The Sun Also Rises (1926). The famous novel of the "lost generation." The hero, Jake Barnes, symbolically emasculated by a war wound, strives to make a new life for himself in which his former passion for Lady Brett Ashley can have no place. The other characters, though not so mutilated as Jake, are equally hard put to find meaning in the life following World War I. Ironically, Jake comes closest to finding a kind of peace by periodically abandoning the bars of Paris for at least a half-life in the mountains and by the sea.

A Farewell to Arms (1929). One of the most famous modern war novels, this tells the story of the American lieutenant Frederic Henry and the English nurse Catherine Barkley on the Italian front during World War I. Henry's growing disillusion with the war parallels his deepening love for Catherine. Finally he makes his "separate peace," deserts his ambulance corps, and flees to Switzerland with Catherine. Their life is idyllic until they must come back to reality when Catherine's child is born. Both she and the child die, and the novel closes with one of Hemingway's most bitter and nihilistic comments: Henry likens human life to that of ants caught in a fire and ignored by God.

"A Clean, Well-Lighted Place" (1933). One of the most compressed of Hemingway's stories and one that shows clearly his philosophy and one of his favorite techniques. The well-lighted bar and the old man who drinks there suggest the characteristic Hemingway theme of man's need for some kind of temporary escape from a black, probably meaningless world. The old man and the older waiter are two of Hemingway's initiates. Both are aware of the nothingness *(nada)* of the world and thus the importance of the clean, well-lighted bar, which is a kind of substitute daylight. The younger waiter is not initiated: He believes that ordinary things—sex, a wife, a home—are what constitute human life.

The Old Man and the Sea (1952). The short novel that reestablished Hemingway's reputation after the failure of *Across the River and into the Trees*.

It retells with great force the old Hemingway story of man's courage and his ultimate defeat. Here, with biblical overtones, the old story emerges as the great battle between an old Cuban fisherman and a giant marlin. Both fight well, but both are finally defeated—the marlin by the old man, and the old man by the sharks that eat away the marlin's body. As so often in Hemingway, the courage and endurance of the fight are magnified by being misunderstood by outsiders, here the tourists.

THOMAS WOLFE (1900–1938)

Wolfe's work is unique in American literature. The great homogeneous mass of autobiographical fiction and reminiscence that he wrote has called into question the basic problem of form in fiction.

Life. Wolfe was born in Asheville, North Carolina (the Altamont of his fiction), graduated from the University of North Carolina, and received his M. A. from Harvard. He taught intermittently at New York University and made several trips abroad, where he did much of his early writing and where (unlike the expatriate writers of the time) he discovered that he was an American writer and that his material must be American. In 1925 he met Mrs. Aline Bernstein, who became his mistress and an important figure in his later work. He contracted tuberculosis of the brain and died in 1938, leaving a great mass of unfinished and unpublished manuscripts. Approximately half of his work was published posthumously.

The Problem of Wolfe's Fiction. Even before Wolfe's early death his work had aroused controversy among readers and critics. There is still no general agreement on the form, content, themes, and techniques of his work. He has passionate admirers and passionate detractors but relatively few nonpartisan critics. The major objections to Wolfe's work are that it is relatively formless, that it is marred by highly rhetorical poetic passages, and that it is far too autobiographical.

In a long essay, "The Story of a Novel" (1936), Wolfe confirmed a great deal about his work that critics had already inferred. He was a compulsive writer; he felt driven to write, as if some great demon was locked within his sensibility and was seeking release. And he was an expansive writer; his urge was never to delete but always to write more. He remarked that he had something like total recall of his past—not only of events but of the sights, sounds, odors, the very feel of the things happening to him. It was this gigantic totality that he felt driven to record. The people and places from his experience existed in his mind on a heroic scale, and he could never say enough about them, never re-create his experience in all its enormous complexity. But such was his attempt; and this was the reason that he was not really aware when a certain novel or story was finished. He did not think of his work in those formal categories but rather as a single immense opus that would be finished when his life was finished and that would have the same plan, or lack of plan, as his life. Maxwell Perkins, his editor at Scribner's, helped him to reshape large segments of his first novel, *Look Homeward, Angel* (1929) and simply told him when his second (*Of Time and the River,* 1935) was finished. Similarly, his next editor, Edward C. Aswell of Harper's, put together a vast mass of Wolfe's material after Wolfe's death and published it in the form of two novels—*The Web and the Rock* (1939) and *You Can't Go Home Again* (1940)—and *The Hills Beyond* (1943), a collection of short pieces that relate to the novels and that may originally have been part of them.

What is clear from Wolfe's essay and from his whole work is that he was a romantic strongly reminiscent of Whitman (whether or not he consciously thought of himself as a follower of Whitman). He felt his own experience as somehow interwoven with that of America, and his compulsion to experience everything and then record it takes the form of what Whitman called "tallying" America. Both writers (and Hart Crane as well) were struck by the country's hugeness and variety and equally struck by the infinite variety of human experience. It is perhaps not an overstatement to say that for all three writers America became the public vehicle of the private search. All this, of course, is the essence of a certain kind of romanticism, recalling Wordsworth and Keats as well as various American romantics. The identification of oneself with a larger entity—a country, even humanity in general—has always been the romantic's defense of autobiographical writing.

For the reader and critic, however, after a certain interval has passed it is no longer important whether or not a writer's work is autobiographical. Where he got his material is less important than what he did with it. Hemingway and Fitzgerald are probably just as autobiographical as Wolfe. One difference between their work and Wolfe's is that Wolfe used his life comprehensively, they selectively. Another difference is that they embodied in their work certain ideas and attitudes toward life that are distinguishable parts of that work. Here is where Wolfe differs importantly from them and from other contemporary writers such as Faulkner. The immense bulk and enormous sensuous detail in his work obscure any easily recognizable pattern of idea or attitude except a rather generalized sense of sadness about the elements of time and death in the human condition. And often even this attitude is to be found not so much in the narrative itself as in the poetic asides and interpolations.

So, in the long run, it is not whether Wolfe is autobiographical that matters but whether he is a good artist in fiction or a rhetorician working within a rather loose form of fiction. If the latter, a further question is whether his poetic prose, if it is not organically related to his narrative, is good enough to stand by itself. These are large questions indeed, and one may satisfy himself about them only by reading Wolfe in bulk, as he intended his work to be read.

Representative Works

Look Homeward, Angel (1929). Wolfe's first and most famous novel. Basically an initiation story, it depicts Eugene Gant's youth in a small North Carolina town and his gropings toward maturity. Chronologically, it traces his life from the time he is a newsboy to his days at the state university. It is generally considered Wolfe's best novel because in it his rhapsodic rendering of sensuous detail and his poetic apostrophes are held within the sensibility of a sensitive, romantic boy. The novel introduces three unforgettable characters who recur intermittently in Wolfe's later work: Eugene's brother Ben, who died young; his mother, Elizabeth, garrulous and domineering; and his father, W. O. Gant, a stonecutter by trade but an artist and rhetorician by destiny. Mixing fine realistic scenes with torrents of rhetoric, Wolfe manages to convey Eugene's story but also, more memorably, the Christ-like figure of his brother Ben and the larger-than life figure of his father. In fact, W. O. Gant, in his hunger for love and for all experience, and in the fustian rhetoric that is his defense against life, is much more like Wolfe himself than Eugene Gant is. In his essay "The Story of a Novel," Wolfe (echoing Joyce) said that all men's search was for a father, an authority figure outside themselves. Although this notion is not often a shaping theme in Wolfe's fiction, it is certainly psychologically evident in his first novel.

"The Lost Boy" (1941). A reminiscence, or short story, in four parts, written in the 1930s and published posthumously as part of *The Hills Beyond*. It shows Wolfe doing what he did best, recalling and re-creating his past in poetic prose that evokes the sadness of passing time and the sorrow of inevitable death. The piece depicts a brief period in Altamont, then a period of several months in 1904 when Wolfe's mother took her children to St. Louis and opened a boardinghouse while the world's fair was in progress there. The opening section is a fine portrayal of Grover Gant (Eugene's older brother) as a young boy in Altamont. The next two sections are told by Mrs. Gant and Eugene's sister Daisy. They fill out the character of Grover for Eugene, too young to remember Grover, who died of typhoid at age twelve. The fourth part depicts Eugene returning to St. Louis, finding the boardinghouse, and recalling the feel of the past. This story illustrates Wolfe's characteristic mixture of realistic depiction of event and character and the authorial rhetoric that colors the narrative. The first part, recording a boy's actions, is heightened by the boy's ideas of time and eternity. The third part, told by the sister, rhetorically questions the meaning of life. And the fourth part (Eugene's), though mainly straightforward narrative, is in language that lifts the events from mere particularity to a kind of lament for the human condition that recalls Donne and Sir Thomas Browne.

JOHN STEINBECK (1902–1968)

As novelist, dramatist, and social critic, Steinbeck seems assured of a permanent place in American letters. He worked successfully with the long novel, the novella, and the short story.

Life. Steinbeck was born in Salinas, California; lived most of his life in that region; and used the locale in much of his best work. He attended Stanford University but never took a degree. In his early years as a struggling writer, he often worked as an unskilled laborer, and even after he became relatively well known he occasionally worked with migrant fruit pickers to keep in touch with the common man who was the subject of much of his work. As late as 1960 he was still trying to capture the feel of common America by means of a long, rambling auto trip through the countrysides and small towns of New England, the West Coast, and the Deep South (a trip recorded in *Travels with Charley,* 1962). Among many literary honors, he received the Pulitzer Prize for *The Grapes of Wrath* (1939) and the Nobel Prize for literature in 1962 for his work as a whole.

Shaping Forces of Steinbeck's Fiction. Steinbeck's fiction has been variously labeled naturalistic, social realistic, proletarian, romantic, pragmatic, pseudoscientific, and mythic. All the adjectives are accurate in the sense that they describe parts of Steinbeck's work, but not the whole. Steinbeck had no single and settled view of life or art, nor did he believe that any single view could be completely true. He was primarily a passionate observer of human life; but he was also an amateur scientist and philosopher, and he assimilated many of the literary, philosophical, and scientific ideas of his time. The assimilation, however, was not merely imitation; it was provisional, a using and testing of these ideas, a depicting of experience in certain forms in order to see if the forms could contain the experience.

To illustrate briefly: Certain works, or parts of them, seem easily labeled. *The Grapes of Wrath* may be called naturalistic in the classic sense of that term. The characters seem driven by interior and exterior forces to do what they do. They react instinctively to basic animal drives in man: fear, hunger, and sex. The same may be said of the characters in *Tortilla Flat, Cannery Row,* "Flight," and "The Snake." Further, in all these works the characters tend to be the simple characters favored by naturalists: They are poorly educated and unaware of the social, psychological, and economic forces that move them. But *The Grapes of Wrath* is also a socially realistic and even a proletarian novel, like Steinbeck's *In Dubious Battle.* In scenes reminiscent of Dos Passos, Upton Sinclair, and Sandburg, Steinbeck implies the possibility of common men, exploited workers, becoming a single unit, joining in a movement that will attempt to alleviate their social and economic deprivation. But the novel, like much of Steinbeck's work, has another dimension. The ex-preacher Jim Casy and, later, Tom Joad both arrive at inarticulate conclusions that recall Emerson and Whitman's transcendental views and also William James's view of religion expressed in *Varieties of Religious Experience* (see the F. I. Carpenter articles listed in the Bibliography). Casy and Joad speak haltingly of a mystical unity of life in which past, present, and future coexist. And throughout the book the characters do not so much believe in God as (in James's terms) they use him according to their needs. Corollary to these religious views, or half-views, is the ecological scientific view that is also one of the main threads of the novel and much of Steinbeck's other work as well. This view echoes the transcendental belief that all beings are interdependent; men, animals, and plants are related as parts of a single whole. The migrating Okies are seen partly as a movement caused by environment and affecting environment. Finally, the Joads, like the characters in *Tortilla Flat, The Pastures of Heaven,* and *East of Eden,* are given a dimension beyond that of realistic characters by being placed in a mythical framework. Steinbeck sometimes seems to echo Frazer and Jung in his evocation of a racial memory and the notion of inherited psychological characteristics, and he was certainly heavily indebted to Freud's view of orthodox religion having originally sprung from fear. Yet he frequently used myths drawn from the Judeo-Christian tradition to give his characters depth: for example, the Exodus and Promised Land myths in *The Grapes of Wrath* and the Cain and Abel myth in *East of Eden.*

Some critics, looking for the key to Steinbeck's work, believe it is to be found in *Sea of Cortez* (1941). There are good reasons for this belief, especially if one reads the 1951 edition of the book, which opens with Steinbeck's tribute to his longtime friend Ed Ricketts, who operated a small marine biology laboratory in Monterey and was killed in 1948. Steinbeck depicted him in several works, most notably as Doc in *Cannery Row* and *Sweet Thursday. Sea of Cortez* is the record of an expedition made in 1940 by Steinbeck, Ricketts, and a few others into the Gulf of California, where they collected and labeled specimens of marine invertebrate fauna. The book exemplifies what Steinbeck calls "Is," or "nonteleological," thinking. Reduced to its simplest terms, this point of view considers the "how" and the "what" of things without reference to the ultimate "why." Abandoning religious and philosophical preconceptions, it tries to discover the relationships between life and nonlife, between animal life in whatever form and the environment in which this life either lives or dies. In marine life the process of cause and effect may be traced—one species survives and another dies because of certain ecological conditions—but one can find no purposive order there. One cannot discern any chain of cause and effect that will lead logically to the postulation of a supreme being, good or bad. One can see only the hint of a great interlocking relationship between life and nonlife. Because of the scarcity of evidence this kind of thinking can be applied to human life only by analogy. But Steinbeck does draw analogies, and many of his examples recall the naturalistic and romantic views of the

Okies' odyssey in *The Grapes of Wrath* and the man–nature relationships in *The Pastures of Heaven* and *To a God Unknown*.

But *Sea of Cortez* should be read in conjunction with the rest of Steinbeck's work. Late works like *Travels with Charley* show that the purely scientific view of reality never completely satisfied Steinbeck, any more than the naturalistic or romantic views did. His work as a whole depicts reality from a number of limited points of view, and to the end of his life he remained a seeker. Perhaps the most important single idea underlying much of his work is that of unity—the essential oneness of all men and of all men with the universe. But whether this unity exists (biologically, socially, mystically, or mythically) or whether it is something that man must work toward is never really clear. This was a teasing problem for Steinbeck as it is for other thinkers of various persuasions. The naturalist, the Emersonian romantic, the proletarian writer, the mythic writer all postulate this notion of unity, and all are faced with the difficulty of whether it is or ought to be—and thus are faced with the corollary problems of fate and free will. No one has presented a universally satisfactory answer to these problems; Steinbeck is in good company.

But behind the intellect and technical skill of the writer lies the sensibility of the artist. There can be no doubt that Steinbeck's besetting sin as an artist is sentimentality. He weeps over many of his characters (like Dickens) and tries, often unsuccessfully, to make the reader weep with him. Significantly, this weakness exists no matter what intellectual or literary approach he uses. To all the adjectives applied to his work one might add the noun *sentimentalist,* for sentimentality mars much of his best work and helps ruin his worst.

Representative Works

The Grapes of Wrath (1939). Steinbeck's most famous novel. It depicts the flight of the Okies from Oklahoma, Texas, and Arkansas to the Promised Land of California. Driven from their homes by drought and mortgage foreclosures during the 1930s' depression, thousands of small farmers emigrated to California, lured by handbills and gossip that assured them of work and possibly land there. The novel is panoramic, with interchapters and asides recalling Dos Passos's *U.S.A.* There are impressionistic portrayals of the large-scale emigration, the exploitation of the farmers by used-car dealers and other merchants along the way, the inhuman attitude of the banks, and the wholesale rejection of the emigrants by the California landowners. Against this background of social and economic catastrophe Steinbeck tells the story of one family caught up in it. But the exodus of the Joad family is not only a story of individuals but also a symbolic account of the movement itself. The Joads suffer all the hardships of the thousands they represent—the deaths of the old folks, the desperate search for work, the bitterness of the dispossessed, the growing sense that some kind of solidarity is necessary to combat the system. Jim Casy (a former fundamentalist preacher) and Tom Joad are the characters who speak out most strongly for the rather vague notion of human unity and the more precise idea of the need for economic reform. The novel is a mixture of social commentary, realistic depiction of poverty and hunger and a few well-realized characters, and a kind of generalized mythic or religious atmosphere. Its effectiveness lies more in its parts than in the book as a totality.

The Red Pony. (1937). Four long related stories that are best called initiation stories. In the first three, young Jody Tiflin becomes aware of the quality of life and death by witnessing the birth and death of a colt and its mother. In the fourth story when his grandfather comes to visit the ranch, Jody learns from the old man's tales something of the American dream of the West and of man's perennial search for virgin land—something new and unspoiled. Well-written and relatively unsentimental, the stories reflect Steinbeck's vision of life as a puzzling mixture of the physical and the spiritual.

RICHARD WRIGHT (1908–1960)

The most famous American black fiction writer, Wright stands as a symbol of racial pride and integrity and as an important influence on such later writers as Ralph Ellison, James Baldwin, and many others.

Life. Wright's life is the archetypal story of the poor black boy who overcomes incredible handicaps to succeed in the white man's world. His autobiography *Black Boy* (1945) movingly depicts his first seventeen years: the early days in a Mississippi sharecropper's cabin, his father's desertion of the family, his mother's lingering illness, the numerous moves from Natchez to Jackson to Arkansas and finally to Memphis. As a teenager, Wright managed to sneak books out of the "white" Memphis library and read voraciously in Mencken, Dreiser, Lewis, Sherwood Anderson, and other critics of established society. He finally escaped the South for Chicago, where he encountered more poverty in the depression years, joined the Communist party (which he later left), and finally achieved recognition with his *Uncle Tom's Children* (1938), a collection of four long stories. A Guggenheim Fellowship allowed him to work on his first novel, *Native Son* (1940), which was successful not only as a novel but also as a play and a movie. In 1941 he wrote the text for a photographic history of the American Negro, *Twelve Million Black Voices,* and in 1945 he produced *Black Boy.* Thereafter he spent much of his life in France, where he came under the influence of postwar existentialism, then best voiced by Jean-Paul Sartre. His last works, though generally inferior to his earlier, are nonetheless honest depictions of black conditions in Asia, Africa, and Spain.

Achievement and Influence. Wright's best work, like Dreiser's, succeeds not by any obvious literary skills but by his passionate obsession with a certain aspect of the human condition and his absolute honesty in dealing with it. Like Dreiser, he was not a stylist, not a writer anyone would want to imitate. Even in his best work there are arid stretches of discursive commentary. Yet the cumulative effect of *Native Son,* several short stories, and *Black Boy* is undeniable. The mighty theme that Melville felt necessary for a mighty novel emerges in Wright's best work: the tragic dichotomy of black and white in America. Ellison's *Invisible Man,* probably one of the finest novels of the century, is much more sophisticated in technique than any of Wright's work, but it is clearly indebted to Wright. Ellison, James Baldwin, and other black writers have paid tribute to Wright's work, as well they should. As Pound said of Whitman, certain writers are beginners: They project an area of life and an attitude toward it in a large and often unsophisticated way. And it is on this work that later writers build. Of Wright it may be said that out of his own life he projected not only the great theme of American racial animosity but even many of the basic metaphors (invisibility, Negro role playing, subterranean life) by which later writers have dramatized this situation. In short, his work is the source book for a great portion of modern American black fiction.

Representative Works

Native Son (1940). Wright's first novel, the work that in its original form and its play and movie versions brought him fame and economic security. Probably indebted directly to Dreiser's *An American Tragedy* for both its basic plot and its naturalistic viewpoint, it has come to be a landmark in black American fiction. With the passion that marks all of Wright's early work, it tells the story of Bigger Thomas, a product of Chicago's ghetto. Through a series of circumstances over which he has little control, Bigger becomes involved with whites and with the Communist party, kills a white woman, becomes a fugitive, kills his own black sweetheart, and is finally caught and condemned to death. His lawyer, in a long courtroom speech reminiscent of Dreiser's argument in *An American Tragedy,* condemns all American society for Bigger's fate. Bigger himself, however, is paradoxically unconvinced of his victimization; he feels free and even "creative" after his murders. Critics have often noted the contradictory influences of Dreiser and Dostoevski in the novel.

Black Boy (1945). Perhaps Wright's best book, a brief autobiography of his early years in the South and his final escape to Chicago. Nowhere else in Wright's work is his understanding of black rage so evident as in this book. In its straightforward account of black Southern life in the early 1900s and of Wright's personal fight for identity, it is more moving than much "social fiction," including Wright's. The paralyzing effect of white supremacy is unforgettably depicted in Wright's dealings with white workers and the irony of his grandfather's being refused a pension although he had fought bravely for the North in the Civil War. Particularly revealing is the pattern of fear and flight that tears apart Wright's family relationships. The fear, hatred, and pathetic yet terrifying religiosity of his grandmother become the trap Wright fights desperately to escape by going North. One understands much better his later flight further "north" to France and existentialism after reading this account of his early years.

EUDORA WELTY (b.1909)

Like the two other Southern writers whom she most resembles, Faulkner and Flannery O'Connor, Welty has made her fictional southern world both solidly real and regional and at the same time universal, mainly by her use of myth. Although Welty has published several successful novels, her most consistently fine work is in the form of the short story.

Life. Welty was born in Jackson, Mississippi, and although she attended the University of Wisconsin and Columbia University and has traveled abroad on various fellowships, Mississippi has remained her spiritual and physical home and the locale of most of her fiction. Her work has brought her many honors and awards: She is a member of the National Institute of Arts and Letters, has received the William Dean Howells Fiction Award from that society, and has served as Honorary Consultant of the Library of Congress. She has lectured and taught at several American universities, and her important essay "Place in Fiction" was first presented as a lecture at Cambridge University.

Fictional World. More than her obvious talents as a fiction writer, it was Eudora Welty's interest in myth that brought her to critical prominence in the 1950s and 1960s. It was during those years that Myth-Archetype Criticism emerged as a serious critical angle of vision, and much of Welty's fiction has reference to a world beyond the ordinary one, whether the reference is to a specific myth or to a more general and eclectic fusing of archetypal characters and situations. The connected stories of *The Golden Apples,* for example, use elements of the familiar Greek myth of Hercules' search for the golden apples of the sun. But much of her work depends for added dimension of meaning not upon a single specific myth but rather upon what might be called generalized myth: bits and fragments from Greek and Roman mythology, from the Bible, and from old romances and fairy tales. The purpose of using myth in fiction is generally to suggest that the characters and their situations are universal, that behind them lies the long foreground of all human experience and behavior. Generally speaking, Welty's early work utilizes this concept of generalized myth as opposed to the more specific references of later works such as *The Golden Apples* and *The Bride of the Innisfallen.* Examples of her use of generalized myth are "Death of a Traveling Salesman," "A Curtain of Green," and "A Worn Path" from *A Curtain of Green* (1941); the novel *The Robber Bridegroom*

(1942); and "The Wide Net" and "A Still Moment" from *The Wide Net* (1943).

In addition to Welty's mythic fiction, and sometimes overlapping it, is a considerable part of her work that falls within the category of psychological realism firmly grounded in solid specification of place and character—fiction that at its best reminds us of the work of Katherine Anne Porter, who encouraged Welty in her early work and for whom Welty has always professed the highest admiration. Stories such as "Keela the Outcast Indian Maiden," "Petrified Man," "Livvie," and "No Place for You, My Love" are of this kind. They reveal not only Welty's interest in character but also her sense of history and tragedy.

But Welty is perhaps most brilliant in comic fiction, whether in the mythic or the realistic mode or in a combination of the two. It ranges from the incredibly good farce of "Why I Live at the P. O." and *The Ponder Heart*, through the more subtle humor of *The Robber Bridegroom*, to the comic elements of stories that are not primarily designed to evoke laughter—"Keela the Outcast Indian Maiden," "Old Mr. Marblehall," and "A Worn Path." Her work seems to show, as Dr. Johnson said of Shakespeare's work, that she is a natural humorist but a comparatively artificial tragic writer. As Seymour L. Gross has so well illustrated (see Bibliography), she delights in the unpredictability of human nature and its capacity for eluding easy classification.

Representative Works

"Death of a Traveling Salesman" (1941). Welty's first published short story and by consensus one of her best. The story exemplifies her use of generalized myth as a backdrop against which her solidly realistic story is played. An ailing traveling salesman loses his way in backwoods Mississippi while trying to reach the town of Beulah. He meets and is helped by a man and his wife who seem to be simply country people but who are given certain mythic characteristics. They offer him the ease of mind and soul he is seeking (the land of Beulah in Bunyan's *Pilgrim's Progress* is the pleasant land that the fortunate find before death). But the drab commercial habits of a lifetime drive him away from them, and he dies alone of a heart attack. The story realistically and skillfully probes the salesman's mind as he nears death and can be admired as psychological fiction even if the reader is unaware of the mythic overtones.

"Keela the Outcast Indian Maiden" (1941). Superficially a Southern grotesque story, actually a subtle delineation of guilt and moral bewilderment and almost a parable of the American white man's mistreatment of both the black and the Indian. The wandering protagonist, having been an accessory to the dehumanization of a black man in a freak show, is compelled to tell his story over and over, without understanding it, as he searches for the victim in order somehow to compensate him. When he does find the black, history is verified: He has nothing to give him, and even if he had something, the black man is now unable to benefit by it.

"A Worn Path" (1941). One of Welty's most brilliant and moving stories and one of her most effective handlings of generalized myth. Phoenix Jackson is among her most successful archetypal figures, suggesting in her consciousness and behavior not only the experience of blacks in America but the wider experience of all mankind that has loved, been loyal to others, and struggled courageously against a world of nature and society full of frightening dangers. The old black woman's trek to Natchez to get medicine and a Christmas toy for her grandson is given universal resonance by the mythic qualities of the dangers and difficulties she encounters. Rather like Psyche going through Hades to complete a divine mission ordained by the gods, old Phoenix struggles through woods and swamp, survives an encounter with a white hunter and his menacing dog, and succeeds in reaching the hospital in Natchez where she is given her "reward": medicine for her grandchild. Her struggle is spiritual as well as physical: the journey of the soul in a spiritual world, as suggested by her communion with the things and creatures of nature. Neither Phoenix nor the world she travels through is simply natural; they are also historical and mythic. As her name and other elements of the story suggest, her present journey is the center of a series of superimposed spiritual circles: the circle of her own "real life," the circle of history, and the circle of timeless human existence, or myth.

SAUL BELLOW (b.1915)

Serious critics have called Bellow our finest living novelist. In 1976 he won the Nobel Prize for Literature.

Life. Bellow was born in Montreal to parents of Russian-Jewish descent. The family moved to Chicago when he was nine, and his formative years were spent there. He attended the University of Chicago and received a B. S. from Northwestern University. He began publishing short fiction as early as 1941 in such journals as *Partisan Review*. His first novel, *Dangling Man,* was published in 1944. *The Adventures of Augie March* (1953) won a National Book Award. It was followed by *Henderson the Rain King* (1959), another fine novel, and then by *Herzog* (1964), which won another National Book Award. His latest novels are *Mr. Sammler's Planet* (1970) and *Humboldt's Gift* (1975).

Evolution of the Bellow Hero. Perhaps Bellow's greatest achievement is to have written what George Meredith called the highest kind of comedy: that which moves the reader to thoughtful laughter. He has done this largely through the creation of a succession of protagonists who are partly stereotyped Jewish clowns—pathetic, grotesque, yet funny—and partly serious and sensitive individuals who seek answers to the great questions about the human condition. The combination is a striking one and has been imitated by Bernard Malamud, Philip Roth, and other Jewish writers. But the mixture has varied as Bellow's work has progressed. Although all his protagonists are in James's term "intense perceivers," that is, persons of marked sensitivity and intense self-awareness, Bellow's early characters are not formal intellectuals. Tommy Wilhelm (*Seize the Day,* 1956), Augie March, and Henderson are average sensual men. They feel an enormous but largely emotional pressure to determine who they are and why they exist in a bizarre and painful world. Bereft of formal religion and failing to find answers in human relationships—love or family ties—they feel empty. In Henderson's terms, they feel an inarticulate *want.* Foregoing straightforward realism, Bellow sends these characters on symbolic missions—to funeral parlors, to Mexico, to Africa. In every case they arrive at a destination that is a kind of answer to their questions. But their affirmations are completely personal and subjective. Henderson, for example, discovers that some kind of good life is possible, but his taking on the young lives of a primitive child and a lion cub are symbols of this discovery, not explanations of it.

By contrast, Bellow's later books and protagonists are not only symbolic but discursive attempts to answer his continuing questions. Moses Herzog and Artur Sammler are scholars and intellectuals. Bellow's characteristic irony often makes them grotesques and figures of fun, much like his earlier people. But they are many levels above Augie March and Henderson in their intellectual approach to the perennial questions. Although their wants and needs are as lacerating as those of Tommy Wilhelm and Henderson, they are able to articulate these feelings in terms that the earlier characters would never have understood. In brief, Bellow's hero has evolved from a relatively naïve seeker—a sad but funny clown—to a relatively sophisticated seeker—but still a sad and funny clown.

Interestingly, as Bellow's heroes have become increasingly intellectual, his plots have become increasingly realistic. Neither Herzog nor Sammler undergoes the surrealistic experiences of Augie March or Henderson. For perceivers like them the world as it is is absurd enough; there is no need to hyperbolize it by symbolic quests and grotesque trappings. Herzog and Sammler do little, but think a great deal, mostly about the failure of love all about them and the increasingly barbaric quality of modern life. Yet their final affirmations are as personal, cryptic, and emotional as that of Henderson. In the face of unremitting evil, Bellow seems to be saying, any reaction other than a mere recognition of that evil will have to be purely personal, "a separate peace."

Representative Works

Henderson the Rain King (1959). One of Bellow's best novels, perhaps the turning point from the earlier work that depicted the protagonist as relatively passive and victimized by overwhelming social and psychological forces. Henderson, a middle-aged millionaire, is driven by a need for beauty and for some sense of life as meaningful. At home in America he can only raise pigs, play his violin, and feel a burning want for something more. He decides to go to Africa, and the literal story of his journey contains many echoes of Conrad's *Heart of Darkness*. But his journey is clearly symbolic: Like Thoreau's *Walden*, it is a journey into the self. He meets and learns much from an African king who is both civilized and savage. Said simply, what he learns is courage and a belief in the possibility of human goodness. He returns to civilization with a savage infant and a lion cub and a determination to enter medical school, despite his age. Symbolically, what he has learned is that he has powers of charity and humaneness that the world he lived in called impossible.

Herzog (1964). A novel dramatizing Moses Herzog's anguished battle with himself and the world. A history professor driven to near breakdown by two unhappy marriages and the larger problem of what it means to be human, Herzog in his anguish takes to writing imaginary letters to everyone who figures in his situation: dead philosophers, friends, wives, mistresses, and ultimately God. Like all Bellow's heroes, he has a tremendous need to love, but he cannot find an object for it except in his children. Driven finally to action, he plans to murder his second wife and her lover but discovers he cannot. He finally retreats to a run-down farmhouse in the Berkshire hills and there arrives at a kind of reconciliation with himself and God. The end of the novel shows him waiting for a woman to come to dinner, a woman who will not satisfy him but who will try. More importantly at the end he has achieved a willingness to wait things out and live as best he can, taking and giving what love is possible.

FLANNERY O'CONNOR (1925–1964)

Despite her early death and her relatively small body of fiction, O'Connor achieved a reputation as one of the finest of modern Southern fiction writers.

Life. O'Connor was born in Savannah, Georgia, the only child of Roman Catholic parents. When she was thirteen the family moved to rural Milledgeville, Georgia, and three years later her father died of a collagen type of disease. In 1945 she was graduated from the Georgia State College for Women, received a fellowship in creative writing from the University of Iowa, and began to publish her first stories. In 1950 she was stricken by the disease that had killed her father, and the combination of the illness and the medication she took for it began to cripple her. However, she published her first novel, *Wise Blood,* in 1952, lectured frequently at universities and writers' workshops, published *A Good Man Is Hard to Find* (a collection of stories) in 1955 and her second novel, *The Violent Bear It Away,* in 1960. Her last work, a collection of short stories, was published posthumously in 1965.

Southern Gothicism. Read literally, O'Connor's work is the very epitome of what is sometimes called Southern gothic writing. It abounds in horrors and what seems to be sensationalism. But her work, like that of other writers also called Southern gothicists (including Faulkner, Eudora Welty, and Carson McCullers), is clearly not meant to operate only on a literal level. Like these writers—and like Nathanael West, with whom she is often compared—she used her horrors and grotesques for symbolic purposes. Her work is a model of surface realism masking what often actually is sheer allegory. What makes her work unique in Southern writing is that her allegorical or symbolic intention is resolutely Christian and, more specifically, Roman Catholic. Using the world she knew best, the mostly rural life of Georgia and the Protestant Fundamentalism that was its major religious expression, she nevertheless wrote Roman Catholic fiction. The material she had to deal with—the life around her—prevented her from being a Catholic novelist in the sense that Evelyn Waugh or Graham Greene are Catholic novelists. She could not deal with Catholicism in action because, in her world, there was none. Thus she dealt with what was at hand and in effect wrote Catholic renditions of Southern Protestant life. Such an explanation is, of course, an oversimplification of her work. Although she was a religious writer, she was more than that. Like most other good fiction writers, she projected a realistic world that in its local customs and manners was a microcosm of the larger human world. She did not write homilies. She wrote of a certain part of the southern United States, giving us this world in all its uniqueness and complexity, giving us that sense of time and place that James called the hallmark of realistic fiction. Her special talent was also to give us more—this world, just as it is, but carrying with it a meaning that that world did not suspect.

Representative Works

"A Good Man Is Hard To Find" (1955). Perhaps O'Connor's best-known and most discussed story. Characteristically, the action of the story is both violent and grotesque. A Southern family—mother, father, children, and grandmother—are waylaid by an escaped convict called the Misfit, and eventually all are slain. What saves the story from being a horribly grotesque murder tale is the conversation between the grandmother and the Misfit at the end of the story. Unwittingly, he preaches to her the doctrine of the Atonement. Christ, he says, has thrown everything off balance by raising the dead and by his own resurrection. He has made possible the choice between good and evil in a world that otherwise would offer nothing but brief pleasure and pain, then death. The Misfit's words go directly to the grandmother's heart, or soul, and despite her fear she reaches out to him and calls him one of her children. At this point he kills her; but, dying, she has for the first time found life. The Misfit, who in his grotesque way also believes in Christ, makes this clear by his final statement: There is no real pleasure in anything, not even in killing, because (again) Christ has thrown everything off balance.

The Violent Bear It Away (1960). Generally regarded as the finer of O'Connor's two novels. It depicts the struggle between old Mason Tarwater, a backwoods fundamentalist "prophet," and his rationalistic, agnostic nephew Rayber over the life of Francis Marion Tarwater, Old Tarwater's grandson and Rayber's nephew. The blood relationship indicates the boy's affinities for both viewpoints. But the relationship to the mad old prophet is the stronger, and struggling all the while, young Tarwater finally succumbs to his grandfather—in effect, to religion. Like one driven, or chosen, he carries out his grandfather's order: to baptize Rayber's idiot son, ironically named Bishop. But the story is not as simple as this summary may imply. Young Tarwater drowns Bishop while he baptizes him and is later sodomized by a satanic figure. Full of his grandfather's religious "madness," he leaves for the city to preach the salvation he himself has found. Only a careful probing beneath the horrific and grotesque elements of the story reveals that the old man's religious "madness" is not that at all, but rather what might be called genuine religious fervor, and that his grandson's actions are hyperbolic renderings of the workings of grace.

11
Modern Dramatists

EUGENE O'NEILL (1888–1953)

By consensus O'Neill is America's greatest playwright and probably one of the great modern playwrights of world literature. Although he wrote many different kinds of plays, he was essentially a tragedian.

Life. O'Neill was born in New York City, the second son of a well-known actor, James O'Neill. His early years were ones of tension and unhappiness (later vividly dramatized in *Long Day's Journey into Night*), culminating in a brief and unfortunate marriage. Like Melville, he escaped his troubles by going to sea for two years and continuing the life of a sailor ashore for several years. After a siege of tuberculosis, during which he wrote his earliest plays, he attended George Pierce Baker's famous classes on playwriting and began his association with the Provincetown Players, who produced his early plays. In 1918 he married Agnes Boulton (the mother of Shane and Oona, who married Charlie Chaplin). In the next few years he became a successful and prolific playwright, winning Pulitzer prizes for *Beyond the Horizon* (1920) and *Anna Christie* (1921). He was divorced from Agnes Boulton and in 1929 married Carlotta Monterey. After *Mourning Becomes Electra* (1931) and *Ah, Wilderness!* (1933) his reputation declined, although he was awarded the Nobel Prize for literature in 1936. He contracted Parkinson's disease some time in the late 1940s, after he had written his last great plays, only one of which (*The Iceman Cometh,* 1946) was produced on Broadway before his death. He was posthumously awarded a third Pulitzer Prize in 1957 for *Long Day's Journey into Night*.

O'Neill's Greatness. To a foreigner beginning to study American drama it would hardly be an exaggeration to say: Forget the eighteenth and nineteenth centuries; American drama begins with O'Neill. Such an approach would stress two facts: (1) There was very little good American drama before O'Neill; and (2) the intellectual and dramatic influences on

O'Neill's work are European. One can easily see in his work the influences of Nietzsche, Schopenhauer, Ibsen, and especially Strindberg. The exceptions to this generalization are some echoes from Emerson and Thoreau (although O'Neill may as easily have been echoing the English or German transcendentalists) and, more important, his occasional use of the New England Puritan past in plays like *Desire Under the Elms* and *Mourning Becomes Electra.*

To view O'Neill as the fountainhead of American drama implies not only his excellence but also a large and varied body of work. Both criteria are true. O'Neill was above all else a playwright, one to whom ideas, attitudes, and social and religious problems existed in dramatic form. Reading his letters and occasional jottings one is not struck by any remarkable quality of thought. He was an intelligent man, but he never said anything that others had not said before. As a certain kind of poet apparently thinks in images (for example, William Carlos Williams: no ideas but in things), so O'Neill seems to have thought only in terms of scenes, character, and dialogue. Early in his career he wrote of his "feeling for the impelling, inscrutable forces behind life which it is my ambition to at least faintly shadow at their work in my plays."[1] It is the kind of comment that nearly any playwright or novelist might make. The value of an idea must exist not as a general statement but as a dramatized examination of life. And in O'Neill's best work this is exactly the way his thought operates.

But O'Neill's status as America's greatest playwright lies not only in his dramatic imagination but in the numerous forms and techniques that he employed. The bulk of his work is realistic in form, but he experimented with a number of antirealistic forms and techniques. Two of his best-known plays *(The Emperor Jones* and *The Hairy Ape)* are expressionistic: Scenery, character, and dialogue are deliberately distorted to provide particular atmosphere and meaning. Another successful play, *The Great God Brown,* has its major characters wearing masks, as in Greek tragedy, and O'Neill thought that some of his other plays (for example, *All God's Chillun Got Wings* and *Marco Millions,)* might benefit from the same device. In addition, some of his work is deliberately mythical, retelling in modern terms the great fables of antiquity: *Mourning Becomes Electra,* for example, is based on the Aeschylus trilogy about the decline and fall of the house of Atreus. And in a daring and surprisingly successful experiment, O'Neill in *Strange Interlude* allows his characters to express their secret thoughts to the audience in stream-of-consciousness asides. In short, there is hardly a serious dramatic form or device in twentieth-century drama that O'Neill did not utilize, usually for the first time in American theater.

---

1. Letter to Barrett Clark, 1919; quoted from Oscar Cargill, N.B. Fagin and W.J. Fisher, eds., *O'Neill and His Plays: Four Decades of Criticism* (New York: New York University Press, 1961), p. 100.

The Pattern of O'Neill's Work. O'Neill's work does not easily fall into such categories as stages or phases. Although he developed as an artist, he did fine work from beginning to end. It is true that his late works are more obviously autobiographical than his early ones, but this fact in itself has no bearing on their merits. His early one-act plays of the sea (the S.S. *Glencairn* group) are obviously romantic dramas within a realistic framework, as are *Beyond the Horizon* and *Anna Christie.* The characters are somewhat sentimentalized in all these plays, and the search for an answer "beyond the horizon" is too obvious in the play of that name and to some extent in all of them. The Glencairn plays, however, remain remarkable evocations of the loneliness and strange beauty of the seaman's life; they have reminded many readers of Melville, high praise indeed.

After this early romanticism, O'Neill moved steadily ahead in his long investigation of new forms and contents. In the expressionistic form he examined the destruction of a single human mind *(The Emperor Jones)* and told a kind of social-class fable *(The Hairy Ape).* He probed into the psychological complexities of interracial marriage *(All God's Chillun Got Wings),* then wrote one of his finest realistic tragedies, *Desire Under the Elms.* In *Marco Millions* and *The Great God Brown* he depicted the shallowness of American materialism, then moved to a semimystical view of life in *Lazarus Laughed* (which was a Broadway failure). *Strange Interlude* and *Mourning Becomes Electra,* which followed, are probably his most ambitious plays, each running for several hours. After the failure of *Days Without End* (1934) O'Neill's name disappeared from Broadway, and there was speculation that he had written himself out. What in fact was happening was that he was writing the plays that were probably his greatest, although they did not achieve popularity until after his death.

These last plays, especially *The Iceman Cometh* and *Long Day's Journey into Night,* must be regarded as among the finest of O'Neill's work. In them he returns to earlier parts of his life—his sailor days at Jimmy the Priest's saloon and his early adult life with his parents and his brother Jamie. He is less concerned with experimentation than with the "inscrutable forces" that he had been dramatizing in one way or another for nearly forty years. If these late plays are heavily autobiographical, it is surely because O'Neill came to see that the answers to the questions of human life must be found, if at all, within the context of one's own life. They are answers that one has lived. Oddly, these last plays have been regarded as bleakly pessimistic and also as relatively optimistic. What O'Neill seems to have done is to dramatize as powerfully as he could the life he knew best, and in capturing the quality of that life he captured also its enigma. Some parts of life seem patterned; others not. Sometimes it seems that man controls events; other times the reverse. Like Melville, O'Neill seemed to have felt that the counterimplications do not cancel each other out but are rather parts of something larger, not a pattern understandable to man, but a mystery. Beginning his work with the most obvious kind of romanticism, he ended it with something like the more profound romanticism of Coleridge: *Omnia exeunt in mysterium.*

Representative Works

The Hairy Ape (1922). One of O'Neill's most often produced plays, even now. In eight highly expressionistic scenes the play depicts the awakening consciousness of Yank, a stoker on a transatlantic liner. Scenery, dialogue, and characters are distorted in order to underline the message of the play. The stokers are variously depicted as caged animals, prisoners, and robots. Yank is at first content to be part of the ship's machinery that makes it go. But when Mildred Douglas, the spoiled daughter of a steel magnate, takes a guided tour of the stoke hole she recoils from him in terror, calling him a "filthy beast." From that point on Yank begins to brood, wondering who he is and what kind of world he lives in. In a Fifth Avenue Sunday morning scene it becomes clear that he literally does not exist for the rich people leaving church. Trying to find where he belongs, he finally verbalizes his question to a policeman, who tells him indifferently to go to hell. He wanders to the zoo, talks to a gorilla, opens the cage to shake hands with and free it—and is crushed to death.

Yank is often seen as the common man (or the American workingman) or the proletarian masses asserting their humanity and searching for their rightful place in a repressive capitalistic society. But on a psychological rather than social plane, Yank can be viewed as any man, or Everyman, seeking his own identity; knowing this, he will know all he needs to know of the world. But the play is a series of rejections, and the question is never answered.

Desire Under the Elms (1924). One of the shortest and most effective of O'Neill's tragedies. The action of the play consists of two elemental human drives: Sexual passion and the desire for land. These twin drives motivate the three central characters: old Ephraim Cabot, his son Eben, and Abbie Putnam, the young girl Ephraim takes as his third wife. Ephraim wants a child to inherit his land; Abbie wants security (land); but inevitably Abbie and Eben are drawn to each other. In a heavily Freudian scene Abbie seduces Eben in a parlor that was his mother's special room, and Eben even seems to blur the distinction between his mother and Abbie. Abbie bears a son that she claims is Ephraim's and Ephraim believes to be his, although everyone else knows the child is Eben's. After a tragic misunderstanding between Abbie and Eben, Abbie kills the child, and she and Eben face the consequences together. Although the time is 1850 and the place New England, the play manages to suggest an older life and a simpler and more primitive set of human values. Whether mythic, biblical, or Freudian in conception, it dramatizes the elemental level of human life that all civilizations and moral codes must contend with.

Long Day's Journey Into Night (1956). One of O'Neill's last plays, written in 1940 but not produced until after his death. Strongly autobiographical and remarkably compressed, it portrays a day and night in the life of the Tyrone family in their run-down summer house. Although the action begins quietly on a lovely summer morning, one is aware of the tensions among the members of the family—the father, his wife, and the two sons, Jamie and Edmund (Eugene). Less sensational than Albee's *Who's Afraid of Virginia Woolf?* which resembles it, the play progressively reveals the family's tragic life as a mixture of circumstance and character that no one can fathom. The father, a talented actor, has spent years cultivating a stage role that has made him wealthy but ruined him as an artist. The mother has been addicted to morphine since the birth of Edmund, when she was accompanying her husband on the road and a hotel doctor gave her the drug. Jamie is a drunkard and wastrel; Edmund is suffering from tuberculosis. Day turns to night as the mother, after one of her many "cures," resumes her morphine habit and the sons and the father get drunk in their individual ways. A series of violent arguments about blame and responsibility comes to nothing. The father and his sons bitterly review the past, while listening apprehensively for the mother's movements upstairs, trying to gauge whether, like some mysterious fate, she will come down. The dramatic impact of the work is enormous. It shows O'Neill at his best, depicting the shifting and mysterious interplay of circumstance, character, human responsibility, and the ambivalent love-hate quality of emotion. A triumph of realistic drama, it has been considered by many critics the greatest American play.

ELMER RICE (1892–1967)

One of the most productive and accomplished modern American playwrights, Rice was born in New York City to a relatively poor Jewish family. Despite early hardships, he attended law school and was admitted to the bar. He did not practice law, but his legal background provided the material for his first successful Broadway play, *On Trial* (1914), and figures prominently in several of his later plays. Although he sensed early in his career that drama was his special talent, he was not content simply to be a playwright. Theater in all its aspects was his larger love, and at various times he was not only writer but director and producer as well. This general sense of theater led him in 1937 to organize the Playwrights' Company, which included such noted figures as Maxwell Anderson, Robert Sherwood, Sidney Howard, and S. N. Behrman. Like many other American writers of the 1920s and 1930s, he became associated with radical causes, and today a good deal of his work does not seem to rise above the level of dramatic propaganda. Yet the plays generally considered his best are two social criticism works, indictments of American life under the capitalistic system. *The Adding Machine* (1923), which is often revived, is one of the best American examples of expressionistic drama. Avoiding any attempt at dramatic illusion, it depicts its protagonist (Mr. Zero) as a victim of the machine age. A bookkeeper reduced to an automaton by the drudgery of his work, he is replaced by an automatic adding machine. In a series of events surrealistically depicted by symbolic staging, he kills his employer, is convicted of murder, and goes to an afterlife that is spoiled for him by his earthly robotism. *Street Scene* (1929) illustrates the other side of Rice's talent. Wholly realistic in its stage presentation, it depicts the lives of several families living in a New York tenement. It is often called a naturalistic play, and indeed it could well be a dramatization of a Dreiser or Farrell novel. A cross section of lower-class Americans—Jews, Italians, Irish, and others—are jammed together, driven into unendurable situations by their closeness, the summer heat, and the social system that makes escape impossible. Murder, the failure of social idealism, and the impossibility of human love are the seemingly inevitable consequences of this situation. Though somewhat melodramatic, the play, like *The Adding Machine,* indicts American society for its neglect of "the little people" and abandonment of the American democratic ideal. The bulk of Rice's work, in fact, dramatizes the failure of the American way of life. Much of his later work probably will not survive, despite his theatrical talent. But plays as different in technique as *The Adding Machine* and *Street Scene* seem likely to retain the dramatic vitality that ensures their place in modern American drama. (*Street Scene* not only won the Pulitzer Prize and was made into a movie, but nearly twenty years later it was turned into a remarkably successful opera by Rice, Langston Hughes, and Kurt Weill.)

TENNESSEE WILLIAMS (b. 1911)

At various times accused of sensationalism, obscenity, and obscurity, Williams has become one of the best-known contemporary playwrights.

Life. Born Thomas Lanier Williams in Columbus, Mississippi, Williams was brought up in the South, mainly Mississippi, Tennessee, and Missouri. His early life seems one of classic insecurity, a portrait of the artist as a sensitive, lonely, introspective person who turned early to writing as a partial substitute for life. He was educated erratically at the University of Missouri, Washington University of St. Louis, and the University of Iowa. He has received numerous awards, including the Pulitzer Prize for both *The Glass Menagerie* (1945) and *Cat on a Hot Tin Roof* (1955).

Gothic Drama. Williams is to American drama roughly what Faulkner is to American fiction. He is capable of writing perfectly realistic, illusionistic drama not essentially different in presentation from the classic illusionism of Ibsen or O'Neill. But, like Faulkner, he has not been content to work within these limitations. In his staging directions, for example, he often demands symbolic settings such as walls that seem to exist only by suggestion and rooms without ceilings so that the sky may be seen. In *Summer and Smoke* (1948) he calls for the presiding presence of the statue of an angel who is to suggest eternity. His directions also often call for musical themes to recur at appropriate times, and his *Camino Real* (1953) is as unrealistic in setting and action as Wilder's *Skin of Our Teeth* or O'Neill's *Great God Brown*. But whether writing as illusionist or symbolist, Williams presents us with a vision of life that may accurately be called gothic. Like Poe and Rimbaud he writes of the horrors of the soul. For example, in *Suddenly Last Summer* (1958), the protagonist is dead before the play begins, but we learn that, like Melville, he has visited the hellish islands of the Galapagos and witnessed the hatching of great sea turtles. He has seen the young turtles break out of their eggs in the hot sand and watched the hordes of black vulturelike birds swoop down and kill them before they can reach the sea that is their home. Symbolically, this same protagonist, a homosexual, is attacked and devoured by hordes of dark children with whom he has had sexual relations. (These horrors are reported, not dramatized.) The play is probably Williams's most extreme dramatization of his view of the human condition, but many of his other plays support it. Many of Williams's major characters are grotesques who have perceived the horror of human existence that lies partly in the condition in which man finds himself but more in man's very nature. Williams's most typical characters are atoms whirling in a void, intuiting the nothingness of human life, and therefore psychic mutes, unable to relate to other characters. Many of them long for love and understanding, but few of them find either; most are what Melville called *isolatoes,* cripples either physically or symbolically (or both) who have perceived their ultimate defeat. Among them may be listed Laura *(The Glass Menagerie),* Sebastian Venable *(Suddenly Last Summer),* Shannon (*The Night of the Iguana,* 1961), Alexandra del Lago and Chance Wayne (*Sweet Bird of Youth,* 1959), and Brick Pollitt *(Cat on a Hot Tin Roof).* Occasionally Williams touches on contemporary social problems (such as political corruption and racism in *Sweet Bird of Youth*), but his major concern is to dramatize poetically the essential horror of human life as such—the strange urge among people to speak to each other when there is really nothing to say, the menacing brevity of youth and beauty, the inevitability of pain and death. If a critic were to trace out the figure in the carpet, the overall meaning of Williams's work, he might well point out Big Daddy *(Cat on a Hot Tin Roof),* in love with life but dying of cancer; Chance Wayne *(Sweet Bird of Youth),* wanting love but facing castration; and Sebastian Venable *(Suddenly Last Summer),* seeing providence operative and prophetic in the slaughter of turtles. Such a view of life may well issue in tragedy, but as

Williams dramatizes it, it must be called gothic tragedy. It is tragedy stemming from the deliberately distorting imagination of the playwright, in contrast with the tragedy of O'Neill's last works, where the horror arises not only from the characters themselves but from commonplace reality itself. Reality for Williams is never commonplace. Even in his plays that most closely approach illusionism his characters are larger than life. Reality in a Williams play is always strained through the sieve of a poetic imagination that registers human life in sensational hyperbole.

ARTHUR MILLER (b. 1915)

A follower of Ibsen, Miller, though an accomplished theatrical craftsman, is primarily a dramatist of ideas.

Life. Born in New York City to a middle-class Jewish family, Miller attended the University of Michigan, where his apprentice plays won several awards and where he met his first wife. His first Broadway success was *All My Sons* (1947), which won the New York Drama Critics' Circle Award. It was quickly followed by *Death of a Salesman* (1949), which won a Pulitzer Prize and is generally considered his best play. In the early 1950s Miller became associated with a number of left-wing causes and (like many other prominent writers) became a target for Senator Joseph McCarthy's Communist-hunting committee. Miller's play *The Crucible* (1953), based on the Salem witch trials, reflects some of the turmoil he found himself in. In 1956 he divorced his wife and married Marilyn Monroe, at that time Hollywood's major sex symbol, but the marriage lasted only four years. In 1962 he married Ingeborg Morath, a Swiss photographer. His *After the Fall* (1964) was assumed to be autobiographical, a revelation of much of his early life and especially of his troubled marriage to Marilyn Monroe (who by then had committed suicide). His play *The Price* (1968) received mixed reviews.

Miller as a Contemporary Ibsen. Miller has often acknowledged his debt to Ibsen, from whom he apparently learned one of his most frequently used devices—the gradual revelation of past events that changes the present situation. In one way or another he uses this technique in *All My Sons, Death of a Salesman, After the Fall,* and *The Price.* Sometimes, as in the first- and last-named plays, the revelation takes the form of mere information. Sometimes, as in the other two, he merges the past and present by reenacting earlier events, either directly or in the mind of his protagonist. More important is the fact that both Ibsen and Miller play the part of "playwright as thinker." Miller sees himself, as Ibsen saw himself, as a modern, enlightened intellectual, with psychological and sociological resources not available to earlier dramatists. Miller's early flirtation with Marxism gave way to a more personal and less systematic view of man and history, one that mixes depth psychology and a strong historical sense with a general vision of man that has been called, loosely, "existential." But the main point is that much of Miller's work, like much of Ibsen's, gives the impression of problem solving. But the theatrical skills of both men prevent much of their work from being taken simply as problem plays like the "agit-prop" plays of Odets and other dramatists of the 1930s.

It is true that a good deal of modern American drama, including the work of O'Neill, Rice, Williams, and Albee "argues" in the sense that it presents a given dramatic situation and implies that this situation is somehow wrong or unhealthy. But with the exception of expressionistic or absurdist techniques, or the anti-illusion devices of Brecht, which are meant to be obvious and which work only because they *are* obvious, most of the best modern drama has kept its argument within the dramatic framework of the play. Miller's work, like Ibsen's, manages to remain basically realistic and yet to seem somewhat disputatious—to argue seriously as Shaw does ironically. It is drama that seems to set up a given dramatic situation in order to make a fairly clear and logical point. Obvious examples from Ibsen are *A Doll's House, The Wild Duck,* and *An Enemy of the People* (which Miller adapted for the American stage). Examples from Miller are *All My Sons, The Crucible,* and of course, *Death of a Salesman.*

In *All My Sons,* which is replete with Ibsenesque revelations from the past, Joe Keller kills himself to illustrate the rather doctrinaire point that all men must live as brothers if civilization is to survive. In *The Crucible* John Proctor is given twentieth-century insights into human motivation and mob psychology in order to show that situations like that of seventeenth-century Salem can be understood and forestalled. Willy Loman's suicide in *Death of a Salesman* is generally taken to be evidence that the American dream of material success is simply a dream. But the ending of the play does not have the usual Miller "conclusion" to it. The remaining major characters—and many viewers—cannot agree on the simple question of whether or not Willy Loman failed, whether his suicide is redemptive or damning. The play is probably the most moving of Miller's works, perhaps because it seems to transcend his usual logic.

Something similar may be said of *After the Fall* and *The Price.* In both plays there is the usual reliance on new knowledge as evidence of advance in sympathy and understanding. Quentin, in *After the Fall,* virtually psychoanalyzes himself and comes to the conclusion that perhaps the knowing is all, that there are no ultimate norms, only endless information about particulars. *The Price* is almost dialectal in structure, arguing the difference between necessary and unnecessary human sacrifice, between martyrdom and self-delusion as a way of life. But neither play ends syllogistically. Like *Death of a Salesman,* they argue large problems but come to only tentative conclusions. Although neither of the last two plays deserves to stand with *Death of a Salesman,* all three plays share the same quality. In them Miller is still the playwright thinking, but he is not giving any easy professorial answers. Mirroring the complexity of human existence, he also catches (especially in *Death of a Salesman*) what James called the strange irregular rhythm of life.

EDWARD ALBEE (b. 1928)

Brought up from infancy by wealthy foster parents who apparently gave him more material than emotional security, Albee in his life and work provides rich hunting ground for the psychoanalytical critic. A major recurring theme in his work is the near impossibility of human love against a background of man's alienation from whatever force or person (if any) directs the universe. Philosophically he has often been called an existentialist; dramatically he has often been described as an absurdist, but also as an heir to the symbolic realism of O'Neill's later plays.

Some of Albee's best-known plays, especially *The Sandbox* (1959) and *The American Dream* (1960), are absurdist in the obvious way that much of Beckett's and Ionesco's work is. Put in its simplest terms, this kind of writing echoes the meaninglessness (therefore the absurdity) of human existence in the form of the work itself. An apparently senseless world is echoed in a senseless imitation; form is meaning, or nonmeaning. Neither *The American Dream* nor *The Sandbox* bothers to be realistic or illusionistic in the sense of depicting life as it appears to ordinary vision. They go to the heart of the matter (meaninglessness), ignoring the traditional realism which depicts life as it seems to be but which may suggest by dramatic action that life is without purpose or design. However, few of Albee's works can be called "nonplays" in the sense that many of Beckett's and Brecht's can be so called. His first work, *The Zoo Story* (1959), for example, is often termed absurdist, as it certainly is in its philosophical point of view. Briefly, the play seems to say that animals do not desire spiritual communication either with their own species or with a God whom they cannot conceive; yet man is an animal, and he desires both. The play in its form of presentation, however, is not absurdist but quite illusionistic. The given situation, the setting, even the tragic action are realistic in the traditional theatrical way. The absurdity lies in the conclusion, not in the presentation. The same thing is true of what is probably Albee's most important play to date, *Who's Afraid of Virginia Woolf?* (1962) To read the play only as a realistic-symbolic play such as O'Neill's *Long Day's Journey into Night* is to miss much of its meaning, which is often conveyed by mythic allusions and reenactments. Yet in parts it reminds the viewer of the late O'Neill plays. The characters are not absurdist symbols but people, grotesque and obviously symbolic but nonetheless people. Like most of Albee's work, the play is iconoclastic. One by one, illusions are stripped away until man is left in an essentially absurd position: Martha and George lose their fictitious son, who has been the real meaning of their marriage. Honey seemingly hopes for a real son by

Nick, but Albee implies that such a son would be as emasculated and empty as the son mutilated and killed in *The American Dream*. Later works, including *Tiny Alice* (1965) and the two short, connected plays *Box* and *Quotations from Chairman Mao Tse-Tung* (1969) suggest that Albee, whether working as absurdist or absurdist-realist, is satirizing not simply anything as simple as American materialism but the essential nihilism of existence itself.

12
Modern Literary Criticism

Literary criticism of some sort is surely as old as literature; yet there is some justification for calling the twentieth century the age of criticism. In sheer bulk, if in no other way, criticism has joined poetry, fiction, and drama as one of the major literary products of our time. Critics of the stature of Edmund Wilson, Lionel Trilling, and F. O. Matthiessen are as much a part of the literary scene as are creative writers. Why criticism should have assumed its current dignity and prestige is an interesting and complex question which cannot be discussed here. Perhaps the truest comment is in another name for our time—the Age of Analysis. Most areas of modern human life have come under the scrutiny of systematic investigation, and literature, too, has had to undergo this intensified scrutiny. An interesting aspect of this increased investigation is that so much of it has come from artists who are also critics—Pound, Eliot, Allen Tate, Karl Shapiro, Ralph Ellison, James Baldwin. Earlier artists were sometimes serious critics, but with rare exceptions (Sidney, Ben Jonson, Samuel Johnson, Coleridge, Arnold) their criticism was "occasional." The implication seems to be that modern artists are aware of the need for sophisticated examination of literature.

Part of the complexity of the current critical scene stems from the fact that older approaches to literature have survived but in modified forms. No modern criticism is really new. Older critical thought—particularly that of Plato, Aristotle, Longinus, and Coleridge—survives in much modern critical theory. And the older historical-biographical approach to a writer lives on, modified by newer views of history and views of biography that have been enhanced by the work of Freud and depth psychology in general. Eliot's argument that all good new art is a continuation of tradition is also true of criticism. New Critics, psychoanalytical critics, cultural-historical critics, myth-archetype critics, and New Humanists all have their roots in antiquity and later. That they do is a tribute to them; for otherwise they would be literary "sports" or mutations, a category that has been historically without value.

Most attempts to survey modern American criticism have understandably been impelled to distinguish various approaches by giving them distinctive labels. Thus the terms New Humanism and New Criticism have become part of the current literary vocabulary. The weakness of such labeling is that the label almost always makes the critical approach seem more rigid and doctrinaire than it generally is in practice. Critics have a way of sliding out of categories when they find the formal tenets too restricting. The reader consulting such summaries of criticism is likely to find that a given critic appears in two or three different categories. Yet certain approaches to literature exist in what may be called their pure form. It is useful to sketch out these approaches, occasionally indicating critics who have used more than one approach, or who have combined different approaches.

NEW HUMANISTS

New Humanists (including primarily Irving Babbitt, Paul Elmer More, and Norman Foerster) viewed literature from a moral and even religious point of view. Like Matthew Arnold, whom they often echo, they held that literature is a moral force, almost a secular religion. Opposed to both nineteenth-century romantic views of the perfectibility of man and to current naturalistic thought, which sharply curtailed his moral freedom, they suggested an older, humanistic view of man and of literature. Taking their name and some of their attitudes from such sixteenth-century humanists as More and Erasmus, they viewed great literature as the best of ancient writing combined with the best writing of the Christian era. This combination produced a kind of new classicism, which saw man as limited, yet free and dignified; not naturally good, yet on occasion capable of greatness. Inevitably these critics condemned most of the literature of their own time, seeing it as romantic naturalism, with either Rousseau or Zola at its source. Like much of Arnold's work, their criticism is hardly aesthetic at all. It condemns or praises a religious or philosophical point of view. Eliot and T. E. Hulme both have affinities with New Humanists, Eliot having studied with Babbitt at Harvard. T. E. Hulme's famous essay "Romanticism and Classicism," though often associated with New Criticism, reads in many places like a highly contentious version of much of Babbitt's work.

NEW CRITICISM

New Criticism is perhaps the easiest approach to describe in its pure form and is a convenient norm against which to measure other approaches that are less easily depicted. Sometimes called *formalism,* it is perhaps best described by one of its adherents, Cleanth Brooks, in his famous essay

"The Formalist Critic." One of the things New Criticism did was to stress that the artwork is a thing in itself, distinct from everything else in the world, including its author's life and intention, his historical and cultural milieu, and even the subject matter of the artwork itself. The work, in fact, is its own world and ought to be so regarded. The function of the critic is to scrutinize the work; to examine its parts and the ways they are united; to indicate the function of particular imagery, rhythm, rhyme, and tone. Since the work is unique, it cannot really be paraphrased; in MacLeish's famous terms it should not "mean" but "be." What it says is what it is; the form and the content are not separable, for the basis of the work is metaphor or symbol, a single indivisible figure. Such intense analysis, such concentration on the work itself, lends itself best to poetry and to short fiction or drama. With the novel it has less to do—or, rather, too much to do. (Mark Schorer's famous essay "Technique As Discovery" is a remarkable example of this approach applied to the novel form.)

Critics usually associated with New Criticism include Brooks, Robert Penn Warren, Allen Tate, R. P. Blackmur, and sometimes Yvor Winters and I. A. Richards. Pound and Eliot, because of their early intense study of not only English but foreign verse techniques, are also often connected with the movement. The movement reached its height in the 1940s, and the famous textbook anthology *Understanding Poetry,* by Brooks and Warren, became almost a classroom bible for perhaps a decade, producing countless thousands of pseudo-New Critics among the teachers and students who used it. Though sometimes debunked as remedial reading, and though clearly open to abuse—gratuitous antihistoricism and antibiography, for example—it performed and continues to perform an invaluable function, that of forcing attention to the text itself.

OTHER SCHOOLS

Outside the New Critical world of the artwork, of course, lies the great world itself—everything in any way having to do with the work. Other modern critical approaches have concerned themselves in various ways with this outside but impinging world. Although for purposes of aesthetic analysis one may regard the work of art as autonomous, in fact, of course, it is no such thing. It is a construct produced by a certain kind of person living at a certain historical moment in a particular cultural situation. And this person, like the rest of us, believed certain things and disbelieved others; was conscious of some things and unconscious of others; was partly shaped by family, friends, marriage, books, and physiology. Examination of the world outside the work can obviously tell us much about the work that the work itself cannot reveal. The investigation of everything that impinges on the artwork is the function of schools that may be labeled the psychoanalytical school, the cultural-historical school, and the myth-archetype school. The terms are clumsy and the functions of the schools sometimes overlap, but perhaps the general approaches may be made clear.

Psychoanalytical Criticism. Freud, of course, is the fountainhead of the psychoanalytical school, which is now, if not pure Freud, then some kind of modified Freudianism, generally using one of three approaches. (1) The psychoanalytical critic may concern himself with a given writer's life in relation to his work (for example, Joseph Wood Krutch's and Marie Bonaparte's biographies of Poe). Or (2) he may deal simply with a work in itself, analyzing it as a Freudian psychiatrist analyzes a dream (F. C. Crews's analysis of Hawthorne's "Roger Malvin's Burial"). Or (3) he may discuss larger aspects of literature from a generally psychoanalytical point of view (Simon O. Lesser's *Fiction and the Unconscious*).

In the first approach, the psychoanalysis of an individual writer naturally works best when the critic has a wealth of relevant biographical material at hand so that he can illuminate certain aspects of the work by citing real psychological evidence from the writer's life. This kind of criticism can of course be clumsily done or done simply for sensational reasons, and few critics are competent to do it at all, although many try. But no one who has read Henry Murray's introduction to Melville's *Pierre,* for example, can deny the remarkable light that Murray's discussion of Melville throws on that strange book.

In the second approach, when the critic puts a work to the psychoanalytical test without any special reference to the author's life, the results tend to be more debatable. The most famous example of this type of criticism is Wilson's Freudian reading of James's *The Turn of the Screw,* which is far from being generally accepted as valid, although no one denies its cleverness. The critical danger in applying psychoanalytical techniques to a given work lies in Freud's own insistence on the constant character of symbolism. Kings and queens *always* mean father and mother; houses *always* mean the feminine body; elongated objects such as staffs or canes *always* mean the phallus, and so on. A further weakness of this kind of approach is that straight Freudian analysis is always reductive: The dream or story only *seems* to mean what it appears to mean on the surface; what it *really* means is what the Freudian analysis reveals. Conversely, the greatest strength of such analysis lies in the critic's awareness that he may be adding meaning to a work, that he may be showing a further dimension which the writer may or may not have been aware of but which is nevertheless there. A purely Freudian reading of *Moby-Dick,* for example, is hardly more than a joke; yet to ignore the elements in the work that cry out for Freudian interpretation is indefensible.

In the third approach, when the critic discusses some large aspect of literature from a psychoanalytical point of view, all depends upon his awareness of Freud's basically antiliterary bias and upon his own sensitivity to literature. Although Freud had much good to say about literature, to the end he apparently regarded it as a kind of surrogate neurosis. On this point, Lionel Trilling's discussion of Freud and literature in *The Liberal Imagination* is admirable, as are many of the articles in the collection *Art and Psychoanalysis,* edited by William Phillips.

One rather obvious point should be added to this discussion: Psychoanalytical criticism must exist now if for no other reason than that so much of modern literature utilizes the insights of formal psychology. Perhaps we could do without Ernest Jones's psychoanalytical study of *Hamlet,* since we assume that, whatever Shakespeare may have been trying to do, he was not concerning himself with Freud's view of the Oedipus complex. But O'Neill, Faulkner, Fitzgerald, Albee, and others have obviously read Freud and his followers; therefore they in turn must be read in this light.

Cultural-Historical Criticism. The cultural-historical approach to criticism overlaps both the psychoanalytical and the myth-archetype, depending upon the emphasis it places on biography (which may be psychoanalytical) or on the element of unconscious myth produced by a given historical culture. This approach does not evaluate the work but attempts to describe it, to place it, as a part of a given time and culture. F. O. Matthiessen's *American Renaissance* is one of the most brilliant examples of this approach. Important aspects of the work of Emerson, Thoreau, Hawthorne, Melville, and Whitman are revealed by an examination of the cultural milieu in which these writers worked. An equally famous example, revealing some of the dangers of this approach, is V. L. Parrington's *Main Currents in American Thought,* which describes and places writers according to a doctrinaire left-wing view of history and economics. The next step from Parrington may be to some even more doctrinaire view of history, such as the rigid Marxist one espoused by Granville Hicks and Christopher Caudwell. Further, whatever view of history and culture this kind of critic adopts, he is susceptible to the temptation to historico-cultural determinism so well illustrated by Taine, for whom the artwork was sufficiently described by placing it in its triple matrix of the author's national character, his moment in history, and his cultural setting (sometimes abbreviated to race, moment, and milieu). Even when this kind of critic escapes the trap of Taine's determinism (assuming he wants to escape it), he must nevertheless work more as historian than critic: That is, he must inevitably work outward and away from the work itself to the milieu, the investigation of which can be endless. And if he moves away from a relatively brief segment of history, or a relatively recognizable milieu, he runs the very real risk of oversimplification, of imposing historico-cultural patterns rather than finding them.

Whether or not what Kenneth Lynn calls the American dream of success began with seventeenth-century American culture and endures in some identifiable form until the present is an interesting question. But it is mainly a historical and cultural question; it cannot actually be found in literature, although it may be verified there. If the function of the cultural-historical approach is to show that important American writing is partly explainable by reference to this enduring dream, it is of great value. But unless used by someone with Matthiessen's aesthetic sense, the approach tends to be that of cultural history, in which individual works are seen as representative, as illustrations or documents rather than artworks to be taken seriously in their own right. These dangers are mainly connected with hypothetical larger views of history and culture. In general, however, this kind of criticism can be enormously helpful in the examination of a given artwork by providing specific historical or cultural knowledge that the work assumes but does not explain. In this sense cultural-historical criticism is scholarly in a way that none of the other approaches is.

Myth-Archetype Criticism. The approach here called myth-archetype is the hardest of all to describe. It is partly psychoanalytical in its orientation but uses Jung much more than Freud. It also overlaps the cultural-historical approach in that what a historian might call a historical milieu, myth-archetype critics often call myth. In fact (again in the terms used here), there is probably no myth-archetype critic who is not also in some way a cultural-historical critic. Both schools assume that there is an underlying pattern to literature and that this pattern at least partly shapes the literary work. For the cultural-historical critic it is likely to be an identifiable and nameable pattern—the American dream of success or the moral innocence that R. W. B. Lewis sees as marking nineteenth-century American writing (*The American Adam*). For the myth-archetype critic the pattern is likely to be less obvious and less easily identified. The two approaches are hard to distinguish because the cultural-historical critic believes he has discovered a pattern (real history) that the myth-archetype critic finds exemplified originally in prehistory, in myth, in actions or stories that often precede written literature. In Leslie Fiedler's terms, the myth-archetype critic is concerned with the "archetype," while the cultural-historical critic is concerned with the "signature," the personal use of the ideal, or mythic, situation. The cultural-historical critic is a historian, while the myth-archetype critic attempts to point out the great underlying patterns of human behavior and belief, whatever literary work they may appear in. Thus the American dream of success is sufficient for a cultural-historical critic, while for a myth-archetype critic it is rather a localized and culturized version of a timeless human aspiration.

The myth-archetype critic, though never denying the insights of Freudian analysis, is generally more indebted to Jung and to anthropologists and comparative religionists such as Sir James Frazer, F. M. Cornford, Edwin Hatch, and more recently Mircea Eliade. In Jung and in the work of the other scholars mentioned he finds evidence of the attitudes, beliefs, and basic human actions and reactions that he sees as the wellsprings of human life and literature. All life and literature, for many myth-archetype critics, is a reenactment of primitive, preliterary, perhaps even pretemporal, life. Jung is particularly important in this respect, because his argument for a collective unconscious mind allows for and partly explains modern man's reenacting (in various modes) the most primitive life of the race. (Northrop Frye, generally a myth-archetype critic, illustrates modern man's relation to ancient man in "The Theory of Fictional Modes," a section of his *Anatomy of Criticism*. He sees imitative literature as descending from myth, to romance, to Renaissance tragedy, to realistic fiction, and so on. The scale also indicates the difficulty of keeping myth and history apart, for it starts with preliterary matter and moves to literature, which is obviously historical and culturally oriented.)

The question often raised about the myth-archetype approach is what it has to say about the artwork. Certainly it has much to say about modern life. As Eliade has pointed out, modern man routinely performs actions that were once ritualized, religious, and meaningful. In literature, presumably the same thing happens: Birth, marriage, and death have lost their ritual and religious significance. Aside from the fact that this approach does not evaluate a work—since birth, marriage, and death occur in all kinds of literature, good and bad—what does this approach do for literature that the cultural-historical approach does not do? An obvious answer is that it underscores the cosmic pointlessness of modern literature. A more significant answer is that it underlines the fact that this seemingly pointless modern literature is really the only possible ritual reenactment of ancient religious beliefs and that (ironically) it does what Arnold said poetry ultimately would do—replace religion. Literature, especially drama, may be modern man's only way back to (or forward to) ritual, which is the existential manifestation of religion.

There is also the question of how a mythic or archetypal situation operates in a work. The myth-archetype critic sometimes seems to assume that its mere presence in a work will produce an aesthetic reaction in the reader. But as one of the earlier myth-archetype critics, Maud Bodkin, pointed out in her *Archetypal Patterns in Poetry* (1934), the "rebirth archetype" in "The Ancient Mariner" operates only because Coleridge has skillfully placed it in a number of effectively dramatic contexts. Melville in *Moby-Dick* and Stephen Crane in "The Open Boat" have certainly used archetypal situations—man afloat in a flimsy craft at the mercy of the mighty sea—with tremendous effect, but here too the question of individual art (Fiedler's "signature") must play a part, for the basic situation has been used with indifferent or no success by other writers.

CONCLUSION

Looking over areas of critical approach as they have been sketched out here, the reader may well feel impelled to ask, "What is the function of criticism? What is it supposed to *do*?" As the diversity of critical opinion shows, the answer is not easy. But certainly one of its functions is to "inform" the reader's reaction to the work, to save the reader from mere impressionism. As James said, no critical theory can ever entirely replace the old-fashioned reaction of simply liking or disliking a work; but one of the approaches discussed here (or a combination of them) may make the reader more aware of the reasons for his likes and dislikes. It is worth noting, though, that none of these approaches (with the possible exception of New Humanism) is evaluative except in the material that it chooses to deal with.

13
Compiling and Updating Your Own Bibliography

To supplement the various bibliographies in this book, consult the sources listed below. For dictionaries, indexes, and other reference tools see the General Bibliography.

SECONDARY BIBLIOGRAPHIES

The bibliographies in this section are designed to help you discover writings *on* American authors and their works. Although a few of these compilations come from other fields or take an interdisciplinary approach, most deal primarily with American literature. Those with the widest scope, i.e., those that treat *all* American authors, genres, and literary periods, have been starred (*); and four of the most useful have been double starred (**). Note, however, that under certain circumstances the unstarred sources may prove equally valuable. For example, if you are looking merely for explications of a poem and have no present need for biographical or cultural background studies, you would profit most from consulting, not the starred items, but Kuntz and *The Explicator*.

Starting Points

**LHUS (commonly known as Spiller): the third volume (ed. Thomas H. Johnson) of Spiller, Robert E.; Thorp, Willard; Johnson, Thomas H.; Canby, Henry Seidel, eds. *Literary History of the United States*. (See General Bibliography for vols. 1–2.) An indispensable bibliography in paragraph form with some annotations. Published in 1948, it covers material through 1946. The first half treats periods, types, arts and language, folk materials, popular literature, regionalism, and so on. The second half contains bibliographies of individual authors. Should not be used alone but with

** Ludwig, Richard M., ed. *Literary History of the United States: Bibliography Supplement*. New York: Macmillan, 1959. Covers through 1957. Sometimes bound with the 1948 bibliography (above) and sometimes with the 1972 supplement (below); in such cases a single index may serve the several volumes.

**Spiller, Robert E.; Thorp, Willard; Johnson, Thomas H.; Canby, Henry Seidel; Ludwig, Richard M., eds. *Literary History of the United States: Bibliography Supplement II.* New York: Macmillan, 1972. Covers 1958–1970.

*Leary, Lewis. *Articles on American Literature.* 2 vols. Durham, N.C.: Duke University Press. Vol. 1 (1954) lists articles published from 1900 to 1950; vol. 2 (1970), from 1950 to 1967. Has sections on individual authors (including many lesser-known figures) and on subjects like biography, humor, black writers, and science.

Gohdes, Clarence. *Bibliographical Guide to the Study of the Literature of the United States.* 3d ed., rev. and enl. Durham, N.C.: Duke University Press, 1970. Annotated. No author bibliographies but a good variety of subjects.

Update the Above Bibliographies With

*"Articles on American Literature Appearing in Current Periodicals," a quarterly bibliography in *American Literature* since November 1929. Anyone interested in completeness should check each issue at least as far back as the latest edition of Leary, which is the only cumulation of this bibliography. Authors are grouped alphabetically within periods: (a) 1607–1800, (b) 1800–1870, (c) 1870–1920, (d) 1920–. A "General" section includes topics that straddle these periods.

**MLA International Bibliography.* Reprint. New York: Kraus, 1964–. An annual compilation issued through 1968 as part of *PMLA* but since 1969 in separate format. Annual coverage begins with 1921. Has an American section divided into periods. Unlike the *American Literature* bibliography (above) it lists books, festschriften, and dissertation abstracts as well as articles.

MLA Abstracts of Articles in Scholarly Journals. New York: Modern Language Association of America, 1971–. Articles abstracted in this annual are marked with an asterisk in the *MLA International Bibliography.*

American Literary Scholarship: An Annual. Durham, N.C.: Duke University Press, 1965–. Bibliographical essays by various authorities reviewing the year's work on American literature. Coverage starts with 1963.

American Literature Abstracts, a semiannual publication begun in 1967. Author-prepared abstracts of current articles on American literature. Also contains a "Book Review Consensus" section.

Modern Humanities Research Association. *Annual Bibliography of English Language and Literature* (1921–). Coverage begins with 1920. Arranged by period. British and American authors are alphabetized together. Also lists book reviews.

For Explications of Poems, Short Stories, Novels, Plays

Kuntz, Joseph M. *Poetry Explication: A Checklist of Interpretation since 1925 of British and American Poems Past and Present.* Rev. ed. Chicago: Swallow, 1962. Covers 1925–1959.

Walker, Warren S. *Twentieth-Century Short Story Explication: Interpretations, 1900–1966, of Short Fiction since 1800.* 2d ed. Hamden, Conn.: Shoe String, 1967. Supplements published in 1970, 1973.

Thurston, Jarvis; Emerson, O. B.; Hartman, Carl; and Wright, Elizabeth V. *Short

Fiction Criticism: A Checklist of Interpretations since 1925 of Stories and Novelettes (American, British, Continental) 1800–1958. Chicago: Swallow, 1960.

Gerstenberger, Donna, and Hendrick, George. *The American Novel, 1789–1959: A Checklist of Twentieth-Century Criticism.* Chicago: Swallow, 1961. A supplementary volume is *A Checklist of Criticism on Novels Written since 1789, Volume II: Criticism Written 1960–1968.* Chicago: Swallow, 1970.

Palmer, Helen H., and Dyson, Jane A. *American Drama Criticism: Interpretations, 1890–1965 Inclusive, of American Drama since the First Play Produced in America.* Hamden, Conn.: Shoe String, 1967. *Supplement I.* Hamden, Conn.: Shoe String, 1970.

Ryan, Pat M. *American Drama Bibliography: A Checklist of Publications in English.* Fort Wayne, Ind.: Fort Wayne Public Library, 1969.

Update These Genre Bibliographies With

"A Check List of Explication," an annual bibliography in *The Explicator* since 1944. Mostly concerned with poetry.

"Bibliography [of Short Fiction Criticism]," in the summer issues of *Studies in Short Fiction.* Annual March through March coverage except for the first bibliography (Summer 1964), which covers 1960 through March 1964.

For an Interdisciplinary, American Studies Approach

"Articles in American Studies," annual bibliography in the summer issues of the *American Quarterly* since 1955 (for 1954). Only articles of an interdisciplinary nature are listed. They are grouped in sections denoting their primary field (e.g., literature, geography, mass culture, music, philosophy, psychiatry) but are also given initials denoting their secondary fields. Thus an article on myth in Willa Cather's works receives a full listing in the literature section but bears the initials *F, H,* and *R* to indicate its pertinence to folklore, history, and religion. Annotated.

Harvard Guide to American History. Edited by Frank Freidel, with the assistance of Richard K. Showman. 2 vols. Rev. ed. Cambridge, Mass: Harvard University Press, Belknap Press, 1974. Contains sections on travel books, serials, biographies, language, popular literature, and the arts. The original edition of the *Harvard Guide to American History,* edited by Oscar Handlin and others (Cambridge, Mass.: Harvard University Press, 1954) is also useful, with sections on historical fiction and poems.

Library of Congress. *A Guide to the Study of the United States of America.* Washington, D.C.: Library of Congress, 1960. 6,487 entries under such headings as literature, language, literary history and criticism, periodicals and journalism, the American Indian, travel, entertainment, books and libraries, science, and law. Paragraph-size annotations.

America: History and Life: A Guide to Periodical Literature (1964–). Abstracts and bibliography.

Other Bibliographies of Secondary Sources

Clark, Harry H. *American Literature: Poe through Garland.* Goldentree Bibliographies in Language and Literature. Northbrook, Ill.: AHM Publishing Corp., 1971.

Cline, Gloria Stark, and Baker, Jeffrey A. *An Index to Criticisms of British and American Poetry*. Metuchen, N.J.: Scarecrow, 1973.

Eichelberger, Clayton L. *A Guide to Critical Reviews of United States Fiction, 1870–1910*. 2 vols. Metuchen, N.J.: Scarecrow, 1971, 1974.

Emanuel, James A., and Gross, Theodore L., eds. *Dark Symphony: Negro Literature in America*. New York: Free Press, 1968. Anthology with a substantial bibliography of primary and secondary sources (pp. 564–600).

Gohdes, Clarence. *Literature and Theater of the States and Regions of the U. S. A.: An Historical Bibliography*. Durham, N.C.: Duke University Press, 1967. Geographical arrangement.

Jones, Howard Mumford, and Ludwig, Richard M. *Guide to American Literature and Its Backgrounds since 1890*. 4th ed. Cambridge, Mass.: Harvard University Press, 1972. Lists (1) social and intellectual background studies and (2) the major works of the period.

Porter, Dorothy B. *The Negro in the United States: A Selected Bibliography*. Washington, D.C.: Library of Congress, 1970. Includes sections on literature, folklore, and art.

Rubin, Louis, D., Jr., ed. *A Bibliographical Guide to the Study of Southern Literature*. Baton Rouge: Louisiana State University Press, 1969. Supplemented by "Bibliography: A Checklist of Scholarship on Southern Literature," published annually since 1969 in *Mississippi Quarterly*.

Turner, Darwin T. *Afro-American Writers*. Goldentree Bibliographies in Language and Literature. Northbrook, Ill.: AHM Publishing Corp., 1970.

Woodress, James. *Dissertations in American Literature, 1891–1966*. Durham, N.C.: Duke University Press, 1968. Lists Ph.D. dissertations (completed and in progress) on individual authors and on subjects like criticism, nonfictional prose, Puritanism, and travel. Supplemented by

"Research in Progress," published quarterly in *American Literature*. A list of current Ph.D. dissertations and other scholarly projects.

Extensive bibliographies also appear in the following books listed in the General Bibliography: Blair (1937, 1960), *CHAL* (1917–1921), Hubbell (1954), Quinn et al. (1951), Taylor (1936), *Eight American Authors* (1971), *Fifteen American Authors before 1900* (1971), *Sixteen Modern American Authors* (1973).

PRIMARY BIBLIOGRAPHIES

To gather bibliography of works *by* an American author, consult the following sources:

LHUS, vol. 3, and supplements. The bibliographies of separate works under individual authors will usually prove adequate unless you need to know the name of the publisher, the number of pages, and the like. In such cases go to

BAL, Jacob Blanck's multivolume *Bibliography of American Literature*. New Haven: Yale University Press, 1955–. Technical, detailed information.

Cumulative Book Index (1898–). An ongoing list of recently published books. Still more current registries of publication are *American Book Publishing Record* (a monthly) and *Publishers Weekly*.

Whiteman, Maxwell. *A Century of Fiction by American Negroes, 1853–1952: A Descriptive Bibliography*. West Orange, N.J.: Saifer, 1955.

Wright, Lyle H. *American Fiction: 1851–1875*. San Marino, Calif.: Huntington Library, 1957. *American Fiction: 1876–1900*. San Marino, Calif.: Huntington Library, 1966.

Primary bibliographies also appear in several sources listed above with the secondary bibliographies: Jones and Ludwig, Emanuel and Gross.

MISCELLANEOUS TOOLS

Altick, Richard D., and Wright, Andrew. *Selective Bibliography for the Study of English and American Literature*. 5th ed. New York: Macmillan, 1975.

Dictionary of American Biography. Edited by Allen Johnson and Dumas Malone. 20 vols. and index. New York: Scribner, 1928–1937. Plus supplements.

Nilon, Charles H. *Bibliography of Bibliographies in American Literature*. New York: Bowker, 1970.

Resources for American Literary Study (1971–). Twice yearly. Contains bibliographical essays, checklists, and reviews of primary and secondary sources.

General Bibliography

Although this general bibliography (GB) offers the reader a chance to browse, it is designed primarily as a list of books cited in short form in two or more of the chapter bibliographies. Arrangement is alphabetical by author or editor, though a few books are also cross-referenced by title. For individual authors and for such topics as local color, naturalism, modern fiction, poetry, and criticism the relevant chapter bibliographies should be consulted.

Aarne, Antti, and Thompson, Stith. *The Types of the Folktale*. 2d revision. Folklore Fellows Communications, no. 184. Helsinki: Suomalainen Tiedeakatemia, Academia Scientiarum Fennica, 1961.

Aaron, Daniel. *The Unwritten War: American Writers and the Civil War*. New York: Knopf, 1973.

Altick, Richard D., and Wright, Andrew (see chap. 13).

Anderson, Charles R., ed. *American Literary Masters*. 2 vols. New York: Holt, Rinehart & Winston, 1965.

Auchincloss, Louis. *Pioneers and Caretakers: A Study of Nine American Women Novelists*. Minneapolis: University of Minnesota Press, 1965.

Austin, James C., and Koch, Donald A., eds. *Popular Literature in America: A Symposium in Honor of Lyon N. Richardson*. Bowling Green, Ohio: Bowling Green University Popular Press, 1972.

Baldwin, James. *Nobody Knows My Name*. New York: Dial, 1961.

———. *Notes of a Native Son*. Boston: Beacon, 1955.

Basler, Roy P. *Sex, Symbolism and Psychology in Literature*. New Brunswick, N. J.: Rutgers University Press, 1948.

Baym, Max I. *A History of Literary Aesthetics in America*. New York: Ungar, 1973.

Berthoff, Warner. *The Ferment of Realism: American Literature, 1884–1919*. New York: Free Press, 1965.

Bewley, Marius. *The Complex Fate: Hawthorne, Henry James and Some Other American Writers*. London: Chatto & Windus, 1952.

———. *Eccentric Design: Form in the Classic American Novel*. New York: Columbia University Press, 1959.

174

————. *Masks & Mirrors*. New York: Atheneum, 1970.

Bier, Jesse. *The Rise and Fall of American Humor*. New York: Holt, Rinehart & Winston, 1968.

Blackmur, R. P. *The Double Agent*. New York: Arrow Editions, 1935.

Blair, Walter. *Horse Sense in American Humor*. 1942. Reprint. New York: Atheneum, Russell & Russell, 1962.

————. *Native American Humor (1800–1900)*. New York: American Book, 1937.

————. *Native American Humor*. San Francisco: Chandler, 1960. Lacks the individual author bibliographies of the 1937 edition, but the general bibliography and introduction are updated.

Blotner, Joseph. *The Modern American Political Novel, 1900–1960*. Austin: University of Texas Press, 1966.

Bluefarb, Sam. *The Escape Motif in the American Novel: Mark Twain to Richard Wright*. Columbus: Ohio State University Press, 1972.

Bone, Robert A. *The Negro Novel in America*. New Haven: Yale University Press, 1958.

Botkin, B. A., ed. *A Treasury of American Folklore*. New York: Crown, 1944.

Bowen, James K., and Van Der Beets, Richard, eds. *American Short Fiction: Readings and Criticism*. Indianapolis: Bobbs-Merrill, 1970.

Bradbury, John M. *The Fugitives: A Critical Account*. Chapel Hill: University of North Carolina Press, 1958.

Bridgman, Richard. *The Colloquial Style in America*. New York: Oxford University Press, 1966.

Brooks, Cleanth. *The Hidden God: Studies in Hemingway, Faulkner, Yeats, Eliot and Warren*. New Haven: Yale University Press, 1963.

Brooks, Cleanth, and Warren, Robert Penn. *The Scope of Fiction*. New York: Appleton, 1960.

Brooks, Van Wyck. *The Confident Years: 1885–1915*. New York: Dutton, 1952.

————. *New England: Indian Summer, 1865–1915*. New York: Dutton, 1940.

Brooks, Van Wyck, and Bettmann, Otto L. *Our Literary Heritage: A Pictorial History of the Writer in America*. New York: Dutton, 1956.

Brown, Clarence A., ed. *The Achievement of American Criticism*. New York: Ronald, 1954.

Brown, Sterling. *The Negro in American Fiction* [and] *Negro Poetry and Drama*. New York: Arno, 1969.

Browne, Ray B., and Light, Martin, eds. *Critical Approaches to American Literature*. 2 vols. New York: T. Y. Crowell, 1965.

Bruccoli, Matthew J., ed. *The Chief Glory of Every People: Essays on Classic American Writers*. Carbondale: Southern Illinois University Press, 1973.

Bryer, Jackson R., ed. *Sixteen Modern American Authors: A Survey of Research and Criticism*. New York: Norton, 1973.

Burgum, Edwin B. *The Novel and the World's Dilemma*. New York: Oxford University Press, 1947.

Burke, John G., ed. *Regional Perspectives: An Examination of America's Literary Heritage*. Chicago: American Library Association, 1973.

Burr, Nelson R. *A Critical Bibliography of Religion in America*. Vol. 4, pts. 1 and 2 of *Religion in American Life,* edited by James Ward Smith and A. Leland Jamison. Princeton: Princeton University Press, 1961.

Cady, Edwin H. *The Light of Common Day: Realism in American Fiction*. Bloomington: Indiana University Press, 1971.

Callow, James T. *Kindred Spirits: Knickerbocker Writers and American Artists, 1807–1855*. Chapel Hill: University of North Carolina Press, 1967.

Cambridge History of American Literature (see Trent et al.).

Cargill, Oscar. *Intellectual America*. New York: Macmillan, 1941.

Carpenter, Frederic I. *American Literature and the Dream*. New York: Philosophical Library, 1955.

Cawelti, John G. *Apostles of the Self-Made Man*. Chicago: University of Chicago Press, 1965.

Chase, Richard [Volney]. *The American Novel and Its Tradition*. New York: Doubleday, 1957.

Clark, Harry Hayden, ed. *Major American Poets*. New York: American Book, 1936.

———, ed. *Transitions in American Literary History*. Durham, N.C.: Duke University Press, 1953.

Cline, Gloria S., and Baker, J. A. (see chap. 13).

Cohen, Hennig, ed. *Landmarks of American Writing*. New York: Basic Books, 1969.

Conner, Frederick W. *Cosmic Optimism: A Study of the Interpretation of Evolution by American Poets from Emerson to Robinson*. Gainesville: University of Florida Press, 1949.

Cowan, Louise. *The Fugitive Group: A Literary History*. Baton Rouge: Louisiana State University Press, 1959.

Cowie, Alexander. *The Rise of the American Novel*. New York: American Book, 1948.

Cowley, Malcolm, ed. *After the Genteel Tradition: American Writers Since 1910*. New York: Norton, 1937.

Cowley, Malcolm. *Exile's Return*. New York: Viking, 1951.

———. *A Many-Windowed House: Collected Essays on American Writers and American Writing*. Edited by Henry D. Piper. Carbondale: Southern Illinois University Press, 1970.

Cunliffe, Marcus, ed. *American Literature to 1900* and *American Literature since 1900*. Vols. 8 and 9 of *History of Literature in the English Language*. London: Barrie & Jenkins, 1973.

Current-Garcia, Eugene, and Patrick, Walton R., eds. *Realism and Romanticism in Fiction: An Approach to the Novel*. Glenview, Ill.: Scott, Foresman, 1962.

Curtis, Richard. *The Genial Idiots: The American Saga as Seen by Our Humorists*. New York: Crowell Collier Macmillan, 1968.

Davis, Arthur P. *From the Dark Tower: Afro-American Writers, 1900 to 1960*. Washington, D. C.: Howard University Press, 1974.

Deakin, Motley, and Lisca, Peter, eds. *From Irving to Steinbeck: Studies of American Literature in Honor of Harry R. Warfel*. Gainesville: University of Florida Press, 1972.

DeMille, George E. *Literary Criticism in America*. New York: L. MacVeagh, 1931.

Dorson, Richard M. *American Folklore*. Chicago: University of Chicago Press, 1959.

Downs, Robert B. *Books that Changed America*. New York: Macmillan, 1970.

Duffey, Bernard I. *The Chicago Renaissance in American Letters*. East Lansing: Michigan State University Press, 1954.

Dunlap, George A. *The City in the American Novel, 1789-1900*. 1934. Reprint. New York: Atheneum, Russell & Russell, 1965.

Edel, Leon. *The Psychological Novel, 1900–1950*. Philadelphia: Lippincott, 1955.

Ehrenpreis, Irvin, ed. *American Poetry*. Stratford-upon-Avon Studies, no. 7. Leeds, England: E. J. Arnold, 1965.

Eichelberger, Clayton L. (see chap. 13).

Eight American Authors (see Woodress).

The Explicator Cyclopedia (see Walcutt and Whitesell).

Falk, Robert. *The Victorian Mode in American Fiction, 1865–1885*. East Lansing: Michigan State University Press, 1965.

Feidelson, Charles, Jr. *Symbolism and American Literature*. Chicago: University of Chicago Press, 1953.

Feidelson, Charles, Jr., and Brodtkorb, Paul, Jr., eds. *Interpretations of American Literature*. New York: Oxford University Press, 1959.

Fiedler, Leslie A. *An End to Innocence*. Boston: Beacon, 1955.

———. *Love and Death in the American Novel*. New York: Criterion, 1960.

Fifteen American Authors before 1900 (see Rees and Harbert).

Finkelstein, Sidney. *Existentialism and Alienation in American Literature*. New York: International Publishers, 1965.

Foerster, Norman. *American Criticism: A Study in Literary Theory from Poe to the Present*. Boston: Houghton Mifflin, 1928.

———. *The Reinterpretation of American Literature*. New York: Harcourt, 1928.

Folsom, James K. *The American Western Novel*. New Haven: College and University Press, 1966.

Fraiberg, Louis. *Psychoanalysis and Literary Criticism*. Detroit: Wayne State University Press, 1960.

Franklin, H. Bruce. *Future Perfect: American Science Fiction of the Nineteenth Century*. New York: Oxford University Press, 1966.

Frederick, John T. *The Darkened Sky: Nineteenth Century American Novelists and Religion*. Notre Dame, Ind.: University of Notre Dame Press, 1969.

Freidel, Frank (see chap. 13).

French, Warren, ed. *The Fifties: Fiction, Poetry, Drama*. Deland, Fla : Everett/Edwards, 1969.

———, ed. *The Forties: Fiction, Poetry, Drama*. Deland, Fla.: Everett/Edwards, 1967.

———, ed. *The Thirties: Fiction, Poetry, Drama*. Deland, Fla.: Everett/Edwards, 1967.

French, Warren, and Kidd, Walter E., eds. *American Winners of the Nobel Literary Prize*. Norman: University of Oklahoma Press, 1968.

Frohock, Wilbur M. *The Novel of Violence in America*. 1950. 2d ed., rev. & enl. Dallas, Tex.: Southern Methodist University Press, 1958.

Fussell, Edwin. *Lucifer in Harness: American Meter, Metaphor, and Diction*. Princeton: Princeton University Press, 1973.

Gaines, Francis P. *The Southern Plantation*. New York: Columbia University Press, 1925.

Gardiner, H. C., ed. *Fifty Years of the American Novel: A Christian Appraisal*. New York: Scribner, 1951.

Gardner, Rufus H. *The Splintered Stage: The Decline of the American Theater*. New York: Macmillan, 1965.

Gayle, Addison, Jr., ed. *The Black Aesthetic*. New York: Doubleday, 1971.

Geismar, Maxwell. *The Last of the Provincials*. Boston: Houghton Mifflin, 1943.

————. *Rebels and Ancestors: The American Novel 1890–1915.* Boston: Houghton Mifflin, 1953.

Gerstenberger, Donna, and Hendrick, George (see chap. 13).

Gibson, D. B., ed. *Five Black Writers: Essays on Wright, Ellison, Baldwin, Hughes and LeRoi Jones.* New York: New York University Press, 1970.

Gibson, Walker. *Tough, Sweet & Stuffy: An Essay on Modern American Prose Styles.* Bloomington: Indiana University Press, 1966.

Glicksberg, Charles I., ed. *American Literary Criticism, 1900–1950.* New York: Hendricks House, 1951.

Gohdes, Clarence, ed. *Essays on American Literature in Honor of Jay B. Hubbell.* Durham, N. C.: Duke University Press, 1967.

Gordon, Walter K., ed. *Literature in Critical Perspectives: An Anthology.* New York: Appleton, 1968.

Gross, Seymour L., and Hardy, John Edward, eds. *Images of the Negro in American Literature.* Chicago: University of Chicago Press, 1966.

Gross, Theodore L. *The Heroic Ideal in American Literature.* New York: Free Press, 1971.

Hall, Wade. *The Smiling Phoenix: Southern Humor from 1865 to 1914.* Gainesville: University of Florida Press, 1965.

Hall, Wade H. *Reflections of the Civil War in Southern Humor.* Monographs, Humanities. Gainesville: University of Florida Press, 1962.

Hart, James D. *Oxford Companion to American Literature.* 4th ed., rev. & enl. New York: Oxford University Press, 1965.

Hartwick, Harry. *The Foreground of American Fiction.* 1934. Reprint. Staten Island: Gordian, 1967.

Hatcher, Harlan. *Creating the Modern American Novel.* 1935. Reprint. New York: Russell & Russell, 1965.

Hauck, Richard B. *A Cheerful Nihilism: Confidence and "The Absurd" in American Humorous Fiction.* Bloomington: Indiana University Press, 1971.

Hazard, Lucy L. *The Frontier in American Literature.* New York: Barnes & Noble, 1941.

Herron, Ima H. *The Small Town in American Drama.* Dallas, Tex.: Southern Methodist University Press, 1969.

————. *The Small Town in American Literature.* Durham, N.C.: Duke University Press, 1939.

Herzberg, Max J., and the staff of the T. Y. Crowell Co. *Reader's Encyclopedia of American Literature.* London: Methuen, 1963.

Hicks, Granville. *The Great Tradition.* New York: Macmillan, 1933.

————, ed. *The Living Novel.* New York: Macmillan, 1957.

Hilfer, Anthony C. *The Revolt from the Village, 1915–1930.* Chapel Hill: University of North Carolina Press, 1969.

Hill, Herbert, ed. *Anger and Beyond.* New York: Harper & Row, 1966.

Hoffman, Daniel. *Form and Fable in American Fiction.* New York: Oxford University Press, 1961.

Hoffman, Frederick J. *The Twenties.* New York: Collier, 1962.

Horton, Rod W., and Edwards, Herbert W. *Background of American Literary Thought.* 2d ed. New York: Appleton, 1967.

Howard, Leon. *Literature and the American Tradition.* New York: Doubleday, 1960.

Howe, Irving. *A World More Attractive.* New York: Horizon, 1963.

Hubbell, Jay B. *The South in American Literature: 1607–1900.* Durham, N.C.: Duke University Press, 1954.

———. *Who Are the Major American Writers? A Study of the Changing Literary Canon.* Durham, N.C.: Duke University Press, 1972.

Hughes, Glenn. *A History of the American Theatre, 1700–1950.* New York: French [1951].

Ives, Sumner. "A Theory of Literary Dialect." *TSE* 2 (1950): 137–182.

Jones, Howard Mumford. *The Age of Energy: Varieties of American Experience, 1865–1915.* New York: Viking, 1971.

———. *Belief and Disbelief in American Literature.* Chicago: University of Chicago Press, 1967.

———. *The Theory of American Literature.* Ithaca, N.Y.: Cornell University Press, 1965.

Jones, Howard Mumford, and Ludwig, Richard M. (see chap. 13).

Kaplan, Harold. *Democratic Humanism and American Literature.* Chicago: University of Chicago Press, 1972.

Karanikas, Alexander. *Tillers of a Myth: Southern Agrarians as Social and Literary Critics.* Madison: University of Wisconsin Press, 1966.

Kazin, Alfred. *On Native Grounds: An Interpretation of Modern American Prose Literature.* 1942. Reprint. New York: Harcourt Brace Jovanovich, 1972.

Kerr, Howard. *Mediums, and Spirit-Rappers, and Roaring Radicals: Spiritualism in American Literature, 1850–1900.* Urbana: University of Illinois Press, 1972.

Knight, Grant. *The Critical Period in American Literature.* Chapel Hill: University of North Carolina Press, 1951. Concentrates on the 1890s.

Kolodny, Annette. *The Lay of the Land.* Chapel Hill: University of North Carolina Press, 1975.

Kramer, Aaron. *The Prophetic Tradition in American Poetry, 1835–1900.* Cranbury, N.J.: Fairleigh Dickinson University Press, 1968.

Kramer, Dale. *Chicago Renaissance: The Literary Life in the Midwest, 1900–1930.* New York: Appleton, 1966.

Krapp, George Philip. *The English Language in America.* 1925. Reprint. 2 vols. New York: Ungar, 1960.

Krause, Sydney J., ed. *Essays on Determinism in American Literature.* Kent, Ohio: Kent State University Press, 1964.

Kreymborg, Alfred. *Our Singing Strength: An Outline of American Poetry (1620–1930).* New York: Coward-McCann, 1929.

Kuhlmann, Susan. *Knave, Fool, and Genius: The Confidence Man as He Appears in Nineteenth-Century American Fiction.* Chapel Hill: University of North Carolina Press, 1973.

Kuntz, Joseph M. (see chap. 13).

Leary, Lewis. (see chap. 13).

Leisy, Ernest E. *The American Historical Novel.* Norman: University of Oklahoma Press, 1950.

Lieber, Todd M. *Endless Experiments: Essays on the Heroic Experience in American Romanticism.* Columbus: Ohio State University Press, 1973.

Liptzin, Sol. *The Jew in American Literature.* New York: Bloch [1966].

Littlejohn, David. *Black on White.* New York: Viking, 1966.

Loggins, Vernon. *The Negro Author: His Development in America to 1900.* 1931. Reprint. Port Washington, N. Y.: Kennikat, 1964.

Lovell, John, Jr. *Digests of Great American Plays*. New York: T. Y. Crowell, 1961.

Lubbock, Percy. *The Craft of Fiction*. New York: Viking, 1957.

Lynn, Kenneth S. *The Dream of Success*. Boston: Little, Brown, 1955.

————. *Visions of America: Eleven Literary Historical Essays*. Westport, Conn.: Greenwood, 1973.

McGiffert, Michael, ed. *Puritanism and the American Experience*. Reading, Mass.: Addison-Wesley, 1969.

McIlwaine, Shields. *The Southern Poor-White from Lubberland to Tobacco Road*. Norman: University of Oklahoma Press, 1939.

McKerrow, Ronald B. *An Introduction to Bibliography for Literary Students*. Oxford, Eng.: Clarendon, 1927.

McNeir, Waldo, and Levy, Leo B., eds. *Studies in American Literature*. Baton Rouge: Louisiana State University Press, 1960.

Marckwardt, Albert H. *American English*. New York: Oxford University Press, 1958.

Margolies, Edward. *Native Sons*. Philadelphia: Lippincott, 1968.

Martin, Jay. *Harvests of Change: American Literature, 1865–1914*. Englewood Cliffs, N.J.: Prentice-Hall, 1967.

Marx, Leo. *The Machine in the Garden: Technology and the Pastoral Ideal in America*. New York: Oxford University Press, 1964.

Mathews, Mitford M., ed. *A Dictionary of Americanisms on Historical Principles*. 2 vols. Chicago: University of Chicago Press, 1951.

May, John R. *Toward a New Earth: Apocalypse in the American Novel*. Notre Dame, Ind.: University of Notre Dame Press, 1972.

Mencken, Henry L. *The American Language*. 4th ed., cor., enl., and rewritten. New York: Knopf, 1936. With supplements in 1945, 1948.

Merrill, Dana K. *American Biography*. New York: Bowker, 1957.

Miller, Ruth, ed. *Backgrounds to Blackamerican Literature*. San Francisco: Chandler, 1971.

Millgate, Michael. *American Social Fiction: James to Cozzens*. New York: Barnes & Noble, 1964.

Milne, Gordon. *The American Political Novel*. Norman: University of Oklahoma Press, 1966.

Minter, David L. *The Interpreted Design as a Structural Principle in American Prose*. New Haven: Yale University Press, 1969.

Mitchell, Loften. *Black Drama: The Story of the American Negro in the Theatre*. New York: Hawthorn, 1967.

Mizener, Arthur. *Twelve Great American Novels*. Cleveland: World Publishing, 1969.

Moses, Montrose J. *The American Dramatist*. 1925. Reprint. New York: Blom, 1964.

Mott, Frank Luther. *Golden Multitudes: The Story of Best Sellers in the United States*. 1947. Reprint. New York: Bowker, 1960.

————. *A History of American Magazines*. 5 vols. Cambridge, Mass.: Harvard University Press, 1957–1968.

Murphy, Rosalie, and Vinson, James. *Contemporary Poets in the English Language*. London: St. James, 1970.

Nannes, Caspar H. *Politics in the American Drama (1890–1960)*. Washington, D. C.: Catholic University Press, 1960.

Narasimhaiah, C. D., ed. *Asian Response to American Literature*. New York: Barnes & Noble, 1972.

Nelson, Benjamin, ed. *Freud and the Twentieth Century*. New York: Meridian, 1957.

Nemerov, Howard. *Poetry and Fiction: Essays*. New Brunswick, N. J.: Rutgers University Press, 1963.

Nilon, Charles H. (see chap. 13).

Noble, David W. *The Eternal Adam and the New World Garden: The Central Myth in the American Novel since 1830*. New York: Braziller, 1968.

O'Neill, Edward H. *A History of American Biography, 1800–1935*. 1935. Reprint. New York: Atheneum, Russell & Russell, 1968.

Orians, G. Harrison. *A Short History of American Literature Analyzed by Decades*. New York: Appleton, 1940.

Palmer, Helen H., and Dyson, Jane A. (see chap. 13).

Parks, Edd W. *Ante-Bellum Southern Critics*. Athens: University of Georgia Press, 1962.

Parrington, Vernon L. *Main Currents in American Thought*. New York: Harcourt, 1930.

Pattee, Fred Lewis. *The Development of the American Short Story*. 1923. Reprint. New York: Biblo & Tannen, 1966.

———. *The First Century of American Literature, 1770–1870*. 1935. Reprint. New York: Cooper Square, 1966.

———. *A History of American Literature since 1870*. 1915. Reprint. New York: Cooper Square, 1968.

Pavese, Cesare. *American Literature: Essays and Opinions*. Berkeley: University of California Press, 1970.

Pearce, Roy Harvey. *The Continuity of American Poetry*. Princeton: Princeton University Press, 1961.

Pizer, Donald. *Realism and Naturalism in Nineteenth-Century American Literature*. Crosscurrents. Carbondale: Southern Illinois University Press, 1966.

Pochmann, Henry A. *German Culture in America: Philosophical and Literary Influences, 1600–1900*. Madison: University of Wisconsin Press, 1957.

Pritchard, John Paul. *Return to the Fountains: Some Classical Sources of American Criticism*. Durham, N.C.: Duke University Press, 1942.

———. *Criticism in America*. Norman: University of Oklahoma Press, 1956.

Quinn, Arthur Hobson. *American Fiction: An Historical and Critical Survey*. New York: Appleton, 1936.

———. *A History of American Drama: From the Civil War to the Present Day*. 2 vols. New York: Harper, 1927.

Quinn, Arthur Hobson; Murdock, Kenneth B.; Gohdes, Clarence; and Whicher, George F. *The Literature of the American People*. New York: Appleton, 1951.

Redding, Saunders. *To Make a Poet Black*. Chapel Hill: University of North Carolina Press, 1939.

Reed, Perley Isaac. *The Realistic Presentation of American Characters in Native Plays prior to Eighteen Seventy*. Contributions in Language and Literature, no. 1. Columbus: Ohio State University Press, 1918.

Rees, Robert A., and Harbert, E. N., eds. *Fifteen American Authors before 1900: Bibliographic Essays on Research and Criticism*. Madison: University of Wisconsin Press, 1971.

Rideout, Walter B. *The Radical Novel in the United States, 1900–1954*. Cambridge, Mass.: Harvard University Press, 1964.

Robinson, Cecil. *With the Ears of Strangers: The Mexican in American Literature*. Tuscon: University of Arizona Press, 1963.

Rourke, Constance. *American Humor*. 1931. Reprint. New York: Doubleday, 1953.

Rubin, Louis D, Jr., ed. *The Comic Imagination in American Literature*. New Brunswick, N. J.: Rutgers University Press, 1973.

Rubin, Louis D., Jr., ed. (see chap. 13).

Rubin, Louis D., Jr., and Jacobs, R. D., eds. *South: Modern Southern Literature in Its Cultural Setting*. New York: Doubleday, 1961.

Sanford, Charles. *The Quest for Paradise*. Urbana: University of Illinois Press, 1961.

Schraufnagel, Noel. *From Apology to Protest: The Black American Novel*. Deland, Fla.: Everett/Edwards, 1973.

Shapiro, Charles, ed. *Twelve Original Essays on Great American Novels*. Detroit: Wayne State University Press, 1958.

Shapiro, Karl; Miller, James E.; and Slote, Bernice. *Start with the Sun: Studies in Cosmic Poetry*. Lincoln: University of Nebraska Press, 1960.

Simon, Myron, and Parsons, Thornton H., eds. *Transcendentalism and Its Legacy*. Ann Arbor: University of Michigan Press, 1966.

Simonini, R. C., Jr. *Southern Writers: Appraisals in Our Time*. Charlottesville: University Press of Virginia, 1964.

Simpson, Lewis P. *The Man of Letters in New England and the South: Essays on the History of the Literary Vocation in America*. Baton Rouge: Louisiana State University Press, 1973.

Sixteen Modern American Authors (see Bryer).

Skard, Sigmund, ed. *USA in Focus*. Oslo: Universitetsforlaget, 1966.

Smith, Henry Nash. *Virgin Land: The American West as Symbol and Myth*. Cambridge, Mass.: Harvard University Press, 1950.

Snell, George. *The Shapers of American Fiction, 1789–1947*. 1947. Reprint. New York: Cooper Square, 1961.

Spiller, Robert E.; Thorp, Willard; Johnson, Thomas H.; and Canby, Henry Seidel, eds. *Literary History of the United States*. Rev. ed. in one vol. New York: Macmillan, 1953. A comprehensive history written by fifty-five scholars. (When originally published in 1948, this history formed vols. 1 and 2 of a 3-vol. set; for vol. 3 and supplements see chap. 13 above.)

Spiller, Robert E. *The Cycle of American Literature*. New York: Free Press, 1955.

Sprague, Rosemary. *Imaginary Gardens: A Study of Five American Poets*. Philadelphia: Chilton, 1969.

Starke, Catherine J. *Black Portraiture in American Fiction: Stock Characters, Archetypes, and Individuals*. New York: Basic Books, 1971.

Stegner, Wallace E., ed. *The American Novel from James Fenimore Cooper to William Faulkner*. New York: Basic Books [1965].

Stewart, John L. *The Burden of Time: The Fugitives and Agrarians*. Princeton: Princeton University Press. 1965.

Stewart, Randall. *American Literature and Christian Doctrine*. Baton Rouge: Louisiana State University Press, 1958.

Stovall, Floyd, ed. *The Development of American Literary Criticism*. Chapel Hill: University of North Carolina Press, 1955.

Straumann, Heinrich. *American Literature in the Twentieth Century*. 3d rev. ed. New York: Harper & Row, 1965.

Tandy, Jennette. *Crackerbox Philosophers in American Humor and Satire*. 1925. Reprint. Port Washington, N.Y.: Kennikat, 1964.

Tanner, Tony. *The Reign of Wonder: Naivety and Reality in American Literature*. New York: [Cambridge] University Press, 1965.

Tate, Allen, ed. *A Southern Vanguard*. Englewood Cliffs, N.J.: Prentice-Hall, 1947.

Taylor, Walter F. *The Economic Novel in America*. 1942. Reprint. New York: Octagon, 1964.

————. *A History of American Letters, with Bibliographies by Harry Hartwick*. New York: American Book, 1936.

————. *The Story of American Letters*. Chicago: Regnery, 1956.

Thompson, Stith. *Motif-Index of Folk-Literature*. 6 vols. Rev. & enl. ed. Bloomington: Indiana University Press, 1955–1958.

Thorp, Willard. *American Writing in the Twentieth Century*. Cambridge, Mass.: Harvard University Press, 1960.

Thrall, William Flint; Hibbard, Addison; and Holman, C. Hugh. *A Handbook to Literature*. Rev. & enl. ed. New York: Odyssey, 1960.

Thurston, Jarvis, and others (see chap. 13).

Trent, William P.; Erskine, John; Sherman, Stuart P.; and Van Doren, Carl. *Cambridge History of American Literature*. 4 vols. New York: Putnam, 1917–1921.

Trilling, Lionel. *The Liberal Imagination*. New York: Viking, 1950.

Tuttleton, James W. *The Novel of Manners in America*. Chapel Hill: University of North Carolina Press, 1972.

Van Doren, Carl C. *The American Novel, 1789–1939*. New York: Macmillan, 1940.

Van Doren, Mark. *Introduction to Poetry*. New York: Dryden, 1951.

Van Nostrand, A. D. *Everyman His Own Poet: Romantic Gospels in American Literature*. New York: McGraw-Hill, 1968.

————, ed. *Literary Criticism in America*. New York: Liberal Arts Press, 1957.

Vogel, Dan. *The Three Masks of American Tragedy*. Baton Rouge: Louisiana State University Press, 1974.

Voss, Arthur. *The American Short Story: A Critical Survey*. Norman: University of Oklahoma Press, 1973.

Wagenknecht, Edward. *Cavalcade of the American Novel*. New York: Holt, Rinehart & Winston, 1952.

Wager, Willis. *American Literature: A World View*. New York: New York University Press, 1968.

Waggoner, Hyatt H. *American Poets from the Puritans to the Present*. Boston: Houghton Mifflin, 1968.

Wagner, Jean. *Black Poets of·the United States: From Paul Laurence Dunbar to Langston Hughes*. Urbana: University of Illinois Press, 1973.

Walcutt, C. C., and Whitesell, J. E. *The Explicator Cyclopedia*. 3 vols. New York: Quadrangle, 1966–1968.

Walker, Warren S. (see chap. 13).

Warren, Austin. *The New England Conscience*. Ann Arbor: University of Michigan Press, 1966.

————. *Rage for Order*. Chicago: University of Chicago Press, 1948.

Weimer, David R. *The City as Metaphor*. New York: Random House, 1966.

Wells, Henry W. *The American Way of Poetry*. New York: Columbia University Press, 1943.

Welsch, Erwin K. *The Negro in the United States: A Research Guide*. Bloomington: Indiana University Press, 1965.

West, Ray B., Jr. *The Short Story in America, 1900–1950*. Chicago: Regnery, 1952.

Whitlow, Roger. *Black American Literature: A Critical History*. Chicago: Nelson-Hall, 1973.

Williams, Stanley. *The Spanish Background of American Literature*. 2 vols. New Haven: Yale University Press, 1955.

Wilson, Edmund. *Axel's Castle: A Study in the Imaginative Literature of 1870–1930*. New York: Scribner, 1931.

———. *Patriotic Gore: Studies in the Literature of the American Civil War*. London: Andre Deutsch, 1962.

———. *The Triple Thinkers*. New York: Oxford University Press, 1948.

Wilson, Garff B. *Three Hundred Years of American Drama and Theatre: From Ye Bear and Ye Cubb to Hair*. Englewood Cliffs, N.J.: Prentice-Hall, 1973.

Winters, Yvor. *In Defense of Reason*. Chicago and New York: Swallow & Morrow, 1947.

———. *Primitivism and Decadence*. New York: Arrow Editions, 1937.

Woodress, James, ed. *Eight American Authors: A Review of Research and Criticism*. Rev. ed. New York: Norton, 1971.

Woodress, James, ed., with the assistance of Townsend Ludington and Joseph Arpad. *Essays Mostly on Periodical Publishing in America: A Collection in Honor of Clarence Gohdes*. Durham, N.C.: Duke University Press, 1973.

Wright, Nathalia. *American Novelists in Italy: The Discoverers: Allston to James*. Philadelphia: University of Pennsylvania Press, 1965.

Yates, Norris, W. *The American Humorist: Conscience of the Twentieth Century*. Ames: Iowa State University Press, 1964.

Yatron, Michael. *America's Literary Revolt*. New York: Philosophical Library, 1959.

Young, Philip. *Three Bags Full: Essays in American Fiction*. New York: Harcourt Brace Jovanovich [1972].

Young, Thomas D., and Fine, Ronald E., eds. *American Literature: A Critical Survey*. 2 vols. New York: American Book, 1968.

Zesmer, David M. *Guide to English Literature from Beowulf through Chaucer and Medieval Drama*. New York: Barnes & Noble, 1961.

Ziff, Larzer. *The American 1890s*. New York: Viking, 1966.

Chapter-by-Chapter
Bibliographies

These bibliographies are designed to supplement and document the discussions in the text of this guide. To gather further bibliography the reader should consult chapter 13.

See pp. vii–x for list of abbreviations used.

1: EMILY DICKINSON

TEXTS. *The Poems of Emily Dickinson,* ed. Thomas H. Johnson, 3 vols. (Cambridge, Mass.: Harvard University Press, 1955); *The Letters of Emily Dickinson,* ed. Thomas H. Johnson and Theodora Ward, 3 vols. (Cambridge, Mass.: Harvard University Press, 1958).

BIOGRAPHY AND CRITICISM. Charles R. Anderson, *Emily Dickinson's Poetry* (New York: Holt, 1960), especially perceptive; Millicent Todd Bingham, *Ancestor's Brocades* (1945; reprint ed., New York: Dover, 1967), on the early editing of Dickinson's work; Jack L. Capps, *Emily Dickinson's Reading: 1836–1886* (Cambridge, Mass.: Harvard University Press, 1966); Richard Chase, *Emily Dickinson* (New York: Sloane, 1951); John Cody, *After Great Pain: The Inner Life of Emily Dickinson* (Cambridge, Mass.: Harvard University Press, Belknap, 1971); Denis Donoghue, *Emily Dickinson* (UMPAW: 1969); Douglas Duncan, *Emily Dickinson* (Edinburgh: Oliver & Boyd, 1965); Thomas W. Ford, *Heaven Beguiles the Tired: Death in the Poetry of Emily Dickinson* (University: University of Alabama Press, 1966); R. W. Franklin, *The Editing of Emily Dickinson: A Reconsideration* (Madison: University of Wisconsin Press, 1967); Albert J. Gelpi, *Emily Dickinson: The Mind of the Poet* (Cambridge, Mass.: Harvard University Press, 1965); Clark Griffith, *The Long Shadow: Emily Dickinson's Tragic Poetry* (Princeton: Princeton University Press, 1964); David Higgins, *Portrait of Emily Dickinson: The Poet and Her Prose* (New Brunswick, N.J.: Rutgers University Press, 1967), a study of the letters; Thomas H. Johnson, *Emily Dickinson: An Interpretive Biography* (Cambridge, Mass.: Harvard University Press, 1955), standard life, useful for criticism, too; Salamatullah Khan, *Emily Dickinson's Poetry: The Flood Subjects* (New Delhi: Aarti Book

Centre, 1969); Inder N. Kher, *The Landscape of Absence: Emily Dickinson's Poetry* (New Haven: Yale University Press, 1974); Jay Leyda, *The Years and Hours of Emily Dickinson,* 2 vols. (New Haven: Yale University Press, 1960), an important collection of biographical materials chronologically arranged; Brita Lindberg-Seyersted, *The Voice of the Poet: Aspects of Style in the Poetry of Emily Dickinson* (Cambridge, Mass.: Harvard University Press, 1968), useful for technical matters like rhyme, diction, syntax; Klaus Lubbers, *Emily Dickinson: The Critical Revolution* (Ann Arbor: University of Michigan Press, 1968), a study of the American and British reactions to Dickinson since 1862; Dolores Dyer Lucas, *Emily Dickinson and Riddle* (DeKalb: Northern Illinois University Press, 1969), on her use of an ancient mode of slantwise expression; Archibald MacLeish, Louise Bogan, and Richard Wilbur, *Emily Dickinson: Three Views,* with an introduction by Reginald F. French (Amherst, Mass.: Amherst College Press, 1960); Ruth Flanders McNaughton, *The Imagery of Emily Dickinson* (University of Nebraska Studies, 1949; n.s. no. 4); Ruth Miller, *The Poetry of Emily Dickinson* (Middletown, Conn.: Wesleyan University Press, 1968); Jean M. Mudge, *Emily Dickinson & the Image of Home* (Amherst: University of Massachusetts Press, 1975); John B. Pickard, *Emily Dickinson: An Introduction and Appreciation* (AACS, New York: Barnes & Noble, 1967), especially valuable for its many explications and its chapters on nature, immortality, and other themes; David T. Porter, *The Art of Emily Dickinson's Early Poetry* (Cambridge, Mass.: Harvard University Press, 1966), covering up to 1862; Richard B. Sewall, *The Life of Emily Dickinson,* 2 vols. (New York: Farrar, Straus & Giroux, 1974); William R. Sherwood, *Circumference and Circumstance in the Mind and Art of Emily Dickinson* (New York: Columbia University Press, 1968); Genevieve Taggard, *The Life and Mind of Emily Dickinson* (1930; reprint ed., New York: Cooper Square, 1967); Donald E. Thackrey, *Emily Dickinson's Approach to Poetry* (University of Nebraska Studies, 1954; n.s. no. 13); John E. Todd, *Emily Dickinson's Use of the Persona* (The Hague: Mouton, 1973); John E. Walsh, *The Hidden Life of Emily Dickinson* (New York: Simon & Schuster, 1971); Theodora Ward, *The Capsule of the Mind: Chapters in the Life of Emily Dickinson* (Cambridge, Mass.: Harvard University Press, 1961); Robert Weisbuch, *Emily Dickinson's Poetry* (Chicago: University of Chicago Press, 1975); Henry W. Wells, *Introduction to Emily Dickinson* (Chicago: Packard, 1947); George Frisbie Whicher, *This Was a Poet: A Critical Biography of Emily Dickinson* (1938; reprint ed., Ann Arbor: University of Michigan Press, 1957), still worth consulting for its explications and its chapters relating Dickinson to Puritanism, Emerson, and American humor.

COLLECTIONS OF CRITICISM. *Emily Dickinson: A Collection of Critical Essays,* ed. Richard B. Sewall (Englewood Cliffs, N.J.: Prentice-Hall, 1963), covering scholarship from 1924–1961; *The Recognition of Emily Dickinson: Selected Criticism since 1890,* ed. Caesar R. Blake and Carlton F. Wells (Ann Arbor: University of Michigan Press, 1964); *Critics on Emily Dickinson,* ed. Richard H. Rupp (Coral Gables: University of Miami Press, 1972).

EXPLICATIONS OF INDIVIDUAL POEMS. Thomas M. Davis has edited *14 by Emily Dickinson* (Glenview, Ill.: Scott, Foresman, 1964), a valuable collection of explications. Miscellaneous explications of thirty-one Dickinson poems are collected in *Expl Cyc* (GB), 1:55–88. Following are selected explications arranged alphabetically according to the title of the poem explicated: John P.

Kirby, "Dickinson's 'A Bird Came Down the Walk,' " *Expl* 2 (1944), item 61; Laurence Perrine, *Sound and Sense,* 2d ed. (New York: Harcourt, 1963), pp. 138–139 (for "Apparently with No Surprise"); Eugene Hollahan, "Dickinson's 'I Heard a Fly Buzz When I Died,' " *Expl* 25 (1966), item 6, which sees the fly as Satan's representative; James T. Connelly, "Dickinson's 'I Heard a Fly Buzz When I Died,' " *Expl* 25 (1966), item 34, on the symbolism of blue; Ronald Beck, "Dickinson's 'I Heard a Fly Buzz When I Died,' " *Expl* 26 (1967), item 31; William Howard, "Dickinson's 'I Never Saw a Moor,' " *Expl* 21 (1962), item 13; Zahava Karl Dorinson, " 'I Taste a Liquor Never Brewed': A Problem in Editing," *AL* 35 (1963): 363–365; A. Scott Garrow, "A Note on Manzanilla," *AL* 35 (1963): 366; Cecil D. Eby, " 'I Taste a Liquor Never Brewed': A Variant Reading,"*AL* 36 (1965): 516–518, suggesting that the *I* of the poem is a hummingbird; Leyda, 2:20, which notes passages from Emerson's "The Poet" that probably inspired this poem; Lloyd M. Davis, "Dickinson's 'I Taste a Liquor Never Brewed,' " *Expl* 23 (1965), item 53; Raymond G. Malbone, "Dickinson's 'I Taste a Liquor Never Brewed,' " *Expl* 26 (1967), item 14; Whicher, pp. 201–203 (for "Success Is Counted Sweetest"); Raymond J. Jordan, "Dickinson's 'The Bustle in a House,' " *Expl* 21 (1963), item 49; Henry F. Pommer, "Dickinson's 'The Soul Selects Her Own Society,' " *Expl* 3 (1945), item 32; M. Van Doren (GB), pp. 39–42; Paul Faris, "Dickinson's 'The Soul Selects Her Own Society,' " *Expl* 25 (1967), item 65; Simon Tugwell, "Dickinson's 'The Soul Selects Her Own Society,' " *Expl* 27 (1969), item 37; Will C. Jumper, "Dickinson's 'The Soul Selects Her Own Society,' " *Expl* 29 (1970), item 5; Elizabeth Bowman, "Dickinson's 'The Soul Selects Her Own Society,' " *Expl* 29 (1970), item 13. Other explications may be found by checking Kuntz, the annual checklist in *Expl,* and the following:

BIBLIOGRAPHIES. James Woodress in *Fifteen American Authors before 1900* (GB), pp. 139–168, an essay; Willis J. Buckingham, *Emily Dickinson: An Annotated Bibliography: Writings, Scholarship, Criticism, and Ana, 1830–1968* (Bloomington: Indiana University Press, 1970); Sheila T. Clendenning, *Emily Dickinson: A Bibliography, 1850–1966* (Serif Series; Kent, Oh.: Kent State University Press, 1968); *ALS;* and the annual checklist in the *Emily Dickinson Bulletin,* a quarterly (1968–).

CONCORDANCE. S. P. Rosenbaum has compiled *A Concordance to the Poems of Emily Dickinson* (Ithaca, N.Y.: Cornell University Press, 1964).

2: AMERICAN HUMORISTS, 1850–1900

Blair (GB: 1937) is still the best introduction to the subject. Also see the essays in Rubin (GB: 1973).

Charles Farrar Browne (Artemus Ward)

Artemus Ward: His Book (Santa Barbara, Calif.: Wallace Hebberd, 1964) has a seven-page introduction by Robert M. Hutchins. Helpful books are Don C. Seitz, *Artemus Ward* (New York: Harper, 1919) and James C. Austin, *Artemus Ward* (TUSAS: 1964). Austin stresses Browne's use of anecdotes, his Down East affinities, his accomplishment as a lecturer, and his influence on other humorists. Shorter studies include Curtis Dahl, "Artemus Ward: Comic Panoramist," *NEQ* 32 (1959):

476–485; David S. Hawes, "Artemus Ward Will Speak a Piece," *QJS* 50 (1964): 421–431, a good survey of the comic lectures; John J. Pullen, "Artemus Ward: The Man Who Made Lincoln Laugh," *Saturday Review,* February 7, 1976, pp. 19–24; John Q. Reed, "Artemus Ward: The Minor Writer in American Studies," *MQ* 7 (1966): 241–251. See James C. Austin, "Charles Farrar Browne (1834–1867)," *ALR* 5 (1972): 151–165 for bibliography.

Henry Wheeler Shaw

Uncle Sam's Josh, or Josh Billings on Practically Everything (Boston: Little, Brown, 1953) is edited by Donald Day. David B. Kesterson has written the fullest study: *Josh Billings (Henry Wheeler Shaw)* (TUSAS: 1973). Also see Joseph Jones, "Josh Billings' Notions on Humor," *Studies in English, University of Texas* (1943), pp. 148–161.

3. LOCAL COLOR

ANTHOLOGIES. *American Local Color Stories,* edited with an introduction by Harry R. Warfel and G. Harrison Orians (New York: American Book, 1941); *The Local Colorists: American Short Stories, 1857–1900,* edited with an introduction by Claude M. Simpson (New York: Harper, 1960).

STUDIES. Wallace Stegner, "Tales That Grew by the Village Green," *NYTBR,* May 22, 1960, pp. 1, 16, an essay-review of Simpson's anthology; Richard M. Weaver, "Realism and the Local Color Interlude," *GaR* 22 (1968): 301–305; Babette M. Levy, "Mutations in New England Local Color," *NEQ* 19 (1946): 338–358; Perry Westbrook, *Acres of Flint: Writers of Rural New England, 1870–1900* (Metuchen, N.J.: Scarecrow, 1951), on Jewett, Freeman, Stowe, and others; Claud B. Green, "The Rise and Fall of Local Color in Southern Literature," *Miss Q* 18 (1965): 1–6; Merrill A. Skaggs, *The Folk of Southern Fiction* (Athens: University of Georgia Press, 1972).

Also see Berthoff (GB: 1965), pp. 90–103.

BIBLIOGRAPHY. *LHUS* 3: 304–325; Lud, pp. 62–64; Simpson (above), pp. 17–20; Leary, s.v. *regionalism;* Rubin (GB: 1969), pp. 79–81.

Bret Harte

TEXTS. *The Writings of Bret Harte,* 20 vols. (Boston: Houghton Mifflin, 1896–1914); *Representative Selections* (New York: American Book, 1941), with introduction, annotated bibliography, and notes by Joseph B. Harrison; *The Letters of Bret Harte,* ed. Geoffrey Bret Harte (London: Hodder and Stoughton, n.d.); *Sketches of the Sixties by Bret Harte and Mark Twain,* 2d ed. (San Francisco: John Howell, 1927).

STUDIES. George R. Stewart, Jr.'s *Bret Harte: Argonaut and Exile* (Boston: Houghton Mifflin, 1931), an indispensable critical biography, should be supplemented with Stewart's entry on Harte in the *DAB* and with Franklin Walker, *San Francisco's Literary Frontier* (New York: Knopf, 1939). Also see Gustave O. Arlt, "Bret Harte—the Argonaut," *SoCalQ* 44 (1962): 17–30 and Patrick Morrow, *Bret Harte* (Western Writers Series; Boise, Id.: Boise State College, 1972). According to Margaret Duckett's exhaustive *Mark Twain and Bret Harte*

(Norman: University of Oklahoma Press, 1964), Twain was chiefly to blame for the rift between these former friends who had coauthored the play *Ah Sin* (1877).
"THE LUCK OF ROARING CAMP." Blair (GB: 1937), pp. 131–132, identifies its humorous elements. Cleanth Brooks, John T. Purser, and Robert Penn Warren, *An Approach to Literature,* 3d ed. (New York: Appleton, 1952), pp. 86–87, accuse Harte of sentimentalizing. Allen B. Brown's "The Christ Motif in *The Luck of Roaring Camp,*" *PMASAL* 46 (1961): 629–633, points to numerous biblical and Christian images. According to J. R. Boggan's "The Regeneration of 'Roaring Camp,' " *NCF* 22 (1967): 271–280, these images are intended as irony.
"TENNESSEE'S PARTNER." In "Harte's 'Tennessee's Partner,' " *Expl* 22 (1963), item 10, E. R. Hutchison takes issue with Brooks and Warren (1960), pp. 161–164.
BIBLIOGRAPHY. Patrick Morrow, "Bret Harte (1836–1902)," *ALR* 3 (1970): 167–177, an essay-review of Harte scholarship; Linda D. Barnett, "Bret Harte: An Annotated Bibliography of Secondary Comment," *ALR* 5 (1972): 189–320, 331–484.

George Washington Cable

TEXTS. Five first editions of Cable's books, including *Old Creole Days,* have been reprinted with introductions by Arlin Turner (Richmond, Va.: Garrett, 1970). Turner has also written the introduction to *The Grandissimes* (New York: Sagamore, 1957) and has edited Cable's *The Negro Question: A Selection of Writings on Civil Rights in the South* (Garden City, N.Y.: Doubleday, 1958) and *Cajuns and Creoles: Stories of Old Louisiana* (Garden City, N.Y.: Doubleday, 1959).
BOOKS ON CABLE. Lucy Leffingwell Cable Biklé (Cable's daughter), *George W. Cable: His Life and Letters* (New York: Scribner, 1928); Kjell Ekström, *George Washington Cable: A Study of His Early Life and Work* (Cambridge: Harvard University Press, American Institute in the University of Upsala, 1950), especially useful for Cable's treatment of the Creoles; Guy A. Cardwell, *Twins of Genius* (East Lansing: Michigan State College Press, 1953), on Cable's association with Twain; Arlin Turner, *George W. Cable: A Biography* (Durham, N.C.: Duke University Press, 1956), valuable for comments on individual writings; Philip Butcher, *George W. Cable: The Northampton Years* (New York: Columbia University Press, 1959); Arlin Turner, *Mark Twain and George W. Cable* (East Lansing: Michigan State University Press, 1960), letters by Twain and Cable with interchapters and notes by Turner; Philip Butcher, *George Washington Cable* (TUSAS: 1962), a good introduction; Louis D. Rubin, Jr., *George W. Cable* (Indianapolis: Bobbs-Merrill, Pegasus, 1969).
SHORTER STUDIES. Arlin Turner, *George W. Cable* (SoWS; Austin, Tx.: Steck-Vaughn, 1969); Howard W. Fulweiler, "Of Time and the River: 'Ancestral Nonsense' vs. Inherited Guilt in Cable's 'Belles Demoiselles Plantation,' " *MASJ* 7 (1966): 53–59.
BIBLIOGRAPHY. Philip Butcher, "George Washington Cable (1844–1925)," *ALR* 1 (1967): 13–19; Rubin (GB: 1969), pp. 165–166.

Joel Chandler Harris

TEXTS. *The Complete Tales of Uncle Remus,* with foreward by Richard Chase (Boston: Houghton Mifflin, 1955), the fullest one-vol. edition; *Joel Chandler Harris, Editor and Essayist: Miscellaneous Literary, Political and Social Writ-*

ings, ed. Julia Collier Harris (Chapel Hill: University of North Carolina Press, 1931).

BIOGRAPHY. Three important books are Julia Collier Harris, *The Life and Letters of Joel Chandler Harris* (Boston: Houghton Mifflin, 1918), by Harris's daughter-in-law; Robert L. Wiggins, *The Life of Joel Chandler Harris from Obscurity in Boyhood to Fame in Early Manhood* (1918; reprint ed., Detroit: Gale, 1969); and Paul M. Cousins, *Joel Chandler Harris: A Biography* (Baton Rouge: Louisiana State University Press, 1968).

COMMENTARY. John Stafford, "Patterns of Meaning in *Nights with Uncle Remus,*" *AL* 18 (1946): 89–108; Louise Dauner, "Myth and Humor in the Uncle Remus Fables," *AL* 20 (1948): 129–143; Bernard Wolfe, "Uncle Remus and the Malevolent Rabbit," *Commentary* 8 (July 1949): 31–41; Stella Brewer Brookes, *Joel Chandler Harris—Folklorist* (Athens: University of Georgia Press, 1950), with chapters on folk genres but with no mention of Thompson motif or Aarne-Thompson tale-type numbers; Sumner Ives, "Dialect Differentiation in the Stories of Joel Chandler Harris," *AL* 27 (1955): 88–96, proof that Harris's dialects identify a speaker's social class as well as his region; David A. Walton, "Joel Chandler Harris as Folklorist: A Reassessment," *KFQ* 11 (1966): 21–26; David A. Walton, "Folklore as Compensation: A Content Analysis of the Negro Animal Tale," *Journal of the Ohio Folklore Society* 1 (1966): 15–25; Darwin T. Turner, "Daddy Joel Harris and His Old-Time Darkies," *SLJ* 1 (1968): 20–41.

BIBLIOGRAPHY. Rubin (GB: 1969), pp. 212–214; Arlin Turner, "Joel Chandler Harris," *ALR* [1] no. 3 (1968): 18–23.

Sarah Orne Jewett

TEXTS. *The Uncollected Short Stories of Sarah Orne Jewett,* ed. Richard Cary (Waterville, Me.: Colby College Press, 1971); *The World of Dunnet Landing,* ed. David B. Green (Lincoln: University of Nebraska Press, 1962), containing the Pointed Fir sketches, plus five essays on Jewett and this work; *Deephaven and Other Stories,* edited with a seventeen-page introduction by Richard Cary (New Haven: College & University Press, 1966); *Sarah Orne Jewett Letters,* ed. Richard Cary, rev. & enl. ed. (Waterville, Me.: Colby College Press, 1967).

FULL-LENGTH STUDIES. The standard critical biography, *Sarah Orne Jewett* (Boston: Houghton Mifflin, 1929), is by Francis O. Matthiessen. Richard Cary's authoritative *Sarah Orne Jewett* (TUSAS: 1962) analyzes her work as a whole and her individual writings.

SHORTER STUDIES. Eleanor M. Smith, "The Literary Relationship of Sarah Orne Jewett and Willa Sibert Cather," *NEQ* 29 (1956): 472–492; Margaret F. Thorp, *Sarah Orne Jewett* (UMPAW: 1966), a useful pamphlet; Paul J. Eakin, "Sarah Orne Jewett and the Meaning of Country Life," *AL* 38 (1967): 508–531.

The Country of the Pointed Firs. Warner Berthoff, "The Art of Jewett's *Pointed Firs,*" *NEQ* 32 (1959): 598–632; Hyatt H. Waggoner, "The Unity of *The Country of the Pointed Firs,*" *TCL* 5 (1959): 67–73; Francis Fike, "An Interpretation of *Pointed Firs,*" *NEQ* 34 (1961): 478–491; Robin Magowan, "Pastoral and the Art of Landscape in *The Country of the Pointed Firs,*" *NEQ* 36 (1963): 229–240; Robin Magowan, "The Outer Island Sequence in *Pointed Firs,*" *CLQ,* ser. 6 (1964): 418–424, on the significance of chaps. 5–15.

BIBLIOGRAPHY. Cary, *Sarah Orne Jewett,* pp. 165–171 (annotated); John E. Frost,

"Sarah Orne Jewett Bibliography: 1949–1963," *CLQ,* ser. 6, no. 10 (1964): 405–417; Richard Cary, "Sarah Orne Jewett," *ALR* 1 (1967): 61–66; Clayton L. Eichelberger, "Sarah Orne Jewett (1849–1909): A Critical Bibliography of Secondary Comment," *ALR* 2 (1969): 189–262 (fully annotated).

Mary E. Wilkins Freeman

TEXTS. *The Best Stories of Mary E. Wilkins,* ed. Henry W. Lanier (New York: Harper, 1927); *A Humble Romance and Other Stories,* ed. Clarence Gohdes (Richmond, Va.: Garrett, 1969).

STUDIES. Edward Foster, *Mary E. Wilkins Freeman* (New York: Hendricks, 1956); Perry D. Westbrook, *Mary Wilkins Freeman* (TUSAS: 1967).

BIBLIOGRAPHY. Foster (above); Westbrook (above, annotated); Perry D. Westbrook, "Mary E. Wilkins Freeman" *ALR* 2 (1969): 139–142.

4: SOCIAL CRITICS

John William De Forest

TEXTS AND STUDIES. *Honest John Vane* (1960), *Playing the Mischief* (1961), and *Kate Beaumont* (1963) have been issued in the Monument edition of De Forest's works (State College, Pa.: Bald Eagle). All are edited with introductions by Joseph Jay Rubin. Posthumous books compiled from De Forest's many magazine contributions include *Witching Times* (a novel on the Salem witch trials), edited with introduction by Alfred Appel, Jr. (New Haven: College & University Press, 1967), and the autobiographical *A Volunteer's Adventures* (useful background for *Miss Ravenel's Conversion*), ed. James H. Crovshore, with introduction by Stanley T. Williams (New Haven: Yale University Press, 1946). *Miss Ravenel's Conversion from Secession to Loyalty* (New York: Rinehart, 1955) contains an important introduction by the editor, Gordon S. Haight. A full-length interpretive study is James F. Light, *John William De Forest* (TUSAS: 1965).

ANNOTATED BIBLIOGRAPHIES. Light (above); James F. Light. "John William De Forest (1826–1906)," *ALR*[1] no. 1 (1967): 32–35; "John William De Forest . . . A Critical Bibliography of Secondary Comment," *ALR* [1] no. 4 (1968): 1–56, compiled by the editors of *ALR*.

Henry Adams

TEXTS. *The Education of Henry Adams,* ed. with introduction and notes by Ernest Samuels (RivEd; Boston: Houghton Mifflin, 1974) is the best text; the Modern Library edition of *The Education* (New York: Random House, 1931) contains a useful index. *Esther* has been reprinted (Gainesville, Fla.: Scholars' Facsimiles & Reprints, 1938) with an introduction by Robert E. Spiller.

SOME COLLECTIONS OF LETTERS. *A Cycle of Adams Letters, 1861–1865* (1920), *Letters of Henry Adams, 1858–1891* (1930), and *Letters of Henry Adams, 1892–1918* (1938) were all edited by Worthington C. Ford and published by Houghton Mifflin (Boston and New York). Also see *Henry Adams and His Friends,* ed. Harold Dean Cater (Boston: Houghton Mifflin, 1947).

BIOGRAPHIES. The fullest life is a trilogy by Ernest Samuels: *The Young Henry Adams* (1948), *Henry Adams, The Middle Years* (1958), and *Henry Adams, the Major*

Phase (1964), all Cambridge, Mass.: Harvard University Press. Also see Elizabeth Stevenson, *Henry Adams, a Biography* (New York: Macmillan, 1956).

FULL-LENGTH COMMENTARIES. A good starting point is George Hochfield's *Henry Adams: An Introduction and Interpretation* (AACS; New York: Barnes & Noble, 1962), which devotes a chapter to each of the important works. Other interpretive books are Max I. Baym, *The French Education of Henry Adams* (New York: Columbia University Press, 1951); John J. Conder, *A Formula of His Own: Henry Adams's Literary Experiment* (Chicago: University of Chicago Press, 1970); Robert A. Hume, *Runaway Star: An Appreciation of Henry Adams* (Ithaca, N.Y.: Cornell University Press, 1951); William H. Jordy, *Henry Adams: Scientific Historian* (New Haven: Yale University Press, 1952); J. C. Levenson, *The Mind and Art of Henry Adams* (Boston: Houghton Mifflin, 1957); Melvin Lyon, *Symbol and Idea in Henry Adams* (Lincoln: University of Nebraska Press, 1970); Ernst Scheyer, *The Circle of Henry Adams: Art & Artists* (Detroit: Wayne State University Press, 1970); Vern Wagner, *The Suspension of Henry Adams* (Detroit: Wayne State University Press, 1969), noteworthy for its attention to Adams's humor.

SHORTER STUDIES. Anderson (GB: 1965): 317–341, a perceptive analysis of *Chartres* and *The Education;* Louis Auchincloss, *Henry Adams* (UMPAW: 1971); Gerrit H. Roelofs, "Henry Adams: Pessimism and the Intelligent Use of Doom," *ELH* 17 (1950): 214–239, especially useful on the function of Adams's assertions of failure; Kenneth MacLean, "Window and Cross in Henry Adams' *Education,*" *UTQ* 28 (1959): 322–344, an interesting study of imagery.

BIBLIOGRAPHY. Charles Vandersee, "Henry Adams (1838–1918)," *ALR* 2 (1969): 89–120; and *ALR* 8 (1975): 13–34; Earl N. Harbert, "Henry Adams," in *Fifteen American Authors before 1900* (GB), pp. 3–36.

5: LITERARY REALISTS

Especially pertinent, since it concentrates on Twain, Howells, and James, is *The Illusion of Life: American Realism as a Literary Form* (Charlottesville: University Press of Virginia, 1969), by Harold H. Kolb, Jr. Also see *American Literary Realism, 1870–1910* (a periodical begun in 1963); William R. Linneman's "Satires of American Realism, 1880–1900," *AL* 34 (1962): 80–93; and the following items in our General Bibliography: Current-Garcia and Patrick (1962); Ziff (1966); Knight (1951); Pizer (1966); Berthoff (1965); Cady (1971); Robert Falk, "Rise of Realism, 1871–1891," in Clark, *Transitions,* pp. 379–442.

Samuel Clemens (Mark Twain)

TEXTS. *Works of Mark Twain,* published jointly by the presses of the universities of Iowa and California (1972–), is designed to be definitive. *The Mark Twain Papers,* ed. Frederick Anderson (Berkeley: University of California Press, 1967–) is a much-needed collection of previously maledited and unpublished works. In *Mark Twain's Hannibal, Huck & Tom* (Berkeley: University of California Press, 1969) editor Walter Blair provides manuscript sources for the stories about Huckleberry Finn, Tom Sawyer, and their world. Edited texts of the novels and other writings, too numerous for listing here, may be found in such bibliographies as Beebe and Feaster (below). *Mark Twain's Autobiography,* ed. Albert B. Paine, 2 vols. (New York: Harper, 1924), is entertaining but frequently unreliable.

BIOGRAPHY. An excellent starting point is DeLancey Ferguson, *Mark Twain, Man and Legend* (1943; reprint ed., New York: Atheneum, Russell & Russell, 1965). Also see Albert B. Paine, *Mark Twain: A Biography,* 3 vols. (New York: Harper, 1912); Van Wyck Brooks, *The Ordeal of Mark Twain* (1920; rev. ed., New York: Dutton, 1933), which began a widespread controversy by maintaining that Twain was hindered by his mother, his wife, and his frontier environment from becoming a first-rate artist; Clara Clemens, *My Father, Mark Twain* (New York: Harper, 1931); Bernard DeVoto, *Mark Twain's America* (Boston: Little, Brown, 1932), which attacks Brooks by viewing Twain as primarily a frontier humorist; Minnie M. Brashear, *Mark Twain, Son of Missouri* (1934; reprint ed., New York: Atheneum, Russell & Russell, 1964); Ivan Benson, *Mark Twain's Western Years* (Stanford, Calif.: Stanford University Press, 1938); Kenneth R. Andrews, *Nook Farm: Mark Twain's Hartford Circle* (Cambridge, Mass.: Harvard University Press, 1950); Henry S. Canby, *Turn West, Turn East* (Boston: Houghton Mifflin, 1951), on Twain and James; Dixon Wecter, *Sam Clemens of Hannibal* (Boston: Houghton Mifflin, 1952), the best work on Twain's youth; Hamlin Hill, *Mark Twain: God's Fool* (New York: Harper & Row, 1973), on Twain's last decade; Justin Kaplan, *Mark Twain and His World* (New York: Simon & Schuster, 1974), copiously illustrated; Caroline T. Harnsberger, *Mark Twain, Family Man* (New York: Citadel, 1960); Milton Meltzer, *Mark Twain Himself: A Pictorial Biography* (New York: T. Y. Crowell, 1960); *A Casebook on Mark Twain's Wound,* ed. Lewis Leary (New York: T. Y. Crowell, 1962), documents in the Brooks-DeVoto controversy and its aftermath; Paul Fatout, *Mark Twain in Virginia City* (Bloomington: Indiana University Press, 1964); Edward Wagenknecht, *Mark Twain, the Man and His Work* (1935; 3d ed., Norman: University of Oklahoma Press, 1967); Dewey Ganzel, *Mark Twain Abroad: The Cruise of the "Quaker City"* (Chicago: University of Chicago Press, 1968).

COLLECTIONS OF CRITICISM. *Mark Twain: Selected Criticism,* ed. Arthur L. Scott (Dallas, Tex.: Southern Methodist University Press, 1955); *Mark Twain: A Collection of Critical Essays,* ed. Henry Nash Smith (TCV; Englewood Cliffs, N. J.: Prentice-Hall, 1963); *Discussions of Mark Twain,* ed. Guy A. Cardwell (Lexington, Mass.: Heath, 1963); *Mark Twain: A Profile,* ed. Justin Kaplan (New York: Hill & Wang, 1967); *Mark Twain: The Critical Heritage,* ed. Frederick Anderson (New York: Barnes & Noble, 1971); *Critics on Mark Twain,* ed. David B. Kesterson (Coral Gables, Fla.: University of Miami Press, 1973).

STUDIES. Howard G. Baetzhold, *Mark Twain and John Bull* (Bloomington: Indiana University Press, 1970); Frank Baldanza, *Mark Twain: An Introduction and Interpretation* (AACS; New York: Barnes & Noble, 1961); Gladys C. Bellamy, *Mark Twain as a Literary Artist* (Norman: University of Oklahoma Press, 1950); Blair (GB:1937), pp. 147–162, analysis of Twain's humor; Thomas Blues, *Mark Twain & the Community* (Lexington: University Press of Kentucky, 1970); Edgar M. Branch, *The Literary Apprenticeship of Mark Twain* (Urbana: University of Illinois Press, 1950); *Clemens of The Call: Mark Twain in San Francisco,* ed. Edgar M. Branch (Berkeley: University of California Press, 1969); Louis J. Budd, *Mark Twain: Social Philosopher* (Bloomington: Indiana University Press, 1962); Pascal Covici, Jr., *Mark Twain's Humor: The Image of a World* (Dallas, Tex.: Southern Methodist University Press, 1962); James M.

Cox, *Mark Twain: The Fate of Humor* (Princeton: Princeton University Press, 1966); Bernard DeVoto, *Mark Twain at Work* (Cambridge, Mass.: Harvard University Press, 1942), standard; Allison Ensor, *Mark Twain & the Bible* (Lexington: University of Kentucky Press, 1969); Paul Fatout, *Mark Twain on the Lecture Circuit* (Bloomington: Indiana University Press, 1960); Philip S. Foner, *Mark Twain, Social Critic* (New York: International Publishers, 1958); William M. Gibson, *The Art of Mark Twain* (New York: Oxford University Press, 1976); Sydney J. Krause, *Mark Twain as Critic* (Baltimore: Johns Hopkins Press, 1967); Lewis Leary, *Mark Twain* (UMPAW: 1960), a pamphlet; S. B. Liljegren, *The Revolt against Romanticism in American Literature as Evidenced in the Works of S. L. Clemens* (1947; reprint ed., New York: Haskell, 1964); E. Hudson Long, *Mark Twain Handbook* (New York: Hendricks, 1957), with chapters on biographies, "Backgrounds," "The Man of Letters," "Mind and Art," "Fundamental Ideas," and "Mark Twain's Place in Literature"; Fred W. Lorch, *The Trouble Begins at Eight: Mark Twain's Lecture Tours* (Ames: Iowa State University Press, 1968); Kenneth S. Lynn, *Mark Twain and Southwestern Humor* (Boston: Little, Brown, 1960), stimulating; D. M. McKeithan, *Court Trials in Mark Twain and Other Essays* (The Hague: Martinus Nijhoff, 1958); Arthur G. Pettit, *Mark Twain and the South* (Lexington: University Press of Kentucky, 1974); Robert Regan, *Unpromising Heroes: Mark Twain and His Characters* (Berkeley: University of California Press, 1966); Franklin R. Rogers, *Mark Twain's Burlesque Patterns* (Dallas, Tex.: Southern Methodist University Press, 1960); Roger B. Salomon, *Twain and the Image of History* (New Haven: Yale University Press, 1961); Arthur L. Scott, *Mark Twain at Large* (Chicago: Regnery, 1969), on the effect of Twain's life abroad; Henry Nash Smith, *Mark Twain: The Development of a Writer* (Cambridge, Mass.: Harvard University Press, 1962), an important genetic study; William C. Spengemann, *Mark Twain and the Backwoods Angel: The Matter of Innocence in the Works of Samuel L. Clemens* (Kent, Oh.: Kent State University Press, 1966); Albert E. Stone, Jr., *The Innocent Eye: Childhood in Mark Twain's Imagination* (New Haven: Yale University Press, 1961); Victor R. West, *Folklore in the Works of Mark Twain* (Studies in Language, Literature, and Criticism, no. 10; Lincoln: University of Nebraska, 1930), an eighty-seven-page survey; Robert A. Wiggins, *Mark Twain: Jackleg Novelist* (Seattle: University of Washington Press, 1964).

"THE CELEBRATED JUMPING FROG OF CALAVERAS COUNTY." Edgar M. Branch, " 'My Voice Is Still for Setchell': A Background Study of 'Jim Smiley and His Jumping Frog,' " *PMLA* 82 (1967): 591–601, with a full bibliographical note.

Innocents Abroad. In his review for the *Overland Monthly* 4 (1870): 100–101 Bret Harte noted that Twain's "mock assumption of a righteous indignation" was "always ludicrously disproportionate to the cause." Several studies analyze the differences between this book and the original travel letters: L. T. Dickinson, "Mark Twain's Revisions in Writing *The Innocents Abroad*," *AL* 19 (1947): 139–157; Calder M. Pickett, "Mark Twain as Journalist and Literary Man: A Contrast," *JQ* 38 (1961): 59–66. These letters have been collected in *Traveling with the Innocents Abroad: Mark Twain's Original Reports from Europe and the Holy Land,* ed. Daniel M. McKeithan (Norman: University of Oklahoma Press, 1958).

The Gilded Age. The definitive study is Bryant Morey French, *Mark Twain and "The Gilded Age"* (Dallas, Tex.: Southern Methodist University Press, 1965).

Roughing It. Franklin R. Rogers, "The Road to Reality: Burlesque Travel Literature and Mark Twain's *Roughing It,*" *BNYPL* 67 (1963): 155–168; *Mark Twain's Frontier,* ed. James E. Camp and X. J. Kennedy (New York: Holt, 1963), a sourcebook; Rodman W. Paul's introduction to the Rinehart edition (1953) of *Roughing It.*

The Adventures of Tom Sawyer. Walter Blair's theory that the story achieves unity through Tom's maturation ("On the Structure of Tom Sawyer," *MP* 37 [1939]: 75–88) is upheld by Hamlin Hill's study of the manuscript: "The Composition and the Structure of *Tom Sawyer,*" *AL* 32 (1961): 380–392. In chapter 4 of *Mark Twain & Huck Finn* Blair later showed how the Hannibal material that went into *Tom Sawyer* was modified by Twain's deceptive memory, his moods, reading, and previous writing. Other studies include "Tom Sawyer and His Cousins," chapter 3 of Albert E. Stone's *Innocent Eye;* Robert Tracy, "Myth and Reality in *The Adventures of Tom Sawyer,*" *SoR,* n.s. 4 (1968): 530–541; William B. Dillingham, "Setting and Theme in *Tom Sawyer,*" *MTJ* 12, no. 2 (1964): 6–8; Howard S. Mott, Jr., "The Origin of Aunt Polly," *PW* 134 (1938): 1821–1823.

Life on the Mississippi. Salomon, *Twain and the Image of History,* pp. 74–94; Paul Schmidt, "River vs. Town: Mark Twain's *Old Times on the Mississippi,*" *NCF* 15 (1960): 95–111; Dewey Ganzel, "Twain, Travel Books, and *Life on the Mississippi,*" *AL* 34 (1962): 40–55; Barriss Mills, "*Old Times on the Mississippi* as an Initiation Story," *CE* 25 (1964): 283–289.

Adventures of Huckleberry Finn. Scholars cited in our analysis are represented in the following collections of criticism: *Mark Twain's "Huckleberry Finn,"* ed. Barry A. Marks (Problems in American Civilization; Lexington, Mass.: Heath, 1959); *Huckleberry Finn: Text, Sources, and Criticism,* ed. Kenneth S. Lynn (New York: Harcourt, 1961); *Adventures of Huckleberry Finn: An Annotated Text, Backgrounds and Sources, Essays in Criticism,* ed. Sculley Bradley, Richmond Croom Beatty, and E. Hudson Long (Norton Critical Ed.; New York: Norton, n.d.); *Huck Finn and His Critics,* ed. Richard Lettis, Robert F. McDonnell, and William E. Morris (New York: Macmillan, 1962); *Twentieth Century Interpretations of "Adventures of Huckleberry Finn,"* ed. Claude M. Simpson (Englewood Cliffs, N.J.: Prentice-Hall, 1968); *The Art of Huckleberry Finn: Text, Sources, Criticism,* ed. Hamlin Hill and Walter Blair, 2d ed. (San Francisco: Chandler, 1969); *Adventures of Huckleberry Finn,* ed. James K. Bowen and Richard Van Der Beets (Glenview, Ill.: Scott, Foresman, 1970), containing abstracts of criticisms; *The Merrill Studies in Huckleberry Finn,* ed. John C. Gerber (Columbus, Oh.: Merrill, 1971). Other studies cited are Helmut E. Gerber, "Twain's *Huckleberry Finn,*" *Expl* 12 (1954), item 28; Hoffman, *Form and Fable,* pp. 317–350; Jose Barchilon and Joel S. Kovel, "*Huckleberry Finn:* A Psychoanalytic Study," *Journal of the American Psychoanalytic Association* 14 (1966): 775–814; Olin H. Moore, "Mark Twain and Don Quixote," *PMLA* 37 (1922): 324–346; James P. McIntyre, "Three Practical Jokes: A Key to Huck's Changing Attitude toward Jim," *MFS* 14 (1968): 33–37; Victor A. Doyno, "Over Twain's Shoulder: The Composition and Structure of *Huckleberry Finn,*" *MFS* 14 (1968): 3–9. Also see George C. Carrington, Jr., *The Dramatic Unity of "Huckleberry Finn"* (Columbus: Ohio State University Press, 1976); Walter Blair's *Mark Twain & "Huck Finn"* (Berkeley: University of California Press, 1960), an exhaustive look into the background of this novel, has chapters on such topics as the Duke and the Dauphin, the Grangerfords, the Bricksville mob, and the Wilks "funeral orgies." On pp. 424–427 there is a large unannotated bibliography of *Huckleberry Finn* studies.

The Connecticut Yankee. Blair (GB: 1942), pp. 202–209, explains that Twain was satirizing policies opposed by Grover Cleveland. In "A Connecticut Yankee in King Arthur's Court: The Machinery of Self-Preservation," *YR* 50 (1960): 89–102, James M. Cox sees the ending of the novel as symbolizing the death of Twain's obsession with the Paige typesetting machine. Charles S. Holmes in "*A Connecticut Yankee in King Arthur's Court:* Mark Twain's Fable of Uncertainty," *SAQ* 61 (1962): 462–472 finds Twain retreating into the world of childhood and dreams as he worried about mankind and his own career. Also see Henry Nash Smith, *Mark Twain's Fable of Progress: Political and Economic Ideas in "A Connecticut Yankee"* (New Brunswick, N.J.: Rutgers University Press, 1964); James D. Williams, "The Use of History in Mark Twain's *A Connecticut Yankee*," *PMLA* 80 (1965): 102–110, on Twain's reading; Reid Maynard, "Mark Twain's Ambivalent Yankee," *MTJ* 14, no. 3 (1968–1969): 1–5, which reviews the criticism.

Pudd'nhead Wilson. Especially comprehensive is Robert Rowlette, *Twain's "Pudd'nhead Wilson": The Development and Design* (Bowling Green, Oh.: Bowling Green University Popular Press, 1971). Also see Florence B. Leaver, "Mark Twain's Pudd'nhead Wilson," *MTJ* 10, no. 2 (1956): 14–20; Frederick Anderson's introduction (pp. vii–xxxii) to a facsimile edition of this novel (San Francisco: Chandler, 1968); George M. Spangler, "*Pudd'nhead Wilson:* A Parable of Property," *AL* 42 (1970): 28–37. Philip C. Kolin has compiled "Mark Twain's *Pudd'nhead Wilson:* A Selected Checklist," *BB* 28 (1971): 58–59.

The Mysterious Stranger. John S. Tuckey's *Mark Twain's Mysterious Stranger and the Critics* (Belmont, Calif.: Wadsworth, 1968), a collection of criticism, was preceded by his *Mark Twain and Little Satan* (West Lafayette, Ind.: Purdue University Studies, 1963), an admirable piece of detective work that reversed Bernard DeVoto's dating of the various manuscripts and revealed the fraudulent nature of the Paine-Duneka version. Tuckey's findings are corroborated in *Mark Twain's Mysterious Stranger Manuscripts,* edited with an informative introduction by William M. Gibson (Mark Twain Papers; Berkeley: University of California Press, 1969), which prints the holograph versions for the first time.

OTHER STORIES. Clinton S. Burhans, Jr., "The Sober Affirmation of Mark Twain's Hadleyburg," *AL* 34 (1962): 375–384; Darwin H. Shrell, "Twain's Howl and His Bluejays," in *Essays in Honor of Esmond Linworth Marilla,* ed. Thomas A. Kirby and William J. Olive (Baton Rouge: Louisiana State University Press, 1970), pp. 283–290, on "Baker's Blue-Jay Yarn"; John A. Burrison, *"The Golden Arm": The Folk Tale and Its Literary Use by Mark Twain and Joel C. Harris* (Atlanta: Georgia State University Research Paper, 1968).

BIBLIOGRAPHIES. Merle Johnson, *A Bibliography of the Works of Mark Twain,* rev. ed. (New York: Harper, 1935); Roger Asselineau, *The Literary Reputation of Mark Twain from 1910 to 1950* (Paris: Didier, 1954), containing a critical essay (pp. 19–65) and annotated bibliography of 1,333 items arranged chronologically; Harry Hayden Clark, "Mark Twain," in Woodress, ed., *Eight American Authors* (GB), pp. 273–320, a bibliographical essay; E. H. Long, *Mark Twain Handbook,* annotated bibliographies supplementing each chapter; Wagenknecht, *Mark Twain,* pp. 247–264; Maurice Beebe and John Feaster, "Criticism of Mark

Twain: A Selected Checklist," *MFS* 14 (1968): 93–139; *BAL; ALS,* with an annual chapter on Twain.

OTHER TOOLS. Useful summaries are in Robert L. Gale, *Plots and Characters in the Works of Mark Twain,* 2 vols. (Hamden, Conn.: Archon, 1973). *A Mark Twain Lexicon,* compiled by Robert L. Ramsay and Frances G. Emberson (1938; reprint ed., New York: Atheneum, Russell & Russell, 1963) has sections on Twain's Americanisms, new words, and archaisms.

William Dean Howells

TEXTS. "Howells's Unpublished Prefaces" to Harper's library edition were edited by George Arms in *NEQ* 17 (1944): 580–591. *A Selected Edition of William Dean Howells* (Bloomington: Indiana University Press, 1968–) is under the general editorship of Edwin H. Cady. Clara M. and Rudolf Kirk have edited a good one-volume collection: *William Dean Howells: Representative Selections, with Introduction, Bibliography and Notes* (1950; rev. ed., American Century series, New York: Hill & Wang, 1961). Among various editions of *The Rise of Silas Lapham* are those introduced by E. H. Cady (RivEd; Boston: Houghton Mifflin, 1957), Rudolf and Clara M. Kirk (New York: Collier, 1962), George Arms (Rinehart ed.; New York: Holt, Rinehart & Winston, 1949), and Harry Hayden Clark (New York: Modern Library, 1951). Also see *A Hazard of New Fortunes,* with an introduction by Tony Tanner (New York: Oxford University Press, 1965) and by George W. Arms (New York: Dutton, Everyman, 1952); *Indian Summer,* with an introduction by William M. Gibson (New York: Dutton, Everyman, 1958); *Criticism and Fiction and Other Essays,* ed. Clara M. and Rudolf Kirk (New York: New York University Press, 1959); *My Mark Twain: Reminiscences and Criticisms,* ed. Marilyn A. Baldwin (Baton Rouge: Louisiana State University Press, 1967); *A Modern Instance,* ed. William M. Gibson (Riv Ed; Boston: Houghton Mifflin, 1957). *Life in Letters of William Dean Howells,* 2 vols. (1928; reprint ed., New York: Atheneum, Russell & Russell, 1968), edited by his daughter Mildred Howells, is an important collection of letters.

BIOGRAPHIES. Two volumes by Edwin H. Cady comprise the definitive critical biography of Howells: *The Road to Realism: The Early Years, 1837–1885* (Syracuse, N.Y.: Syracuse University Press, 1956) and *The Realist at War: The Mature Years, 1885–1920* (Syracuse, N.Y.: Syracuse University Press, 1958). It should be consulted for literary explication as well as background. Also see Edward Wagenknecht, *William Dean Howells: The Friendly Eye* (New York: Oxford University Press, 1969), a psychograph, and Kenneth S. Lynn, *William Dean Howells: An American Life* (New York: Harcourt Brace Jovanovich, 1971).

COLLECTIONS OF CRITICISM. *Howells: A Century of Criticism,* ed. Kenneth E. Eble (Dallas, Tex.: Southern Methodist University Press, 1962); *The War of the Critics over William Dean Howells,* ed. Edwin H. Cady and David L. Frazier (Evanston, Ill.: Row, 1962).

COMMENTARY. George N. Bennett, *William Dean Howells: The Development of a Novelist* (Norman: University of Oklahoma Press, 1959); George N. Bennett, *The Realism of William Dean Howells, 1889–1920* (Nashville, Tenn.: Vanderbilt University Press, 1973); George C. Carrington, Jr., *The Immense Complex*

Drama: The World and Art of the Howells Novel (Columbus: Ohio State University Press, 1966); Everett Carter, *Howells and the Age of Realism* (Philadelphia: Lippincott, 1954); Delmar G. Cooke, *William Dean Howells: A Critical Study* (1922; reprint ed., New York: Atheneum, Russell & Russell, 1967); James L. Dean, *Howells' Travels toward Art* (Albuquerque: University of New Mexico Press, 1970), on the travel writings; Oscar W. Firkins, *William Dean Howells: A Study* (1924; reprint ed., New York: Russell & Russell, 1963); Olov W. Fryckstedt, *In Quest of America: A Study of Howells' Early Development as a Novelist* (Cambridge, Mass.: Harvard University Press, 1958), which concludes with the year 1882; William McMurray, *The Literary Realism of William Dean Howells* (Crosscurrents; Carbondale: Southern Illinois University Press, 1967); Kermit Vanderbilt, *The Achievement of William Dean Howells* (Princeton: Princeton University Press, 1968). Also see William M. Gibson, *William Dean Howells* (UMPAW: 1967); Clara M. and Rudolf Kirk, *William Dean Howells* (TUSAS: 1962); James L. Woodress, Jr., *Howells and Italy* (Durham, N.C.: Duke University Press, 1952); Robert L. Hough, *The Quiet Rebel: William Dean Howells as Social Commentator* (Lincoln: University of Nebraska Press, 1959); Clara M. Kirk, *W. D. Howells, Traveler from Altruria, 1889–1894* (New Brunswick, N.J.: Rutgers University Press, 1962), useful background for the Altrurian novels; Clara M. Kirk, *W. D. Howells and Art in His Time* (New Brunswick, N.J.: Rutgers University Press, 1965), an interesting study of Howells's relations with art and artists.

The Rise of Silas Lapham. Donald Pizer, "The Ethical Unity of *The Rise of Silas Lapham*," *AL* 32 (1960): 322–327; William R. Manierre II, "*The Rise of Silas Lapham:* Retrospective Discussion as Dramatic Technique," *CE* 23 (1962): 357–361; L. E. Scanlon, "*The Rise of Silas Lapham:* Literalism or Art?" *NEQ* 35 (1962): 376–390; Kermit Vanderbilt, "Howells among the Brahmins: Why 'The Bottom Dropped Out' during *The Rise of Silas Lapham*," *NEQ* 35 (1962): 291–317; John E. Hart, "The Commonplace as Heroic in *The Rise of Silas Lapham*," *MFS* 8 (1962–1963): 375–383; Richard Coanda, "Howells' *The Rise of Silas Lapham*," *Expl* 22 (1963), item 16, an analysis of diabolic motifs; James E. Bryan, "The Chronology of *Silas Lapham*," *AN&Q* 4 (1965): 56; G. Thomas Tanselle, "The Architecture of *The Rise of Silas Lapham*," *AL* 37 (1966): 430–457, exhaustive proof of this novel's careful structure; G. T. Tanselle, "The Boston Seasons of Silas Lapham," *SNNTS* 1 (1969): 60–66.

STUDIES OF OTHER INDIVIDUAL WORKS. Alma J. Payne, "The Family in the Utopia of William Dean Howells," *GaR* 15 (1961): 217–229 on the "Altrurian" novels; William J. Free, "Howells' 'Editha' and Pragmatic Belief," *SSF* 3 (1966): 285–292; Alexander Evanoff, "William Dean Howells' Economic Chance-World in *A Hazard of New Fortunes:* An American Classic Reviewed," *Discourse* 5 (1962): 382–388; Kermit Vanderbilt, "Marcia Gaylord's Electra Complex: A Footnote to Sex in Howells," *AL* 34 (1962): 365–374; James W. Gargano, "*A Modern Instance:* The Twin Evils of Society," *TSLL* 4 (1962): 399–407.

BIBLIOGRAPHY. William M. Gibson and George Arms, *A Bibliography of William Dean Howells* (New York: New York Public Library, 1948); James Woodress and Stanley P. Anderson, "A Bibliography of Writing about William Dean Howells," *ALR* special no. (1969): 1–139, annotated; Vito J. Brenni, *William Dean Howells: A Bibliography* (Metuchen, N.J.: Scarecrow, 1973); George Fortenberry, "William Dean Howells," in *Fifteen American Authors before 1900* (GB), pp. 229–244.

Henry James

TEXTS. There is no single edition of James's work that includes all the areas he worked in. There are two major editions of his fiction. The twenty-four-volume New York edition (New York: Scribner, 1907–1909) includes James's final revisions and his Prefaces; two volumes were added after his death, so that the complete edition consists of twenty-six volumes. The edition edited by Percy Lubbock, 35 vols. (New York: Macmillan, 1921–1923) is based on the New York edition but adds all the fiction published in James's lifetime that he did not include in the New York edition. The New York edition was gradually reissued and completed in 1964. For a comparison of the two editions see Leon Edel and Dan H. Laurence, *A Bibliography of Henry James* (London: R. Hart-Davis, 1961). Edel edited *The Complete Tales of Henry James,* 12 vols. (Philadelphia: Lippincott, 1962–1965). Specialized collections of the fiction include *The Ghostly Tales of Henry James,* ed. Leon Edel (New York: Grossett & Dunlap, 1963); *Stories of Writers and Artists,* ed. F. O. Matthiessen (New York: New Directions, 1946); *The Portable Henry James,* ed. M. D. Zabel (New York: Viking, 1951); and *The Henry James Reader,* ed. Leon Edel (New York: Scribner, 1965). Edel also edited *The Complete Plays of Henry James* (Philadelphia: Lippincott, 1949). James's unfinished autobiography has been edited by F. J. Dupee (New York: Criterion, 1956).

A fair amount of James's criticism has been collected. R. P. Blackmur edited and commented on James's Prefaces in *The Art of the Novel* (New York: Scribner, 1934). F. O. Matthiessen and Kenneth Murdock edited *The Notebooks of Henry James* (New York: Oxford University Press, 1947). Edel edited essays, reviews, and articles by James in *The Future of the Novel* (New York: Knopf, Vintage, 1956), *The American Essays of Henry James* (New York: Knopf, Vintage, 1956), and *The House of Fiction* (London: R. Hart-Davis, 1957). James E. Miller collected many of James's comments on fiction and arranged them according to subject matter in *Theory of Fiction: Henry James* (Lincoln: University of Nebraska Press, 1972).

STUDIES. For bibliography see Robert L. Gale's comprehensive bibliographical essay in *Eight American Authors* that discusses James scholarship through 1969 and Beatrice Ricks's *Henry James* (Metuchen, N.J.: Scarecrow, 1975). In addition see Edel and Laurence (above); *Modern Fiction Studies* for Spring 1957 and Spring 1966; and the June 1957 issue of *Nineteenth Century Fiction*. Introductions to James's work are Bruce McElderry, *Henry James* (TUSAS: 1965) and D. W. Jefferson, *Henry James* (New York: Grove, 1962). The most important biography of James is Edel's monumental five-volume study (Philadelphia: Lippincott, 1953–1972). Other biographical studies include F. W. Dupee, *Henry James* (New York: Sloane, 1951); H. M. Hyde, *Henry James at Home* (New York: Farrar, Straus & Giroux, 1969); F. O. Matthiessen, *The James Family* (New York: Knopf, 1947); C. H. Grattan, *The Three Jameses* (New York: New York University Press, 1932); and Simon Nowell-Smith, *The Legend of the Master* (New York: Scribner, 1948). Criticism of James's work is voluminous.

Important early studies are J. W. Beach, *The Method of Henry James* (New Haven: Yale University Press, 1918; enlarged ed., West Orange, N.J.: A. Saifer, 1954) and Van Wyck Brooks, *The Pilgrimage of Henry James* (New York: Dutton, 1925). Of major importance are F. O. Matthiessen, *Henry James: The Major Phase* (New York: Oxford University Press, 1944); Oscar Cargill, *The Novels of Henry James* (New York: Macmillan, 1961); and Dorothea Krook, *The Ordeal of Consciousness in Henry James* (New York: Cambridge University Press, 1962). Other full-length studies are listed below in alphabetical order; generally the subtitle indicates the critic's special emphasis. Quentin Anderson, *The American Henry James* (New Brunswick, N. J.: Rutgers University Press, 1957); Martha Banta, *Henry James and the Occult* (Bloomington: Indiana University Press, 1972); Theodora Bosanquet, *Henry James at Work* (Honolulu: Hogarth, 1927); Peter Buitenhuis, *The Grasping Imagination: The American Writings of Henry James* (Toronto: Toronto University Press, 1970); Seymour Chatman, *The Later Style of Henry James* (Oxford: Blackwell, 1972); J. A. Clair, *The Ironic Dimension in the Fiction of Henry James* (Pittsburgh: Duquesne University Press, 1965); F. C. Crews, *The Tragedy of Manners* (New Haven: Yale University Press, 1957); Leon Edel, ed., *Henry James and H. G. Wells* (Urbana: University of Illinois Press, 1958); Michael Egan, *Henry James: The Ibsen Years* (London: Vision Press, 1972); R. L. Gale, *The Caught Image: Figurative Language in the Fiction of Henry James* (Chapel Hill: University of North Carolina Press, 1964); Maxwell Geismar, *Henry James and the Jacobites* (Boston: Houghton Mifflin, 1963); Richard A. Hocks, *Henry James and Pragmatistic Thought* (Chapel Hill: University of North Carolina Press, 1974); L. B. Holland, *The Expense of Vision: Essays on the Craft of Henry James* (Princeton: Princeton University Press, 1964); R. Kossmann, *Henry James: Dramatist* (Groningen: Wölters-Noordhoff, 1969); Cornelia P. Kelley, *The Early Development of Henry James* (Urbana: University of Illinois Press, 1965); Naomi Lebowitz, *The Imagination of Loving: Henry James's Legacy to the Novel* (Detroit: Wayne State University Press, 1965); Manfred MacKenzie, *Communities of Love and Honor in Henry James* (Cambridge, Mass.: Harvard University Press, 1976); D. S. Maini, *Henry James: The Indirect Vision—Studies in Themes and Techniques* (New York: McGraw-Hill, 1973); Carl Maves, *Sensuous Pessimism: Italy in the Works of Henry James* (Bloomington: Indiana University Press, 1973); Donald L. Mull, *Henry James's 'Sublime Economy': Money as Symbolic Center in the Fiction* (Middletown, Conn.: Wesleyan University Press, 1973); John P. O'Neill, *Workable Design: Action and Situation in the Fiction of Henry James* (Port Washington, N.Y.: Kennikat, 1973); Richard Poirier, *The Comic Sense of Henry James* (New York: Oxford University Press, 1960); Lyall H. Powers, *Henry James* (New York: Holt, Rinehart & Winston, 1970); Morris Roberts, *Henry James's Criticism* (Cambridge, Mass.: Harvard University Press, 1929); Charles T. Samuels, *The Ambiguity of Henry James* (Urbana: University of Illinois Press, 1971); Sallie Sears, *The Negative Imagination: Form and Perspective in the Novels of Henry James* (Ithaca, N.Y.: Cornell University Press, 1968); Oral Segal, *The Lucid Reflector: The Observer in Henry James's Fiction* (New Haven: Yale University Press, 1970); Muriel G. Shine, *The Fictional Children of Henry James* (Chapel Hill: University of North Carolina Press, 1970); J. A. Smith, *Henry James and Robert Louis Stevenson* (London: R. Hart-Davis, 1948); Elizabeth Stevenson, *The Crooked Corridor: A Study of Henry James*

(New York: Macmillan, 1949); William Veeder, *Henry James—the Lessons of the Master* (Chicago: University of Chicago Press, 1975); Ronald Wallace, *Henry James and the Comic Form* (Ann Arbor: University of Michigan Press, 1975); J. A. Ward, *The Imagination of Disaster: Evil in the Fiction of Henry James* (Lincoln: University of Nebraska Press, 1961) and *Search for Form: Studies in the Structure of James's Fiction* (Chapel Hill: University of North Carolina Press, 1967); Christof Wegelin, *The Image of Europe in Henry James* (Dallas, Tex.: Southern Methodist University Press, 1958); Philip M. Weinstein, *Henry James and the Requirements of the Imagination* (Cambridge, Mass.: Harvard University Press, 1971); Viola H. Winner, *Henry James and the Visual Arts* (Charlottesville: University Press of Virginia, 1970); and W. F. Wright, *The Madness of Art: A Study of Henry James* (Lincoln: University of Nebraska Press, 1962).

There are numerous collections of critical articles on James's work. Collections of a general nature are F. J. Dupee, ed., *The Question of Henry James* (New York: Holt, 1945); Naomi Lebowitz, ed., *Discussions of Henry James* (Lexington, Mass.: Heath, 1962); Leon Edel, ed., *Henry James: A Collection of Critical Essays* (Englewood Cliffs, N.J.: Prentice-Hall, 1963); Roger Gard, comp., *Henry James: The Critical Heritage* (New York: Barnes & Noble, 1968); Tony Tanner, ed., *Henry James: Modern Comments* (New York: Macmillan, 1968); John A. Goode, ed., *The Air of Reality: New Essays on Henry James* (New York: Harper & Row, 1972); and Lyall H. Powers, ed., *Henry James's Major Novels: Essays in Criticism* (East Lansing: Michigan State University Press, 1973). More specialized collections include Wm. T. Stafford, comp., *Merrill Studies in The American* (Columbus, Oh.: Merrill, 1971); Wm. T. Stafford, ed., *Perspectives on James's Portrait of A Lady* (New York: New York University Press, 1967); Peter Buitenhuis, ed., *Twentieth Century Interpretations of Portrait of A Lady* (Englewood Cliffs, N.J.: Prentice-Hall, 1968); Lyall H. Powers, comp., *Merrill Studies in Portrait of A Lady* (Columbus, Oh.: Merrill, 1970); G. Willen, ed., *A Casebook on Henry James's The Turn of the Screw* (New York: T. Y. Crowell, 1960); T. A. Cranfill and R. L. Clark, eds., *An Anatomy of The Turn of the Screw* (Austin: University of Texas Press, 1965); Robert Kimbrough, ed., *The Turn of the Screw: An Authoritative Text, Backgrounds, and Sources* (New York: Norton, 1966); Jane P. Tompkins, ed., *Twentieth Century Interpretations of The Turn of the Screw* (Englewood Cliffs, N.J.: Prentice-Hall, 1970); Wm. T. Stafford, ed., *James's Daisy Miller: The Story, the Play, the Critics* (New York: Scribner, 1963); S. P. Rosenbaum, ed. *The Ambassadors* (Norton Critical Ed., New York: Norton, 1964); and Albert E. Stone, ed., *Twentieth Century Interpretations of The Ambassadors* (Englewood Cliffs, N.J.: Prentice-Hall, 1969).

6: NATURALISM

Lars Ahnebrink, *The Beginnings of Naturalism in American Fiction* (Cambridge, Mass.: Harvard University Press, 1950); John W. Aldridge, ed., *Critiques and Essays in Modern Fiction* (New York: Ronald, 1952); Malcolm Cowley, *The Literary Situation* (New York: Viking, 1954); James T. Farrell, *Literature and Morality* (New York: Vanguard, 1947) and *Reflections at Fifty* (New York: Vanguard, 1954); F. J. Hoffman, *Freudianism and the Literary Mind* (Baton Rouge: Louisiana State University

Press, 1945); Richard Hofstadter, *Social Darwinism in American Thought* (Philadelphia: University of Pennsylvania Press, 1944); Sydney J. Krause, *Essays on Determinism in American Literature* (Kent, Oh.: Kent State University Press, 1964); Stow Persons, ed., *Evolutionary Thought in America* (New Haven: Yale University Press, 1950); Philip Rahv, *Image and Idea* (New York: New Directions, 1949); Edward Stone, ed., *What Was Naturalism?* (New York: Appleton, 1959); C. C. Walcutt, *American Literary Naturalism: A Divided Stream* (Minneapolis: University of Minnesota Press, 1956); Émile Zola, *The Experimental Novel and Other Essays,* trans. Belle M. Sherman (London: Cassell, 1894); *The Naturalist Novel,* ed. Maxwell Geismar (Montreal: Harvest House, 1964). See also in the GB the following: Cargill, Chase, Clark (Transitions), Kazin, Lynn, Millgate, Parrington, Pizer, Stovall, Taylor, and Thorp.

Stephen Crane

TEXTS. Currently the standard edition of Crane's prose is *The Work of Stephen Crane,* ed. Wilson Follett, 12 vols. (New York: Knopf, 1925–1927; reprint ed., New York: Atheneum, Russell & Russell, 1963). The Virginia edition is in preparation under the editorship of Fredson Bowers but to date has produced only two of ten projected volumes, *Bowery Tales* and *Tales of Whilomville* (Charlottesville: University Press of Virginia, 1969). The standard edition of the verse is *The Collected Poems of Stephen Crane,* ed. Wilson Follett (New York: Knopf, 1930). There have been many editions of parts of Crane's work; among them are *The Poems of Stephen Crane: A Critical Edition,* ed. Joseph Katz (New York: Cooper Square, 1966); *The Complete Novels of Stephen Crane,* ed. Thomas A. Gullason (Garden City, N.Y.: Doubleday, 1967); *The Complete Short Stories and Sketches of Stephen Crane,* ed. Thomas A. Gullason (Garden City, N.Y.: Doubleday, 1963); *The Portable Stephen Crane,* ed. Joseph Katz (New York: Viking, 1969); *The Stephen Crane Reader,* ed. R. W. Stallman (Glenview, Ill.: Scott, Foresman, 1972); *The New York City Sketches of Stephen Crane and Related Pieces,* eds., R. W. Stallman and E. R. Hagemann (New York: New York University Press, 1966); *Stephen Crane: Sullivan County Tales and Sketches,* ed., R. W. Stallman (Ames: Iowa State University Press, 1968); the Norton Critical Edition of *The Red Badge of Courage,* eds. S. Bradley et al. (New York: Norton, 1962); three useful editions of *Maggie*—Maurice Bassan, ed. (Belmont, Calif.: Wadsworth, 1966), Donald Pizer, ed. (San Francisco, Calif.: Chandler, 1968), and Joseph Katz, ed. (Gainesville, Fla.: Scholars' Facsimiles and Reprints, 1969); *The War Dispatches of Stephen Crane,* eds. R. W. Stallman and E. R. Hagemann (New York: New York University Press, 1964); *Stephen Crane: Uncollected Writings,* ed. O. W. Fryckstedt (Uppsala: Acta Universitatis Upsaliensis, 1963); and *Stephen Crane in the West and Mexico,* ed. Joseph Katz (Kent, Oh.: Kent State University Press, 1971).

STUDIES. The most useful survey of Crane scholarship through 1970 is that by Donald Pizer in *Fifteen American Authors Before 1900* (GB). Also valuable are A. W. Williams and Vincent Starrett, *Stephen Crane: A Bibliography* (Glendale, Calif.: John Valentine, 1948); R. W. Stallman, *Stephen Crane: A Critical Bibliography* (Ames: Iowa State University Press, 1972); and Maurice Beebe and Thomas A. Gullason, "Criticism of Stephen Crane: A Selected Checklist with an Index to Studies of Separate Works," *Modern Fiction Studies* (1959): 282–291. Additional bibliographical material may be found in the quarterly *Stephen Crane Newsletter* and in *Thoth,* an annual bibliography published since 1963 by Syracuse University. An interesting introduction is by a French critic, Jean Cazemajou, *Stephen Crane* (UMPAW: 1969). Book-length biographical studies include Thomas Beer, *Stephen Crane: A Study in American Letters* (New York: Knopf, 1923); John Berryman, *Stephen Crane* (New York: Sloane, 1950); Corwin K. Linson, *My Stephen Crane,* ed. Edwin H. Cady (Syracuse, N.Y.: Syracuse University Press, 1958); Lillian Gilkes, *Cora Crane: A Biography of Mrs. Stephen Crane* (Bloomington: University of Indiana Press, 1960); Edwin H. Cady, *Stephen Crane* (TUSAS: 1962); Eric Solomon, *Stephen Crane in England* (Columbus: Ohio State University Press, 1964); and R. W. Stallman, *Stephen Crane: A Biography* (New York: Braziller, 1968). Edwin H. Cady and Lester G. Wells edited *Stephen Crane's Love Letters to Nellie Crouse* (Syracuse, N.Y.: Syracuse University Press, 1954), and R. W. Stallman and Lillian Gilkes edited *Stephen Crane: Letters* (New York: New York University Press, 1960). Surprisingly few book-length critical studies exist; they include Daniel G. Hoffman, *The Poetry of Stephen Crane* (New York: Columbia University Press, 1957); Eric Solomon, *Stephen Crane: From Parody to Realism* (Cambridge, Mass.: Harvard University Press, 1966); Donald B. Gibson, *The Fiction of Stephen Crane* (Carbondale: Southern Illinois University Press, 1968); Marston LaFrance, *A Reading of Stephen Crane* (Oxford: Clarendon, 1971); Milne Holton, *Cylinder of Vision: The Fiction and Journalistic Writing of Stephen Crane* (Baton Rouge: Louisiana State University Press, 1972); and Frank Bergon, *Stephen Crane's Artistry* (New York: Columbia University Press, 1975). Collections of short criticism include Joseph Katz, ed., *Stephen Crane: The Blue Hotel* (Columbus, Oh.: Merrill, 1969); Maurice Bassan, ed., *Stephen Crane: A Collection of Critical Essays* (Englewood Cliffs, N.J.: Prentice-Hall, 1967); Joseph Katz, ed., *Stephen Crane in Transition: Centenary Essays* (DeKalb: Northern Illinois University Press, 1972); and Richard M. Weatherford, ed., *Stephen Crane: The Critical Heritage* (London: Routledge & Kegan Paul, 1973).

Frank Norris

TEXTS. The standard edition of the work is *The Complete Edition of Frank Norris,* 10 vols. (Garden City, N.Y.: Doubleday, Doran, 1928). Important individual titles follow: *Moran of the Lady Lettie* (Garden City, N.Y.: Doubleday and McClure, 1898); *Blix* (Garden City, N.Y.: Doubleday and McClure, 1899); *A Man's Woman* (Garden City, N.Y.: Doubleday and McClure, 1900); *The Octopus* (Garden City, N.Y.: Doubleday, Page, 1901); *The Pit* (Garden City, N.Y.: Doubleday, Page, 1903); *The Responsibilities of the Novelist and Other Literary Essays* (Garden City, N.Y.: Doubleday, Page, 1903); *Vandover and the Brute* (Garden City, N.Y.: Doubleday, Page, 1914); *The Literary Criticism of Frank Norris,* ed. Donald Pizer (Austin: University of Texas Press, 1964).

STUDIES. The best review of Norris scholarship is William B. Dillingham's bibliographical essay in *Fifteen American Authors before 1900.* See also Kenneth A. Lohf and Eugene P. Sheehy, *Frank Norris: A Bibliography* (Georgetown, Calif.: Talisman, 1959). A good critical introduction is W. M. Frohock, *Frank Norris* (UMPAW: 1968). The only complete biography is Franklin D. Walker, *Frank Norris: A Biography* (Garden City, N.Y.: Doubleday, Doran, 1932). Full-length studies of his work are Ernest Marchand, *Frank Norris: A Study* (Stanford, Calif.: Stanford University Press, 1942); Lars Ahnebrink, *The Beginnings of Naturalism in American Fiction* (Cambridge, Mass.: Harvard University Press, 1950); Warren French, *Frank Norris,* (TUSAS: 1962); Donald Pizer, *The Novels of Frank Norris* (Bloomington: Indiana University Press, 1966); and William B. Dillingham, *Frank Norris: Instinct and Art* (Lincoln: University of Nebraska Press, 1969). Representative short articles of general interest are Charles G. Hoffmann, "Norris and the Responsibility of the Novelist," *SAQ* 54 (1955):508–515 and Arnold L. Goldsmith, "The Development of Frank Norris's Philosophy" in *Studies in Honor of John Wilcox* ed. A. D. Wallace and W. O. Ross (Detroit: Wayne State University Press, 1958). Representative discussions of *The Octopus* (his most widely discussed work) are H. W. Reninger, "Norris Explains *The Octopus:* A Correlation of His Theory and Practice," *AL* 12 (1940): 218–227; George W. Meyer, "A New Interpretation of *The Octopus,*" *CE* 4 (1943): 351–359; Donald Pizer, "Another Look at *The Octopus,*" *NCF* 10 (1955): 217–224; and Kenneth S. Lynn, introduction to *The Octopus* (Riv Ed, Boston: Houghton Mifflin, 1958). Franklin D. Walker has edited *The Letters of Frank Norris* (San Francisco: Book Club of California, 1956).

Theodore Dreiser

TEXTS. There is no standard edition of Dreiser's work. Novels: *Sister Carrie* (Garden City, N.Y.: Doubleday, Page, 1900); *Jennie Gerhardt* (New York: Harper, 1911); *The Financier* (New York: Harper, 1912); *The Titan* (New York: John Lane, 1914); *The "Genius"* (John Lane, 1915); *An American Tragedy* (New York: Boni & Liveright, 1925); *The Bulwark* (Garden City, N.Y.: Doubleday, 1946); *The Stoic* (Garden City, N.Y.: Doubleday, 1947). Collections of short stories: *Free, and Other Stories* (New York: Boni & Liveright, 1918); *Chains* (New York: Boni & Liveright, 1927); *Fine Furniture* (New York: Random House, 1930); *The Best Short Stories of Theodore Dreiser,* ed. Howard Fast (Cleveland, Oh.: World Publishing, 1947); *The Best Short Stories of Theodore Dreiser,* ed. James T. Farrell (Cleveland, Oh.: World Publishing, 1956). Autobiography: *A Book About Myself* (New York: Boni & Liveright, 1922); *Dawn* (New York: Liveright, 1931). Criticism and philosophy: *Hey, Rub-A-Dub-Dub!* (New York: Boni & Liveright, 1920); *The Color of a Great City* (New York: Boni & Liveright, 1923); *Tragic America* (New York: Liveright, 1931); *America Is Worth Saving* (New York: Modern Age, 1941); *Selected Poems,* ed. R. P. Saalbach (New York: Exposition, 1969).

STUDIES. The most useful bibliographical essay on Dreiser is that of Robert H. Elias in *Sixteen Modern American Authors*. See also Hugh C. Atkinson, *Theodore Dreiser: A Checklist* (Columbus, Oh.: Merrill, 1971). A useful introduction is Philip L. Gerber, *Theodore Dreiser* (TUSAS: 1964). Biographical work on Dreiser includes H. L. Mencken, *A Book of Prefaces* (New York: Knopf, 1917); Burton Rascoe, *Theodore Dreiser* (New York: McBride, 1926); Dorothy Dudley, *Forgotten Frontiers: Dreiser and the Land of the Free* (New York: H. Smith and R. Haas, 1932); Robert H. Elias, *Theodore Dreiser: Apostle of Nature* (Ithaca, N.Y.: Cornell University Press, 1970); Helen Dreiser (Dreiser's second wife), *My Life with Dreiser* (Cleveland, Oh.: World Publishing, 1951); W. A. Swanberg, *Dreiser* (New York: Scribner, 1965); Marguerite Tjader, *Theodore Dreiser: A New Dimension* (Norwalk, Ct.: Silvermine Publishers, 1965).

Critical work on Dreiser is enormous, although it includes surprisingly few full-length studies; these are F. O. Matthiessen, *Theodore Dreiser* (New York: Sloane, 1951); Charles Shapiro, *Theodore Dreiser: Our Bitter Patriot* (Carbondale: Southern Illinois University Press, 1962); John J. McAleer, *Theodore Dreiser* (New York: Barnes and Noble, 1968); Ellen Moers, *Two Dreisers* (New York: Viking, 1969); Ruth E. Kennell, *Theodore Dreiser and the Soviet Union, 1927–1945* (New York: International Publishers, 1969); Richard D. Lehan, *Theodore Dreiser: His World and His Novels* (Carbondale: Southern Illinois University Press, 1969); Robert Penn Warren, *Homage to Theodore Dreiser* (New York: Random House, 1971); and Donald Pizer, *The Novels of Theodore Dreiser* (Minneapolis: University of Minnesota Press, 1976). Collections of short criticism include Alfred Kazin and Charles Shapiro, eds., *The Status of Theodore Dreiser* (Bloomington: Indiana University Press, 1955); John Lydenberg, ed., *Dreiser: A Collection of Critical Essays* (Englewood Cliffs, N.J.: Prentice-Hall, 1971); Jack Salzman, ed., *Theodore Dreiser: The Critical Reception* (New York: David Lewis, 1972) and The Merrill Studies in *An American Tragedy* (Columbus, Oh.: Merrill, 1971).

Jack London

TEXTS. There is no standard edition of London's work, which runs to more than fifty volumes. Two English editions are currently in progress: the Fitzroy edition of the works of Jack London and the Bodley Head Jack London. Following is a highly selective list of his fiction, essays, and travel literature. Fiction: *The Son of the Wolf, Tales of the Far North* (Boston: Houghton Mifflin, 1900); *A Daughter of the Snows* (Philadelphia: Lippincott, 1902); *The Call of the Wild* (New York: Macmillan, 1903); *The Sea Wolf* (New York: Macmillan, 1904); *White Fang* (New York: Macmillan, 1906); *The Iron Heel* (New York: Macmillan, 1907); *Martin Eden* (New York: Macmillan, 1909); *South Sea Tales* (New York: Macmillan, 1911); *Smoke Bellew Tales* (New York; Century, 1912); *The Valley of the Moon* (New York: Macmillan, 1913); *The Star Rover* (New York: Macmillan, 1915); *The Little Lady of the Big House* (New York: Macmillan, 1916). Polemics: *The People of the Abyss* (New York: Macmillan, 1903); *War of the Classes* (New York: Macmillan, 1905); *Revolution and Other Essays* (New York: Macmillan, 1910). Travel: *The Cruise of the Snark* (New York: Macmillan, 1911).

STUDIES. An excellent bibliography is H. C. Woodbridge, John London, and George H. Tweney, *Jack London: A Bibliography* (Georgetown, Calif.: Talisman, 1966). A good introduction is C. C. Walcutt, *Jack London* (UMPAW: 1966). Biographical material is plentiful and varied. Full-length works include Martin Johnson, *Through the South Seas with Jack London* (New York: Dodd, Mead, 1913); Charmian London (his wife), *The Book of Jack London*, 2 vols. (New York: Century, 1921) and *Our Hawaii* (New York: Macmillan, 1922); Edward B. Payne, *The Soul of Jack London* (New York: Rider, 1926); Joan London (his daughter), *Jack London: An Unconventional Biography* (Garden City, N.Y.: Doubleday, 1939; 1968); Joseph Noel, *Footloose in Arcadia* (New York: Carrick, 1940); Irving Stone, *Jack London, Sailor on Horseback: A Biographical Novel* (Garden City, N.Y.: Doubleday, 1947); and Richard O'Connor, *High Jinks on the Klondike* (Indianapolis: Bobbs-Merrill, 1954) and *Jack London: A Biography* (Boston: Little, Brown, 1964). Criticism of London's work has consisted mainly of short articles and essays. Longer work includes H. L. Mencken, *Prejudices: First Series* (New York: Knopf, 1921); William McDevitt, *Jack London as Poet* (San Francisco: Recorder-Sunset Press, 1947); Philip S. Foner, *Jack London: American Rebel* (New York: Citadel, 1964); and King Hendricks, *Jack London: Master Craftsman of the Short Story* (Logan: Utah State University Press, 1966). King Hendricks and Irving Shepard edited *Letters from Jack London* (New York: Odyssey, 1965). For reviews and studies of individual works see Woodbridge, London, and Tweney, pp. 358–373.

7: SOCIAL PROTEST AND REALISM

Hamlin Garland

TEXTS. There is no collected edition of Garland's work. Following is a highly selective list of what is generally regarded as his most important work; the publishers and dates are those of original publication: *Main-Travelled Roads* (New York: Harper, 1890), stories; *Prairie Folks* (Chicago: Stone and Kimball, 1892), stories; *Rose of Dutcher's Cooly* (Chicago: Stone and Kimball, 1895), novel; *Crumbling Idols* (Chicago: Stone and Kimball, 1894), essays on literature, especially veritism and local color; *Boy Life on the Prairie* (New York: Macmillan, 1899), sketches and reminiscences. Four interconnected volumes of biography and reminiscences involving himself and his family are *A Son of the Middle Border* (New York: Macmillan, 1917); *A Daughter of the Middle Border* (New York: Macmillan, 1921); *Trail-Makers of the Middle Border* (New York: Macmillan, 1926); and *Back-Trailers from the Middle Border* (New York: Macmillan, 1928).

STUDIES. The most useful brief survey of scholarship on Garland is that by Donald Pizer in *ALR 1870–1910* 1 (1967–1968): 45–51. The fullest listing of commentary on Garland, well annotated, is Jackson R. Bryer and Eugene Harding, "Hamlin Garland (1860–1940): A Bibliography of Secondary Comment," *ALR 1870–1910* 3 (1970): 290–387. See also Jackson R. Bryer and Eugene Harding, *Hamlin Garland and the Critics: An Annotated Bibliography* (Troy, N.Y.: Whitston, 1973). There are two full-length studies of Garland: Jean Holloway, *Hamlin Garland: A Biography* (Austin: University of Texas Press, 1960) and Donald Pizer, *Hamlin Garland's Early Work and Career* (Berkeley: University of California Press, 1960). Pizer also edited Garland's diaries (San Marino, Calif.: Huntington Library, 1968). Lloyd A. Arvidson edited *Hamlin Garland: Centennial Tributes and a Checklist of the Hamlin Garland Papers in the University of Southern California Library* (Los Angeles: University of Southern California Library, 1962). Among dozens of articles listed in Spiller, Pizer, and elsewhere, a few representative specimens may be mentioned: Bernard I. Duffey, "Hamlin Garland's 'Decline' from Realism," *AL* 25 (1953): 69–74; Donald Pizer, "Romantic Individualism in Garland, Norris and Crane," *AQ* 10 (1958): 463–475, reprinted in *Realism and Naturalism in Nineteenth Century American Literature* (Carbondale: Southern Illinois University Press, 1966); Clyde E. Henson, "Joseph Kirkland's Influence on Hamlin Garland," *AL* 23 (1952): 458–463; Bruce R. McElderry, Jr., "Hamlin Garland and Henry James," *AL* 23 (1952): 433–446. Pizer discusses articles on individual works on p. 50 (see above). Three standard views of Garland are to be found in Lars Ahnebrink, *The Beginnings of Naturalism in American Fiction* (New York: Atheneum,

Russell & Russell, 1961); C. C. Walcutt, *American Literary Naturalism: A Divided Stream* (Minneapolis: University of Minnesota Press, 1956); and V. L. Parrington, *Main Currents in American Thought,* vol. 3 (New York: Harcourt, 1930).

Edith Wharton

TEXTS. Novels: *The Touchstone* (New York: Scribner, 1900); *The Valley of Decision* (New York: Scribner, 1902); *Sanctuary* (New York: Scribner, 1903); *The House of Mirth* (New York: Scribner, 1905); *The Fruit of the Tree* (New York: Scribner, 1907); *Madame de Treymes* (New York: Scribner, 1907); *Ethan Frome* (New York: Scribner, 1911); *The Reef* (New York: Appleton, 1912); *The Custom of the Country* (New York: Scribner, 1913); *Summer* (New York: Appleton, 1917); *The Marne* (New York: Appleton, 1918); *The Age of Innocence* (New York: Appleton, 1920); *The Glimpses of the Moon* (New York: Appleton, 1922); *A Son at the Front* (New York: Scribner, 1923); *Old New York* (New York: Appleton, 1924); *The Mother's Recompense* (New York: Appleton, 1925); *Twilight Sleep* (New York: Appleton, 1927); *The Children* (New York: Appleton, 1928); *Hudson River Bracketed* (New York: Appleton, 1929); *The Gods Arrive* (New York: Appleton, 1932); *The Buccaneers* (New York: Appleton, 1938). Collections of short stories: *The Greater Inclination* (New York: Scribner, 1899); *Crucial Instances* (New York: Scribner, 1901); *The Descent of Man* (New York: Scribner, 1904); *The Hermit and the Wild Woman* (New York: Scribner, 1908); *Tales of Men and Ghosts* (New York: Scribner, 1910); *Xingu* (New York: Scribner, 1916); *Here and Beyond* (New York: Appleton, 1926); *Certain People* (New York: Appleton, 1930); *Human Nature* (New York: Appleton, 1933); *The World Over* (New York: Appleton, 1936); *Ghosts* (New York: Appleton, 1937); *An Edith Wharton Treasury,* ed. A. H. Quinn (New York: Appleton, 1950); *Best Short Stories of Edith Wharton,* ed. Wayne Andrews (New York: Scribner, 1958); *The Edith Wharton Reader,* ed. Louis Auchincloss (New York: Scribner, 1965). Autobiography. *A Backward Glance* (New York: Appleton, 1934).

STUDIES. For bibliography see Vito J. Brenni, *Edith Wharton, A Bibliography* (Morgantown: West Virginia University Library, 1966), a fairly thorough but unannotated listing of Wharton criticism. A good introduction is Louis Auchincloss, *Edith Wharton* (UMPAW: 1961). Full-length biographies are Percy Lubbock, *Portrait of Edith Wharton* (New York: Appleton 1947); Olivia Coolidge, *Edith Wharton 1862–1937* (New York: Scribner, 1964); Grace Kellogg, *The Two Lives of Edith Wharton: The Woman and Her Work* (New York: Appleton, 1965); R. W. B. Lewis, *Edith Wharton: A Biography* (New York: Harper & Row, 1975); Millicent Bell, *Edith Wharton and Henry James: The Story of Their Friendship* (New York: Braziller, 1965); and Louis Auchincloss, *Edith Wharton, A Woman of Her Time* (New York: Viking, 1971). Book-length studies are Robert Morss Lovett, *Edith Wharton* (New York: McBride, 1925); Blake Nevius, *Edith Wharton: A Study of Her Fiction* (Berkeley: University of California Press, 1953); Marilyn J. Lyde, *Edith Wharton: Convention and Morality in the Work of a Novelist* (Norman: University of Oklahoma Press, 1959); Geoffrey Walton, *Edith Wharton: A Critical Interpretation* (Rutherford, N.J.: Fairleigh Dickinson University Press, 1971); and Margaret B. McDowell, *Edith Wharton* (TUSAS; 1976). Good shorter studies are Anne Fremantle's in *Fifty Years of the American Novel: A Christian Appraisal,* ed. H. C. Gardiner (New York:

Scribner, 1951); Arthur Mizener's discussion of *The Age of Innocence* in *Twelve Great American Novels* (New York: New American Library, 1967); and Josephine L. Jessup, *The Faith of Our Feminists* (New York: R. R. Smith, 1950). Useful collections of criticism are Irving Howe, ed., *Edith Wharton: A Collection of Critical Essays* (Englewood Cliffs, N.J.: Prentice-Hall, 1962) and Blake Nevius, ed., *Edith Wharton's Ethan Frome: The Story with Sources and Commentary* (New York: Scribner, 1968).

William Vaughn Moody

TEXTS. *The Poems and Plays of William Vaughn Moody,* ed. John M. Manly, 2 vols. (Boston: Houghton Mifflin, 1912); *Selected Poems of William Vaughn Moody,* ed. Robert M. Lovett (Boston: Houghton Mifflin, 1931).

STUDIES. A helpful introduction and reevaluation is Martin Halpern, *William Vaughn Moody* (TUSAS: 1964). The fullest biographical and critical treatments are D. D. Henry, *William Vaughn Moody: A Study* (Somerville, Mass.: Humphries, 1934) and Maurice F. Brown, *Estranging Dawn: The Life and Works of William Vaughn Moody* (Carbondale: Southern Illinois University Press, 1973). Shorter studies are F. O. Matthiessen, *The Responsibilities of the Critic* (New York: Oxford University Press, 1952); Hyatt H. Waggoner, *American Poets from the Puritans to the Present* (Boston: Houghton Mifflin, 1966); F. W. Conner, *Cosmic Optimism: A Study of the Interpretation of Evolution by American Poets from Emerson to Robinson* (Gainesville: University of Florida Press, 1949); and Howard Mumford Jones, *The Bright Medusa* (Urbana: University of Illinois Press, 1952), which places Moody in the poetic situation of the turn of the century. Daniel G. Mason has edited *Some Letters of William Vaughn Moody* (Boston: Houghton Mifflin, 1913), and Percy MacKaye has edited Moody's letters to his wife, *Letters to Harriet* (Boston: Houghton Mifflin, 1935).

Edgar Lee Masters

TEXTS. *Spoon River Anthology* (New York: Macmillan, 1963); *The New Spoon River* (New York: Collier, 1968); *Selected Poems* (New York: Putnam, 1933).

STUDIES. An early evaluation of the poetry is Amy Lowell, *Tendencies in Modern Poetry* (New York: Macmillan, 1917). Later studies are Michael Yatron, *America's Literary Revolt* (New York: Philosophical Library, 1959); A. W. Derleth, "Masters and the Revolt from the Village," *Colorado Quarterly* 8 (1959):164–167 and *Three Literary Men: A Memoir of Sinclair Lewis, Sherwood Anderson and Edgar Lee Masters* (New York: Candlelight Press, 1963); Lois Hartley, *Spoon River Revisited* (Ball State Monograph no. 1; Muncie, Ind.: Ball State University Press, 1963); and John T. Flanagan, *Edgar Lee Masters: The Spoon River Poet and His Critics* (Metuchen, N.J.: Scarecrow, 1975).

Edwin Arlington Robinson

TEXTS. *Collected Poems* (New York: Macmillan, 1937); *Selected Early Poems and Letters,* ed. C. T. Davis (New York: Holt, Rinehart & Winston, 1960); *Selected Poems,* ed. M. D. Zabel (New York: Macmillan, 1965).

STUDIES. The most helpful bibliography is Ellsworth Barnard's review of Robinson scholarship in *Sixteen Modern American Authors.* See also Charles B. Hogan, *A Bibliography of Edwin Arlington Robinson* (New Haven: Yale University Press,

1936); L. Lippincott, *A Bibliography of the Writings and Criticisms of Edwin Arlington Robinson* (Westwood, Mass.: Faxon, 1937); and William White, *Edwin Arlington Robinson: A Supplemental Bibliography* (Kent, Oh.: Kent State University Press, 1971). Introductions to the work are Charles Cestre, *An Introduction to Edwin Arlington Robinson* (New York: Macmillan, 1930); Louis O. Coxe, *E. A. Robinson* (UMPAW: 1962); and Hoyt C. Franchere, *Edwin Arlington Robinson* (TUSAS: 1968). Biographies include Rollo W. Brown, *Next Door to a Poet* (New York: Appleton, 1937); Hermann Hagedorn, *Edwin Arlington Robinson* (New York: Macmillan, 1938); Daniel G. Mason, *Music in My Time, and Other Reminiscences* (New York: Macmillan, 1938); and Chard P. Smith, *Where the Light Falls* (New York: Macmillan, 1965). Full-length studies include Lloyd R. Morris, *The Poetry of Edwin Arlington Robinson* (Garden City, N.Y.: Doran, 1923); Ben Ray Redman, *Edwin Arlington Robinson* (New York: McBride, 1926); Mark Van Doren, *Edwin Arlington Robinson* (New York: Literary Guild of America, 1927); Lucius M. Beebe, *Aspects of the Poetry of Edwin Arlington Robinson* (Cambridge, Mass.: Harvard University Press, 1928); Laura E. Richards, *E. A. R.* (Cambridge, Mass.: Harvard University Press, 1936); R. P. T. Coffin, *New Poetry of New England: Frost and Robinson* (New York: Athereum, Russell & Russell, 1938); Estelle Kaplan, *Philosophy in the Poetry of Edwin Arlington Robinson* (New York: Columbia University Press, 1940); Yvor Winters, *Edwin Arlington Robinson* (New York: New Directions, 1946); Emery Neff, *Edwin Arlington Robinson* (New York: Sloane, 1948); Ellsworth Barnard, *Edwin Arlington Robinson: A Critical Study* (New York: Macmillan, 1952); Edwin S. Fussell, *Edwin Arlington Robinson: The Literary Background of a Traditional Poet* (Berkeley: University of California Press, 1954); William R. Robinson, *Edwin Arlington Robinson: A Poetry of the Act* (Cleveland: Western Reserve Press, 1967); Wallace L. Anderson, *Edwin Arlington Robinson: A Critical Introduction* (Boston: Houghton Mifflin, 1967); and Louis O. Coxe, *Edwin Arlington Robinson: The Life of Poetry* (Indianapolis: Bobbs-Merrill, Pegasus, 1969). Collections of shorter criticism of his work are the *Colby Library Quarterly* (Waterville, Me.: Colby College Press, 1969); Ellsworth Barnard, ed., *Edwin Arlington Robinson: Centenary Essays* (Athens: University of Georgia Press, 1969); Richard Cary, ed., *Appreciation of Edwin Arlington Robinson* (Waterville, Me.: Colby College Press, 1969); and Francis Murphy, ed., *Edwin Arlington Robinson* (Englewood Cliffs, N.Y.: Prentice-Hall, 1970). Robinson's letters have been variously collected: Ridgely Torrence has edited *Selected Letters of Edwin Arlington Robinson* (New York: Macmillan, 1940). Carl J. Weber has edited *Letters of Edwin Arlington Robinson to Howard George Schmitt* (Waterville, Me.: Colby College Library, 1943). Denham Sutcliffe has edited *Untriangulated Stars: Letters of Edwin Arlington Robinson to Harry deForest Smith, 1890–1905* (Cambridge, Mass.: Harvard University Press, 1947). Richard Cary has edited *Edwin Arlington Robinson's Letters to Edith Brower* (Cambridge, Mass.: Harvard University Press, 1968).

8: THE MODERN TEMPER

Poetry

D. C. Allen, ed., *The Moment of Poetry* (Baltimore: Johns Hopkins Press, 1962); Charles F. Altieri; *Modern Poetry* (Arlington Heights, Ill.: AHM Publishing Corporation, 1976); Owen Barfield, *Poetic Diction* (Middletown, Conn.: Wesleyan University Press, 1973); J. W. Beach, *Obsessive Images: Symbolism in Poetry of the 1930's and 1940's* (Minneapolis: University of Minnesota Press, 1960); R. P. Blackmur, *Form and Value in Modern Poetry* (Garden City, N.Y.: Doubleday, Anchor, 1957); Louise Bogan, *Achievement in Modern Poetry* (Chicago: Regnery, 1951); Cleanth Brooks, *Modern Poetry and the Tradition* (Chapel Hill: University of North Carolina Press, 1939); Glauco Cambon, *The Inclusive Flame* (Bloomington: Indiana University Press, 1963) and *Recent American Poetry* (UMPAW: 1962); Paul Carroll, *The Poem in Its Skin* (Chicago: Follett, 1968); Stanley K. Coffman, *Imagism: A Chapter for the History of Modern Poetry* (Norman: University of Oklahoma Press, 1951); L. S. Dembo, *Conceptions of Reality in Modern American Poetry* (Berkeley: University of California Press, 1966); Babette Deutsch, *Poetry in Our Time* (New York: Holt, Rinehart & Winston, 1952); James Dickey, *Babel to Byzantium: Poets and Poetry Now* (New York: Farrar, Straus & Giroux, 1968) and *The Suspect in Poetry* (Madison, Minn.: Sixties Press, 1964); Denis Donoghue, *Connoiseurs of Chaos: Ideas of Order in Modern American Poetry* (New York: Macmillan, 1965); Lloyd Frankenberg, *Pleasure Dome: On Reading Modern Poetry* (Boston; Houghton Mifflin, 1949); Paul Goodman, *Speaking of Language: Defense of Poetry* (New York: Random House, 1972); Harvey Gross, *Sound and Form in Modern Poetry* (East Lansing; University of Michigan Press, 1963); John Hollander, ed., *Modern Poetry* (New York: Oxford University Press, 1968); Richard Howard, *Alone With America: Essays on the Art of Poetry in the United States Since 1950* (New York: Atheneum, 1959); Glenn Hughes, *Imagism and the Imagists* (Stanford, Calif.: Stanford University Press, 1931); Edward Hungerford, ed., *Poets in Progress* (Evanston, Ill.: Northwestern University Press, 1967); J. Isaacs, *The Background of Modern Poetry* (New York: Dutton, 1952); Randall Jarrell, *Poetry and the Age* (New York: Knopf, 1953); Frank Kermode, *The Romantic Image* (New York: Macmillan, 1958); Amy Lowell, *Tendencies in Modern Poetry* (New York: Macmillan, 1917); Karl Malkoff, *Crowell's Handbook of Contemporary American Poetry* (New York: T. Y. Crowell, 1973); Louis L. Martz, *The Poem of the Mind* (New York: Oxford University Press, 1966); William Martz, *Distinctive Voice: Twentieth Century American Poetry* (Glenview, Ill.: Scott, Foresman, 1965); Jerome Mazzaro, ed., *Modern American Poetry* (New York: McKay, 1970); Howard Nemerov, ed., *Poets on Poetry* (New York: Basic Books, 1966); William Van O'Connor, *Sense and Sensibility in Modern Poetry* (Chicago: University of Chicago Press, 1948); David Ossman, comp., *This Sullen Art* (New York: Corinth Books, 1963); Anthony Ostroff, ed., *The Contemporary Poet as Artist and Critic* (Boston: Little, Brown, 1964); Robert Phillips, *The Confessional Poets* (Carbondale: Southern Illinois University Press, 1973); Ezra Pound, *The ABC of Reading* (New York: New Directions, 1960); Sr. Bernetta Quinn, *The Metamorphic Tradition in Modern Poetry* (New Brunswick, N.J.: Rutgers University Press, 1955); Kenneth Rexroth, *American Poetry in the Twentieth Century* (New York: Herder and Herder, 1971); M. L. Rosenthal, *The New American Poetry* (New York: Macmillan, 1967) and *The New Poets* (New York: Oxford University Press, 1967); Karl Shapiro, *In Defense of Ignorance* (New York: Knopf, Vintage, 1965); James G. Southworth, *Some Modern American Poets* (Oxford: Blackwell, 1950); Stephen Stepanchev, *American Poetry Since 1945* (New York: Harper & Row, 1965); Wallace Stevens, *The Necessary Angel* (New York: Knopf, 1951); Walter Sutton, *American Free Verse: The Modern Revolution in Poetry* (New York: New Directions, 1973); Peter Viereck, *The Last Decade in Poetry* (Bureau of

Publications; Nashville, Tenn.: George Peabody College for Teachers, 1954); Hyatt H. Waggoner, *The Heel of Elohim* (Norman: University of Oklahoma Press, 1950); W. C. Williams, *Selected Essays* (New York: Random House, 1954); Yvor Winters, *On Modern Poets* (New York: Meridian, 1959).

Fiction

John W. Aldridge, *Critiques and Essays in Modern Fiction* (New York: Ronald, 1952) and *Time to Murder and Create: The Contemporary Novel in Crisis* (New York: McKay, 1966); Walter Allen, *The Modern Novel in Britain and the United States* (New York: Dutton, 1964); Jonathan Baumbach, *The Landscape of Nightmare* (New York: New York University Press, 1965); Joseph W. Beach, *The Twentieth Century Novel* (New York: Century, 1932) and *American Fiction, 1920–1940* (New York: Macmillan, 1941); N. M. Blake, *Novelists' America: Fiction as History, 1910–1940* (Syracuse, N.Y.: Syracuse University Press, 1969); Percy H. Boynton, *America in Contemporary Fiction* (Chicago: University of Chicago Press, 1940); Stanley Cooperman, *World War I and the American Novel* (Baltimore: Johns Hopkins Press, 1967); Malcolm Cowley, *The Literary Situation* (New York: Viking, 1954) and *A Second Flowering: Works and Days of the Lost Generation* (New York: Viking, 1973); Chester E. Eisinger, *Fiction of the Forties* (Chicago: University of Chicago Press 1963); Ralph Ellison, *Shadow and Act* (New York: Random House, 1964); Nick A. Ford, *The Contemporary Negro Novel* (Washington, D. C.: McGrath, 1968); Warren French, *The Social Novel at the End of an Era* (Carbondale: Southern Illinois University Press, 1966); David D. Galloway, *The Absurd Hero in American Fiction* (Austin: University of Texas Press, 1966); Addison Gayle, Jr., *The Way of the New World: The Black Novel in America* (Garden City, N.Y.: Doubleday, 1976); Maxwell Geismar, *American Moderns: From Rebellion to Conformity* (New York: Hill & Wang, 1958) and *Writers in Crisis: The American Novel Between Two Wars* (Boston: Houghton Mifflin, 1942); Blanche Gelfante, *The American City Novel* (Norman: University of Oklahoma Press, 1954); James B. Gilbert, *Writers and Partisans: A History of Literary Radicalism in America* (New York: Wiley, 1968); Louise Y. Gossett, *Violence in Recent Southern Fiction* (Durham, N.C.: Duke University Press, 1965); Allen Guttman, *The Jewish Writer in America* (New York: Oxford University Press, 1971); Howard M. Harper, comp., "General Studies of Recent American Fiction: A Selected Checklist," *MFS* 19 (1973): 127–133; Howard M. Harper, *Desperate Faith* (Chapel Hill; University of North Carolina Press, 1967); Ihib Hassan, *Radical Innocence* (Princeton: Princeton University Press, 1961); Herbert Hill, ed., *Anger and Beyond: The Negro Writer in the United States* (New York: Harper & Row, 1966); F. J. Hoffman, *The Modern Novel in America* (Chicago: Regnery, 1951) and *The Art of Southern Fiction* (Carbondale: Southern Illinois University Press, 1967); C. Hugh Holman. *The American Novel through Henry James* (New York: Appleton, 1966); Carl M. Hughes, *The Negro Novelist* (New York: Citadel, 1953); N. J. Karolides, *The Pioneer in the American Novel, 1900–1950* (Norman: University of Oklahoma Press, 1967); Alfred Kazin, *Bright Book of Life: American Novelists and Storytellers from Hemingway to Mailer* (Boston: Little, Brown, 1973); Marcus Klein, *After Alienation: American Novels in Mid-Century* (New York: Meridian, 1963); Marcus Klein, ed., *The American Novel Since World*

War II (New York: Fawcett, 1969); Wesley Kort, *Shriven Selves: Religious Problems in Recent American Fiction* (Philadelphia: Fortress, 1972); Richard Lehan, *A Dangerous Crossing: French Literary Existentialism and the Modern American Novel* (Carbondale: Southern Illinois University Press, 1973); R. W. B. Lewis, *The Picaresque Saint: Representative Figures in American Fiction* (Philadelphia: Lippincott, 1958); John O. Lyons, *The College Novel in America* (Carbondale: Southern Illinois University Press, 1962); Harold T. McCarthy, *The Expatriate Perspective: American Novelists and the Idea of America* (Rutherford, N.J.: Fairleigh Dickinson University Press, 1973); Dave Madden, ed., *Proletarian Writers of the Thirties* (Carbondale: Southern Illinois University Press, 1968); Irving Malin, *New American Gothic* (Carbondale: Southern Illinois University Press, 1962); Irving Malin, comp., *Contemporary American-Jewish Literature: Critical Essays* (Bloomington: Indiana University Press, 1973); R. W. Meyer, *The Middle Western Farm Novel in the Twentieth Century* (Lincoln: University of Nebraska Press, 1965); Arthur Mizener, *The Sense of Life in the Modern Novel* (Boston: Houghton Mifflin, 1964); Harry T. Moore, ed., *Contemporary Novelists* (Carbondale: Southern Illinois University Press, 1964); Blake Nevius, *The American Novel: Sinclair Lewis to the Present* (New York: Appleton, 1970); William Peden, *The American Short Story* (Boston: Houghton Mifflin, 1964); Louis D. Rubin, *The Faraway Country: Writers of the Modern South* (Seattle: University of Washington Press, 1963) and *The Curious Death of the Novel* (Baton Rouge: Louisiana State University Press, 1967); Richard H. Rupp, *Celebration in Postwar American Fiction, 1945–1967* (Coral Gables: University of Miami Press, 1970); Robert Scholes, *The Fabulators* (New York: Oxford University Press, 1967); Max F. Schulz, *Radical Sophistication: Studies in Contemporary Jewish-American Novelists* (Athens: Ohio University Press, 1969) and *Black Humor Fiction of the Sixties* (Athens: Ohio University Press, 1973); Bernard Sherman, *The Invention of the Jew: Jewish-American Education Novels* (Cranbury, N.J.: Yoseloff, 1969); Harry Slochower, *No Voice Is Wholly Lost* (New York: Creative Age, 1945); Edward Stone, ed., *What Was Naturalism?* (New York: Appleton, 1959); Walter Sullivan, *Death By Melancholy: Essays on Modern Southern Fiction* (Baton Rouge: Louisiana State University Press, 1972); Tony Tanner, *City of Words: American Fiction, 1950–1970* (New York: Harper & Row, 1971); Nancy M. Tischler, *Black Masks: Negro Characters in Modern Southern Fiction* (University Park: Pennsylvania State University Press, 1969); Darwin T. Turner, *Afro-American Writers* (New York: Appleton, 1970); A. D. Van Nostrand, *The Denatured Novel* (Indianapolis: Bobbs-Merrill, 1960); Arthur Voss, *The American Short Story: A Critical Survey* (Norman: University of Oklahoma Press, 1973); C. C. Walcutt, *American Literary Naturalism: A Divided Stream* (Minneapolis: University of Minnesota Press, 1956); Joseph J. Waldmeir, ed., *Recent American Fiction* (Boston: Houghton Mifflin, 1963); Helen A. Weinberg, *The New Novel in America: The Kafkan Mode in Contemporary Fiction* (Ithaca, N.Y.: Cornell University Press, 1969); Walter Wells, *Tycoons and Locusts: A Regional Look at Hollywood Fiction of the 1930's* (Carbondale: Southern Illinois University Press, 1973); Max Westbrook, *The Modern American Novel* (New York: Random House, 1966); Austin M. Wright, *The American Short Story in the Twenties* (Chicago: University of Chicago Press, 1961); Émile Zola, *The Experimental Novel and Other Essays,* trans. Belle M. Sherman (London: Cassell, 1894). In addition see GB entries for Auchincloss, Berthoff, Bewley, Blotner, Bone, Cowley, Duffey, Edel, Fiedler, Folsom, Frohock, Gross and Hardy, Kazin, Leisy, Margolies, Martin, Millgate, Pattee, Rubin, Taylor, and West.

Drama

Doris E. Abramson, *Negro Playwrights in the American Theatre, 1925–1959* (New York: Columbia University Press, 1969); Brooks Atkinson, *Broadway* (New York: Macmillan, 1970); Eric Bentley, *The Playwright as Thinker* (New York: Harcourt, 1946) and *In Search of Theater* (New York: Knopf, 1953); C. W. E. Bigsby, *Confrontation and Commitment: A Study of Contemporary American Drama, 1959–1966* (Columbia: University of Missouri Press, 1968); Anita Block, *The Changing World in Plays and Theater* (Boston: Little, Brown, 1939); Jane F. Bonin, *Prize-Winning American Drama: A Bibliographical and Descriptive Guide* (Metuchen, N.J.: Scarecrow, 1973); Louis Broussard, *American Drama: Contemporary Allegory from Eugene O'Neill to Tennessee Williams* (Norman: University of Oklahoma Press, 1962); Robert Brustein, *The Theater of Revolt* (Boston: Little, Brown, 1964); *Seasons of Discontent* (New York: Simon & Schuster, 1967), and *The Third Theatre* (New York: Knopf, 1969); Harold Clurman, *Lies Like Truth* (New York: Grove, 1958) and *The Naked Image* (New York: Macmillan, 1966); Denis Donoghue, *The Third Voice* (New Brunswick, N.J.: Rutgers University Press, 1959); Alan S. Downer, *Fifty Years of American Drama: 1900–1950* (Chicago: Regnery, 1951) and *Recent American Drama* (UMPAW: 1961); Alan S. Downer, ed., *American Drama and Its Critics* (Chicago: University of Chicago Press, 1965) and *The American Theatre Today* (New York: Basic Books, 1967); Earl Jerome Ellison, *God on Broadway* (Richmond, Va.: John Knox Press, 1973); Lehman Engel, *The American Musical Theater: A Consideration* (New York: Macmillan, 1967); Horst Frenz, ed., *American Playwrights on Drama* (New York: Hill & Wang, 1965); John Gassner, *The Theatre in Our Times* (New York: Crown, 1954); *Masters of the Drama* (New York: Dover, 1954); and *Theatre at the Crossroads* (New York: Holt, Rinehart & Winston, 1960); Richard Gilman, *Common and Uncommon Masks* (New York: Random House, 1971); Joseph Golden, *The Death of Tinker Bell: The American Theatre in the Twentieth Century* (Syracuse, N.Y.: Syracuse University Press, 1967); Martin Gottfried, *A Theatre Divided: The Postwar American Stage* (Boston: Little, Brown, 1968); Jean Gould, *Modern American Playwrights* (New York: Dodd, Mead, 1966); Morgan Y. Himelstein, *Drama Was a Weapon: The Left-Wing Theater in New York, 1929–1941* (New Brunswick, N.J.: Rutgers University Press, 1963); Walter Kerr, *Pieces at Eight* (New York: Simon & Schuster, 1951); *The Theater in Spite of Itself* (New York: Simon & Schuster, 1963); *Tragedy and Comedy* (New York: Simon & Schuster, 1967); and *Thirty Plays Hath November* (New York: Knopf, 1969); J. W. Krutch, *American Drama Since 1918,* rev. ed. (New York: Braziller, 1957); Allan Lewis, *American Plays and Playwrights of the Contemporary Theatre* (New York: Crown, 1965); Frederick Lumley, *New Trends in 20th Century Drama* (New York: Oxford University Press, 1972); Jane Mathews, *The Federal Theatre, 1935–1939: Plays, Relief, and Politics* (Princeton: Princeton University Press, 1967); Lofton Mitchell, *Black Drama: The Story of the American Negro in the Theatre* (New York: Hawthorn, 1967); Thomas G. Moore, *The Economics of the American Theatre* (Durham, N.C.: Duke University Press, 1968); Thomas E. Porter, *Myth and Modern American Drama* (Detroit: Wayne State University Press, 1969); Julia S. Price, *The Off-Broadway Theater* (Metuchen, N.J.: Scarecrow, 1962); Gerald Rabkin, *Drama and Commitment: Politics in the American Theater of the Thirties* (Bloomington: Indiana University Press, 1964); James M. Salem, *A Guide to Critical Reviews. Part One: American Drama from O'Neill to Albee* (Metuchen, N.J.: Scarecrow, 1966);

Stanley Schatt, "Contemporary Afro-American Drama: An Annotated Checklist of Primary and Secondary Sources, 1950–1972," *West Coast Review* 8:2 (1973): 41–44; Richard Schechner, *Public Domain* (Indianapolis: Bobbs-Merrill, 1969); W. D. Sievers, *Freud on Broadway* (New York: Hermitage House, 1955); Cecil M. Smith, *Musical Comedy in America* (New York: Theatre Arts Books, 1950); Kenneth Tynan, *Curtains* (New York: Atheneum, 1961); Mardi Valgemae, *Accelerated Grimace: Expressionism in the American Drama of the 1920's* (Carbondale: Southern Illinois University Press, 1972); Gerald Weales, *American Drama Since World War II* (New York: Harcourt, 1962) and *The Jumping-Off Place: American Drama in the 1960's* (New York: Macmillan, 1969); Raymond Williams, *Modern Tragedy* (Stanford, Calif.: Stanford University Press, 1966).

9: MODERN POETS

Amy Lowell

TEXTS. *The Complete Poetical Works of Amy Lowell*, ed. Louis Untermeyer (Boston: Houghton Mifflin, 1955); *A Critical Fable* (Boston: Houghton Mifflin, 1922); *Tendencies in Modern American Poetry* (New York: Macmillan, 1917).

STUDIES. Frances Kemp, "Bibliography of Amy Lowell," *Bulletin of Bibliography* 15 (1933–1934): 8–9, 25–26, 50–53. Biographical and critical studies include Clement Wood, *Amy Lowell* (New York: H. Vinal, 1926); S. Foster Damon, *Amy Lowell: A Chronicle, with Extracts from Her Correspondence* (Boston: Houghton Mifflin, 1935); Horace Gregory, *Amy Lowell: Portrait of the Poet in Her Time* (Camden, N.J.: T. Nelson, 1958); and Jean Gould, *Amy: The World of Amy Lowell and the Imagist Movement* (New York: Dodd, Mead, 1975). Shorter studies include Margaret Widdemer, "The Legend of Amy Lowell," *Texas Quarterly*, 6 (1963): 193–200 and Rosemary Sprague, *Imaginary Gardens* (Philadelphia: Chilton, 1970), a study of Dickinson, Millay, Lowell, Teasdale, and Moore.

Robert Frost

TEXTS. *Collected Poems* (New York: Holt, 1930; 1939) includes the essay "The Figure a Poem Makes." *The Poems of Robert Frost* (New York: Modern Library, 1946) includes the essay "The Constant Symbol." *Complete Poems* (New York: Holt, 1949) is the most inclusive collection to 1949. *In the Clearing* (New York: Holt, Rinehart & Winston, 1962) collects the later poems. *The Poetry of Robert Frost*, ed. Edward R. Lathem (New York: Holt, Rinehart & Winston, 1969) is the most nearly complete edition. *Selected Prose of Robert Frost*, eds. Hyde Cox and Edward R. Lathem (New York: Holt, Rinehart & Winston, 1966) and *Robert Frost on Writing*, ed. Elaine Berry (New Brunswick, N.J.: Rutgers University Press, 1973) are two useful texts.

STUDIES. The most helpful review of Frost scholarship is Reginald L. Cook in *Sixteen Modern American Authors*. Also helpful are Esther Mertins, *The Intervals of Robert Frost: A Critical Bibliography* (Berkeley: University of California Press, 1947) and Donald J. Greiner, *The Merrill Checklist of Robert Frost* (Columbus, Oh.: Merrill, 1969). Useful introductions to the work are Lawrance Thompson, *Robert Frost* (UMPAW: 1959); Robert A. Greenberg and James G. Hepburn, eds., *Robert Frost: An Introduction* (New York: Holt, Rinehart & Winston, 1961); Elizabeth Isaacs, *An Introduction to Robert Frost* (Chicago: Swallow, 1962); Philip L. Gerber, *Robert Frost* (TUSAS: 1966); and Elizabeth Jennings, *Frost* (New York: Barnes & Noble, 1966). Biographical material is plentiful and includes Lawrance Thompson, *Robert Frost: The Early Years, 1874–1915* and *Robert Frost: The Years of Triumph, 1915–1938* (New York: Holt, Rinehart & Winston, 1966 and 1970), the first two volumes of a projected three-volume biography; Elizabeth S. Sergeant, *Robert Frost: The Trial by Existence* (New York: Holt, Rinehart & Winston, 1960); Sidney Cox, *A Swinger of Birches* (New York: New York University Press, 1960); Jean Gould, *The Aim Was Song* (New York: Dodd, Mead, 1964); Edward C. Lathem and Lawrance Thompson, eds., *Robert Frost: Farm Poultryman* (Hanover, N.H.: Dartmouth Publications, 1963); Edward C. Lathem, ed., *Interviews with Robert Frost* (New York: Holt, Rinehart & Winston, 1966); Louis Mertins, ed., *Robert Frost: Life and Talks— Walking* (Norman: University of Oklahoma Press, 1965); Daniel Smythe, *Robert Frost Speaks* (New York: Twayne, 1964); F. D. Reeve, *Robert Frost in Russia* (Boston: Little, Brown, 1964); Robert Francis, *Frost: A Time to Talk: Conversations and Indiscretions Recorded by Robert Francis* (Amherst: University of Massachusetts Press, 1972). There are three collections of letters: *Selected Letters of Robert Frost,* ed. Lawrance Thompson (New York: Holt, Rinehart & Winston, 1964); *Family Letters of Robert and Elinor Frost,* ed. Arnold Grade (Albany: State University of New York Press, 1972); and *The Letters of Robert Frost to Louis Untermeyer* (New York: Holt, Rinehart & Winston, 1963). Book-length studies of Frost are as follows: Gorham B. Munson, *Robert Frost: A Study in Sensibility and Good Sense* (Garden City, N.Y.: Doran, 1927); Robert P. T. Coffin, *New Poetry of New England: Frost and Robinson* (New York: Atheneum, Russell & Russell, 1938); Lawrance Thompson, *Fire and Ice: The Art and Thought of Robert Frost* (New York: Atheneum, Russell & Russell, 1942); Reginald L. Cook, *The Dimensions of Robert Frost* (New York: Rinehart, 1958); George W. Nitchie, *Human Values in the Poetry of Robert Frost* (Durham, N.C.: Duke University Press, 1960); John F. Lynen, *The Pastoral Art of Robert Frost* (New Haven: Yale University Press, 1960); John R. Doyle, Jr., *The Poetry of Robert Frost* (Darien, Conn.: Hafner, 1962); Radcliffe Squires, *The Major Themes of Robert Frost* (Ann Arbor: University of Michigan Press, 1963); Reuben A. Brower, *The Poetry of Robert Frost: Constellations of Intention* (New York: Oxford University Press, 1963); Edward C. Lathem, ed., *A Concordance to the Poetry of Robert Frost* (New York: Holt, Rinehart & Winston, 1971); and Frank Lentricchia, *Robert Frost: Modern Poetics and the Landscapes of Self* (Durham, N.C.: Duke University Press, 1975). Collections of short criticism include Richard Thornton, ed., *Recognition of Robert Frost* (New York: Holt, 1937); James M. Cox, ed., *Robert Frost: A Collection of Critical Essays* (Englewood Cliffs, N.J.: Prentice-Hall, 1962); and Lewis P. Simpson, ed., *Profile of Robert Frost* (Columbus, Oh.: Merrill, 1971).

Carl Sandburg

TEXTS. *Complete Poems* (New York: Harcourt, 1950); *The Sandburg Range* (New York: Harcourt, 1957), excerpts from his novel, autobiography, his Lincoln biography, selections from his poems, children's stories, and so on; *Re-*

membrance Rock (New York: Harcourt, 1948), a very long novel; *Always the Young Strangers* (New York: Harcourt, 1953), autobiography.
STUDIES. W. P. Schenk, "Carl Sandburg: A Bibliography," *Bulletin of Bibliography* 16 (1936): 4–7 and Thomas P. Shaw, *Carl Sandburg: A Bibliography* (Washington, D.C.: Library of Congress, 1948) are two good sources. A good introduction to Sandburg's work is Richard Crowder, *Carl Sandburg* (TUSAS: 1964). Biographical studies are K. W. Detzer, *Carl Sandburg: A Study in Personality and Background* (New York: Harcourt, 1941); Harry Golden, *Carl Sandburg* (Cleveland: World Publishing, 1961); Hazel Durnell, *The America of Carl Sandburg* (Riverton, Va.: University Press of Washington, D.C., 1965); Joseph Haas and Gene Lovitz, *Carl Sandburg: A Pictorial Biography* (New York: Putnam, 1967); and N. Callahan, *Carl Sandburg: The Lincoln of Our Literature* (New York: New York University Press, 1970). Herbert Mitgang has edited *The Letters of Carl Sandburg* (New York: Harcourt, 1968). Serious criticism of Sandburg's poetry is relatively sparse. An early estimate is Amy Lowell, *Tendencies in Modern American Poetry* (New York: Macmillan, 1917). Later comments are Oscar Cargill, "Carl Sandburg: Crusader and Mystic," *CE* 1 (1940): 649–657; W. C. Williams, "Carl Sandburg's Complete Poems," in *Selected Essays* (New York: Random House, 1954); Michael Yatron, *America's Literary Revolt* (New York: Philosophical Library, 1959); Gay Wilson Allen, "Carl Sandburg: Fire and Smoke," *SAQ* 59 (1960): 315–331; and Mark Van Doren, *Carl Sandburg* (Washington, D.C.: Library of Congress, 1969), which includes a bibliography of Sandburg materials in the Library of Congress collections.

Vachel Lindsay

TEXTS. *Collected Poems* (New York: Macmillan, 1923; 1925). *Selected Poems of Vachel Lindsay,* ed. Hazelton Spencer (New York: Macmillan, 1931); *Selected Poems of Vachel Lindsay,* ed. Mark Harris (New York: Macmillan, 1963); *Adventures While Preaching the Gospel of Beauty* (New York: Macmillan, 1914); *A Handy Guide for Beggars* (New York: Macmillan, 1916).
STUDIES. Biographical studies of Lindsay include Stephen Graham, *Tramping with a Poet in the Rockies* (New York: Appleton, 1922); Albert E. Trombly, *Vachel Lindsay, Adventurer* (Columbia, Mo.: Lucas Bros., 1929); Edgar Lee Masters, *Vachel Lindsay: A Poet in America* (New York: Scribner, 1935); Mark Harris, *City of Discontent* (Indianapolis: Bobbs-Merrill, 1952); and Eleanor Ruggles, *The West-Going Heart: A Life of Vachel Lindsay* (New York: Norton, 1959). Among critical studies of Lindsay are E. L. Davison, *Some Modern Poets and Other Critical Essays* (New York: Harper, 1928); Davis Edwards, "The Real Source of Vachel Lindsay's Poetic Technique," *QJS* 33 (1947): 182–195; N. E. Enkvist, "The Folk Element in Vachel Lindsay's Poetry," *ES* 32 (1951): 241–249; and Michael Yatron, *America's Literary Revolt* (New York: Philosophical Library, 1959). Other comments on Lindsay include Peter Viereck, "Vachel Lindsay, the Dante of the Fundamentalists: The Suicide of America's Faith in Technology," in *Friendship's Garland: Essays Presented to Mario Praz on His Seventieth Birthday,* ed. V. Gabrieli (Rome: Edizioni di Storia e Letteratura, 1966), 2: 207–232 and John T. Flanagan, "Vachel Lindsay: An Appraisal," in *Essays on American Literature in Honor of Jay B. Hubbell,* ed. Clarence Gohdes (Durham, N.C.: Duke University Press, 1967), pp. 273–281.

Wallace Stevens

TEXTS. *The Collected Poems of Wallace Stevens* (New York: Knopf, 1954); *Poems by Wallace Stevens,* intro. by Samuel F. Morse (New York: Knopf, Vintage, 1959); *The Necessary Angel: Essays on Reality and the Imagination* (New York: Knopf, 1951; Vintage, 1965). *Opus Posthumous,* ed. Samuel F. Morse (New York: Knopf, 1957) includes poems omitted from *Collected Poems,* later poems, translations, miscellaneous prose, and "Adagia" (brief and often cryptic comments on poetry, imagination, and reality).

STUDIES. The most helpful bibliography is Joseph N. Riddel's essay reviewing Stevens scholarship in *Sixteen Modern American Authors.* See also Samuel F. Morse, *Wallace Stevens: A Preliminary Checklist of His Published Writings, 1898–1954* (New Haven: Yale University Library, 1954); Jackson R. Bryer and J. N. Riddel, "A Checklist of Stevens Criticism," *TCL* 8, nos. 3–4 (October 1962–January 1963): 124–142; J. M. Edelstein, *Wallace Stevens: A Descriptive Bibliography* (Pittsburgh: University of Pittsburgh Press, 1973); T. L. Huguelet, *The Merrill Checklist of Wallace Stevens* (Columbus, Oh.: Merrill, 1970); and *The Wallace Stevens Newsletter* (1969–). Introductions to this difficult poet are William York Tindall, *Wallace Stevens* (UMPAW: 1961); Henry W. Wells, *Introduction to Wallace Stevens* (Bloomington: Indiana University Press, 1964); and William Burney, *Wallace Stevens* (TUSAS: 1968). A biographical study is Samuel F. French, *Wallace Stevens: Poetry as Life* (Indianapolis: Bobbs-Merrill, Pegasus, 1970). Holly Stevens has edited *Letters of Wallace Stevens* (New York: Knopf, 1966). Criticism of Stevens's work is plentiful and indicates continued and growing interest in his achievement. The following book-length studies are listed in alphabetical order: James Baird, *The Dome and the Rock: Structure in the Poetry of Wallace Stevens* (Baltimore: Johns Hopkins Press, 1968); Michel Benamou, *Wallace Stevens and the Symbolist Imagination* (Princeton: Princeton University Press, 1972); James Benziger, *Images of Eternity* (Carbondale: Southern Illinois University Press, 1962); Richard Blessing, *Wallace Stevens's "Whole Harmonium"* (Syracuse, N.Y.: Syracuse University Press, 1970); Robert Buttell, *Wallace Stevens: The Making of Harmonium* (Princeton: Princeton University Press, 1967); Frank Doggett, *Stevens' Poetry of Thought* (Baltimore: Johns Hopkins Press, 1966); John J. Enck, *Wallace Stevens: Images and Judgements* (Cardondale: Southern Illinois University Press, 1964); Daniel Fuchs, *The Comic Spirit of Wallace Stevens* (Durham, N.C.: Duke University Press, 1962); Frank Kermode, *Wallace Stevens* (New York: Grove, 1961); Edward Kessler, *Images of Wallace Stevens* (New Brunswick, N.J.: Rutgers University Press, 1972); A. W. Litz, *Introspective Voyager: The Poetic Development of Wallace Stevens* (New York: Oxford University Press, 1972); E. P. Nassar, *Wallace Stevens: An Anatomy of Figuration* (Philadelphia: University of Pennsylvania Press, 1965); William Van O'Connor, *The Shaping Spirit: A Study of Wallace Stevens* (Chicago: Regnery, 1950); Robert Pack, *Wallace Stevens: An Approach to His Poetry and Thought* (New Brunswick, N.J.: Rutgers University Press, 1958); Joseph N. Riddel, *The Clairvoyant Eye* (Baton Rouge: Louisiana State University Press, 1965); H. J. Stern, *Wallace Stevens: Art of Uncertainty* (Ann Arbor: University of Michigan Press, 1966); Ronald Sukenick, *Wallace Stevens: Musing the Obscure* (New York: New York University Press, 1967); Helen Vendler, *On Extended Wings: Wallace Stevens's Longer Poems* (Cambridge, Mass.: Harvard University Press, 1969);

and Thomas F. Walsh, *Concordance to the Poetry of Wallace Stevens* (University Park: Pennsylvania State University Press, 1963). Briefer studies are Sr. M. Bernetta Quinn, *The Metamorphic Tradition in Modern Poetry* (New Brunswick, N.J.: Rutgers University Press, 1955); J. Hillis Miller, *Poets of Reality* (Cambridge, Mass.: Harvard University Press, 1965); Frank Lentricchia, *The Gaiety of Language: An Essay on the Radical Poetics of W. B. Yeats and Wallace Stevens* (Berkeley: University of California Press, 1968); and Suzanne Juhasz, *Metaphor and the Poetry of Williams, Pound and Stevens* (Lewisburg, Pa.: Bucknell University Press, 1973). Useful collections of short criticism are Ashley Brown and Robert S. Haller, eds., *The Achievement of Wallace Stevens* (Philadelphia: Lippincott, 1962); Marie Boroff, ed., *Wallace Stevens: A Collection of Critical Essays* (Englewood Cliffs, N.J.: Prentice-Hall, 1963); Roy H. Pearce and J. Hillis Miller, eds., *The Act of the Mind: Essays on the Poetry of Wallace Stevens* (Baltimore: Johns Hopkins Press, 1965); and Peter L. McNamara, ed., *Critics on Wallace Stevens* (Coral Gables: University of Miami Press, 1972).

William Carlos Williams

TEXTS. *Collected Earlier Poems of William Carlos Williams* (New York: New Directions, 1951); *Collected Later Poems of William Carlos Williams* (New York: New Directions, 1963); *Complete Collected Poems of William Carlos Williams 1906–1938* (New York: New Directions, 1938); *Selected Poems of William Carlos Williams* (New York: New Directions, 1963); *Pictures from Brueghel and Other Poems,* including "The Desert Music" and "Journey to Love" (New York: New Directions, 1962); *Paterson,* books 1–5 (New York: New Directions, 1963); *I Wanted to Write a Poem,* ed. Edith Heal (Boston: Beacon, 1958). Williams's comments on many of his own works; *Autobiography* (New York: Random House, 1951); *In the American Grain* (New York: New Directions, 1956), historical sketches and comments on the American past; *Selected Essays* (New York: Random House, 1954); *The William Carlos Williams Reader,* ed. M. L. Rosenthal (New York: New Directions, 1966), poems, fiction, drama, and miscellaneous prose.

STUDIES. The most helpful review of Williams scholarship is Linda W. Wagner's bibliographical essay in *Sixteen Modern American Authors.* Additional bibliographies are Emily M. Wallace, *A Bibliography of William Carlos Williams* (Middletown, Conn.: Wesleyan University Press, 1968) and John Engels, ed., *The Merrill Checklist of William Carlos Williams* (Columbus, Oh.: Merrill, 1969). Helpful biographical and critical introductions are John Malcolm Brinnin, *William Carlos Williams* (UMPAW: 1963) and Thomas R. Whitaker, *William Carlos Williams* (TUSAS: 1968). John C. Thirlwall has edited *Selected Letters of William Carlos Williams* (New York: McDowell, Obolensky, 1950). Full-length studies of Williams (listed here alphabetically) are James Breslin, *William Carlos Williams: An American Artist* (New York: Oxford University Press, 1970); Robert Coles, *William Carlos Williams: The Knack of Survival in America* (New Brunswick, N. J.: Rutgers University Press, 1975); Joel Connaroe, *William Carlos Williams's "Paterson": Language and Landscape* (Philadelphia: University of Pennsylvania Press, 1970); Bram Dijkstra, *The Hieroglyphics of a New Speech: Cubism, Stieglitz, and the Early Poetry of William Carlos Williams*

(Princeton: Princeton University Press, 1968); James Guimond, *The Art of William Carlos Williams* (Urbana: University of Illinois Press, 1968); Suzanne Juhasz, *Metaphor and the Poetry of Williams, Pound, and Stevens* (Lewisburg, Pa.: Bucknell University Press, 1973); Vivienne Koch, *William Carlos Williams* (New York: New Directions, 1950); Jerome Mazzaro, *William Carlos Williams: The Later Poems* (Ithaca, N. Y.: Cornell University Press, 1973); J. Hillis Miller, *Poets of Reality* (Cambridge, Mass.: Harvard University Press, 1965); Alan B. Ostrom, *The Poetic World of William Carlos Williams* (Carbondale: Southern Illinois University Press, 1966); Sherman Paul, *The Music of Survival: A Biography of a Poem by William Carlos Williams* (Urbana: University of Illinois Press, 1968); Walter S. Peterson, *An Approach to Paterson* (New Haven: Yale University Press, 1967); Sr. M. Bernetta Quinn, *The Metamorphic Tradition in Modern Poetry* (New Brunswick, N. J.: Rutgers University Press, 1955); Benjamin Sankey, *A Companion to William Carlos Williams's Paterson* (Berkeley: University of California Press, 1971); Rod Townley, *The Early Poetry of William Carlos Williams* (Ithaca, N.Y.: Cornell University Press, 1975); Linda W. Wagner, *The Poems of William Carlos Williams: A Critical Study* (Middletown, Conn.: Wesleyan University Press, 1964) and *The Prose of William Carlos Williams* (Middletown, Conn.: Wesleyan University Press, 1970); A. K. Weatherhead, *The Edge of the Image* (Seattle: University of Washington Press, 1967); Mike Weaver, *William Carlos Williams: The American Background* (New York: Cambridge University Press, 1971); and Reed Whittemore, *William Carlos Williams: Poet from Jersey* (Boston: Houghton Mifflin, 1975). Collections of critical pieces on the work include J. Hillis Miller, ed., *William Carlos Williams: A Collection of Critical Essays* (Englewood Cliffs, N.J.: Prentice-Hall, 1966); Jerome Mazzaro, ed., *Profile of William Carlos Williams* (Columbus, Oh.: Merrill, 1971); and John Engels, ed., *The Merrill Studies in Paterson* (Columbus, Oh.: Merrill, 1971). Issues of periodicals devoted entirely to Williams include *Briarcliff Quarterly* 3 (October 1946); *Perspective* 6, no. 4 (Autumn–Winter 1953); *Western Review* 17, no. 4 (Summer 1953); *Massachusetts Review* 3, no. 2 (Winter 1962); and *Journal of Modern Literature* 1, no. 4 (1971).

Ezra Pound

TEXTS. The following texts give the heart of Pound's work: *Selected Poems of Ezra Pound*, intro. by T. S. Eliot (London: Faber, 1928); *Selected Poems of Ezra Pound* (New York: New Directions, 1957); *Personae: Collected Shorter Poems of Ezra Pound* (London: Faber, 1952); *The Cantos of Ezra Pound* (New York: New Directions, 1948), which includes "A Draft of XXX Cantos," "Eleven New Cantos, XXXI–XLI," "The Fifth Decad of Cantos, XLII–LI," Cantos LII–LXXI," "The Pisan Cantos, LXXIV–LXXXIV" (Cantos LXXII, and LXXIII have never been published.); *Section: Rock-Drill, 85–95 de los cantares* (New York: New Directions, 1956); *Thrones, 96–109 de los cantares* (New York: New Directions, 1959); *Drafts and Fragments of Cantos CX–CXVII* (London: Faber, 1970); *The Classical Anthology Defined by Confucius* (Cambridge, Mass.: Harvard University Press, 1954); *Confucian Analects* (London: Peter Owen, 1956); *Confucius: The Great Digest and Unwobbling Pivot* (London: Peter Owen, 1952); *Sophocles: Women of Trachis* (London: Neville Spearman, 1956); *Love Poems of Ancient Egypt*, with Noel Stock (New York: New Directions,

1962); *The Translations of Ezra Pound,* ed. Hugh Kenner (New York: New Directions, 1963); *Literary Essays of Ezra Pound,* ed. T. S. Eliot (New York: New Directions, 1954); *The Spirit of Romance* (New York: New Directions, 1952); *ABC of Reading* (New York: New Directions, 1960); *Pavannes and Divagations* (New York: New Directions, 1958); *Patria Mia* and *The Treatise on Harmony* (London: Peter Owen, 1962); *Guide to Kulchur* (New York: New Directions, 1952); *ABC of Economics* (Tunbridge Wells: Peter Russell, 1953); *Jefferson and/or Mussolini* (London: Stanley Nott, 1935); *Impact: Essays on Ignorance and the Decline of American Civilization,* ed. Noel Stock (Chicago: Regnery, 1960); *Selected Prose, 1909–1965,* ed. William Cookson (New York: New Directions, 1973).

STUDIES. The most helpful guide in the sea of Pound studies is John J. Espey, whose bibliographical essay in *Sixteen Modern American Authors* reviews Pound scholarship through 1971. Also helpful are Donald Gallup, *A Bibliography of Ezra Pound* (London: Hart-Davis, 1963) and Marie Henault, *The Merrill Guide to Ezra Pound* (Columbus, Oh.: Merrill, 1970). Useful introductions are G. S. Fraser, *Ezra Pound* (New York: Grove, 1961); William Van O'Connor, *Ezra Pound* (UMPAW: 1963); and Christine Brooke-Rose, *A ZBC of Ezra Pound* (Berkeley: University of California Press, 1971). Biographical material is plentiful but uneven; of the studies listed below, Stock is the most reliable: Charles Norman, *The Case of Ezra Pound* (London: Bodley Head, 1948) and *Ezra Pound* (New York: Macmillan, 1960); E. C. Mullins, *This Difficult Individual, Ezra Pound* (New York: Fleet, 1961); Patricia Hutchins, *Ezra Pound's Kensington* (Chicago: Regnery, 1965); Julian Cornell, *The Trial of Ezra Pound* (New York: Day, 1966); Michael Reck, *Ezra Pound: A Close-Up* (New York: McGraw-Hill, 1967); Harry M. Meacham, *The Caged Panther: Ezra Pound at St. Elizabeths* (New York: Twayne, 1967); Noel Stock, *The Life of Ezra Pound* (New York: Pantheon, 1970); Mary de Rachewiltz, *Discretions* (Boston: Little, Brown, 1971); Catherine Seelye, ed., *Charles Olson & Ezra Pound: An Encounter at St. Elizabeths* (New York: Grossman/Viking, 1975); and C. David Heymann, *Ezra Pound: The Last Rower* (New York: Viking Penguin, 1976). D. D. Paige has edited *The Letters of Ezra Pound* (New York: Harcourt, 1950), and Forrest Read has edited *Pound/Joyce: The Letters of Ezra Pound to James Joyce, with Pound's Essays on Joyce* (New York: New Directions, 1967). The great number of full-length studies of Pound indicates the early and continuing belief in his great importance as poet, critic, and spokesman for his age. Of the studies listed below in alphabetical order, the early assessments by Eliot and Yeats are of obvious interest; others that deserve special praise include those of Edwards and Vasse, Emery, Espey, Stock, Watts, and Yip. The studies are Walter Baumann, *The Rose in the Steel Dust: An Examination of the Cantos of Ezra Pound* (Coral Gables: University of Miami Press, 1970); William B. Chace, *The Political Identities of Ezra Pound and T. S. Eliot* (Stanford, Calif.: Stanford University Press, 1973); Donald Davie, *Ezra Pound: Poet as Sculptor* (New York: Oxford University Press, 1964); Earle Davis, *Vision Fugitive: Ezra Pound and Economics* (Lawrence: University Press of Kansas, 1968); George Dekker, *Sailing after Knowledge: The Cantos of Ezra Pound* (London: Routledge & Kegan Paul, 1963); L. Dembo, *The Confucian Odes of Ezra Pound: A Critical Appraisal* (Berkeley: University of California Press, 1963); N. C. de Nagy, *The Poetry of Ezra Pound: The Pre-Imagist Stage* (Bern: Francke, 1960) and *Ezra Pound's*

Poetics and Literary Tradition (Bern: Francke, 1966); John H. Edwards and William W. Vasse, *Annotated Index to the Cantos of Ezra Pound* (Berkeley: University of California Press, 1957); T. S. Eliot, *Ezra Pound, His Metric and Poetry* (New York: Knopf, 1917); Clark Emery, *Ideas into Action: A Study of Pound's Cantos* (Coral Gables: University of Miami Press, 1958); John J. Espey, *Ezra Pound's Mauberley: A Study in Composition* (Berkeley: University of California Press, 1955); Donald Gallup, *T. S. Eliot and Ezra Pound: Collaborators in Letters* (New Haven: Yale University Press, 1970); K. L. Goodwin, *The Influence of Ezra Pound* (New York: Oxford University Press, 1966); Thomas H. Jackson, *The Early Poetry of Ezra Pound* (Cambridge, Mass.: Harvard University Press, 1968); Hugh Kenner, *The Poetry of Ezra Pound* (New York: New Directions, 1951) and *The Pound Era* (Berkeley: University of California Press, 1971); Gary Lane, *A Concordance to Personae* (New York: Haskell House, 1972); Stuart Y. McDougal, *Ezra Pound and the Troubadour Tradition* (Princeton: Princeton University Press, 1972); Max Nanny, *Ezra Pound: Poetics for an Electric Age* Bern: Francke, 1973); Daniel D. Pearlman, *The Barb of Time: On the Unity of Ezra Pound's Cantos* (New York: Oxford University Press, 1969); M. L. Rosenthal, *A Primer of Ezra Pound* (New York: Macmillan, 1960); K. K. Ruthven, *A Guide to Ezra Pound's Personae* (Berkeley: University of California Press, 1969); Herbert N. Schneidau, *Ezra Pound: The Image and the Real* (Baton Rouge: Louisiana State University Press, 1969); Noel Stock, *Poet in Exile: Ezra Pound* (New York: Barnes & Noble, 1964) and *Reading the Cantos: The Study of Meaning in Ezra Pound* (New York: Pantheon, 1966); J. P. Sullivan, *Ezra Pound and Sextus Propertius: A Study in Creative Translation* (Austin: University of Texas Press, 1964); Harold H. Watts, *Ezra Pound and The Cantos* (Chicago: Regnery, 1952); Hugh Witmeyer, *The Poetry of Ezra Pound: Forms and Renewal, 1908–1920* (Berkeley: University of California Press 1969); W. B. Yeats, "A Packet for Ezra Pound," in *A Vision* (New York: Macmillan, 1961); and Wai-lim Yip, *Ezra Pound's Cathay* (Princeton: Princeton University Press, 1969). Two studies of imagism should also be mentioned: Glenn Hughes, *Imagism and the Imagists* (Stanford, Calif.: Stanford University Press, 1931) and Stanley K. Coffman, *Imagism: A Chapter for the History of Modern Poetry* (Norman: University of Oklahoma Press, 1951). Collections of shorter criticism include Peter Russell, ed., *Ezra Pound* (London: Peter Nevill, 1950); Lewis Leary, ed., *Motive and Method in The Cantos of Ezra Pound* (New York: Columbia University Press, 1954); William Van O'Connor and Edward Stone, eds., *A Casebook on Ezra Pound* (New York: T. Y. Crowell, 1959); Walter Sutton, ed., *Ezra Pound: A Collection of Critical Essays* (Englewood Cliffs, N.J.: Prentice-Hall, 1963); Noel Stock, ed., *Perspectives* (Chicago: Regnery, 1965); Eva Hesse, comp., *New Approaches to Ezra Pound* (Berkeley: University of California Press, 1969); E. San Juan, comp., *Critics on Ezra Pound* (Coral Gables: University of Miami Press, 1972); and Eric Homberger, comp., *Ezra Pound: The Critical Heritage* (London: Routledge & Kegan Paul, 1972).

Robinson Jeffers

TEXTS. *Tamar and Other Poems* (New York: Peter G. Boyle, 1924); *Roan Stallion, Tamar and Other Poems* (New York: Boni & Liveright, 1925), reprinted with new poems by Modern Library, 1935; *The Women at Point Sur* (New York: Liveright, 1927); *Cawdor and Other Poems* (New York: Liveright, 1928); *Dear*

Judas and Other Poems (New York: Liveright, 1929); *Thurso's Landing and Other Poems* (New York: Liveright, 1932); *Give Your Heart to the Hawks and Other Poems* (New York: Random House, 1933); *Solstice and Other Poems* (New York: Random House, 1935); *Such Counsels You Gave to Me and Other Poems* (New York: Random House, 1937); *The Selected Poetry of Robinson Jeffers* (New York: Random House, 1938); *Be Angry at the Sun* (New York: Random House, 1941); *Medea* (New York: Random House, 1946), translation; *The Double Axe and Other Poems* (New York: Random House, 1948); *Hungerfield and Other Poems* (New York: Random House, 1954).

STUDIES. Primary bibliographies are S. S. Alberts, *A Bibliography of the Works of Robinson Jeffers* (New York: Random House, 1933) and a supplement, H. C. Woodbridge, "A Bibliographical Note on Jeffers," *The American Book Collector* 10 (September 1959): 15–18. See also W. H. Nolte, *The Merrill Guide to Robinson Jeffers* (Columbus, Oh.: Merrill, 1970). Good introductions to Jeffers are Lawrence C. Powell, *Robinson Jeffers: The Man and His Work* (Pasadena, Calif.: San Pasqual Press, 1940) and Frederic I. Carpenter, *Robinson Jeffers* (TUSAS: 1962). Carpenter includes a useful bibliography of articles and sections of books dealing with Jeffers. Biographical material on Jeffers includes Melba B. Bennett, *Robinson Jeffers and the Sea* (San Francisco: Gelber, Lilienthal, Inc., 1936); Edith Greenan, *Of Una Jeffers* (Los Angeles: Ward Ritchie Press, 1939); Ann N. Ridgeway, ed., *The Selected Letters of Robinson Jeffers: 1897–1962* (Baltimore: Johns Hopkins Press, 1968). Book-length critical studies of Jeffers are George Sterling, *Robinson Jeffers: The Man and the Artist* (New York: Boni & Liveright, 1926); Rudolph Gilbert, *Shine, Perishing Republic: Robinson Jeffers and the Tragic Sense in Modern Poetry* (New York: Haskell House, 1936, 1965); Radcliffe Squires, *The Loyalties of Robinson Jeffers* (Ann Arbor: University of Michigan Press, 1956); Mercedes C. Monjian, *Robinson Jeffers: A Study in Inhumanism* (Pittsburgh: University of Pittsburgh Press, 1958). Melba B. Bennett, *The Stone Mason of Tor House: The Life and Work of Robinson Jeffers* (Los Angeles: Ward Ritchie Press, 1966) includes a useful secondary bibliography arranged year by year until 1966. An appreciation of Jeffers by one of his disciples is Brother Antoninus, *Robinson Jeffers: Fragments of an Older Fury* (Berkeley: Oyez, 1968). Recently published studies are A. B. Coffin, *Robinson Jeffers, Poet of Inhumanism* (Madison: University of Wisconsin Press, 1971); Louis Adamic, *Robinson Jeffers* (Folcroft, Pa.: Folcroft Library, 1973); and Robert Brophy, *Robinson Jeffers: Myth, Ritual, and Symbol in the Narrative Poems* (Cleveland: Western Reserve Press, 1973).

Marianne Moore

TEXTS. *Selected Poems,* introduction by T. S. Eliot (New York: Macmillan, 1935); *Collected Poems* (New York: Macmillan, 1951); *A Marianne Moore Reader* (New York: Viking, 1961); *The Complete Poems of Marianne Moore* (New York: Macmillan, 1967); *Tell Me, Tell Me* (New York: Viking, 1966); *Predilections* (New York: Viking, 1955); *The Fables of La Fontaine* (New York: Viking, 1954), translation.

STUDIES. For bibliography see E. P. Sheehy and K. A. Lohf, *The Achievement of Marianne Moore: A Bibliography 1907–1957* (New York: New York Public Library, 1958). Introductions to the work are B. F. Engel, *Marianne Moore*

(TUSAS: 1964); Jean Garrigue, *Marianne Moore* (UMPAW: 1965); and G. W. Nitchie, *Marianne Moore: An Introduction to the Poetry* (New York: Columbia University Press, 1970). Book-length studies are Sr. Mary Therese, *Marianne Moore* (Grand Rapids, Mich.: Eerdmans, 1969); and Gary Lane, *A Concordance to the Poems of Marianne Moore* (New York: Haskell House, 1972). Briefer studies are A. K. Weatherhead, *The Edge of the Image* (Seattle: University of Washington Press, 1967), a study of Moore and William Carlos Williams, and R. P. Blackmur, "The Method of Marianne Moore," in *Language as Gesture* (New York: Harcourt, 1950). Collections of short criticism are Jose Garcia Villa, ed., "Marianne Moore Issue," *Quarterly Review of Literature,* 4, no. 2 (1948): 121–223, essays by Brooks, Fowlie, Ransom, Stevens, Williams, and others; T. Tambimuttu, ed., *Festschrift for Marianne Moore's Seventy-Seventh Birthday* (New York: Tambimuttu and Mass, 1964), essays, memoirs, and poems by Herbert Read, John Ciardi, Kenneth Burke, Eberhart, Ginsberg, Lowell, Wilbur, and others; and Charles Tomlinson, ed., *Marianne Moore: A Collection of Critical Essays* (Englewood Cliffs, N.J.: Prentice-Hall, 1970).

T. S. Eliot

TEXTS. The following texts contain the heart of Eliot's work: *Collected Poems 1909–1962* (New York: Harcourt, 1963); *Complete Plays and Poems* (London: Faber, 1969); *Poems Written in Early Youth* (New York: Farrar, Straus & Giroux, 1967); *The Waste Land: A Facsimile and Transcript of the Original Drafts Including the Annotations of Ezra Pound,* ed. Valerie Eliot (New York: Harcourt, 1971); *The Complete Plays* (New York: Harcourt, 1967); *Selected Essays,* rev. ed. (New York: Harcourt, 1950); *Selected Prose,* ed. John Hayward (Baltimore: Penguin, 1953); *The Use of Poetry and the Use of Criticism* (London: Faber, 1955); *On Poetry and Poets* (New York: Farrar, Straus, 1957); *To Criticize the Critic* (New York: Farrar, Straus & Giroux, 1965); *After Strange Gods: A Primer of Modern Heresy* (London: Faber, 1934); *Christianity and Culture* (New York: Harcourt, 1960).

STUDIES. The most helpful bibliographical aid is Richard Ludwig's review of Eliot scholarship in *Sixteen Modern American Authors.* See Donald Gallup, *T. S. Eliot: A Bibliography* (London: Faber, 1969) for the most inclusive listing of Eliot's works. Also helpful are Mildred Martin, *A Half Century of Eliot Criticism: An Annotated Bibliography, 1916–1965* (Lewisburg, Pa.: Bucknell University Press, 1972) and Bradley Gunther, *The Merrill Checklist of T. S. Eliot* (Columbus, Oh.: Merrill, 1970). Useful introductions are Muriel C. Bradbrook, *T. S. Eliot* (Harlow, Essex: Longmans, 1958); Leonard Unger, *T. S. Eliot* (UMPAW: 1961); and Philip R. Headings, *T. S. Eliot* (TUSAS: 1964). Biographical material is contained in the following: Richard March and M. J. Tambimuttu, eds., *T. S. Eliot: A Symposium for His Sixtieth Birthday* (Chicago: Regnery, 1949); Herbert Howarth, *Some Figures Behind T. S. Eliot* (Boston: Houghton Mifflin, 1964); William T. Levy and Victor Scherle, *Affectionately, T. S. Eliot: The Story of a Friendship, 1947–1965* (Philadelphia: Lippincott, 1968); Robert Sencourt, *T. S. Eliot: A Memoir,* ed. D. Adamson (New York: Dodd, Mead, 1971); and Bernard Bergonzi, *T. S. Eliot* (New York: Macmillan, 1972). Further biographical information can be found in many of the following book-length critical studies, listed in alphabetical order: Harry T. Antrim, *T. S. Eliot's*

Concept of Language (Gainesville: University of Florida Press, 1971); Steffan Bergsten, *Time and Eternity: A Study in the Structure and Symbolism of T. S. Eliot's Four Quartets* (Stockholm: Svenska bökforlaget, 1960); Harry Blamires, *Word Unheard: A Guide through Eliot's Four Quartets* (London: Methuen, 1969); Carl Bodelsen, *T. S. Eliot's Four Quartets: A Commentary* (Copenhagen: Copenhagen University Publications Fund, 1958); E. M. Browne, *The Making of T. S. Eliot's Plays* (New York: Cambridge University Press, 1969); Georges Cattaui, *T. S. Eliot,* trans. Claire Pace and Jean Stewart (New York: Funk & Wagnalls, 1968); Joseph Chiari, *T. S. Eliot: Poet and Dramatist* (New York: Barnes & Noble, 1973); Constance De Masirevich, *On the Four Quartets of T. S. Eliot* (New York: Barnes & Noble, 1953); Elizabeth Drew, *T. S. Eliot: The Design of His Poetry* (New York: Scribner, 1949); Johannes Fabricius, *The Unconscious and Mr. Eliot: A Study in Expressionism* (Copenhagen: Nyt Nordisk Forlag, 1967); Northrop Frye, *T. S. Eliot* (New York: Barnes & Noble, 1966); Helen L. Gardner, *The Art of T. S. Eliot* (New York: Dutton, 1959); Arapura G. George, *T. S. Eliot: His Mind and Art* (New York: Asia Publishing House, 1962); David E. Jones, *The Plays of T. S. Eliot* (Toronto: University of Toronto Press, 1960); Genesius Jones, *Approach to the Purpose: A Study of the Poetry of T. S. Eliot* (New York: Barnes & Noble, 1965); Hugh Kenner, *The Invisible Poet: T. S. Eliot* (New York: McDowell Obolensky, 1959); Russell Kirk, *Eliot and His Age* (New York: Random House, 1972); Roger Kojecky, *T. S. Eliot's Social Criticism* (New York: Farrar, Straus & Giroux, 1972); Fei-pai Lu, *T. S. Eliot: The Dialectal Structure of His Theory of Poetry* (Chicago: University of Chicago Press, 1966); Sean Lucy, *T. S. Eliot and the Idea of Tradition* (New York: Barnes & Noble, 1960); John D. Margolis, *T. S. Eliot's Intellectual Development, 1922–1939* (Chicago: University of Chicago Press, 1972); F. O. Matthiessen, *The Achievement of T. S. Eliot,* 3d ed. (New York: Oxford University Press, 1958); D. E. S. Maxwell, *The Poetry of T. S. Eliot* (London: Routledge & Kegan Paul, 1952); Marion Montgomery, *T. S. Eliot: An Essay on the American Magus* (Athens: University of Georgia Press, 1969); S. Musgrove, *T. S. Eliot and Walt Whitman* (New York: Cambridge University Press, 1954); Gertrude Patterson, *T. S. Eliot: Poems in the Making* (New York: Barnes & Noble, 1971); Raymond Preston, *Four Quartets Rehearsed* (New York: Sheed & Ward, 1946); V. Rai, *The Waste Land: A Critical Study* (Varanasi, India: Motilal Banarsidass, 1965); R. H. Robbins, *The T. S. Eliot Myth* (New York: Schuman, 1951); H. L. Sharma, *The Essential T. S. Eliot: A Critical Analysis* (Mystic, Conn.: Verry, 1971); Krishna N. Sinha, *On Four Quartets of T. S. Eliot* (Ilfracombe, Devon: A. H. Stockwell, 1963); Kristian Smidt, *Poetry and Belief in the Work of T. S. Eliot,* rev. ed. (New York: Humanities, 1961); Carol H. Smith, *T. S. Eliot's Dramatic Theory and Practice* (Princeton: Princeton University Press, 1963); Grover A. Smith, Jr., *T. S. Eliot's Poetry and Plays: A Study in Sources and Meaning* (Chicago: University of Chicago Press, 1956); B. C. Southam, *A Guide to the Selected Poems of T. S. Eliot* (New York: Harcourt, 1968); David Ward, *T. S. Eliot Between Two Worlds* (London: Routledge & Kegan Paul, 1973); and George Williamson, *A Reader's Guide to T. S. Eliot* (New York: Noonday, 1957). Collections of short criticism of a general nature are Leonard Unger, ed., *T. S. Eliot: A Selected Critique* (New York: Rinehart, 1948); Neville Braybrooke, ed., *T. S. Eliot: A Symposium for His Seventieth Birthday* (New York: Farrar, Straus, 1958); Hugh Kenner, ed., *T. S. Eliot: A Collection of*

Critical Essays (Englewood Cliffs, N.J.: Prentice-Hall, 1962); B. Rajan, ed., *T. S. Eliot: A Study of His Writings by Several Hands* (New York: Atheneum, Russell & Russell, 1966); Allen Tate, ed., *T. S. Eliot: The Man and His Work* (New York: Delacorte, 1966); and Martin Graham, ed., *Eliot in Perspective: A Symposium* (New York: Humanities, 1970). More specialized collections are C. B. Cox and A. B. Hinchliffe, eds., *T. S. Eliot: The Waste Land: A Casebook* (New York: Macmillan, 1968); Jay Martin, ed., *A Collection of Critical Essays on The Waste Land* (Englewood Cliffs, N.J.: Prentice-Hall, 1968); A. D. Moody, ed., *The Waste Land in Different Voices* (New York: St. Martin's, 1975); E. San Juan, ed., *A Casebook on "Gerontion"* (Columbus, Oh.: Merrill, 1971); David R. Clark, comp., *Twentieth Century Interpretations of Murder in the Cathedral* (Englewood Cliffs, N.J.: Prentice-Hall, 1971); Bernard Bergonzi, ed., *T. S. Eliot: Four Quartets: A Casebook* (New York: Macmillan, 1969); and David E. Jones, ed., *The Plays of T. S. Eliot* (London: Routledge & Kegan Paul, 1960).

John Crowe Ransom

TEXTS. Most of the poems Ransom wanted preserved are to be found in two collections: *Selected Poems* (New York: Knopf, 1945, 1963) and *Poems and Essays* (New York: Knopf, Vintage 1955). His social and religious views are illustrated in two books and an important essay: *God Without Thunder: An Unorthodox Defense of Orthodoxy* (New York: Harcourt, 1930); *The World's Body* (New York: Scribner, 1938); and "Reconstructed but Unregenerate," in *I'll Take My Stand* (New York: Harper, 1930). His influential survey of modern criticism is *The New Criticism* (Norfolk, Conn.: New Directions, 1941). Perhaps his most famous single essay is "Criticism as Pure Speculation," in *The Intent of the Critic*, ed. Donald A. Stauffer (Princeton: Princeton University Press, 1941).

STUDIES. Introductions to Ransom's work are John L. Stewart, *John Crowe Ransom* (UMPAW: 1962) and T. H. Parsons, *John Crowe Ransom* (TUSAS: 1969). Critical studies are K. F. Knight, *The Poetry of John Crowe Ransom: A Study of Diction, Metaphor, and Symbol* (The Hague: Mouton, 1964); Robert Buffington, *The Equilibrist: A Study of John Crowe Ransom's Poems, 1916–1963* (Nashville, Tenn.: Vanderbilt University Press, 1967); J. E. Magner, *John Crowe Ransom: Critical Principles and Preoccupations* (The Hague: Mouton, 1971); and Miller Williams, *The Poetry of John Crowe Ransom* (New Brunswick, N.J.: Rutgers University Press, 1972). *Sewanee Review* 56 (Summer 1948): 365–476 was devoted to Ransom and includes many of the most famous essays on Ransom by Matthiessen, Tate, Cleanth Brooks, and other critics. Thomas D. Young, ed., *John Crowe Ransom: Critical Essays and a Bibliography* (Baton Rouge: Louisiana State University Press, 1968) reprints some of the essays from the *Sewanee Review* collection along with many others. It also includes the most complete bibliography (primary and secondary) to date. W. D. Snodgrass, Leonie Adams, and Muriel Rukeyser discuss Ransom's poem "Master's in the Garden Again," and Ransom answers them in Anthony Ostroff, ed., *The Contemporary Poet as Artist and Critic* (Boston: Little, Brown, 1964). More general studies of Ransom and his connections with the groups of southern writers known as the Fugitives and the Agrarians are as follows: John M. Bradbury, *The Fugitives: A Critical Account* (Chapel Hill: University of North Carolina Press, 1958); Louise Cowan, *The Fugitive Group: A Literary History*

(Baton Rouge: Louisiana State University Press, 1959); John L. Stewart, *The Burden of Time: The Fugitives and Agrarians* (Princeton: Princeton University Press, 1965).

Archibald MacLeish

TEXTS. The bulk of MacLeish's lyric work is included in *New and Collected Poems, 1917–1976* (Boston: Houghton Mifflin, 1976). Verse plays: *Panic* (Boston: Houghton Mifflin, 1935); *The Secret of Freedom, Air Raid,* and *The Fall of the City* in *Three Short Plays* (New York: Dramatists, 1961); *The American Story: Ten Radio Scripts* (New York: Duell, Sloan & Pearce, 1944); *The Trojan Horse* (Boston: Houghton Mifflin, 1952); *This Music Crept by Me upon the Waters* (Cambridge, Mass.: Harvard University Press, 1953); *J. B.* (Boston: Houghton Mifflin, 1957); *Herakles* (Boston: Houghton Mifflin, 1957); *Scratch* (Boston: Houghton Mifflin, 1971). Criticism: *A Time To Speak* (Boston: Houghton Mifflin, 1941); *Poetry and Opinion; the Pisan Cantos of Ezra Pound* (Urbana: University of Illinois Press, 1950); *Poetry and Experience* (Boston: Houghton Mifflin, 1961); *The Dialogues of Archibald MacLeish and Mark Van Doren,* ed. W. V. Bush (New York: Dutton, 1964); *A Continuing Journey* (Boston: Houghton Mifflin, 1967).

STUDIES. Bibliography: Edward Mullaly, *Archibald MacLeish: A Checklist* (Kent, Oh.: Kent State University Press, 1973). Introductions: S. L. Falk, *Archibald MacLeish* (TUSAS: 1965) and Grover Smith, *Archibald MacLeish* (UMPAW: 1972). Shorter discussions are Hyatt Waggoner, *The Heel of Elohim* (Norman: University of Oklahoma Press, 1950) and J. G. Southworth, *Some Modern American Poets* (Oxford: Blackwell, 1950).

Edna St. Vincent Millay

TEXTS. Poetry: The bulk of Millay's lyric work is included in *Collected Sonnets* (New York: Harper, 1941); *Collected Lyrics* (New York: Harper, 1943); and *Collected Poems* (New York: Harper, 1956). Plays: *Aria da Capo,* 1920; *The Lamp and the Bell,* 1921; *Two Slatterns and a King,* 1921, in *Three Plays* (New York: Harper, 1926); *The King's Henchman* (New York: Harper, 1927); *The Princess Marries the Page* (New York: Harper, 1932). Translation: with George Dillon, Baudelaire's *Flowers of Evil* (New York: Harper, 1936).

STUDIES. Karl Yost, *A Bibliography of the Works of Edna St. Vincent Millay* (New York: Harper, 1937). Good introductions to her work are Norman A. Brittin, *Edna St. Vincent Millay* (TUSAS: 1967) and James Gray, *Edna St. Vincent Millay* (UMPAW: 1967). Elizabeth Atkins, *Edna St. Vincent Millay and Her Times* (Chicago: University of Chicago Press, 1936) is consistently laudatory. Biographical studies are Vincent Sheehan, *The Indigo Bunting* (New York: Harper, 1951); Miriam Gurko, *Restless Spirit* (New York: T. Y. Crowell, 1962); and Jean Gould, *The Poet and Her Book* (New York: Dodd, Mead, 1969). Allan R. Macdougall edited *Letters of Edna St. Vincent Millay* (New York: Harper, 1952).

E. E. Cummings

TEXTS. *Poems 1923–1954* (New York: Harcourt, 1954); *95 Poems* (New York: Harcourt, 1958); *73 Poems* (New York: Harcourt, 1963); *100 Selected Poems*

(New York: Grove, 1959); *Complete Poems 1913–1962* (New York: Harcourt Brace Jovanovich, 1972); *Three Plays and a Ballet,* ed. G. J. Firmage (New York: October House, 1967); *E. E. Cummings: A Miscellany Revised,* ed. G. J. Firmage (New York: October House, 1965); *Eimi* (New York: Grove, 1958); *The Enormous Room* (New York: Modern Library, 1934); *i: six nonlectures* (New York: Atheneum, 1953).

STUDIES. Bibliography includes Paul Lauter, *E. E. Cummings: Index to First Lines and Bibliography of Works by and about the Poet* (Chicago: Swallow, 1955); G. J. Firmage, *E. E. Cummings: A Bibliography* (Middletown, Conn.: Wesleyan University Press, 1960); and W. Eckley, *The Merrill Guide to e. e. cummings* (Columbus, Oh.: Merrill, 1970). The best biography is Charles Norman, *The Magic Maker: E. E. Cummings* (New York: Duell, Sloan & Pearce, 1964). F. W. Dupee and George Stade edited *Selected Letters* (New York: Harcourt, 1969). General introductions are B. A. Marks, *E. E. Cummings* (TUSAS: 1964) and Eve Triem, *E. E. Cummings* (UMPAW: 1970). Full-length studies include Norman Friedman, *E. E. Cummings: The Art of His Poetry* (Baltimore: Johns Hopkins Press, 1960) and *E. E. Cummings: The Growth of a Writer* (Carbondale: Southern Illinois University Press, 1964); and R. E. Wegner, *The Poetry and Prose of E. E. Cummings* (New York: Harcourt, 1965). Collections of criticism are Norman Friedman, ed., *E. E. Cummings: A Collection of Critical Essays* (Englewood Cliffs, N.J.: Prentice-Hall, 1972) and S. V. Baum, ed., *Esti: e e c: E. E. Cummings and His Critics* (East Lansing: Michigan State University Press, 1962). Important short criticism is S. V. Baum, "E. E. Cummings: The Technique of Immediacy," *SAQ,* 53 (1954): 70–88 and R. P. Blackmur, "Notes on E. E. Cummings' Language," in *Form and Value in Modern Poetry* (Garden City, N.Y.: Doubleday, Anchor, 1957) and in *Esti.*

Hart Crane

TEXTS. *Complete Poems* (Garden City, N.Y.: Doubleday, Anchor, 1958), including Crane's famous essay "Modern Poetry" and *Complete Poems and Selected Letters and Prose,* ed. Brom Weber (New York: Oxford University Press, 1966).

STUDIES. The most helpful bibliography is Brom Weber's review of Crane scholarship in *Sixteen Modern American Authors.* Also useful are H. D. Rowe, *Hart Crane: A Bibliography* (Chicago: Swallow, 1955); Joseph Schwartz and Robert C. Schwelk, *Hart Crane: A Descriptive Bibliography* (Pittsburgh: University of Pittsburgh Press, 1972); and K. A. Lohf, comp., *The Literary Manuscripts of Hart Crane* (Columbus: Ohio State University Press, 1967). Introductions to the work are Samuel Hazo, *Hart Crane* (New York: Barnes & Noble, 1963); Vincent Quinn, *Hart Crane* (TUSAS: 1963); M. K. Spears, *Hart Crane* (UMPAW: 1965); and H. A. Leibowitz, *Hart Crane* (New York: Columbia University Press, 1968). Biographical studies are Philip Horton, *Hart Crane: The Life of an American Poet* (New York: Norton, 1937; New York: Viking, 1957); Brom Weber, *Hart Crane: A Biographical and Critical Study,* rev. ed. (New York: Atheneum, Russell & Russell, 1970); and John Unterecker, *Voyager: A Life of Hart Crane* (New York: Farrar, Straus & Giroux, 1969). There are three collections of letters: *Letters of Hart Crane, 1916–1932,* ed. Brom Weber (Berkeley: University of California Press, 1952); *Robber Rocks: Letters and Memories of Hart Crane, 1923–1932,* ed. Susan J. Brown (Middletown, Conn.: Wesleyan University Press, 1969); and *Letters of Hart Crane and His Family,* ed. T. S. W. Lewis (New

York: Columbia University Press, 1974). Book-length studies of the work are L. S. Dembo, *Hart Crane's Sanskrit Charge: A Study of The Bridge* (Ithaca, N.Y.: Cornell University Press, 1960); Alan Trachtenberg, *Brooklyn Bridge: Fact and Symbol* (New York: Oxford University Press, 1965); Robert L. Perry, *The Shared Vision of Waldo Frank and Hart Crane* (Lincoln: University of Nebraska Press, 1966); R. W. B. Lewis, *The Poetry of Hart Crane: A Critical Study* (Princeton: Princeton University Press, 1967); R. W. Butterfield, *The Broken Arc: A Study of Hart Crane's Poetry* (Edinburgh: Oliver & Boyd, 1969); Sherman Paul, *Hart's Bridge* (Urbana: University of Illinois Press, 1972); H. Landry and others, *A Concordance to the Poems of Hart Crane* (Metuchen, N.J.: Scarecrow, 1973); and M. D. Uroff, *Hart Crane: The Patterns of His Poetry* (Urbana: University of Illinois Press, 1974). Shorter studies are R. P. Blackmur, *Form and Value in Modern Poetry* (Garden City, N.Y.: Doubleday, Anchor, 1957); Allen Tate, *Collected Essays* (Chicago: Swallow, 1959); Yvor Winters, *On Modern Poets* (New York: Meridian, 1959); James E. Miller, Jr., Karl Shapiro, and Bernice Slote, *Start with the Sun: Studies in Cosmic Poetry* (Lincoln: University of Nebraska Press, 1960); and Thomas A. Vogler, *Preludes to Vision: The Epic Venture in Blake, Wordsworth, Keats, and Hart Crane* (Berkeley: University of California Press, 1972).

Langston Hughes

TEXTS. Poetry: *Weary Blues* (New York: Knopf, 1926); *Fine Clothes to the Jew* (New York: Knopf, 1927); *Scottsboro Limited* (New York: Golden Stair Press, 1932); *Dream Keeper* (New York: Knopf, 1932); *Shakespeare in Harlem* (New York: Knopf, 1942); *Fields of Wonder* (New York: Knopf, 1947); *One Way Ticket* (New York: Knopf, 1949); *Montage of a Dream Deferred* (New York: Holt, 1951); *Selected Poems* (New York: Knopf, 1959); *Ask Your Mama* (New York: Knopf, 1961); *The Panther and the Lash* (New York: Knopf, 1967). Fiction: *Not Without Laughter* (New York: Knopf, 1941), novel; *The Ways of White Folks* (New York: Knopf, 1934), stories; *Laughing to Keep from Crying* (New York: Holt, 1952), stories; *Something in Common* (New York: Hill & Wang, 1963), stories; *The Best of Simple* (New York: Hill & Wang, 1961), stories. Autobiography: *I Wonder As I Wander* (New York: Rinehart, 1956) and *The Big Sea* (New York: Hill & Wang, 1963). Miscellaneous: *A Langston Hughes Reader* (New York: Braziller, 1958).

STUDIES. Valuable for both bibliography and biography is Donald C. Dickinson, *A Bio-Bibliography of Langston Hughes 1902–1967* (Hamden, Conn.: Archon, 1968). Another biography is Milton Meltzer, *Langston Hughes* (New York: T. Y. Crowell, 1968). A full-length study is James Emanuel, *Langston Hughes* (TUSAS: 1967). Shorter studies are Saunders Redding, *To Make a Poet Black* (Chapel Hill: University of North Carolina Press, 1939); Nat Hentoff, "Langston Hughes, He Found Poetry in the Blues," *Mayfair* (1958): 26–27; and Charlemae Rollins, *Famous American Negro Poets* (New York: Dodd, Mead, 1965). Collections of short criticism are the Hughes number of *CLAJour* (1968) and T. B. O'Daniel, ed., *Langston Hughes, Black Genius: A Critical Evaluation* (New York: Morrow, 1971).

Richard Eberhart

TEXTS. The most important collections of Eberhart's poetry are *Poems, New and Selected* (Norfolk, Conn.: New Directions, 1944); *Selected Poems* (New York: Oxford University Press, 1951); *Undercliff: Poems 1946–1953* (New York: Oxford University Press, 1957); *Collected Poems 1930–1960* (New York: Oxford University Press, 1960); *Collected Verse Plays* (Chapel Hill: University of North Carolina Press, 1962); *The Quarry* (New York: Oxford University Press, 1964); *Selected Poems 1930–1965* (New York: New Directions, 1965); and *Thirty One Sonnets* (New York: Eakins Press, 1967).

STUDIES. A good introduction is Ralph J. Mills, Jr., *Richard Eberhart* (UMPAW: 1966). The bibliography lists not only commentaries on Eberhart but also many of his own comments on his own and other poetry. Bernard F. Engel discusses many of the best-known poems in *The Achievement of Richard Eberhart* (Glenview, Ill.: Scott, Foresman, 1968) and more thoroughly in *Richard Eberhart* (TUSAS: 1971). Louise Bogan, Philip Booth, and William Stafford discuss Eberhart's "Am I My Neighbor's Keeper?" and Eberhart answers them in Anthony Ostroff, ed., *The Contemporary Poet as Artist and Critic* (Boston: Little, Brown, 1964). See also Ralph J. Mills, Jr., *Contemporary American Poetry*, (New York: Random House, 1965), pp. 9–31 and Edward Hungerford, ed., *Poets in Progress* (Evanston, Ill.: Northwestern University Press, 1962), pp. 73–91.

Theodore Roethke

TEXTS. *Words for the Wind: The Collected Verse of Theodore Roethke* (Garden City, N.Y.: Doubleday, 1958); *Roethke: Collected Poems* (Garden City, N.Y.: Doubleday, 1966); *On the Poet and His Craft: Selected Prose of Theodore Roethke*, ed. Ralph Mills, Jr. (Seattle: University of Washington Press, 1965); *Straw for the Fire: From the Notebooks of Theodore Roethke*, ed. David Wagoner (Garden City, N.Y.: Doubleday, Anchor, 1974).

STUDIES. Bibliography: J. R. McLeod, *Theodore Roethke: A Bibliography* (Kent, Oh.: Kent State University Press, 1973). Introductions are Ralph Mills, Jr., *Theodore Roethke* (UMPAW: 1963); Edward Hungerford, ed., *Poets in Progress* (Evanston, Ill.: Northwestern University Press, 1962); and William J. Martz, *The Achievement of Theodore Roethke* (Glenview, Ill.: Scott, Foresman, 1966). Full-length studies are Karl Malkoff. *Theodore Roethke: An Introduction to the Poetry* (New York: Columbia University Press, 1966) and Rosemary Sullivan. *Theodore Roethke: The Garden Master* (Seattle: University of Washington Press, 1976). Shorter discussions include Arnold Stein, ed., *Theodore Roethke: Essays on the Poetry* (Seattle: University of Washington Press, 1965); Anthony Ostroff, ed., *The Contemporary Poet as Artist and Critic* (Boston: Little, Brown, 1964); M. L. Rosenthal, *The Modern Poets* (New York: Oxford University Press, 1967); and Nathan A. Scott, Jr., *The Wild Prayer of Longing* (New Haven: Yale University Press, 1971). A good biography is Allan Seager, *The Glass House: The Life of Theodore Roethke* (New York: McGraw-Hill, 1968). Mills has edited *Selected Letters* (Seattle: University of Washington Press, 1968).

Karl Shapiro

TEXTS. Poetry: *Person, Place and Thing* (New York: Reynal & Hitchcock, 1942); *V-Letter and Other Poems* (New York: Reynal & Hitchcock, 1944); *Essay on Rime*

(New York: Reynal & Hitchcock, 1945); *Trial of a Poet and Other Poems* (New York: Reynal & Hitchcock, 1947); *Poems, 1940–1953* (New York: Random House, 1953); *Poems of a Jew* (New York: Random House, 1958); *The Bourgeois Poet* (New York: Random House, 1964); *Selected Poems* (New York: Random House, 1968); *White-Haired Lover* (New York: Random House, 1968). Criticism: *Beyond Criticism* (Lincoln: University of Nebraska Press, 1953); *In Defense of Ignorance* (New York: Random House, 1960); *To Abolish Children* (New York: Quadrangle, 1968); with James E. Miller and Bernice Slote, *Start with the Sun: Studies in Cosmic Poetry* (Lincoln: University of Nebraska Press, 1960).

STUDIES. William White, *Karl Shapiro: A Bibliography* (Detroit: Wayne State University Press, 1960). Most critical commentary on Shapiro's work remains in periodical form; no full-length critical or biographical study yet exists. Stephen Stepanchev, *American Poetry Since 1945* (New York: Harper & Row, 1965) finds the early poetry best. Ralph J. Mills, Jr., *Contemporary American Poetry* (New York: Random House, 1965) comments favorably on the work to that date. Adrienne Rich, Donald Justice, William Dickey, and Shapiro discuss selections from *The Bourgeois Poet* in Anthony Ostroff, ed., *The Contemporary Poet as Artist and Critic* (Boston: Little, Brown, 1964).

Randall Jarrell

TEXT. Poetry: *The Complete Poems* (New York: Farrar, Straus & Giroux, 1968). Criticism: *Poetry and the Age* (New York: Knopf, 1953) and *A Sad Heart at the Supermarket: Essays and Fables* (New York: Atheneum, 1962). Novel: *Pictures From an Institution* (New York: Meridian, 1954).

STUDIES. The best bibliography of Jarrell's work, including lectures, poetry readings, and recordings, is that of Karl Shapiro done for the Library of Congress in 1967. Shapiro's essay accompanying the bibliography is included in *Randall Jarrell 1914–1965,* eds. Robert Lowell, Peter Taylor, and R. P. Warren (New York: Farrar, Straus & Giroux, 1967); the collection prints comments and tributes by twenty-seven writers, including Lowell, Cleanth Brooks, Alfred Kazin, and others. Other generally favorable comments are Sr. M. Bernetta Quinn, *The Metamorphic Tradition in Modern Poetry* (New Brunswick, N.J.: Rutgers University Press, 1955); M. L. Rosenthal, *The Modern Poets: A Critical Introduction* (New York: Oxford University Press, 1960); W. B. Rideout, in *Poets in Progress,* ed. Edward Hungerford (Evanston, Ill.: Northwestern University Press, 1967). Full-length studies include Frederick J. Hoffman. *The Achievement of Randall Jarrell* (Glenview, Ill.: Scott, Foresman, 1970); Suzanne Ferguson, *The Poetry of Randall Jarrell* (Baton Rouge: Louisiana State University Press, 1971); and M. L. Rosenthal, *Randall Jarrell* (UMPAW: 1972).

Robert Lowell

TEXTS. *Land of Unlikeness* (Omaha, Nebr.: Cummington Press, 1944); *Lord Weary's Castle* (New York: Harcourt, 1946); *Poems 1938–1949* (London: Faber, 1950); *The Mills of the Kavanaughs* (New York: Harcourt, 1951); *Life Studies* (New York: Farrar, Straus, 1959); *Imitations* (New York: Farrar, Straus, 1961), translations; *Phaedra* (New York: Farrar, Straus, 1961), translation; *For the Union Dead* (New York: Farrar, Straus & Giroux, 1964); *The Old Glory* (New

York: Farrar, Straus & Giroux, 1965), a trilogy of plays based on three Hawthorne stories, Melville's *Benito Cereno,* and Thomas Morton's early history of New England; *Near the Ocean* (New York: Farrar, Straus & Giroux, 1967); *Prometheus Bound* (New York: Farrar, Straus & Giroux, 1967), translation; *Notebooks 1967–1968* (New York: Farrar, Straus & Giroux, 1969); *The Dolphin* (New York: Farrar, Straus & Giroux, 1973); *History* (New York: Farrar, Straus & Giroux, 1973).

STUDIES. For bibliography see Jerome Mazzaro, *The Achievement of Robert Lowell* (Detroit: University of Detroit Press, 1960), which lists commentary on Lowell through 1959, and the Parkinson collection (listed below), which supplements Mazzaro. Introductions are Jay Martin, *Robert Lowell* (UMPAW: 1970) and Richard J. Fcin, *Robert Lowell* (TUSAS: 1970). Full-length studies are Hugh B. Staples, *Robert Lowell: The First Twenty Years* (New York: Farrar, Straus, 1962); Jerome Mazzaro, *the Poetic Themes of Robert Lowell* (Ann Arbor: University of Michigan Press, 1965); Philip Cooper, *The Autobiographical Myth of Robert Lowell* (Chapel Hill: University of North Carolina Press, 1970); Patrick Cosgrave, *The Public Poetry of Robert Lowell* (London: Gollancz, 1970); Roger K. Meiners, *Everything to Be Endured: An Essay on Robert Lowell and Modern Poetry* (Columbia: University of Missouri Press, 1970); Thomas R. Edwards, *Imagination and Power: A Study of Poetry on Public Themes* (New York: Oxford University Press, 1971); Marjorie G. Perloff, *The Poetic Art of Robert Lowell* (Ithaca, N.Y.: Cornell University Press, 1973). Important shorter studies are Edward B. Hungerford, ed., *Poets in Progress* (Evanston, Ill.: Northwestern University Press, 1962); Glauco Cambon, *The Inclusive Flame* (Bloomington: Indiana University Press, 1963); Anthony Ostroff, ed., *The Contemporary Poet as Artist and Critic* (Boston: Little, Brown, 1964); Ralph J. Mills, Jr., *Contemporary American Poetry* (New York: Random House, 1965); and William J. Martz, ed., *The Achievement of Robert Lowell* (Glenview, Ill.: Scott, Foresman, 1966). Collections of shorter criticism are Thomas Parkinson, ed., *Robert Lowell: A Collection of Critical Essays* (Englewood Cliffs, N.J.: Prentice-Hall, 1968); Michael London and Robert Boyers, eds., *Robert Lowell: A Portrait of the Artist in His Time* (New York: David Lewis, 1970); Jerome Mazzaro, ed., *Profile of Robert Lowell* (Columbus, Oh.: Merrill, 1971); and Jonathan Price, comp., *Critics on Robert Lowell* (Coral Gables: University of Miami Press, 1972).

Gwendolyn Brooks

TEXTS. *A Street in Bronzeville* (New York: Harper, 1945); *Annie Allen* (New York: Harper, 1949); *Maud Martha* (New York: Harper, 1953), novel; *Bronzeville Boys and Girls* (New York: Harper, 1956); *The Bean Eaters* (New York: Harper, 1960); *In the Mecca* (New York: Harper & Row, 1968); *Report from Part One: The Autobiography of Gwendolyn Brooks* (Detroit: Broadside Press, 1972).

STUDIES. Bibliography: Jon N. Loff, "Gwendolyn Brooks: A Bibliography," *CLAJour* 17 (1973): 21–32. Studies are Charlemae Rollins, *Famous American Negro Poets* (New York: Dodd, Mead, 1965) and the following selected articles: Stanley Kunitz, "Bronze by Gold," *Poetry* 76 (1950): 52–56; J. Crockett, "An Essay on Gwendolyn Brooks," *Negro History Bulletin* 19 (1955): 37–39; Frank L. Brown, "Chicago's Great Lady of Poetry," *Negro Digest* 11 (1961): 53–57; Arthur P. Davis, "The Black and Tan Motif in the Poetry of Gwendolyn Brooks," *CLAJour* 6 (1962): 90–97 and "Gwendolyn Brooks: A Poet of the Unheroic," *CLAJour* 7 (1963): 114–125; B. Cutler, "Long Reach, Strong Speech," *Poetry* 103 (1964): 388–389; James A. Emanuel, "A Note on the Future of Negro Poetry," *Negro American Literature Forum* 1 (1967): 2–3; George E. Kent, "The Poetry of Gwendolyn Brooks," *Black Writers* 20 (1972): 30–43, 20 (1973): 36–48, 68–71; and Houston A. Baker, Jr., "The Achievement of Gwendolyn Brooks," *CLAJour* 16 (1972): 25–31.

Richard Wilbur

TEXTS. *The Beautiful Changes and Other Poems* (New York: Harcourt, 1947); *Ceremony and Other Poems* (New York: Harcourt, 1950); *Things of This World* (New York: Harcourt, 1956); *Poems 1943–1956* (London: Faber, 1956); *Advice to a Prophet and Other Poems* (New York: Harcourt, 1961); *The Poems of Richard Wilbur* (New York: Harcourt, 1963); *Walking to Sleep: New Poems and Translations* (New York: Harcourt, 1969); *Opposites* (New York: Harcourt Brace Jovanovich, 1973). Wilbur has translated Molière's *Misanthrope* (New York: Harcourt, 1955) and *Tartuffe* (New York: Harcourt, 1963) and has written lyrics for a comic opera version of Voltaire's *Candide* (New York: Schirmer, 1958). Wilbur has commented on his own poetic beliefs in an essay called "The Genie in the Bottle," in *Mid-Century American Poets,* ed. John Ciardi (New York: Twayne, 1950).

STUDIES. John P. Field, *Richard Wilbur: A Bibliographical Checklist* (Kent, Oh.: Kent State University Press, 1971). A good introduction is Donald L. Hill, *Richard Wilbur* (TUSAS; New York: Twayne, 1967); Hill reads a great many poems very closely and provides a useful bibliography that includes listings of reviews of Wilbur's books. Paul F. Cummins's, *Richard Wilbur: A Critical Essay* (Grand Rapids, Mich.: Eerdmans, 1971) is a book-length study. Randall Jarrell's *Poetry and the Age* (New York: Knopf, Vintage, 1953) finds Wilbur too traditional but nonetheless praises him highly. Ralph J. Mills, Jr., *Contemporary Poetry* (New York: Random House, 1965) is probably the best commentary to date. M. L. Rosenthal, *The Modern Poets: A Critical Introduction* (New York: Oxford University Press, 1960) laments Wilbur's "traditionalism" but nevertheless admires his work. Peter Viereck's views are similar in *The Last Decade in Poetry: New Dilemmas and New Solutions* (Nashville, Tenn.: Bureau of Publications, George Peabody College for Teachers, 1954). Frederic E. Faverty's opinion is more favorable in "Well-Open Eyes: or, The Poetry of Richard Wilbur" in *Poets in Progress,* ed. Edward Hungerford (Evanston, Ill.: Northwestern University Press, 1967). Richard Eberhart, Robert Horan, and May Swenson have commented on Wilbur's "Love Calls Us to the Things of This World," and Wilbur has replied in Anthony Ostroff, ed., *The Contemporary Poet as Artist and Critic* (Boston: Little, Brown, 1964).

James Dickey

TEXTS. Poetry: *Into the Stone* (New York: Scribner, 1960); *Drowning With Others* (Middletown, Conn.: Wesleyan University Press, 1962); *Helmets* (Middletown, Conn.: Wesleyan University Press, 1964); *Buckdancer's Choice* (Middletown, Conn.: Wesleyan University Press, 1965); *Poems 1957–1967* (Middletown, Conn.: Wesleyan University Press, 1967); *The Eye-Beaters, Blood, Victory, Madness, Buckhead, and Mercy* (Garden City, N.Y.: Doubleday, 1970). Prose:

The Suspect in Poetry (Madison, Minn.: The Sixties Press, 1964); *Spinning the Crystal Ball* (Washington, D.C.: Library of Congress, 1967); *Babel to Byzantium* (New York: Farrar, Straus & Giroux, 1968); *Self-Interviews,* recorded and edited by Barbara and James Reiss (Garden City, N.Y.: Doubleday, 1971); *Deliverance* (Boston: Houghton Mifflin, 1970), novel.

STUDIES. Bibliography: Franklin Ashley, *James Dickey: A Checklist* (Detroit: Gale, 1972) and Eileen Glancy, *James Dickey: The Critic as Poet: An Annotated Bibliography* (Troy, N.Y.: Whitston, 1972). A good introduction is Laurence Lieberman, *The Achievement of James Dickey* (Glenview, Ill.: Scott, Foresman, 1968). Other brief studies are Stephen Stepanchev, *American Poetry since 1945* (New York: Harper & Row, 1965); M. L. Rosenthal, *The New Poets* (New York: Oxford University Press, 1967); Paul Carroll, *The Poem in Its Skin* (Chicago: Follett, 1968); and Richard Howard, *Alone With America: Essays on the Art of Poetry in the United States since 1950* (New York: Atheneum, 1969).

Allen Ginsberg

TEXTS. *Howl and Other Poems* (San Francisco: City Lights Books, 1956); *Kaddish and Other Poems 1958–1960* (San Francisco: City Lights Books, 1961); *Empty Mirror: Early Poems* (New York: Totem Press, 1961); *Reality Sandwiches* (San Francisco: City Lights Books, 1963); *Wichita Vortex Sutra* (San Francisco: City Lights Books, 1967); *Planet News* (San Francisco: City Lights Books, 1968); *T.V. Baby Poems* (New York: Grossman, 1968); *The Yage Letters* (San Francisco: City Lights Books, 1963); *Indian Journals* (San Francisco: City Lights Books, 1970).

STUDIES. For bibliography see Edward Z. Menkin, "Allen Ginsberg: A Bibliography and Bibliographical Sketch," *Thoth* 8 (1967): 35–44 and George Dowden, *A Bibliography of Works by Allen Ginsberg: October, 1943–July 1, 1967* (San Francisco: City Lights Books, 1971). The only full-length biography is Jane Kramer, *Allen Ginsberg in America* (New York: Random House, 1968). A balanced critical study with a good bibliography is Thomas F. Merrill, *Allen Ginsberg* (TUSAS: 1969). Other shorter studies in book form are Seymour Krim, ed., *The Beats* (New York: Fawcett, 1960); Thomas Parkinson, ed., *A Casebook on the Beat* (New York: T. Y. Crowell, 1961); Stephen Stepanchev, *American Poetry Since 1945* (New York: Harper & Row, 1965); and M. L. Rosenthal, *The New American Poetry* (New York: Macmillan, 1967). A general study of the beats is John Tytell, *Naked Angels: The Lives and Literature of the Beat Generation* (New York: McGraw-Hill, 1976).

Sylvia Plath

TEXTS. *The Colossus and Other Poems* (New York: Knopf, 1962); *Uncollected Poems* (London: Turret Press, 1965); *Ariel* (New York: Harper & Row, 1966); *Winter Trees* (New York: Harper & Row, 1972); *The Bell Jar* (New York: Harper & Row, 1971).

STUDIES. The most important book on Plath published to date is Charles Newman, ed., *The Art of Sylvia Plath: A Symposium* (Bloomington: Indiana University Press, 1970): it prints seventeen critical and biographical essays and notes by Newman, A. Alvarez, M. L. Rosenthal, Richard Howard, John F. Nims, Ted Hughes, Anne Sexton, Stephen Spender, and others and a checklist of criticism of Plath's work through 1969. The fullest biographical study to date is Edward Butscher's *Sylvia Plath: Method and Madness* (New York: Seabury, 1976). A brief biographical book is Nancy H. Steiner's *A Closer Look at Ariel* (New York: Harper & Row, 1973), and a very brief critical study is Eileen M. Aird, *Sylvia Plath* (New York: Barnes & Noble, 1973). Periodical criticism is abundant from about 1968 to the present. Two important essays are Joyce Carol Oates, "The Death Throes of Romanticism: The Poems of Sylvia Plath," *SoR* 9 (1973): 501–522 and Marjorie G. Perloff, "On the Road to *Ariel:* The 'Transitional' Poetry of Sylvia Plath," *Iowa Review* 4:2 (1973): 94–110. Also see *Letters Home: Correspondence 1950–1963,* selected and edited with commentary by Aurelia Schober Plath (New York: Harper & Row, 1975).

LeRoi Jones (Imamu Amiri Baraka)

TEXTS. Poetry: *Preface to a Twenty Volume Suicide Note* (New York: Totem Press, Corinth Books, 1961); *The Dead Lecturer* (New York: Grove, 1964); *Black Magic: Collected Poetry, 1961–1967* (Indianapolis: Bobbs-Merrill, 1969). Plays: *Dutchman and The Slave* (New York: Morrow, 1964); *Baptism and The Toilet* (New York: Grove, 1967); *Four Black Revolutionary Plays* (Indianapolis: Bobbs-Merrill, 1969). Essays: *Home* (New York: Morrow, 1966) and *In Our Terribleness: Some Elements and Meaning in Black Style* (Indianapolis: Bobbs-Merrill, 1970); *Raise, Race, Rays, Raze: Essays since 1965* (New York: Random House, 1971). Fiction: *The System of Dante's Hell* (New York: Grove, 1965) and *Tales* (New York: Grove, 1967). Commentary on black music: *Blues People* (New York: Morrow, 1963) and *Black Music* (New York: Morrow, 1967).

STUDIES. Bibliography: Letitia Dace, *LeRoi Jones (Imamu Amiri Baraka): A Checklist of Works by and about Him* (London: Nether Press, 1971) and M. Thomas Inge, Jackson R. Bryer and Maurice Duke, eds., *Black American Writers: A Bibliographic Survey,* vol. 2 (New York: St. Martin's, 1976). A full-length study is Theodore R. Hudson, *From LeRoi Jones to Amiri Baraka: The Literary Works* (Durham, N. C.: Duke University Press, 1973). Short studies in book form (dealing with Jones primarily as a poet) are Stephen Stepanchev, *American Poetry Since 1945* (New York: Harper & Row, 1965); M. L. Rosenthal, *The New Poets* (New York: Oxford University Press, 1967); Edward Margolies, *Native Sons* (Philadelphia: Lippincott, 1968); David Littlejohn, *Black on White* (New York: Viking, 1966); and D. B. Gibson, ed., *Five Black Writers: Essays on Wright, Ellison, Baldwin, Hughes and LeRoi Jones* (New York: New York University Press, 1970). Important articles are Denise Levertov, "Poets of the Given Ground," *Nation* 193 (1961): 251–252; George Dennison, "The Demagogy of LeRoi Jones," *Commentary* 39 (1965): 67–70; Clarence Major, "The Poetry of LeRoi Jones," *Negro Digest* 14 (1965): 54–56; Donald Castello, "LeRoi Jones: Black Man as Victim," *Commonweal* 88 (1968): 436–440; and Daphine S. Reed, "LeRoi Jones: High Priest of the Black Arts Movement," *Educational Theatre Journal* 22 (1970): 53–59.

10: MODERN NOVELISTS AND SHORT-STORY WRITERS

Willa Cather

TEXTS. *April Twilights* (New York: Knopf, 1951); rev. ed., edited with introduction by Bernice Slote (Lincoln: University of Nebraska Press, 1962), poems; *The*

Troll Garden (New York: McClure Phillips, 1905), stories; *Alexander's Bridge* (Boston: Houghton Mifflin, 1913), novel; *The Song of the Lark* (Boston: Houghton Mifflin, 1915), novel; *My Ántonia* (Boston: Houghton Mifflin, 1918), novel; *Youth and the Bright Medusa* (New York: Knopf, 1920), stories; *One of Ours* (New York: Knopf, 1922), novel; *A Lost Lady* (New York: Knopf, 1923), novel; *April Twilights and Other Poems* (New York: Knopf, 1923); *The Professor's House* (New York: Knopf, 1925), novel; *My Mortal Enemy* (New York: Knopf, 1926), novel; *Death Comes for the Archbishop* (New York: Knopf, 1927), novel; *Shadows on the Rock* (New York: Knopf, 1931), novel; *Obscure Destinies* (New York: Knopf, 1932), stories; *Lucy Gayhart* (New York: Knopf, 1935), novel; *Not Under Forty* (New York: Knopf, 1936), essays; *Sapphira and the Slave Girl* (New York: Knopf, 1940), novel; *The Old Beauty and Others* (New York: Knopf, 1948), stories; *Willa Cather on Writing* (New York: Knopf, 1949), essays; *Willa Cather's Campus Years,* ed. James R. Shively (Lincoln: University of Nebraska Press, 1950), early writings; *Willa Cather's Collected Short Fiction, 1892–1912,* intro. by Mildred R. Bennett (Lincoln: University of Nebraska Press, 1965); *The Kingdom of Art: Willa Cather's First Principles and Critical Statements, 1893–1896,* ed. Bernice Slote (Lincoln: University of Nebraska Press, 1966); *Uncle Valentine and Other Stories* (Lincoln: University of Nebraska Press, 1973); *The World and the Parish: Willa Cather's Articles and Reviews, 1893–1902,* ed. William M. Curtin (Lincoln: University of Nebraska Press, 1970).

STUDIES. For bibliography, see Phyllis M. Hutchinson, "The Writings of Willa Cather: A List of Works by and about Her," *BNYPL* 60 (1956): 267–288, 338–356, 378–400, a checklist of primary and secondary work to 1956. Later selective bibliographies are to be found in *Willa Cather's Collected Short Fiction* (see above), in Brown and Edel (see below), and in Schroeter (see below). Bernice Slote reviews criticism of Cather through 1968 in *Sixteen Modern American Authors.* Introductions to the work are David Daiches, *Willa Cather: A Critical Introduction* (Ithaca, N.Y.: Cornell University Press, 1951), Dorothy Van Ghent, *Willa Cather* (UMPAW: 1964), and biographical works are Elizabeth Moorhead, *These Too Were Here: Louise Homer and Willa Cather* (Pittsburgh: University of Pittsburgh, 1950), on Cather's years in Pittsburgh; Edith Lewis, *Willa Cather Living* (New York: Knopf, 1953), memories by a close friend of forty years; Mildred R. Bennett, *The World of Willa Cather* (rev. ed., Lincoln: University of Nebraska Press, 1961), a work stressing Cather's Nebraska years; Elizabeth S. Sergeant, *Willa Cather: A Memoir* (rev. ed., Lincoln: University of Nebraska Press, 1963), recollections by a close friend; and James Woodress, *Willa Cather: Her Life and Art* (Indianapolis: Bobbs-Merrill, Pegasus, 1970).

Critical work on Cather is fairly extensive. A good representative sampling of this criticism is James Schroeter, ed., *Willa Cather and Her Critics* (Ithaca, N.Y.: Cornell University Press, 1967), which prints thirty-three reviews, essays, and book sections from before 1920 to the present, including many of the best-known pieces on Cather by Mencken, Wilson, Krutch, Louise Bogan, Trilling, Geismar, Zabel, Rebecca West, Bernice Slote, and others. The book also includes a good selective bibliography of criticism. Another collection is the Cather issue of *WAL* (Spring 1972). Other critical works include Rene Rapin, *Willa Cather* (New York: McBride, 1930), a generally laudatory early study; E. K. Brown, *Willa Cather: A Critical Biography,* completed by Leon Edel (New

York: Knopf, 1953), an indispensable study that is both biographical and critical; Leon Edel, *Willa Cather: The Paradox of Success* (Washington, D.C.: Library of Congress, 1960), a lecture defending Willa Cather's essential conservatism in religion and literature; John H. Randall III, *The Landscape and the Looking Glass: Willa Cather's Search for Value* (Boston: Houghton Mifflin, 1960), a study that finds her early "prairie" work best; Edward A. Bloom and Lillian D. Bloom, *Willa Cather's Gift of Sympathy* (Carbondale: Southern Illinois University Press, 1962), a study of Cather's themes and techniques; and Richard Giannone, *Music in Willa Cather's Fiction* (Lincoln: University of Nebraska Press, 1968). Among many shorter studies dealing with Cather as a regional or local-color writer are Howard Mumford Jones, *The Frontier and American Fiction: Four Lectures on the Relation of Landscape to Literature* (Jerusalem: Magness Press, 1956); D. T. McFarland, *Willa Cather* (New York: Ungar, 1972); Roy W. Meyer, *The Middle Western Farm Novel in the Twentieth Century* (Lincoln: University of Nebraska Press, 1965); and James K. Folsom, *The American Western Novel* (New Haven: College and University Press, 1966). Katherine Anne Porter's essay in *The Days Before* (New York: Delacorte, 1970), reprinted in *The Collected Essays and Occasional Writings of Katherine Anne Porter,* is a sensitive, appreciative estimate that says much about both novelists.

Sherwood Anderson

TEXTS. *Windy McPherson's Son* (New York: John Lane, 1916; Chicago: University of Chicago Press, 1966, intro. by Wright Morris); *Marching Men* (New York: John Lane, 1917; Cleveland: Western Reserve Press, 1972, ed. Ray L. White); *Winesburg, Ohio* (New York: B. W. Huebsch, 1919; New York: Viking, 1916, intro. by Malcolm Cowley; New York: Viking, 1966, ed. J. H. Ferres, with critical essays); *Poor White* (B. W. Huebsch, 1921); *Horses and Men* (New York: B. W. Huebsch, 1923); *A Story Teller's Story* (New York: B. W. Huebsch, 1924; Critical Text ed. Ray L. White, Cleveland: Western Reserve Press, 1968); *Dark Laughter* (New York: Liveright, 1925); *Tar: A Midwest Childhood* (New York: Liveright, 1926; Critical Text ed. Ray L. White, Cleveland: Western Reserve Press, 1969); *Beyond Desire* (New York: Liveright, 1932); *Death in the Woods and Other Stories* (New York: Liveright, 1933); *Kit Brandon* (New York: Scribner, 1936); *Return to Winesburg,* ed. Ray L. White (Chapel Hill: University of North Carolina Press, 1967); *Sherwood Anderson's Memoirs,* ed. Ray L. White (Chapel Hill: University of North Carolina Press, 1969). Recent collections include *The Sherwood Anderson Reader,* ed. Paul Rosenfeld (Boston: Houghton Mifflin, 1947); *The Portable Sherwood Anderson,* ed. Horace Gregory (New York: Viking, 1949); and *Short Stories,* ed. Maxwell Geismar (New York: Hill & Wang, 1962).

STUDIES. The most helpful guide to Anderson scholarship is Walter B. Rideout's bibliographical essay in *Sixteen Modern American Authors.* Of further help are Eugene P. Sheehy and Kenneth A. Lohf, *Sherwood Anderson: A Bibliography* (Georgetown, Calif.: Talisman Press, 1960) and Ray L. White, *The Merrill Checklist of Sherwood Anderson* (Columbus, Oh.: Merrill, 1969). Introductions to the man and his work are Brom Weber, *Sherwood Anderson* (UMPAW: 1964) and Rex Burbank, *Sherwood Anderson* (TUSAS: 1964). Biographical material includes C. B. Chase, *Sherwood Anderson* (New York: McBride, 1927); A. W.

Derleth, *Three Literary Men: A Memoir of Sinclair Lewis, Sherwood Anderson and Edgar Lee Masters* (New York: Candlelight Press, 1963); and Elizabeth Anderson and G. R. Kelly, *Miss Elizabeth: A Memoir* (Boston: Little, Brown, 1969), by Anderson's third wife. Howard M. Jones and Walter P. Rideout have edited *Letters of Sherwood Anderson* (Boston: Little, Brown, 1953); Ray L. White has edited *Sherwood Anderson/Gertrude Stein: Correspondence and Personal Essays* (Chapel Hill: University of North Carolina Press, 1972). Full-length criticism of Anderson includes B. N. Fagin, *The Phenomenon of Sherwood Anderson* (Baltimore: Johns Hopkins Press, 1927); Irving Howe, *Sherwood Anderson* (New York: Sloane, 1951); James Schevill, *Sherwood Anderson: His Life and Work* (Denver: University of Denver Press, 1951); David D. Anderson, *Sherwood Anderson* (New York: Barnes & Noble, 1967); and William A. Sutton, *The Road to Winesburg* (Metuchen, N.J.: Scarecrow, 1972). Important shorter criticism includes F. J. Hoffman, "Anderson: Psychoanalyst by Default," in *Freudianism and the Literary Mind* (Baton Rouge: Louisiana State University Press, 1957); Lionel Trilling, "Sherwood Anderson," in *The Liberal Imagination* (Garden City, N.Y.: Doubleday, Anchor, 1953); Bernard Duffey's treatment of Anderson in *The Chicago Renaissance in American Letters* (East Lansing: Michigan State University Press, 1954); John T. Flanagan, "Hemingway's Debt to Sherwood Anderson," *JEGP* 54 (1955); 507–520; and H. E. Richardson, "Anderson and Faulkner," *AL* 36 (1964): 298–314. Collections of short criticism include *Homage to Sherwood Anderson,* ed. Paul P. Appel (Mamaroneck, N.Y.: Appel, 1970); *Story* 19 (1941); and *The Achievement of Sherwood Anderson,* ed. Ray L. White (Chapel Hill: University of North Carolina Press, 1966).

Sinclair Lewis

TEXTS. *Our Mr. Wrenn* (New York: Harper, 1914); *The Trail of the Hawk* (New York: Harper, 1915); *The Job* (New York: Harper, 1917); *The Innocents* (New York: Harper, 1917); *Free Air* (New York: Harcourt, 1919); *Main Street* (New York: Harcourt, 1920); *Babbitt* (New York: Harcourt, 1922); *Arrowsmith* (New York: Harcourt, 1925); *Mantrap* (New York: Harcourt, 1926); *Elmer Gantry* (New York: Harcourt, 1927); *The Man Who Knew Coolidge* (New York: Harcourt, 1928); *Dodsworth* (New York: Harcourt, 1929); *Ann Vickers* (Garden City, N.Y.: Doubleday, Doran, 1933); *Work of Art* (Garden City, N.Y.: Doubleday, Doran, 1934); *It Can't Happen Here* (Garden City, N.Y.: Doubleday, Doran, 1935); *The Prodigal Parents* (Garden City, N.Y.: Doubleday, Doran, 1938); *Bethel Merriday* (Garden City, N.Y.: Doubleday, Doran, 1940); *Gideon Planish* (New York: Random House, 1943); *Cass Timberlane* (New York: Random House, 1945); *Kingsblood Royal* (New York: Random House, 1947); *The God-Seeker* (New York: Random House, 1949); *World So Wide* (New York: Random House, 1951); *Selected Short Stories* (Garden City, N.Y.: Doubleday, Doran, 1935); *The Man from Main Street: A Sinclair Lewis Reader,* ed. H. E. Maule and M. H. Cane (New York: Random House, 1953).

STUDIES. A good introduction is Mark Schorer, *Sinclair Lewis* (UMPAW: 1963). Full-length biographical material includes two reminiscenses by his first wife, Grace Hegger Lewis: *Half a Loaf* (New York: Liveright, 1931) and *With Love from Gracie* (New York: Harcourt, 1955); Carl Van Doren, *Sinclair Lewis: A Biographical Sketch* (Garden City, N.Y.: Doubleday, Doran, 1933); Mark

Schorer, *Sinclair Lewis: An American Life* (New York: McGraw-Hill, 1961), the best book to date; Vincent Sheean, *Dorothy and Red* (Boston: Houghton Mifflin, 1963); August W. Derleth, *Three Literary Men: A Memoir of Sinclair Lewis, Sherwood Anderson and Edgar Lee Masters* (New York: Candlelight Press, 1963); and James Lundquist, *Sinclair Lewis* (New York: Ungar, 1973). Critical material in book-length form includes Ima H. Herron, *The Small Town in American Literature* (Durham, N.C.: Duke University Press, 1939); Maxwell Geismar, *The Last of the Provincials* (Boston: Houghton Mifflin, 1947); Mark Schorer, ed., *Sinclair Lewis: A Collection of Critical Essays* (Englewood Cliffs, N.J.: Prentice-Hall, 1962), a valuable collection including work by Mencken, Anderson, Parrington, Blackmur, Cowley, and others; S. N. Grebstein, *Sinclair Lewis* (TUSAS: 1962); D. J. Dooley, *The Art of Sinclair Lewis* (Lincoln: University of Nebraska Press, 1967); and R. J. Griffin, ed., *Twentieth Century Interpretations of Arrowsmith* (Englewood Cliffs, N.J.: Prentice-Hall, 1968), eighteen commentaries ranging from early to late. Harrison Smith has edited *From Main Street to Stockholm: Letters of Sinclair Lewis, 1919–1930* (New York: Harcourt, 1952).

Katherine Anne Porter

TEXTS. *Flowering Judas and Other Stories* (New York: Harcourt, 1935); *Pale Horse, Pale Rider: Three Short Novels* (New York: Harcourt, 1939), the title piece, "Old Mortality" and *Noon Wine; The Leaning Tower and Other Stories* (New York: Harcourt, 1944); *The Days Before* (New York: Harcourt, 1952), critical essays; *Ship of Fools* (Boston: Little, Brown, 1962), novel; *The Collected Stories of Katherine Anne Porter* (New York: Harcourt, 1965); *The Collected Essays and Occasional Writings of Katherine Anne Porter* (New York: Delacorte Press, 1970), including all essays in *The Days Before* and many other pieces.

STUDIES. Useful bibliographical studies are Edward Schwartz, "Katherine Anne Porter: A Critical Bibliography," *BNYPL* 57 (1953): 211–247, an annotated listing of both primary and secondary material; and (more comprehensive) Louise Waldrip and Shirley Ann Bauer, *A Bibliography of the Works of Katherine Anne Porter and A Bibliography of the Criticism of the Works of Katherine Anne Porter* (Metuchen, N.J.: Scarecrow, 1969), a valuable work that usually either annotates or quotes from the critical items it lists. Introductions to her work are Ray B. West, *Katherine Anne Porter* (UMPAW: 1963) and George Hendrick, *Katherine Anne Porter* (TUSAS: 1965), the latter also valuable for its critical readings of the stories. Reliable biographical work on Porter is scarce; it includes Glenway Westcott, *Images of Truth: Remembrances and Criticism* (New York: Harper & Row, 1962), Hendrick, Mooney, and Nance (see below). Serious criticism of Porter's work is also relatively rare (she does not appear in either Spiller's bibliography or Ludwig's supplement). Book- or monograph-length studies include Harry J. Mooney, Jr., *The Fiction and Criticism of Katherine Anne Porter* (Pittsburgh: University of Pittsburgh Press, 1957; rev. ed., 1962), a brief but intensive reading of the stories; William L. Nance, *Katherine Anne Porter and the Art of Rejection* (Chapel Hill: University of North Carolina Press, 1964), a fine full-length study; and W. S. Emmons, *Katherine Anne Porter: The Regional Stories* (Southwestern Writers Series; Austin, Tex.: Steck-Vaughn, 1967), a study of the relatively few stories that can be called regional. Later studies are M. M. Liberman, *Katherine Anne Porter's Fiction* (Detroit: Wayne State University Press, 1971) and John E. Hardy, *Katherine Anne Porter* (New York: Ungar, 1973). Many of the finest and best-known short studies have been reprinted, with new studies, in Lodwick Hartley and George Core, eds., *Katherine Anne Porter: A Critical Symposium* (Athens: University of Georgia Press, 1969). Among the best of the shorter general studies are Lodwick Hartley, "Katherine Anne Porter," *SR* 48 (1940): 206–216; R. P. Warren, "Katherine Anne Porter (Irony with a Center)," *KR* 4 (1942): 29–42, reprinted in *Selected Essays* (New York: Random House, 1958); Vernon A. Young, "The Art of Katherine Anne Porter," *New Mexico Quarterly* 15 (1945): 326–341. Lodwick Hartley, "The Lady and the Temple: The Critical Theories of Katherine Anne Porter," *CE* 14 (1953): 386–391, a study of the essays in *The Days Before;* Edward Schwartz, "The Way of Dissent: Katherine Anne Porter's Critical Position," *WHR* 8 (1954): 119–130; James W. Johnson, "Another Look at Katherine Anne Porter," *VQR* 36 (1960): 598–613; Ray B. West, "Katherine Anne Porter and 'Historic Memory'," in *South: Modern Southern Literature in Its Cultural Setting,* eds. L. D. Rubin and R. D. Jacobs (Garden City, N.Y.: Doubleday, 1961); Eudora Welty, "The Eye of the Story," *YR* 55 (1965): 265–275; Louis Auchincloss, "Katherine Anne Porter" in *Pioneers and Caretakers: A Study of Nine American Women Novelists* (Minneapolis: University of Minnesota Press, 1965), pp. 136–151; R. P. Warren, "Uncorrupted Consciousness: The Stories of Katherine Anne Porter," *YR* 55 (1965): 280–290; and Malcolm Marsden, "Love as Threat in Katherine Anne Porter's Fiction," *TCL* 13 (1967): 29–38. Studies of individual stories are listed in Schwartz, Waldrip and Bauer (see above), and Hendrick (see above), pp. 165–169.

F. Scott Fitzgerald

TEXTS. *The Apprentice Fiction of F. Scott Fitzgerald—1909–1917,* ed. John Kuehl (New Brunswick, N.J.: Rutgers University Press, 1965); *This Side of Paradise* (New York: Scribner, 1921), novel; *The Beautiful and Damned* (New York: Scribner, 1922), novel; *Tales of the Jazz Age* (New York: Scribner, 1922); *The Great Gatsby* (New York: Scribner, 1925), novel; *All the Sad Young Men* (New York: Scribner, 1926), stories; *Tender Is the Night* (New York: Scribner, 1934; rev. ed., ed. Malcolm Cowley, New York: Scribner, 1951), novel; *Taps at Reveille* (New York: Scribner, 1935), stories; *The Last Tycoon,* ed. Edmund Wilson (New York: Scribner, 1941), unfinished novel; *The Crack-Up,* ed. Edmund Wilson (New York: New Directions, 1945), nonfiction; *The Stories of F. Scott Fitzgerald* (New York: Scribner, 1951); *Afternoon of an Author; A Selection of Uncollected Stories and Essays,* ed. Arthur Mizener (Princeton: Princeton University Library, 1957); *The Pat Hobby Stories,* ed. Arnold Gingrich (New York: Scribner, 1962); *The Basil and Josephine Stories,* ed. Jackson R. Bryer and John Kuehl (New York: Scribner, 1973); *F. Scott Fitzgerald in His Own Time: A Miscellany,* ed. Matthew J. Bruccoli and Jackson R. Bryer (Kent, Oh.: Kent State University Press, 1971).

STUDIES. Bibliographies of Fitzgerald's work are H. D. Piper, "F. Scott Fitzgerald: A Checklist," *Princeton University Library Chronicle* 12 (1951); Arthur Mizener's appendix to his *Far Side of Paradise* (see below); and Matthew J. Bruccoli, *F. Scott Fitzgerald: A Descriptive Bibliography* (Pittsburgh: University of Pittsburgh Press, 1972). Bibliographies of criticism include Jackson R. Bryer, *The Critical Reputation of F. Scott Fitzgerald: A Bibliographical Study* (Hamden, Conn.: Archon, 1967); Bryer's bibliographical essay in *Sixteen Modern American Authors* (the most helpful single source); and Matthew J. Bruccoli, ed., *The Merrill Checklist of F. Scott Fitzgerald* (Columbus, Oh.: Merrill, 1970). Introductions to the man and his work are Charles E. Shain, *F. Scott Fitzgerald* (TUSAS: 1963) and Milton Hindus, *F. Scott Fitzgerald* (New York: Holt, Rinehart & Winston, 1968). Biographical material is plentiful and includes the following: Arthur Mizener, *The Far Side of Paradise* (Boston: Houghton Mifflin, 1951), the best critical biography; Sheilah Graham and Gerold Frank, *Beloved Infidel* (New York: Holt, 1958), memoirs by Fitzgerald's Hollywood gossip-column mistress; Andrew Turnbull, *Scott Fitzgerald* (New York: Scribner, 1962); Morley Callaghan, *That Summer in Paris: Memories of Tangled Friendships with Hemingway, Fitzgerald, and Some Others* (New York: Coward-McCann, 1963); Ernest Hemingway, *A Moveable Feast* (New York: Scribner, 1964), unkind recollections; H. D. Piper, *F. Scott Fitzgerald: A Critical Portrait* (New York: Holt, Rinehart & Winston, 1965); Nancy Milford, *Zelda* (New York: Harper & Row, 1970); Sara Mayfield, *Exiles from Paradise: Zelda and Scott Fitzgerald* (New York: Delacorte Press, 1971); and Aaron Latham, *Crazy Sundays: F. Scott Fitzgerald in Hollywood* (New York: Viking, 1971). There are three collections of letters: *The Letters of F. Scott Fitzgerald*, ed. Andrew Turnbull (New York: Scribner, 1963); *Dear Scott/Dear Max: The Fitzgerald-Perkins Correspondence*, eds. John Kuehl and Jackson R. Bryer (New York: Scribner, 1971); and *As Ever, Scott-Fitz—Letters Between F. Scott Fitzgerald and His Literary Agent, Harold Ober—1919–1940*, eds. Matthew J. Bruccoli and Jennifer M. Atkinson (Philadelphia: Lippincott, 1972). Book-length critical studies of Fitzgerald are as follows: James E. Miller, Jr., *The Fictional Techniques of Scott Fitzgerald* (New York: New York University Press, 1964); Matthew J. Bruccoli, *The Composition of Tender Is the Night: A Study of the Manuscripts* (Pittsburgh: University of Pittsburgh Press, 1963), indispensable for an understanding of the novel, as is also Malcolm Cowley's introduction to the revised edition of the novel; William F. Goldhurst, *F. Scott Fitzgerald and His Contemporaries* (Cleveland: World Publishing, 1963); Sergio Perosa, *The Art of F. Scott Fitzgerald* (Ann Arbor: University of Michigan Press, 1965); Richard D. Lehan, *F. Scott Fitzgerald and the Craft of Fiction* (Carbondale: Southern Illinois University Press, 1966); Robert Sklar, *F. Scott Fitzgerald: The Last Laocoon* (New York: Oxford University Press, 1967); Milton R. Stern, *The Golden Moment: The Novels of F. Scott Fitzgerald* (Urbana: University of Illinois Press, 1970); Arthur Mizener, *Scott Fitzgerald and His World* (New York: Putnam, 1972); William A. Fahey, *F. Scott Fitzgerald and the American Dream* (New York: T. Y. Crowell, 1973); John A. Higgins, *F. Scott Fitzgerald: A Study of the Stories* (Jamaica, N.Y.: St. John's University Press, 1971); and John F. Callahan, *The Illusions of a Nation—Myth and History in the Novels of F. Scott Fitzgerald* (Urbana: University of Illinois Press 1972). Collections of short criticism of a general nature are Alfred Kazin, ed., *F. Scott Fitzgerald: The Man and His Work* (Cleveland: World Publishing, 1951); Arthur Mizener, ed., *F. Scott Fitzgerald: A Collection of Critical Essays* (Englewood Cliffs, N.J.: Prentice-Hall, 1963); Matthew J. Bruccoli, ed., *Profile of F. Scott Fitzgerald* (Columbus, Oh.: Merrill, 1971); and Kenneth E. Eble, ed., *F. Scott Fitzgerald: A*

Collection of Criticism (New York: McGraw-Hill, 1973). More specialized collections are F. J. Hoffman, ed., *The Great Gatsby: A Study* (New York: Scribner, 1962); E. H. Lockridge, ed., *Twentieth Century Interpretations of The Great Gatsby* (Englewood Cliffs, N.J.: Prentice-Hall, 1968); H. D. Piper, ed., *Fitzgerald's The Great Gatsby: The Novel, the Critics, the Background* (New York: Scribner, 1970); Marvin J. LaHood, ed., *Tender Is the Night: Essays in Criticism* (Bloomington: Indiana University Press, 1969); and Malcolm and Robert Cowley, eds., *Fitzgerald and the Jazz Age* (New York: Scribner, 1966).

John Dos Passos

TEXTS. *One Man's Initiation—1917* (London: Allen and Unwin, 1920); *Three Soldiers* (Garden City, N.Y.: Doran, 1921); *A Pushcart at the Curb* (Garden City, N.Y.: Doran, 1922); *Rosinante to the Road Again* (Garden City, N.Y.: Doran, 1922); *Streets of Night* (Garden City, N.Y.: Doran, 1923); *Manhattan Transfer* (Boston: Houghton Mifflin, 1925); *Facing the Chair* (Boston: Sacco-Vanzetti Defense Committee, 1927); *Orient Express* (New York: Harper, 1927); *In All Countries* (New York: Harcourt, 1934); *Three Plays* (New York: Harcourt, 1934), *Airways, Inc.; Fortune Heights; The Garbage Man; U.S.A.* (New York: Modern Library, 1937), *The 42nd Parallel* (1930), *1919* (1932), *The Big Money* (1936); *Journeys Between Wars* (New York: Harcourt, 1938); *The Ground We Stand On* (New York: Harcourt, 1941); *State of the Nation* (Boston: Houghton Mifflin, 1944); *Tour of Duty* (Boston: Houghton Mifflin, 1946); *District of Columbia* (Boston: Houghton Mifflin, 1952), *Adventures of a Young Man* (1939), *Number One* (1943), *The Grand Design* (1949); *The Prospect Before Us* (Boston: Houghton Mifflin, 1950); *Chosen Country* (Boston: Houghton Mifflin, 1951); *The Head and Heart of Thomas Jefferson* (Garden City, N.Y.: Doubleday, 1954); *Most Likely to Succeed* (Englewood Cliffs, N.J.: Prentice-Hall, 1954); *The Theme Is Freedom* (New York: Dodd, Mead, 1956); *The Men Who Made the Nation* (New York: Doubleday, 1957); *The Great Days* (New York: Sagamore Press, 1958); *Prospects of a Golden Age* (Englewood Cliffs, N.J.: Prentice-Hall, 1959); *Mid-century* (Boston: Houghton Mifflin, 1961); *Mr. Wilson's War* (Garden City, N.Y.: Doubleday, 1962); *Brazil on the Move* (Garden City, N.Y.: Doubleday, 1963); *Occasions and Protests* (Chicago: Regnery, 1964); *Century's Ebb: The Thirteenth Chronicle* (Boston: Gambit, 1975); *The Fourteenth Chronicle: Letters and Diaries of John Dos Passos,* ed. Townsend Ludington (Boston: Gambit, 1973).

STUDIES. An introduction to the work is Robert G. Davis, *John Dos Passos* (UMPAW: 1962). A partial biography is Melvin Landsberg, *Dos Passos' Path to U.S.A.: A Political Biography, 1912–1936* (Boulder: Colorado Associated University Press, 1972). Townsend Ludington has edited *The Fourteenth Chronicle: Letters and Diaries of John Dos Passos* (Boston: Gambit, 1973). Full-length studies of the work are John H. Wrenn, *John Dos Passos* (TUSAS: 1961) and John D. Brantley, *The Fiction of John Dos Passos* (The Hague: Mouton, 1968). Important shorter studies include F. J. Hoffman, *The Modern Novel in America* (Chicago: Regnery, 1951); Malcolm Cowley, *Exile's Return* (New York: Viking, 1951); Blanche Gelfant, *The American City Novel* (Norman: University of Oklahoma Press, 1954); Walter B. Rideout, *The Radical Novel in the United States, 1900–1954* (Cambridge, Mass.: Harvard University Press, 1954); and

John Lydenberg, "Dos Passos's U.S.A.: The Words of the Hollow Men," in *Essays on Determinism in American Literature*, ed. S. J. Krause (Kent, Oh.: Kent State University Press, 1964). Collections of shorter criticism are Max Eastman, ed., *John Dos Passos, An Appreciation* (Englewood Cliffs, N.J.: Prentice-Hall, 1954) and Allen Belkind, ed., *Dos Passos, the Critics, and the Writer's Intention* (Carbondale: Southern Illinois University Press, 1971).

William Faulkner

TEXTS. The following is a list of Faulkner's major works. Editions and reprints of his works are numerous; the dates and publishers listed below are those of the original editions. Also some of Faulkner's fairly long pieces are often printed as short stories, although he intended them as parts of novels; the following list identifies as novels those works that Faulkner apparently intended as such. *The Marble Faun* (Boston: Four Seas, 1924), poems; *Soldier's Pay* (New York: Boni & Liveright, 1926), novel; *Mosquitoes* (New York: Boni & Liveright, 1927), novel; *Sartoris* (New York: Harcourt, Brace, 1929), novel; *The Sound and the Fury* (London: Jonathan Cape and New York: Harrison Smith, 1930), novel; *Sanctuary* (London: Jonathan Cape and New York: Harrison Smith, 1931), novel; *Light in August* (New York: Harrison Smith and Robert Haas, 1932), novel; *A Green Bough* (New York: Harrison Smith and Robert Haas, 1933), poems; *Doctor Martino and Other Stories* (New York: Harrison Smith and Robert Haas, 1934); *Pylon* (New York: Harrison Smith and Robert Haas, 1935), novel; *Absalom, Absalom!* (New York: Random House, 1936), novel; *The Unvanquished* (New York: Random House, 1938), novel; *The Wild Palms* (New York: Random House, 1939), novel; *The Hamlet* (New York: Random House, 1940), novel; *Go Down Moses* (New York: Random House, 1942), novel (including "The Bear"); *Intruder in the Dust* (New York: Random House, 1948), novel; *Knight's Gambit* (New York: Random House, 1949), stories; *Collected Stories of William Faulkner* (New York: Random House, 1950); *Requiem for a Nun* (New York: Random House, 1951), novel, adapted as a play by Ruth Ford; *A Fable* (New York: Random House, 1954), novel; *The Town* (New York: Random House, 1957), novel; *The Mansion* (New York: Random House, 1959), novel; *The Reivers* (New York: Random House, 1962), novel; *Essays, Speeches and Public Letters*, ed. James B. Meriwether (New York: Random House, 1965); *New Orleans Sketches*, intro. Carvel Collins (New Brunswick, N.J.: Rutgers University Press, 1968); *William Faulkner: Early Prose and Poetry*, comp. Carvel Collins (Boston: Little, Brown, 1962).

STUDIES. James B. Meriwether's essay in *Sixteen Modern American Authors* is the most helpful guide in the bewildering world of Faulkner scholarship. He has also compiled *William Faulkner: A Checklist* (Princeton: Princeton University Press, 1957); *The Literary Career of William Faulkner: A Bibliographical Study* (Princeton: Princeton University Press, 1961); and *The Merrill Checklist of William Faulkner* (Columbus, Oh.: Merrill, 1970). Also useful are John Bassett, *William Faulkner: An Annotated Checklist of Criticism* (New York: David Lewis, 1972); Irene L. Sleeth, *William Faulkner: A Bibliography of Criticism* (Chicago: Swallow, 1962); and Maurice Beebe, "Criticism of William Faulkner: A Selected Checklist," *MFS* 13 (1967). Introductions to the work are Michael Millgate, *William Faulkner* (New York: Grove, 1961); Lawrance Thompson,

William Faulkner (New York: Barnes & Noble, 1963); E. L. Volpe, *A Reader's Guide to William Faulkner* (New York: Noonday, 1964); and F. J. Hoffman, *William Faulkner* (TUSAS: 1966). Of the following biographical material the studies by Leary and Blotner are the most extensive: Robert A. Jelliffe, ed., *Faulkner at Nagano* (Tokyo: Kenkyusha, 1956); F. L. Gwynn and J. L. Blotner, *Faulkner in the University* (University Press of Virginia, 1959); Ward L. Miner, *The World of William Faulkner* (New York: Pageant, 1959); John Faulkner, *My Brother Bill: An Affectionate Reminiscence* (New York: Trident, 1963); J. L. Fant and Robert Ashley, eds., *Faulkner at West Point* (New York: Random House, 1964); J. W. Webb and A. W. Green, eds., *William Faulkner of Oxford* (Baton Rouge: Louisiana State University Press, 1967); James B. Meriwether and Michael Millgate, eds., *Lion in the Garden* (New York: Random House, 1968); Lewis Leary, *William Faulkner of Yoknapatawpha County* (New York: T. Y. Crowell, 1973); and Joseph L. Blotner, *Faulkner: A Biography* (New York: Random House, 1974). Book-length criticisms of Faulkner are voluminous. Of the following studies, listed in alphabetical order, the works by Brooks, Brylowski, Howe, Millgate, and Waggoner deserve special mention: Richard P. Adams, *Faulkner: Myth and Motion* (Princeton: Princeton University Press, 1968); Warren Beck, *Man in Motion: Faulkner's Trilogy* (Madison: University of Wisconsin Press, 1961); Melvin Blackman, *Faulkner, the Major Years* (Bloomington: Indiana University Press, 1966); Cleanth Brooks, *William Faulkner: The Yoknapatawpha Country* (New Haven: Yale University Press, 1963); Panthea R. Broughton, *William Faulkner; The Abstract and the Actual* (Baton Rouge: Louisiana State University Press, 1975); Walter Brylowski, *Faulkner's Olympian Laugh* (Detroit: Wayne State University Press, 1968); Lewis M. Dabney, *The Indians of Yoknapatawpha: A Study in Literature and History* (Baton Rouge: Louisiana State University Press, 1974); Elizabeth M. Derr, *Yoknapatawpha: Faulkner's "Little Postage Stamp of Native Soil"* (Bronx, N. Y.: Fordham University Press, 1969); James Early, *The Making of Go Down, Moses* (Dallas: Southern Methodist University Press, 1972); Joseph Gold, *William Faulkner, A Study in Humanism, from Metaphor to Discourse* (Norman: University of Oklahoma Press, 1966); Edward M. Holmes, *Faulkner's Twice-Told Tales: His Re-Use of His Material* (The Hague: Mouton, 1966); Irving Howe, *William Faulkner: A Critical Study* (New York: Knopf, Vintage, 1962); John W. Hunt, *William Faulkner: Art in Theological Tension* (Syracuse, N. Y.: Syracuse University Press, 1965); John Longley, Jr., *The Tragic Mask: A Study of Faulkner's Heroes* (Chapel Hill: University of North Carolina Press, 1963); Irving Malin, *William Faulkner: An Interpretation* (Stanford, Calif.: Stanford University Press, 1957); Michael Millgate, *The Achievement of William Faulkner* (New York: Random House, 1965); Charles H. Nilon, *Faulkner and the Negro* (New York: Citadel, 1965); William Van O'Connor, *The Tangled Fire of William Faulkner* (Minneapolis: University of Minnesota Press, 1954); Sally R. Page, *Faulkner's Women: Characterization and Meaning* (DeLand, Fla.: Everett/Edwards, 1972); Charles D. Peavy, *Go Slow Now. Faulkner and the Race Question* (Eugene: University of Oregon Books, 1972); Joseph W. Reed, Jr., *Faulkner's Narrative* (New Haven: Yale University Press, 1973); Harold E. Richardson, *William Faulkner: The Journey to Self-Discovery* (Columbia: University of Missouri Press, 1969); Kenneth E. Richardson, *Force and Faith in the Novels of William Faulkner* (The Hague: Mouton, 1967); Walter J. Slatoff,

Quest for Failure: A Study of William Faulkner (Ithaca, N.Y.: Cornell University Press, 1960); Peter Swiggart, *The Art of Faulkner's Novels* (Austin: University of Texas Press, 1962); F. L. Utley et al., *Bear, Man, and God: Eight Approaches to William Faulkner's The Bear* (New York: Random House, 1971); Olga W. Vickery, *The Novels of William Faulkner: A Critical Interpretation*, rev. ed. (Baton Rouge: Louisiana State University Press, 1964); and Hyatt H. Waggoner, *William Faulkner: From Jefferson to the World* (Lexington: University Press of Kentucky, 1959). Collections of short criticism of a general nature are F. J. Hoffman and Olga W. Vickery, eds., *William Faulkner: Three Decades of Criticism* (East Lansing: Michigan State University Press, 1960); R. P. Warren, ed., *Faulkner: A Collection of Critical Essays* (Englewood Cliffs, N.J.: Prentice-Hall, 1966); J. Robert Barth, ed., *Religious Perspectives in Faulkner's Fiction* (Notre Dame, Ind.: University of Notre Dame Press, 1972); and Dean M. Schmitter, ed., *William Faulkner: A Collection of Criticism* (New York: McGraw-Hill, 1973). More specialized collections are Michael Cowan, ed., *Twentieth Century Interpretations of The Sound and the Fury* (Englewood Cliffs, N.J.: Prentice-Hall, 1968); James B. Meriwether, ed., *Merrill Studies in The Sound and the Fury* (Columbus, Oh.: Merrill, 1970); M. Thomas Inge, ed., *The Merrill Studies in Light in August* (Columbus, Oh.: Merrill, 1971); John B. Vickery and Olga W. Vickery, eds., *Light in August and the Critical Spectrum* (Belmont, Calif.: Wadsworth, 1971); and Arnold Goldman, ed., *Twentieth Century Interpretations of Absalom! Absalom!* (Englewood Cliffs, N.J.: Prentice-Hall, 1971). A recent study of *The Sound and the Fury* is André Bleikasten's *The Most Splendid Failure* (Bloomington: Indiana University Press, 1976).

Ernest Hemingway

TEXTS. There have been countless editions and reprintings of Hemingway's books. The following are listed by their original publication dates: *In Our Time* (New York: Boni & Liveright, 1925), stories; *The Torrents of Spring* (New York: Scribner, 1926), novel; *The Sun Also Rises* (New York: Scribner, 1926), novel; *Men Without Women* (New York: Scribner, 1927), stories; *A Farewell to Arms* (New York: Scribner, 1929), novel; *Death in the Afternoon* (New York: Scribner, 1932), nonfiction; *Winner Take Nothing* (New York: Scribner, 1933), stories; *Green Hills of Africa* (New York: Scribner, 1935), nonfiction; *To Have and Have Not* (New York: Scribner, 1937), novel; *The Fifth Column and the First Forty-nine Stories* (New York: Scribner, 1938), play plus all the stories in the earlier three collections; *For Whom the Bell Tolls* (New York: Scribner, 1940), novel; *Men at War: The Best War Stories of All Time,* ed. Ernest Hemingway (New York: Crown, 1942), three selections from his own work in a collection of eighty-two pieces; *Across the River and into the Trees* (New York: Scribner, 1950), novel; *The Old Man and the Sea* (New York: Scribner, 1952), novella; *The Wild Years,* ed. Gene Z. Hanrahan (New York: Dell, 1962), seventy-three articles from *The Toronto Star Weekly* and *The Toronto Daily Star,* 1920–1924; *A Moveable Feast* (New York: Scribner, 1964), nonfiction; *By-Line: Ernest Hemingway: Selected Articles and Dispatches of Four Decades,* ed. William White (New York: Scribner, 1967); *Collected Poems* (Folcroft, Pa.: Folcroft Library, 1973); *Islands in the Stream,* novel; (New York: Scribner, 1970); *The Nick Adams Stories,* ed. P. Young (New York: Scribner, 1972).

STUDIES. The most helpful bibliographical survey is that by Fred J. Hoffman (with a supplement by Melvin J. Friedman) in *Sixteen Modern American Authors*. In addition there is Audre Hanneman's meticulous bibliography that lists and annotates Hemingway criticism through 1966, *Ernest Hemingway: A Comprehensive Bibliography* (Princeton: Princeton University Press, 1967). See also William White, *The Merrill Checklist of Ernest Hemingway* (Columbus, Oh.: Merrill, 1970) and the *Fitzgerald/Hemingway Annual*, ed. M. Bruccoli. Useful introductions are Philip Young, *Ernest Hemingway* (UMPAW: 1959); Earl Rovit, *Ernest Hemingway* (TUSAS: 1963); and Sheridan Baker, *Ernest Hemingway* (New York: Holt, Rinehart & Winston, 1967). Biographical material includes the following: Gertrude Stein, *The Autobiography of Alice B. Toklas* (New York: Harcourt, 1933), Hemingway's early years in Paris and Stein's estimate of him; Alfred G. Aronowitz and Peter Hamill, *Ernest Hemingway: The Life and Death of a Man* (New York: Lancer, 1961); Kurt D. Singer, *Hemingway: Life and Death of a Giant* (Los Angeles: Holloway House, 1961); Leicester Hemingway, *My Brother, Ernest Hemingway* (Cleveland: World Publishing, 1962); Marcelline Hemingway Sanford, *At the Hemingways: A Family Portrait* (Boston: Little, Brown, 1962), recollections by Hemingway's older sister; Morley Callaghan, *That Summer in Paris* (New York: Coward-McCann, 1963), recollections of Hemingway, Fitzgerald, and others; Jed Kiley, *Hemingway: An Old Friend Remembers* (New York: Hawthorn, 1965); A. E. Hotchner, *Papa Hemingway: A Personal Memoir* (New York: Random House, 1966), revelations by one who knew Hemingway in the last ten years, called inaccurate by Hemingway's widow; Constance C. Montgomery, *Hemingway in Michigan* (New York: Fleet, 1966); Carlos Baker, *Ernest Hemingway: A Life Story* (New York: Scribner, 1969), unlikely to be soon matched in meticulousness and extent of detail, the official biography to date, approved by Hemingway's widow; James McLendon, *Papa: Hemingway in Key West* (Miami, Fla.: E. A. Seemann, 1972); and Alice H. Sokoloff, *Hadley, the First Mrs. Hemingway* (New York: Dodd, Mead, 1973). Book-length criticism of Hemingway's work follows in alphabetical order: Nelson Algren, *Notes from a Sea Diary: Hemingway All the Way* (New York: Putnam, 1965); John Atkins, *The Art of Ernest Hemingway* (London: Peter Nevill, 1952); Carlos Baker, *The Writer as Artist,* 4th ed. (Princeton: Princeton University Press, 1972); J. J. Benson, *Hemingway: The Writer's Art of Self Defense* (Minneapolis: University of Minnesota Press, 1969); Joseph DeFalco, *The Hero in Hemingway's Short Stories* (Pittsburgh: University of Pittsburgh Press, 1963); Charles A. Fenton, *The Apprenticeship of Ernest Hemingway* (New York: Farrar, Straus 1954); Sheldon N. Grebstein, *Hemingway's Craft* (Carbondale: Southern Illinois University Press, 1973); Leo Gurko, *Ernest Hemingway and the Pursuit of Heroism* (New York: T. Y. Crowell, 1968); Richard B. Hovey, *Hemingway: The Inward Terrain* (Seattle: University of Washington Press, 1968); Nicholas Joost, *Ernest Hemingway and the Little Magazines: The Paris Years* (Barre, Mass.: Barre Publishers, 1968); John Killinger, *Hemingway and the Dead Gods: A Study in Existentialism* (Lexington: University Press of Kentucky, 1960); W. E. Kvam, *Hemingway in Germany: The Fiction, the Legend, and the Critics* (Athens: Ohio University Press, 1973); Robert W. Lewis, Jr., *Hemingway on Love* (Austin: University of Texas Press, 1965); Richard K. Peterson, *Hemingway Direct and Oblique* (The Hague: Mouton, 1969); Nathan A. Scott, *Ernest Hemingway: A Critical Essay* (Grand Rapids,

Mich.: Eerdmans, 1966); Samuel Shaw, *Ernest Hemingway* (New York: Ungar, 1973); Robert O. Stephens, ed., *Hemingway's Nonfiction: The Public Voice* (Chapel Hill: University of North Carolina Press, 1968); Arthur Waldhorn, *A Reader's Guide to Ernest Hemingway* (New York: Farrar, Straus & Giroux, 1972); Emily S. Watts, *Ernest Hemingway and the Arts* (Urbana: University of Illinois Press, 1971); D. B. Wylder, *Hemingway's Heroes* (Albuquerque: University of New Mexico Press, 1970); and Philip Young, *Ernest Hemingway: A Reconsideration* (University Park: Pennsylvania State University Press, 1966). Important shorter studies are R. P. Warren's essay in his *Selected Essays* (New York: Random House, 1958); John Malcolm Brinnin, *The Third Rose: Gertrude Stein and Her World* (Boston: Atlantic–Little, Brown, 1959); and Cleanth Brooks, *The Hidden God: Studies in Hemingway, Faulkner, Yeats, Eliot, and Warren* (New Haven: Yale University Press, 1963). Collections of short criticism are J. K. M. McCaffery, ed., *Ernest Hemingway: The Man and His Work* (Cleveland: World Publishing, 1950); Carlos Baker, ed., *Hemingway and His Critics* (New York: Hill & Wang, 1961) and *Ernest Hemingway: Critiques of Four Major Novels* (New York: Scribner, 1962), twenty-two essays commenting on *The Sun Also Rises, A Farewell to Arms, For Whom the Bell Tolls,* and *The Old Man and the Sea;* Robert P. Weeks, ed., *Hemingway: A Collection of Critical Essays* (Englewood Cliffs, N.J.: Prentice-Hall, 1962); Roger Asselineau, ed., *The Literary Reputation of Hemingway in Europe* (New York: New York University Press, 1965); Arthur Waldhorn, ed., *Ernest Hemingway: A Collection of Criticism* (New York: McGraw-Hill, 1973); Jay Gellens, ed., *Twentieth Century Interpretations of A Farewell to Arms* (Englewood Cliffs, N.J.: Prentice-Hall, 1970); and Katharine T. Jobes, ed., *Twentieth Century Interpretations of The Old Man and the Sea* (Englewood Cliffs, N.J.: Prentice-Hall, 1968).

Thomas Wolfe

TEXTS. *Look Homeward, Angel* (New York: Scribner, 1929), novel; *Of Time and the River* (New York: Scribner, 1935), novel; *From Death to Morning* (New York: Scribner, 1935), short stories; "The Story of a Novel" (New York: Scribner, 1936), essay; *The Web and the Rock* (New York: Harper, 1939), novel; *You Can't Go Home Again* (New York: Harper, 1940), novel; *The Hills Beyond* (New York: Harper, 1943), short pieces. Useful collections are Maxwell Geismar, ed., *The Portable Thomas Wolfe* (New York: Viking, 1946), including selections from the novels, "The Story of a Novel," and six short stories; C. Hugh Holman, ed., *The Short Novels of Thomas Wolfe* (New York: Scribner, 1961); C. Hugh Holman, ed., *The Thomas Wolfe Reader* (New York: Scribner, 1962), selections from the novels, "The Story of a Novel," and seven shorter pieces; and John S. Barnes, ed., *A Stone, A Leaf, A Door* (New York: Scribner, 1945), a selection of Wolfe's poetic prose printed as verse. Richard S. Kennedy and Paschal Reeves have edited *The Notebooks of Thomas Wolfe,* 2 vols. (Chapel Hill: University of North Carolina Press, 1970), which contains selections from notes Wolfe made from 1926 to 1938.

STUDIES. For bibliography see George R. Preston, Jr., *Thomas Wolfe: A Bibliography* (New York: Charles S. Boesen, 1943); C. Hugh Holman, "Thomas Wolfe: A Bibliographical Study," *TSLL* 1 (1959): 427–445; Elmer D. Johnson, *Of Time and Thomas Wolfe: A Bibliography with a Character Index of His Works* (Metuchen,

N.J.: Scarecrow, 1959); Maurice Beebe and Leslie A. Field, "Criticism of Thomas Wolfe: A Selected Checklist," *MFS* 11 (1965): 315–328; and C. Hugh Holman's review of Wolfe scholarship through 1971 in *Sixteen Modern American Authors*, pp. 587–624. Introductions to Wolfe's work are C. Hugh Holman, *Thomas Wolfe* (UMPAW: 1960), a good brief discussion by one of the best Wolfe scholars, who argues that Wolfe's greatest strength lies in the form of the short novel; Richard Walser, *Thomas Wolfe* (New York: Barnes & Noble, 1961); and Bruce R. McElderry, Jr., *Thomas Wolfe* (TUSAS: 1964), a good introduction with a fine selective bibliography. Biographical work on Wolfe is plentiful, if uneven. Three interesting sources are Aline F. Bernstein's *Three Blue Suits* (New York: Equinox Cooperative Press, 1933), *The Journey Down* (New York: Knopf, 1938), and *An Actor's Daughter* (New York: Knopf, 1941), fictional and autobiographical portraits of Wolfe by his mistress, the Esther Jack of his later fiction. Other works include Jonathan Daniels, *Tar Heels* (New York: Dodd, Mead, 1941), reminiscences, including a description of Wolfe's funeral; Hayden Norwood, *The Marble Man's Wife; Thomas Wolfe's Mother* (New York: Scribner, 1947), conversations with Wolfe's mother; Agatha B. Adams, *Thomas Wolfe: Carolina Student* (Chapel Hill: University of North Carolina Library, 1950), Wolfe's days at the university; Thomas C. Pollack and Oscar Cargill, *Thomas Wolfe at Washington Square* (New York: New York University Press, 1954), Wolfe's teaching days at NYU; Floyd C. Watkins, *Thomas Wolfe's Characters: Portraits from Life* (Norman: University of Oklahoma Press, 1957), the factual basis of most of Wolfe's work; Elizabeth Nowell, *Thomas Wolfe: A Biography* (Garden City, N.Y.: Doubleday, 1960), the most detailed and factual biography; Mabel Wolfe Wheaton with Legette Blythe, *Thomas Wolfe and His Family* (Garden City, N.Y.: Doubleday, 1961), a defense of the real Wolfe family by Wolfe's sister; Robert Raynolds, *Thomas Wolfe: Memoir of a Friendship* (Austin: University of Texas Press, 1965); and Andrew Turnbull, *Thomas Wolfe* (New York: Scribner, 1967), a fine recent critical biography. There are four useful collections of Wolfe criticism: Richard Walser, ed., *The Enigma of Thomas Wolfe* (Cambridge: Harvard University Press, 1953), eight biographical and seventeen critical essays; C. Hugh Holman, ed., *The World of Thomas Wolfe* (New York: Scribner, 1962), containing "The Story of a Novel" and thirty critical pieces; Leslie A. Field, ed., *Thomas Wolfe: Three Decades of Criticism* (New York: New York University, Press, 1968), twenty-three critical essays and a selective bibliography; and Paschal Reeves, ed., *Thomas Wolfe and the Glass of Time* (Athens: University of Georgia Press, 1971). Full-length studies of Wolfe include Herbert J. Muller, *Thomas Wolfe* (New York: New Directions, 1947), a study of Wolfe's romanticism; Pamela H. Johnson, *Hungry Gulliver: A Critical Study of Thomas Wolfe* (New York: Scribner, 1948), a generally favorable discussion of the four novels; Louis D. Rubin, Jr., *Thomas Wolfe: The Weather of His Youth* (Baton Rouge: Louisiana State University Press, 1955), a favorable discussion that traces out Wolfe's use of time; Richard S. Kennedy, *The Window of Memory* (Chapel Hill: University of North Carolina Press, 1962), an important study of Wolfe's manuscripts and his professed intentions; C. Hugh Holman, *Three Modes of Southern Fiction: Glasgow, Faulkner, Wolfe* (Athens: University of Georgia Press, 1966), an argument for sane categories in southern fiction; Paschal Reeves, *Thomas Wolfe's Albatross; Race and Nationality in America* (Athens: University of Georgia Press, 1969), a discussion of Wolfe's treatment of Negroes, Jews, foreigners, and Indians; and William Snyder, *Thomas Wolfe: Ulysses and Narcissus* (Athens: Ohio University Press, 1972). Shorter studies of special importance are R. P. Warren, "A Note on the Hamlet of Thomas Wolfe," *American Review* 5 (1935): 191–208, reprinted in his *Selected Essays* (1958) and generally unfavorable; Bernard Devoto, "Genius Is Not Enough," *SRL* 13 (1936): 3–4, 14–15, probably the best-known attack on Wolfe; John Peale Bishop, "The Sorrows of Thomas Wolfe," *KR* 1 (1939): 7–17, reprinted in his *Collected Essays* (1948), a condemnation of Wolfe's failure to structure his work; Nathan L. Rothman, "Thomas Wolfe and James Joyce: A Study in Literary Influence," in *A Southern Vanguard*, ed. Allen Tate (Englewood Cliffs, N.J.: Prentice-Hall, 1947); and Malcolm Cowley, "Thomas Wolfe," *Atlantic Monthly* 200 (1957): 202–12, an argument that Wolfe's compulsive writing indicated a serious emotional illness. There are three collections of letters either by or to Wolfe: John S. Terry, ed., *Thomas Wolfe's Letters to His Mother, Julia Elizabeth Wolfe* (New York: Scribner, 1943); John H. Wheelcock, ed., *Editor to Author: The Letters of Maxwell E. Perkins* (New York: Scribner, 1950); and Elizabeth Nowell, ed., *The Letters of Thomas Wolfe* (New York: Scribner, 1956).

John Steinbeck

TEXTS. The following list contains Steinbeck's most important fiction and two important non-fiction works, *Sea of Cortez* and *Travels with Charley in Search of America*. *Of Mice and Men, The Moon Is Down,* and *Burning Bright* are short novels written as nearly as possible in dramatic form, and all three were produced as plays. *Cup of Gold* (New York: McBride, 1929), novel; *The Pastures of Heaven* (New York: Brewer, Warren and Putnam, 1932), novel; *To a God Unknown* (New York: Ballou, 1933), novel; *Tortilla Flat* (New York: Covici, Friede, 1935), novel; *In Dubious Battle* (New York: Covici, Friede, 1936), novel; *The Red Pony* (New York: Covici, Friede, 1937), originally three connected stories republished as four stories (New York: Viking, 1945); *Of Mice and Men* (New York: Covici, Friede, 1937), novel; *The Long Valley* (New York: Viking, 1938), stories, including those from *The Red Pony; The Grapes of Wrath* (New York: Viking, 1939), novel; *Sea of Cortez* (New York: Viking, 1941), reissued as *The Log from the Sea of Cortez* with Steinbeck's reminiscences of his friend Ed Ricketts (New York: Viking, 1951); *The Moon is Down* (New York: Viking, 1942), novel; *Cannery Row* (New York: Viking, 1945), novel; *The Wayward Bus* (New York: Viking, 1947), novel; *The Pearl* (New York: Viking, 1947), novel; *Burning Bright* (New York: Viking, 1950), novel; *East of Eden* (New York: Viking, 1952), novel; *Sweet Thursday* (New York: Viking, 1954), novel; *The Short Reign of Pippin IV* (New York: Viking, 1957), novel; *The Winter of our Discontent* (New York: Viking, 1961), novel; *Travels with Charley in Search of America* (New York: Viking, 1962). There are two useful collections of Steinbeck's works: Pascal Covici, ed., *The Portable Steinbeck*, intro. Lewis Gannett, rev. ed. (New York: Viking, 1946), selections from *The Long Valley, The Pastures of Heaven, Tortilla Flat, In Dubious Battle, The Grapes of Wrath, Sea of Cortez, The Moon Is Down, Cannery Row,* and *Of Mice and Men* (complete); and *The Short Novels of John Steinbeck* (New York: Viking, 1953) including *Tortilla Flat, The Red Pony, Of Mice and Men, The Moon Is Down, Cannery Row,* and *The Pearl.*

STUDIES. Warren French's review of Steinbeck scholarship in *Sixteen Modern American Authors* is the most helpful general guide to bibliography. Also valuable are Maurice Beebe and Jackson R. Bryer, "Criticism of John Steinbeck: A Selected Checklist," *MFS* 11 (1965): 90–103; and Tetsumaro Hayashi, *A New Steinbeck Bibliography: 1929–1971* and *Steinbeck's Literary Dimensions: A Guide to Comparative Studies* (Metuchen, N.J.: Scarecrow, 1973), including a bibliographical survey to 1971 by Peter Lisca. Introductions to the work are James Gray, *John Steinbeck* (UMPAW: 1971); Warren French, *John Steinbeck* (TUSAS: 1961), a solid work; and Joseph Fontenrose, *John Steinbeck: An Introduction and Interpretation* (New York: Barnes & Noble, 1963), a useful work that stresses Steinbeck's use of myth. Biographical work on Steinbeck is scarce. Two reliable sources are Lewis Gannett's introduction to *The Portable Steinbeck* (see above) and Peter Lisca's article "John Steinbeck: A Literary Biography" in Tedlock and Wicker's collection of criticism (see below). A recent useful book is *Steinbeck: A Life in Letters*, ed. Elaine Steinbeck and Robert Wallsten (New York: Viking, 1975). Although not strictly autobiographical, Steinbeck's *The Log from the Sea of Cortez* (see above), *Travels with Charley* (see above), and *Journal of A Novel: The East of Eden Letters* (New York: Viking, 1969) reveal much about him.

There are four useful collections of Steinbeck criticism. The most general is E. W. Tedlock, Jr., and C. V. Wicker, eds., *Steinbeck and His Critics: A Record of Twenty-Five Years* (Albuquerque: University of New Mexico Press, 1957), hereafter referred to as T & W; the best overall view of his work to date, it includes articles by Peter Lisca, F. I. Carpenter, J. W. Beach, Hyman, Krutch, and others. There are two collections devoted to *The Grapes of Wrath:* Warren French, ed., *A Companion to The Grapes of Wrath* (New York: Viking, 1963), which reprints Steinbeck's newspaper articles on the immigrants and much background material, and Agnes M. Donohue, ed., *A Casebook on The Grapes of Wrath* (New York: T. Y. Crowell, 1968), which reprints a number of articles on the book, some of them dealing with the book as a social document, most of them dealing with it as literature. The two collections nicely complement each other. The most recent collection is R. Astro and T. Hayashi, eds., *Steinbeck, the Man and His Work* (Corvallis: Oregon State University Press, 1971). Full-length studies of Steinbeck's work include Harry T. Moore, *The Novels of John Steinbeck: A First Critical Study* (Chicago: Normandie House, 1939), which deals with the novels of the 1930s; Peter Lisca, *The Wide World of John Steinbeck* (New Brunswick, N. J.: Rutgers University Press, 1958); F. W. Watt, *John Steinbeck* (New York: Grove, 1962), a brief but penetrating study by a British critic; Lester J. Marks, *Thematic Design in the Novels of John Steinbeck* (The Hague: Mouton, 1969); John C. Pratt, *John Steinbeck: A Critical Essay* (Grand Rapids: Eerdmans, 1970); and Howard Levant, *The Novels of John Steinbeck* (Columbia: University of Missouri Press, 1975).

Articles and book sections of special interest are F. I. Carpenter, "John Steinbeck: American Dreamer," *SWR* 26 (1941): 454–467, a comparison of the American myth of the west and Steinbeck's depiction of the reality, and "The Philosophical Joads," *CE* 2 (1941): 315–325, reprinted in his *American Literature and the Dream* (New York: Philosophical Library, 1955), an examination of Steinbeck's indebtedness to Emerson, Whitman, and William James; Edmund Wilson's largely negative discussion of Steinbeck in *The Boys in the Backroom:*

Notes on Californian Novelists (Paterson, N.J.: Colt Press, 1941) reprinted in his *Classics and Commercials* (New York: Farrar, Straus 1950); T. K. Whipple, "Steinbeck: Through a Glass Though Brightly," in his *Study Out the Land* (Berkeley: University of California Press, 1943), an appreciation of Steinbeck's prose techniques; Frederick Bracher, "Steinbeck and the Biological View of Man," *Pacific Spectator* 2 (1948): 14–29; W. O. Ross, "John Steinbeck, Naturalism's Priest," *CE* 10 (1949): 432–438; Michael F. Moloney, "Half-Faiths in Modern Fiction," *Catholic World* 171 (1950): 344–350; John S. Kennedy, "John Steinbeck: Life Affirmed and Dissolved," in *Fifty Years of the American Novel*, ed. H. C. Gardiner (New York: Scribner, 1951); R. W. B. Lewis, "The Steinbeck Perspective," in his *The Picaresque Saint: Representative Figures in Contemporary Fiction* (Philadelphia: Lippincott, 1958) and "John Steinbeck: The Fitful Daemon," in *The Young Rebel in American Literature*, ed. Carl Bode (New York: Praeger, 1960); James Woodress, "John Steinbeck: Hostage to Fortune," *SAQ* 63 (1964): 385–397; and Peter Lisca, "Steinbeck's Image of Man and His Decline as a Writer," *MFS* 11 (1965): 3–10. More general discussions, a few among many, are Maxwell Geismar, *Writers in Crisis: The American Novel between Two Wars* (Boston: Houghton Mifflin, 1942); Frederick J. Hoffman, *The Modern Novel in America, 1900–1950* (Chicago: Regenery, 1951); C. C. Walcutt, *American Literary Naturalism, A Divided Stream* (Minneapolis: University of Minnesota Press, 1956); William Frohock, *The Novel of Violence in America* (Dallas, Tex.: Southern Methodist University Press, 1958); and Maxwell Geismar, *American Moderns, From Rebellion to Conformity* (New York: Hill & Wang, 1958).

Richard Wright

TEXTS. *Uncle Tom's Children* (New York: Harper, 1938); *Native Son* (New York: Harper, 1940); *Twelve Million Black Voices* (New York: Viking, 1941); *Black Boy* (New York: Harper, 1945); *The Outsider* (New York: Harper, 1953); *Savage Holiday* (New York: Avon, 1954); *Black Power* (New York: Harper, 1954); *The Color Curtain* (Cleveland: World Publishing, 1956); *Pagan Spain* (New York: Harper, 1957); *White Man, Listen!* (Garden City, N. Y.: Doubleday, 1957); *The Long Dream* (Garden City, N. Y.: Doubleday, 1958); *Eight Men* (Cleveland: World Publishing, 1961); *Lawd Today* (New York: Avon, 1963).

STUDIES. For bibliography see John M. Reilly, "Richard Wright: An Essay in Bibliography," *Resources for American Literary Study* 1 (1971): 131–180 and M. Thomas Inge, Jackson R. Bryer, and Maurice Duke, eds., *Black American Writers: A Bibliographic Survey*, vol. 2 (New York: St. Martin's, 1976). Introductions are Robert A. Bone, *Richard Wright* (UMPAW: 1969); Russell C. Brignano, *Richard Wright: An Introduction to the Man and His Works* (Pittsburgh: University of Pittsburgh Press, 1970); and Milton and Patricia Rickels, *Richard Wright* (Austin, Tex.: Steck-Vaughn, 1970). Biographies are Constance Webb, *Richard Wright* (New York: Putnam, 1968) and John A. Williams, *The Most Native of Sons* (Garden City, N.Y.: Doubleday, 1970). Full-length studies include Dan McCall, *The Example of Richard Wright* (New York: Harcourt, 1969); Edward Margolies, *The Art of Richard Wright* (Carbondale: Southern Illinois University Press, 1969); Keneth Kinnamon, *The Emergence of Richard Wright* (Urbana: University of Illinois Press, 1972); David Bakish, *Richard Wright* (New York: Ungar, 1973); and Michel Fabre, *The Unfinished Quest of Richard Wright*, trans. Isabel Barzun (New York: Morrow, 1973). Important shorter studies are in Harry Slochower, *No Voice Is Wholly Lost* (New York: Creative Age, 1945); E. B. Bergum, *The Novel and the World's Dilemma* (New York: Oxford University Press, 1947); James Baldwin, *Notes of a Native Son* (Boston: Beacon, 1955) and *Nobody Knows My Name* (New York: Dial, 1961); Robert Bone, *The Negro Novel in America* (New Haven: Yale University Press, 1958); Irving Howe, *A World More Attractive* (New York: Horizon, 1963); Ralph Ellison, *Shadow and Act* (New York: Random House, 1964); Herbert Hill, ed., *Anger and Beyond* (New York: Harper & Row, 1966); and Eldridge Cleaver, *Soul on Ice* (New York: Dell, 1968).

Eudora Welty

TEXTS. *A Curtain of Green and Other Stories* (Garden City, N.Y.: Doubleday, Doran, 1941); *The Robber Bridegroom* (Garden City, N.Y.: Doubleday, Doran, 1942); *The Wide Net and Other Stories* (New York: Harcourt, 1943); *Delta Wedding* (New York: Harcourt, 1946); *The Golden Apples* (New York: Harcourt, 1949); *The Ponder Heart* (New York: Harcourt, 1954); *The Bride of the Innisfallen* (New York: Harcourt, 1955); *The Shoe Bird* (New York: Harcourt, 1964); *Losing Battles* (New York: Random House, 1970); *The Optimist's Daughter* (New York: Random House, 1972); "The Reading and Writing of Short Stories," *Atl* 183 (February 1949): 54–58; "How I Write," *VQR* 31 (Spring 1955): 240–251; "Place in Fiction," *SAQ* 55 (January 1956): 57–72.

STUDIES. Bibliography includes Semour L. Gross, "Eudora Welty: A Bibliography of Criticism and Comment," *Secretary's News Sheet*, Bibliographical Society, University of Virginia, 1960, pp. 1–32 and Noel Polk, "A Eudora Welty Checklist," *MissQ* 26 (1973): 663–693. An introduction is J. A. Bryant, Jr., *Eudora Welty* (UMPAW: 1968). Book-length critical studies are Ruth M. Vande Kieft, *Eudora Welty* (TUSAS: 1962); Alfred Appel, Jr., *A Season of Dreams* (Baton Rouge: Louisiana State University Press, 1965); Neil D. Isaacs, *Eudora Welty* (Austin, Tex.: Steck-Vaughn, 1969); and Zelma T. Howard, *The Rhetoric of Eudora Welty's Short Stories* (Hattiesburg, Miss.: University College Press, 1973). Important shorter studies, among many, are Eunice Glenn, "Fantasy in the Fiction of Eudora Welty," in *A Southern Vanguard*, ed. Allen Tate (Englewood Cliffs, N.J.: Prentice-Hall, 1947); Katherine Anne Porter, introduction to *A Curtain of Green* (New York: Modern Library, 1954); R. P. Warren, "The Love and the Separateness in Miss Welty," *Selected Essays of Robert Penn Warren* (New York: Random House, 1958); Louis D. Rubin, Jr., "The Golden Apples of the Sun," *The Faraway Country: Writers of the Modern South* (Seattle: University of Washington Press, 1963); Louise Y. Gossett, *Violence in Recent Southern Fiction* (Durham, N.C.: Duke University Press, 1965); F. J. Hoffman, *The Art of Southern Fiction* (Carbondale: Southern Illinois University Press, 1967); John E. Hardy, "The Achievement of Eudora Welty," *Southern Humanities Review* 2 (1968): 269–278; and Seymour L. Gross, "Eudora Welty's Comic Imagination," in *The Comic Spirit in American Literature*, ed. Louis D. Rubin, Jr. (New Brunswick, N.J.: Rutgers University Press, 1973).

Saul Bellow

TEXTS. *Dangling Man* (New York: Vanguard, 1944); *The Victim* (New York: Vanguard, 1947); *The Adventures of Augie March* (New York: Viking, 1953); *Seize the Day* (New York: Viking, 1956); *Henderson The Rain King* (New York: Viking, 1959); *Herzog* (New York: Viking, 1964); *Mosby's Memoirs and Other Stories* (Greenwich, Conn.: Fawcett, 1969); *Mr. Sammler's Planet* (New York: Viking, 1970); *Humboldt's Gift* (New York: Viking, 1975). *The Last Analysis* (New York: Viking, 1965), play.

STUDIES. An introduction is Earl Rovit, *Saul Bellow* (UMPAW: 1967). Full-length studies are Tony Tanner, *Saul Bellow* (Edinburgh: Oliver & Boyd, 1965); Keith Opdahl, *The Novels of Saul Bellow* (University Park: Pennsylvania State University Press, 1967); John J. Clayton, *Saul Bellow: In Defense of Man* (Bloomington: Indiana University Press, 1968); Irving Malin, *Saul Bellow's Fiction* (Carbondale: Southern Illinois University Press, 1970); Robert R. Dutton, *Saul Bellow* (TUSAS: 1972); and Brigitte Scheer-Schazler, *Saul Bellow* (New York: Ungar, 1972). Shorter studies are Ihab Hassan, *Radical Innocence* (Princeton: Princeton University Press, 1961); Jonathan Baumbach, *The Landscape of Nightmare* (New York: New York University Press, 1965); David D. Galloway, *The Absurd Hero in American Fiction* (Austin: University of Texas Press, 1966); Howard M. Harper, *Desperate Faith* (Chapel Hill: University of North Carolina Press, 1967); and Nathan A. Scott, Jr., *Three American Moralists: Mailer, Bellow, Trilling* (Notre Dame: University of Notre Dame Press, 1973). Collections of short criticism are Irving Malin, ed., *Saul Bellow and the Critics* (New York: New York University Press, 1967) and Irving Howe, ed., *Herzog by Saul Bellow: Text and Criticism* (New York: Viking, 1976).

Flannery O'Connor

TEXTS. *Wise Blood* (New York: Harcourt, 1952); *A Good Man Is Hard to Find* (New York: Harcourt, 1955); *The Violent Bear It Away* (New York: Farrar, Straus, 1960); *Everything That Rises Must Converge* (New York: Farrar, Straus & Giroux, 1965); *The Complete Stories of Flannery O'Connor* (New York: Farrar, Straus & Giroux, 1971); *Mystery and Manners,* eds. Sally and Robert Fitzgerald (New York: Farrar, Straus & Giroux, 1969), essays and occasional prose.

STUDIES. Helpful bibliographical information is in the collection of critical essays edited by Melvin J. Friedman and Lewis A. Lawson, *The Added Dimension: The Art and Mind of Flannery O'Connor* (Bronx, N.Y.: Fordham University Press, 1966); see also the *Flannery O'Connor Bulletin* (1972–). Introductions are Stanley Edgar Hyman, *Flannery O'Connor* (UMPAW: 1966) and Dorothy Walters, *Flannery O'Connor* (TUSAS: 1973). Book-length critical studies are Carter W. Martin, *The True Country: Themes in the Fiction of Flannery O'Connor* (Nashville, Tenn.: Vanderbilt University Press, 1969); Josephine Hendin, *The World of Flannery O'Connor* (Bloomington: Indiana University Press, 1970); Leon V. Driskell and Joan T. Brittain, *The Eternal Crossroads: The Art of Flannery O'Connor* (Lexington: University Press of Kentucky, 1971); David Eggenschwiler, *The Christian Humanism of Flannery O'Connor* (Detroit: Wayne State University Press, 1972); Kathleen Feeley, *Flannery O'Connor: Voice of the Peacock* (New Brunswick, N.J.: Rutgers University Press, 1972); Gilbert H. Muller, *Nightmares and Visions: Flannery O'Connor and the Catholic Grotesque* (Athens: University of Georgia Press 1972); Miles D. Orvell, *Invisible Parade: The Fiction of Flannery O'Connor* (Philadelphia: Temple University Press, 1972); and Martha Stephens, *The Question of Flannery O'Connor* (Baton Rouge: Louisiana State University Press, 1973). Important shorter studies are

Irving Malin, *New American Gothic* (Carbondale: Southern Illinois University Press, 1962); Louis D. Rubin, Jr., *The Faraway Country: Writers of the Modern South* (Seattle: University of Washington Press, 1963); Jonathan Baumbach, *The Landscape of Nightmare* (New York: New York University Press, 1965); Louise Y. Gossett, *Violence in Recent Southern Fiction* (Durham, N.C.: Duke University Press, 1965); and Richard H. Rupp, *Celebration in Postwar American Fiction 1945–1967* (Coral Gables, Fla.: University of Miami Press, 1970).

11: MODERN DRAMATISTS

Eugene O'Neill

TEXTS. There is no single uniform edition that contains all of O'Neill's plays. *The Plays of Eugene O'Neill*, 3 vols. (New York: Random House, 1951) is the most nearly complete. Volume 1 contains *Strange Interlude, Desire under the Elms, Lazarus Laughed, The Fountain, The Glencairn Series* (the one-acts *The Moon of the Caribbees, In the Zone, Bound East for Cardiff,* and *The Long Voyage Home*), *Ile, Where the Cross Is Made, The Rope, The Dreamy Kid,* and *Before Breakfast.* Volume 2 contains *Mourning Becomes Electra, Ah, Wilderness! All God's Chillun Got Wings, Marco Millions, Welded, Diff'rent, The First Man,* and *Gold.* Volume 3 contains *Anna Christie, Beyond the Horizon, The Emperor Jones, The Hairy Ape, The Great God Brown, The Straw, Dynamo, Days Without End,* and *The Iceman Cometh.* This edition must be supplemented by the later plays, published individually: *A Moon for the Misbegotten* (New York: Random House, 1952); *A Long Day's Journey into Night* (New Haven: Yale University Press, 1956); *A Touch of the Poet* (New Haven: Yale University Press, 1957); *Hughie* (New Haven: Yale University Press, 1959); and *More Stately Mansions* (New Haven: Yale University Press, 1964). Early one-act plays are collected in *Thirst, and Other One-Act Plays* (Boston: Gorham Press, 1914) and *The Lost Plays* (New York: New Fathoms, 1950). *Children of the Sea* (Washington: NCR Microcard Editions, 1972) is a recent collection.

STUDIES. For bibliography see Jackson R. Bryer, "Forty Years of O'Neill Criticism: A Selected Bibliography," *Modern Drama* 4 (1961): 196–216; Oscar Cargill, N. Bryllion Fagin, and William J. Fisher, *O'Neill and His Plays: Four Decades of Criticism* (New York: New York University Press, 1961), hereafter referred to as Cargill; Jordan Y. Miller, *Eugene O'Neill and the American Critic* (Hamden, Conn.: Archon Books, 1962); James M. Salem, *A Guide to Critical Reviews. Part I: American Drama from O'Neill to Albee* (Metuchen, N.J.: Scarecrow, 1966); and John H. Raleigh's review of O'Neill criticism through 1971 in *Sixteen Modern American Authors.* See also Jackson R. Bryer, *Merrill Checklist of Eugene O'Neill* (Columbus, Ohio: Merrill, 1971); Ralph Sanborn and B. H. Clark, eds., *A Bibliography of the Works of Eugene O'Neill together with the Collected Poems of O'Neill* (New York: Blom, 1965); and Jennifer M. Atkinson, *Eugene O'Neill: A Descriptive Bibliography* (Pittsburgh: University of Pittsburgh Press, 1974). Joseph R. Reaver has compiled *An O'Neill Concordance,* 3 vols. (Detroit: Gale, 1969). Introductions to O'Neill's work are Clifford Leech, *Eugene O'Neill* (New York: Grove, 1963); F. I. Carpenter, *Eugene O'Neill* (TUSAS: 1964), a fine introduction that links O'Neill to American transcendentalism; and John Gassner, *Eugene O'Neill* (UMPAW: 1965). Biographical work on O'Neill includes Barrett H. Clark, *Eugene O'Neill: The Man and His Plays* (New York: Dover, 1947), an informal biography; Agnes Boulton, *Part of a Long Story* (Garden City, N. Y.: Doubleday, 1959), a partial and biased account by O'Neill's second wife; Croswell Bowen, *The Curse of the Misbegotten* (New York: McGraw-Hill, 1959), an interesting but undocumented biography utilizing memories by Shane O'Neill, O'Neill's son by Agnes Boulton; Cargill, which prints several short reminiscences; Doris Alexander, *The Tempering of Eugene O'Neill* (New York: Harcourt, 1962), a study of O'Neill to 1920; Arthur and Barbara Gelb, *O'Neill* (New York: Harper & Row, 1962), the fullest biography to date; and Louis Sheaffer, *O'Neill, Son and Playwright* (Boston: Little, Brown, 1968), an account that stresses O'Neill's relations with his parents.

Criticism of O'Neill is plentiful. Cargill is the most comprehensive collection, including general essays, letters, and articles by O'Neill; reviews of the plays; and a good selective bibliography. John Gassner, ed., *O'Neill: A Collection of Critical Essays* (Englewood Cliffs, N.J.: Prentice-Hall, 1964) prints fifteen critical essays. John H. Raleigh edited *Twentieth Century Interpretations of The Iceman Cometh* (Englewood Cliffs, N.J.: Prentice-Hall, 1968). Full-length studies of O'Neill's work include Joseph T. Shipley, *The Art of Eugene O'Neill* (Seattle: University of Washington Chapbooks, 1928), a good brief evaluation of the early work; Alan D. Mickle, *Six Plays of Eugene O'Neill* (New York: Liveright, 1929), high praise for *Anna Christie, The Hairy Ape, The Great God Brown, The Fountain, Marco Millions,* and *Strange Interlude;* Virgil Geddes, *The Melodramadness of Eugene O'Neill* (Brookfield, Conn.: The Brookfield Players, 1934), a negative estimate of the plays through *Strange Interlude;* Edwin A. Engel, *The Haunted Heroes of Eugene O'Neill* (Cambridge: Harvard University Press, 1953), an analysis of O'Neill's pessimism; Doris Falk, *Eugene O'Neill and the Tragic Tension* (New Brunswick, N.J.: Rutgers University Press, 1958), a discussion of Jungian and Freudian psychology in the plays; the December issue of *Modern Drama* 3 (1960): 219–332, containing articles by Engel, Alexander, S. K. Winther, and eleven others; S. K. Winther, *Eugene O'Neill* (New York: Random House, 1934; rev. ed. 1961), general approval of O'Neill's social and philosophical views; Richard D. Skinner, *Eugene O'Neill: A Poet's Quest* (Harlow, Essex: Longmans, 1935, 1964), a discussion of O'Neill's religious beliefs; John H. Raleigh, *The Plays of Eugene O'Neill* (Carbondale: Southern Illinois University Press, 1965), a discussion of O'Neill's development as a dramatist and of his relation to modern American literature; D. V. K. Raghavacharyulu, *Eugene O'Neill* (Bombay: Popular Prakashan, 1965), a technical philosophical analysis of the plays by an Indian thinker; Timo Tiusanen, *O'Neill's Scenic Images* (Princeton: Princeton University Press, 1968), a study stressing the visual form of the plays rather than their meaning; Chester C. Long, *The Role of Nemesis in the Structure of Selected Plays by Eugene O'Neill* (The Hague: Mouton, 1968), the varieties of fate or destiny to be found in the plays; and Emil Tornqvist, *A Drama of Souls: Studies in O'Neill's Super-naturalistic Technique* (New Haven: Yale University Press, 1969), a discussion of the ways O'Neill went beyond realism to depict otherworldly realities. Later studies are Horst Frenz, *Eugene O'Neill* (New York: Ungar, 1971) and Travis Bogard, *Centaur in Time* (New York: Oxford University Press, 1972). Shorter pieces of special interest (among a great many) are Dorothy Alexander, "Strange Interlude and Schopenhauer," *AL* 25 (1953): 213–228; S. K. Winther, "Strindberg and O'Neill: A Study of Influence," *Scandinavian Studies* 31 (1959): 103–120; Edwin A. Engel, "Ideas in the Plays of O'Neill," in *Ideas in the Drama,* ed. John Gassner (New York: Columbia University Press, 1964); William R. Brashear, "O'Neill's Schopenhauer Interlude," *Criticism* 6 (1964): 180–188; and Winifred D. Frazer's monograph, *Love as Death in The Iceman Cometh: A Modern Testament of an Ancient Theme* (Gainesville: University of Florida Press, 1967). Among the discussions of O'Neill in countless books on modern drama may be mentioned George Jean Nathan, *The Intimate Notebooks of George Jean Nathan* (New York: Knopf, 1932); Eric Bentley, *The Playwright as Thinker* (New York: Harcourt, 1946) and *In Search of Theater* (New York: Knopf, 1953); John Gassner, *Masters of the Drama* (New York: Dover, 1954); Joseph Wood Krutch, *American Drama since 1918,* rev. ed. (New York: Braziller, 1957); W. David Sievers, *Freud on Broadway* (New York: Hermitage House, 1955); Harold Clurman, *Lies Like Truth* (New York: Grove, 1958) and *The Naked Image* (New York: Macmillan, 1966); Kenneth Tynan, *Curtains* (New York: Atheneum, 1961); Louis Broussard, *American Drama: Contemporary Allegory from Eugene O'Neill to Tennessee Williams* (Norman: University of Oklahoma Press, 1963); Robert Brustein, *The Theater of Revolt* (Boston: Little, Brown, 1964); Raymond Williams, *Modern Tragedy* (Stanford, Calif.: Stanford University Press, 1966); and Thomas E. Porter, *Myth and Modern American Drama* (Detroit: Wayne State University Press, 1969).

Elmer Rice

TEXTS. Following is a list of Rice's major full-length plays: *On Trial* (New York: French, 1919); *The Adding Machine* (Garden City, N.Y.: Doubleday, Page, 1923); *Close Harmony, or The Lady Next Door,* with Dorothy Parker (New York: French, 1929); *Cock Robin,* with Philip Barry (New York: French, 1929); *Street Scene* (New York: French, 1929); *The Subway* (New York: French, 1929); *See Naples and Die* (New York: French, 1935); *The Left Bank* (New York: French, 1931); *Counsellor-at-Law* (New York: French, 1931); *We, the People* (New York: Coward-McCann, 1933); *Judgment Day* (New York: Coward-McCann, 1934); *American Landscape* (New York: Coward-McCann, 1939); *Two on an Island* (New York: Coward-McCann, 1940); *Flight to the West* (New York: Coward-McCann, 1941); *A New Life* (New York: Coward-McCann, 1944); *Dream Girl* (New York: Coward-McCann, 1946); *Two Plays: Not for Children and Between Two Worlds* (New York: Coward-McCann, 1935), revised version of *Not for Children* (New York: French, 1951); *The Grand Tour* (New York: Dramatists, 1951); *The Winner* (New York: Dramatists, 1954); *Cue for Passion* (New York: Dramatists, 1959); *Love among the Ruins* (New York: Dramatists, 1963). A convenient collection is *Seven Plays by Elmer Rice* (New York: Viking, 1950), which reprints *On Trial, The Adding Machine, Street Scene, Counsellor-at-Law, Judgment Day, Two on an Island,* and *Dream Girl.*

STUDIES. The great bulk of commentary on Rice is in the form of reviews and articles. Only two book-length studies have appeared to date: Robert Hogan, *The Independence of Elmer Rice* (Carbondale: Southern Illinois University Press, 1965) and Frank Durham, *Elmer Rice* (TUSAS: 1970). Shorter studies in book form include Anita Block, *The Changing World in Plays and Theater* (Boston: Little, Brown, 1939); J. W. Krutch, *The American Drama since 1918* (New York: Braziller, 1957); Morgan Y. Himelstein, *Drama Was a Weapon* (New Brunswick, N.J.: Rutgers University Press, 1963); Gerald Rabkin, *Drama and Commitment* (Bloomington: Indiana University Press, 1964); and Allan Lewis, *American Plays and Playwrights of the Contemporary Theater* (New York: Crown, 1965).

Tennessee Williams

TEXTS. *The Glass Menagerie* (New York: Random House, 1945); *You Touched Me!* with Donald Windham (New York: French, 1947); *A Streetcar Named Desire* (New York: New Directions, 1947); *Summer and Smoke* (New York: New Directions, 1948); *American Blues: Five Short Plays* (New York: Dramatists, 1948); *The Rose Tattoo* (New York: New Directions, 1951); *Camino Real* (New York: New Directions, 1953); *27 Wagons Full of Cotton and Other One-Act Plays* (New York: New Directions, 1953); *Hard Candy,* (New York: New Directions, 1954), stories; *One Arm and Other Stories* (New York: New Directions, 1954); *Cat on a Hot Tin Roof* (New York: New Directions, 1955); *Baby Doll* (New York: New Directions, 1956), screenplay; *In The Winter of Cities,* (Norfolk, Conn.: New Directions, 1956), poems; *Orpheus Descending and Battle of Angels* (New York: New Directions, 1958); *Suddenly Last Summer* (New York: New Directions, 1958); *Sweet Bird of Youth* (New York: New Directions, 1959); *Period of Adjustment* (New York: New Directions, 1960); *The Night of the Iguana* (New York: New Directions, 1962); *The Milk Train Doesn't Stop Here Anymore* (New York: New Directions, 1964); *The Eccentricities of the Nightingale* and *Summer and Smoke* (New York: New Directions, 1965), containing the revised version of *Summer and Smoke; Slapstick Tragedy, Two Plays (The Mutilated* and *The Gnädiges Fräulein)* in *Esquire* 64 (1965): 95–102, 130–134; *Small Craft Warnings* (New York: New Directions, 1972); *The Theatre of Tennessee Williams,* 4 vols. (New York: New Directions, 1972); *Eight Mortal Ladies Possessed,* stories (New York: New Directions, 1974); *Moise and the World of Reason* (New York: Simon & Schuster, 1975).

STUDIES. For bibliography see S. L. Falk, *Tennessee Williams* (TUSAS: 1961) and James M. Salem, *A Guide to Critical Reviews. Part One: American Drama from O'Neill to Albee* (Metuchen, N. J.: Scarecrow, 1966). A good introduction is Gerald Weales, *Tennessee Williams* (UMPAW: 1965). Full-length biographical material includes Edwina D. Williams (as told to Lucy Freeman), *Remember Me to Tom* (New York: Putnam, 1963), recollections by Williams's mother, and Gilbert Maxwell, *Tennessee Williams and Friends* (Cleveland: World Publishing, 1965). Full-length critical studies are S. L. Falk (see above); Benjamin Nelson, *Tennessee Williams: The Man and His Work* (New York: Obolensky, 1961); Nancy M. Tischler, *Tennessee Williams: Rebellious Puritan* (New York: Citadel, 1961); Francis Donahue, *The Dramatic World of Tennessee Williams* (New York: Ungar, 1964); Esther M. Jackson, *The Broken World of Tennessee Williams* (Madison: University of Wisconsin Press, 1965); and Norman J. Fedder, *The Influence of D. H. Lawrence on Tennessee Williams* (The Hague: Mouton, 1966). Shorter studies in book form include John Gassner, *The Theatre in Our Times* (New York: Crown, 1954) and *Theatre at the Crossroads* (New

York: Holt, Rinehart & Winston, 1960); Gerald Weales, *American Drama since World War II* (New York: Harcourt, 1962); Louis Broussard, *American Drama: Contemporary Allegory from Eugene O'Neill to Tennessee Williams* (Norman: University of Oklahoma Press, 1962); Allan Lewis, *American Plays and Playwrights of the Contemporary Theatre* (New York: Crown, 1965); R. H. Gardner, *The Splintered Stage: The Decline of the American Theatre* (New York: Macmillan, 1965); Jean Gould, *Modern American Playwrights* (New York: Dodd, Mead, 1966); and T. E. Porter, *Myth and Modern American Drama* (Detroit: Wayne State University Press, 1969). A collection of criticism is Jordan Y. Miller, ed., *Twentieth Century Interpretations of A Streetcar Named Desire* (Englewood Cliffs, N.J.: Prentice-Hall, 1971).

Arthur Miller

TEXTS. *All My Sons* (New York: Reynal, 1947); *Death of a Salesman* (New York: Viking, 1949); *An Enemy of the People* (New York: Viking, 1951), an adaptation of Ibsen's play; *The Crucible* (New York: Viking, 1953); *A View from the Bridge* and *A Memory of Two Mondays* (New York: Viking, 1955), two one-act plays; *The Misfits* (New York: Viking, 1961), a screenplay; *After the Fall* (New York: Viking, 1964); *Incident at Vichy* (New York: Viking, 1965); *The Price* (New York: Viking, 1968); and *The Creation of the World and Other Business* (New York: Viking, 1973). A convenient collection, with a long introduction by Miller, is *Arthur Miller's Collected Plays* (New York: Viking, 1957), including *All My Sons, Death of a Salesman, The Crucible, A Memory of Two Mondays,* and the two-act version of *A View from the Bridge.*

STUDIES. For bibliography see T. Hayashi, *Arthur Miller Criticism, 1930–1967* (Metuchen, N.J.: Scarecrow, 1969), a listing of all primary and secondary material through 1967. A useful introduction is Robert Hogan, *Arthur Miller* (UMPAW: 1964). There is no full-length biography, but brief treatments are numerous (see Hayashi). Book-length critical studies include Dennis Welland, *Arthur Miller* (New York: Grove, 1961); Sheila Huftel, *Arthur Miller: The Burning Glass* (New York: Citadel, 1965); Leonard Moss, *Arthur Miller* (TUSAS: 1967); Edward Murray, *Arthur Miller, Dramatist* (New York: Ungar, 1967); Richard I. Evans, *Psychology and Arthur Miller* (New York: Dutton, 1969); Benjamin Nelson, *Arthur Miller: Portrait of a Playwright* (New York: McKay, 1970); and Ronald Hayman, *Arthur Miller* (New York: Ungar, 1972). Shorter studies in book form include John Gassner, *The Theatre in Our Times* (New York: Crown, 1954), *Form and Idea in Modern Theatre* (New York: Dryden, 1956), and *Theatre at the Crossroads* (New York: Holt, Rinehart & Winston, 1960); Gerald Weales, *American Drama since World War II* (New York: Harcourt, 1962); Louis Broussard, *American Drama: Contemporary Allegory from Eugene O'Neill to Tennessee Williams* (Norman: University of Oklahoma Press, 1962); Allan Lewis, *American Plays and Playwrights of the Contemporary Theatre* (New York: Crown, 1965); R. H. Gardner, *The Splintered Stage: The Decline of the American Theatre* (New York: Macmillan, 1965); Jean Gould, *Modern American Playwrights* (New York: Dodd, Mead, 1966); and T. E. Porter, *Myth and Modern American Drama* (Detroit: Wayne State University Press, 1969). Collections of criticism include Robert W. Corrigan, ed., *Arthur Miller: A Collection of Critical Essays* (Englewood Cliffs, N.J.: Prentice-Hall, 1969); John H. Ferres, ed., *Twentieth Century Interpretations of The Crucible* (Englewood Cliffs, N.J.: Prentice-Hall, 1972); and Walter J. Meserve, ed., *Merrill Studies in Death of a Salesman* (Columbus, Oh.: Merrill, 1972).

Edward Albee

TEXTS. *The Zoo Story* (New York: Coward-McCann, 1959); *The Death of Bessie Smith* (New York: Coward-McCann, 1959); *The Sandbox* (New York: Coward-McCann, 1959); *Fam and Yam* (New York: Coward-McCann, 1960); *The American Dream* (New York: Coward-McCann, 1960); *Who's Afraid of Virginia Woolf?* (New York: Atheneum, 1963); *The Ballad of the Sad Cafe* (New York: Atheneum, 1963), adaptation of the Carson McCullers novella; *Tiny Alice* (New York: Atheneum, 1965); *Malcolm* (New York: Atheneum, 1965), adaptation of the James Purdy novel; *A Delicate Balance* (New York: Atheneum, 1966); *Everything in the Garden* (New York: Atheneum, 1967), adaptation of the Giles Cooper play; *Box* and *Quotations from Chairman Mao Tse-Tung* (New York: Atheneum, 1969); *All Over* (New York: Atheneum, 1971).

STUDIES. For bibliography see Margaret W. Rule, "An Edward Albee Bibliography," *TCL* 14 (1968): 35–44; Richard E. Amacher and Margaret Rule, *Edward Albee at Home and Abroad: A Bibliography* (New York: AMS Press, 1973); and James M. Salem, *A Guide to Critical Reviews. Part One* (Metuchen, N.J.: Scarecrow, 1966). An introduction is Ruby Cohn, *Edward Albee* (UMPAW: 1969). Book-length studies include Gilbert Debusscher, *Edward Albee: Tradition and Renewal* (American Studies Center, 1967); Richard E. Amacher, *Edward Albee* (TUSAS: 1969); Michael E. Rutenberg, *Edward Albee: Playwright in Protest* (New York: Drama Book Specialists, 1969); and Anne Paolucci, *From Tension to Tonic: The Plays of Edward Albee* (Carbondale: Southern Illinois University Press, 1972). Shorter studies in book form are Martin Esslin, *The Theatre of the Absurd* (Garden City, N.Y.: Doubleday, 1961); Allan Lewis, *American Plays and Playwrights of the Contemporary Theatre* (New York: Crown, 1965); Robert Brustein, *Seasons of Discontent* (New York: Simon & Schuster, 1965); Jean Gould, *Modern American Playwrights* (New York: Dodd, Mead, 1966); Brian Way, *American Theatre* (London: Edward Arnold, 1966); C. W. E. Bigsby, *Confrontation and Commitment* (London: MacGibbon and Kee, 1967); William Flanagan, *Writers at Work* (New York: Viking, 1967); and T. E. Porter, *Myth and Modern American Drama* (Detroit: Wayne State University Press, 1969).

12: MODERN AMERICAN LITERARY CRITICISM

SOME IMPORTANT GENERAL WORKS. David Daiches, *Critical Approaches to Literature* (Englewood Cliffs, N.J.: Prentice-Hall, 1956); Stanley Edgar Hyman, *The Armed Vision* (New York: Knopf, 1948); Murray Krieger, *The Play and Place of Criticism* (Baltimore: Johns Hopkins Press 1967); William Van O'Connor, *An Age of Criticism* (Chicago: Regnery, 1952); Walter Sutton, *Modern American Criticism* (Englewood Cliffs, N.J.: Prentice-Hall, 1963). Also see in GB Brown, Foerster *(American Criticism)*, Glicksberg, Jones *(Theory of American Literature)*, Stovall, and Van Nostrand *(Literary Criticism in America)*.

SOME ANTHOLOGIES OF CRITICAL ESSAYS. Monroe C. Beardsley, ed., *The Possibilities of Criticism* (Detroit: Wayne State University Press, 1971); Thomas E.

Berry, ed., *Readings in American Criticism* (New York: Odyssey, 1970); Werner Berthoff, ed., *Fictions and Events: Essays in Criticism and Literary History* (New York: Dutton, 1971); R. S. Crane, ed., *Critics and Criticism* (Chicago: University of Chicago Press, 1957); G. J. and N. M. Goldberg, eds., *The Modern Critical Spectrum* (Englewood Cliffs, N.J.: Prentice-Hall, 1962); O. B. Hardison, Jr., ed., *The Quest for Imagination: Essays in Twentieth-Century Aesthetic Criticism* (Cleveland: Press of Case Western Reserve University, 1971); Geoffrey Hartman, ed., *Beyond Formalism* (New Haven: Yale University Press, 1970); E. D. Hirsch, ed., *Validity in Interpretation* (New Haven: Yale University Press, 1967); Stanley Edgar Hyman, ed., *The Critical Performance* (New York: Knopf, Vintage, 1956); Bernard S. Oldsey and A. O. Lewis, Jr., eds., *Visions and Revisions in Modern American Literary Criticism* (New York: Dutton, 1962); Philip Rahv, ed., *Literature in America* (New York: Meridian, 1957); Wilbur S. Scott, ed., *Five Approaches of Literary Criticism* (New York: Collier, 1962); Donald A. Stauffer, ed., *The Intent of the Critic* (New York: Bantam, 1966); Rene Wellck, ed., *Discriminations* (New Haven: Yale University Press, 1970); Ray B. West, ed., *Essays in Modern Literary Criticism* (New York: Holt, Rinehart & Winston, 1952); Morton D. Zabel, ed., *Literary Opinion in America,* 2 vols. (New York: Harper & Row, 1962). Also see in GB Browne, Foerster *(Reinterpretation),* and Gordon.

THE NEW HUMANISM. Irving Babbitt, *Literature and the American College* (Boston: Houghton Mifflin, 1908); *Rousseau and Romanticism* (Boston: Houghton Mifflin, 1919); and *On Being Creative and Other Essays* (Boston: Houghton Mifflin, 1932); Norman Foerster, *Toward Standards* (New York: Farrar & Rinehart, 1930); Norman Foerster, ed., *Humanism in America* (New York: Farrar & Rinehart, 1930); Paul Elmer More, *Selected Shelburne Essays* (New York: Oxford University Press, 1935).

THE NEW CRITICISM. Cleanth Brooks, *Modern Poetry and the Tradition* (Chapel Hill: University of North Carolina Press, 1939) and *The Well Wrought Urn* (New York: Harcourt, 1947); R. P. Blackmur, *Language as Gesture* (New York: Harcourt, 1943); William Elton, *A Glossary of New Criticism* (Chicago: Modern Poetry Association, 1953); William Empson, *Seven Types of Ambiguity* (New York: New Directions, 1947); Richard Foster, *The New Romantics* (Bloomington: Indiana University Press, 1962); Murray Krieger, *The New Apologists for Poetry* (Minneapolis: University of Minnesota Press, 1956); John Crowe Ransom, *The New Criticism* (New York: New Directions, 1941); William Wimsatt and Monroe C. Beardsley, *The Verbal Icon* (Lexington: University Press of Kentucky, 1954); Yvor Winters, *The Function of Criticism* (Chicago: Swallow, 1957). Also see Richards in GB.

PSYCHOANALYTICAL CRITICISM. Edmund Bergler, *The Writer and Psychoanalysis* (New York: Robert Brunner, 1954); Frederick Crews, ed., *Psychoanalysis and Literary Process* (Cambridge: Winthrop, 1970); Sigmund Freud, *On Creativity and the Unconscious* (New York: Harper, 1958); F. J. Hoffman, *Freudiansim and the Literary Mind* (Baton Rouge: Louisiana State University Press, 1945); Norman N. Holland, *Poems in Persons: An Introduction to the Psychoanalysis of Literature* (New York: Norton, 1973); Suzanne Langer, *Feeling and Form* (New York: Scribner, 1953); Simon O. Lesser, *Fiction and the Unconscious* (New York: Knopf, Vintage, 1962); Leonard and Eleanor Manheim, *Hidden Patterns: Studies in Psychoanalytical Literary Criticism* (New York: Macmillan,

1966); Claudia C. Morrison, *Freud and the Critic* (Chapel Hill: University of North Carolina Press, 1968); William Phillips, ed., *Art and Psychoanalysis* (Cleveland: World Publishing, 1963); Edmund Wilson, *The Wound and the Bow* (Boston: Houghton Mifflin, 1941). See also in GB Basler, Fraiberg, Nelson, and Trilling.

CULTURAL-HISTORICAL CRITICISM. Quentin Anderson, *The Imperial Self: An Essay in American Literary and Cultural History* (New York: Knopf, 1971); V. F. Calverton, *The Liberation of American Literature* (New York: Scribner, 1932); Christopher Caudwell, *Studies in a Dying Culture* (New York: Dodd, Mead, 1938); David Daiches, *Literature and Society* (London: Gollancz, 1938); James T. Farrell, *A Note on Literary Criticism* (New York: Vanguard, 1936); Leslie Fiedler, *Love and Death in the American Novel* (New York: Criterion, 1960); Philip Rahv, *Image and Idea* (New York: New Directions, 1949). See also in GB Brooks, Hicks, Kazin, Lewis, Matthiessen, Parrington, Trilling, and Wilson.

MYTH-ARCHETYPE CRITICISM. Maud Bodkin, *Archetypal Patterns in Poetry* (New York: Oxford University Press, 1934); Joseph Campbell, *The Hero with a Thousand Faces* (New York: Pantheon, 1949); Richard Chase, *Quest for Myth* (Baton Rouge: Louisiana State University Press, 1949); Mircea Eliade, *Images and Symbols* (New York: Sheed & Ward, 1961); Sir James Frazer, *The New Golden Bough,* ed. T. H. Gaster (New York: Criterion, 1959); Northrop Frye, *An Anatomy of Criticism* (Princeton: Princeton University Press, 1957) and *Fables of Identity* (New York: Harcourt, 1963); C. G. Jung, *Two Essays on Analytical Psychology,* trans. R. F. C. Hull (New York: Meridian, 1956); Henry Murray, ed., *Myth and Myth Making* (New York: Braziller, 1960); R. M. Ohman, ed., *The Making of Myth* (New York: Putnam, 1962); Lord Raglan, *The Hero: A Study in Tradition, Myth, and Drama* (New York: F. Watts, 1936); T. A. Sebeok, ed., *Myth: A Symposium* (Bloomington: Indiana University Press, 1965).

Index

ABC of Reading, 78

Absalom! Absalom! 64, 117, 129, 130–131

Absurdism, 158, 159–160

Across the River and into the Trees, 132, 134

Adams, Henry, 24–26, 191–192

Adding Machine, The, 66, 155

Adeler, Max, 6

Adventures of Augie March, The, 145

Adventures of Huckleberry Finn, The, 28, 32, 33–34

Adventures of Tom Sawyer, The, 32

"After Apple-Picking," 69–70

"After Great Pain a Formal Feeling Comes," 4

After the Fall, 157, 158

Ah, Wilderness! 150

Albee, Edward, 47, 66, 158, 159–160, 165, 258

Aldington, Richard, 78

Allen, James Lane, 12, 29

All God's Chillun Got Wings, 151, 152

All My Sons, 157, 158

Ambassadors, The, 41, 43–44, 57, 119

American, The, 40, 41

American Claimant, The, 31, 72

American Dream, The, 159, 160

"American Ideals," 25

American Renaissance, 165

American Tragedy, An, 46, 51, 53, 58, 142

Anderson, Sherwood, 46, 52, 58, 81, 115–117, 118, 127, 141, 236–237

Animal tale, 15–17, 32

Anna Christie, 150, 151

Anticlimax, 4, 6, 8, 34

Antoninus, Brother (William Everson), 64

"anyone lived in a pretty how town," 93

"Apparently with No Surprise," 5

Arp, Bill, 6, 22

"Arrival of the Bee Box, The," 111

Arrowsmith, 118

"*Ars Poetica,*" 90

Artemus Ward: His Book, 7

Artemus Ward: His Travels, 7

"Artemus Ward among the Mormons," 7

Artemus Ward in London, 7

Artemus Ward's Panorama, 7
"Art of Fiction, The," 40, 52
As I Lay Dying, 65, 129
"As Imperceptibly as Grief," 2 n.1
Atherton, Gertrude, 12
Atlantic Monthly, The, 11, 13
Autobiography, 24, 33, 56, 57, 116, 135–136, 141, 152–154

Babbitt, 118
Babbitt, Irving, 84, 162
"Babylon Revisited," 123, 124
"Baker's Blue-Jay Yarn," 32
Baldwin, James, 65, 141, 142, 161
Bayou Folk, 12
"Bean Eaters, The," 103–104
"Bear, The," 65, 129, 131
"Beast in the Jungle, The," 43, 44, 120
"Because I Could Not Stop for Death," 4
Bellamy, Edward, 23
"Belles Demoiselles Plantation," 15
Bell Jar, The, 109, 110
Bellow, Saul, 64, 145–147, 251–252
"Bells for John Whiteside's Daughter," 88
Ben-Hur, 29
Beyond the Horizon, 150, 151
Bierce, Ambrose, 29, 46
"Big Two-Hearted River," 133–134
Billings, Josh, 8–9, 188
"Birches," 70
"Bird Came Down the Walk, A," 4
Black Boy, 141, 142–143
Black literature, 65, 95, 103, 112–113, 141–142
"Black Man Is Making New Gods, The," 113
Blackmur, R. P., 163
"Blue Girls," 88
"Blue Hotel, The," 49
Bodkin, Maud, 167
Bonaparte, Marie, 164
"Brain within It's Groove, The," 2 n.1
Breadwinners, The, 22
Bride of the Innisfallen, The, 143
Bridge, The, 93, 94
"Broken Tower, The," 94–95
Brooks, Cleanth, 88, 162, 163

Brooks, Gwendolyn, 64, 65, 95, 103–104, 231–232
Brown, Alice, 11
Browne, Charles Farrar, 7–8, 187–188
"Buffalo Bill's defunct," 92
Bunner Sisters, 57
Burlesque, 31, 33, 35
"Bustle in a House, The," 5

Cable, George Washington, 12, 14–15, 189
Cacography, 6, 8
Call of the Wild, The, 54
Camino Real, 156
Cannery Row, 138, 139
Cantos, The, 76, 77, 79–80, 89, 93
"Capital of the World, The," 133
Capote, Truman, 53
Castle Nowhere, 12
Cather, Willa, 20, 48, 114–115, 234–236
Cat on a Hot Tin Roof, 155, 156
Caudwell, Christopher, 165
"Celebrated Jumping Frog of Calaveras County, The," 30, 31
Century Magazine, The, 11
Chesnutt, Charles W., 12
"Chicago," 71
"*Chicago Defender* Sends a Man to Little Rock, The," 104
Chopin, Kate, 12
"Christmas-Night in the Quarters," 11
Clark, Charles Heber, 6
"Clean, Well-Lighted Place, A," 134
Clemens, Samuel Langhorne, 14, 15, 22, 28, 29–36, 122, 128, 129, 133, 192–197
Cliff-Dwellers, The, 22
"Clock Stopped, A," 2 n.1
Cocktail Party, The, 86
Coleridge, Samuel Taylor, 73, 128, 152, 161, 167
"Colloquy in Black Rock," 102
Common Lot, The, 22
Common meter, 3
Conjure Woman, The, 12
Connecticut Yankee in King Arthur's Court, A, 35
"Conscientious Objector, The," 100
"Constant Symbol, The," 70
Cooke, Rose Terry, 11

"Cool Tombs," 71
Cooper, James Fenimore, 28
"Cop and the Anthem, The," 21
Corso, Gregory, 64, 107
Country of the Pointed Firs, The, 19
"Courting of Sister Wisby, The," 19
Cowley, Malcolm, 127, 128
Craddock, Charles Egbert, 12
Crane, Hart, 63, 64, 79, 93–95, 136, 227–228
Crane, Stephen, 22, 36, 46, 47–50, 55, 117, 128, 167, 202–203
Crawford, Francis Marion, 29
"Crazy Sunday," 123
Creoles, 14–15
Crèvecoeur, St. John de, 11
Crews, F. C., 164
Criticism and Fiction, 37, 39
Crucial Instances, 57
Crucible, The, 157, 158
Cultural-Historical Criticism, 161, 163, 165, 260
Cummings, E. E., 62, 64, 82, 91–93, 226–227
"Curtain of Green, A," 143

"Daddy," 110
Daisy Miller, 41, 42
Damnation of Theron Ware, The, 23, 29
"Damned Human Race, The," 30
Darwin, Charles, 13, 22–23, 45, 46, 52, 54, 81
Daughter of the Middle Border, A, 56
"Daybreak in Alabama," 96
Days Without End, 152
Death, 2, 4, 5, 88
"Death and the Negro Man," 16 n.3
Death in the Afternoon, 133
Death of a Salesman, 119, 157, 158, 159
"Death of a Toad, The," 105
"Death of a Traveling Salesman," 143, 144
"Death of the Ball Turret Gunner, The," 100–101
"Death of the Hired Man, The," 69
Deephaven, 18
De Forest, John William, 23–24, 191
Deland, Margaret, 11, 23

Democracy, 24
Derby, George Horatio, 6
"Desirée's Baby," 12
Desire Under the Elms, 151, 152, 153
Detective story, 35
Dialect, 17–21 passim, 29, 32
Dickens, Charles, 12
Dickey, James, 105–107, 232–233
Dickinson, Emily, 1–5, 82, 88, 109, 110, 185–187
Dr. Lavendar's People, 11
Dodsworth, 119
Dooley, Mr., 6
Dos Passos, John, 46, 52, 55, 64, 65, 125–127, 241–242
Drama, 29. *See also* Experimental drama
Dramatic monologue, 86
"Dream Variations," 96
Dreiser, Theodore, 22, 46, 50, 51–53, 55, 81, 116, 117, 126, 141, 142, 204–205
"Dulham Ladies, The," 19
Dunbar, Paul Laurence, 95
Dunne, Finley Peter, 6
Dutchman, 111

East of Eden, 139
Eberhart, Richard, 96–97, 229
Edgewater People, 20
"Editha," 39
"Editor's Easy Chair, The," 36
"Editor's Study, The," 36, 39
Education of Henry Adams, The, 24, 25, 26
Edwards, Harry Stillwell, 12
Edwards, Jonathan, 102
Eggleston, Edward, 12
Elder Statesman, The, 86
"Elegy for a Dead Soldier," 99–100
Eliade, Mircea, 166, 167
Eliot, T. S., 59, 62, 63, 67, 68, 75, 76, 77, 78, 79, 80, 82, 83–87, 89, 90, 93, 94, 95, 96, 99, 101, 102, 104, 129, 132, 133, 161, 163, 223–225
Ellison, Ralph, 47, 62, 65, 141, 142, 161
"Elysium Is as Far as to," 2 n.1
Emerson, Ralph Waldo, 3, 73, 81, 91, 94, 98, 132, 138, 140, 151, 165
Emperor Jones, The, 151, 152

"Emperor of Ice-Cream, The," 74

Enormous Room, The, 91

"Equilibrists, The," 88

"Eros Turannos," 61

"Essa on the Muel," 8–9

Essay on Rime, 99

Esther, 22–23, 24

Ethan Frome, 58

Euphemism, 9, 13

Evans, Mari, 95

Experimental drama, 66, 151–152, 155, 156

Experimental fiction, 64–65, 125–127, 129–130

Experimental poetry, 75, 82–83, 91–93, 106

Expressionism, 66, 151, 153, 155

"Exultation Is the Going," 2 n.1

Fable, A, 129

Farewell to Arms, A, 131, 133, 134

Farrell, James T., 46, 55, 116

Faulkner, William, 47, 64, 65, 69, 87, 117, 120, 121, 125, 127–131, 133, 136, 143, 148, 156, 165, 242–244

"Fenimore Cooper's Further Literary Offenses," 30 n.1

"Fenimore Cooper's Literary Offenses," 30 n.1

Ferlinghetti, Lawrence, 107

Fiedler, Leslie, 166, 167

"Figure a Poem Makes, The," 70

Financier, The, 53

Fine arts, 7, 30, 31, 33, 38–39, 95

"Firebombing, The," 106

Fitzgerald, F. Scott, 52, 64, 120, 121–124, 128, 129, 133, 136, 165, 239–241

"Flight," 138

"Flowering Judas," 120–121

Foerster, Norman, 162

Folklore, 29, 33, 34

Folktales, 15–17; Aarne-Thompson types, 16, 32; motifs, 16, 35

Following the Equator, 31 n.2

Fool's Errand, A, 22

"For a Dead Lady," 61

"For a Lamb," 97

Ford, Paul L., 22

Formalism. *See* New Criticism

"Formalist Critic, The," 163

"For the Last Wolverine," 106–107

"For the Union Dead," 102

For Whom the Bell Tolls, 132, 133

"Four for Sir John Davies," 98–99

Four Million, The, 21

Four Quartets, 84, 85, 86–87

Fox, John, Jr., 12

Frame story, 30, 31, 32, 33

Franklin, Benjamin, 9

Frederic, Harold, 23, 29, 36

Free Joe and Other Georgian Sketches, 17

"Free Joe and the Rest of the World," 17

Freeman, Mary E. Wilkins, 19–20, 191

Free verse, 59, 68, 71, 75, 80–81, 83, 93, 95–96, 99, 103, 106, 108–109, 111–112; in imagism, 78; in the New Poetry, 63

"Frescoes from the Past," 32

Freud, Sigmund, 44, 45, 46, 52, 60, 81, 98, 111, 123, 139, 153, 161, 164, 165, 166

Frost, Robert, 59, 60, 62, 67–70, 74, 77, 83, 105, 106, 214–215

Frye, Northrop, 167

Fugitive, The, 87

Fuller, Henry Blake, 22

"Further in Summer Than the Birds," 2 n.1

"Fury of Aerial Bombardment, The," 97

Garland, Hamlin, 22, 36, 46, 55–57, 206–207

George, Henry, 56

"George's Mother," 48

"Gerontion," 120

"Gift of the Magi, The," 21

Gilded Age, The, 32

Ginsberg, Allen, 64, 93, 99, 107–109, 112, 233

Glass Menagerie, The, 155, 156

Go Down, Moses, 131

"Golden Arm, The," 35

Golden Apples, The, 143

Golden Bowl, The, 41
"Good Man Is Hard to Find, A," 148–149
Gothicism, 65, 117, 148, 155–157
"Grandfather's Old Ram," 32
Grandissimes, The, 15
Grapes of Wrath, The, 51, 57, 138, 139, 140–141
"Grave, A," 83
Greater Inclination, The, 57
Great Gatsby, The, 122, 123, 124, 126
Great God Brown, The, 151, 152, 156
Green Hills of Africa, The, 131
Gross, Seymour L., 144
"Groundhog, The," 97

Hairy Ape, The, 66, 151, 152, 153
"Hamlet and His Problems," 84
Harper's Magazine, 11
Harris, George Washington, 22
Harris, Joel Chandler, 15–17, 189–190
Harte, Bret, 12–14, 188–189
Hawthorne, Nathaniel, 15
Hay, John, 11, 22, 24
Hayden, Robert, 64
Hazard of New Fortunes, A, 22
H. D. (Hilda Doolittle), 78
"He Ate and Drank the Precious Words," 2 n.1
"Heathen Chinee, The," 14
Heller, Joseph, 65
Hemingway, Ernest, 23, 47, 64, 69, 77, 87, 117, 118, 120, 121, 123, 129, 131–135, 136, 244–246
Henderson the Rain King, 145, 146–147
"He Preached upon 'Breadth' Till It Argued Him Narrow," 2 n.1
Herne, James A., 29
Herrick, Robert, 22
Herzog, 145, 147
Hicks, Granville, 165
"High-Toned Old Christian Woman, A," 74
Hills Beyond, The, 136, 137
"Hiltons' Holiday, The," 18
History of the United States of America

during the Administrations of Jefferson and Madison, 25
Honest John Vane, 23
Honorable Peter Stirling, The, 22
Hoosier Schoolmaster, The, 12
House of Mirth, The, 58
Howe, E. W., 29, 36
Howells, Willian Dean, 22, 23, 27, 28, 36–39, 50, 197–199
"How Happy Is the Little Stone," 2 n.1
Howl, 107
"How Many Times These Low Feet Staggered," 2 n.1
"How Mr. Rabbit Saved His Meat," 16 n.3
"How Mr. Rabbit Was Too Sharp for Mr. Fox," 16 n.3
"How to Tell a Story," 35
Hughes, Langston, 64, 65, 95–96, 103, 155, 228
Hughes, Ted, 109
Hugh Selwyn Mauberley, 79, 86
Hulme, T. E., 64, 78, 84, 162
Humble Romance and Other Stories, A, 19, 20 n.9
Humor, 3, 6–9, 12–14, 15–17, 18–19, 20, 29–36, 187–188
Hyperbole, 26

"I Cannot Live with You," 2 n.1
Iceman Cometh, The, 150, 152
"Idea of Order at Key West, The," 74
"I Died for Beauty—but Was Scarce," 2 n.1
Ideogram, 76, 77, 79
"I Dreaded That First Robin, So," 2 n.1
"I Felt a Funeral, in My Brain," 2 n.1
"If You Were Coming in the Fall," 2 n.1
"I Heard a Fly Buzz When I Died," 4
"I Know That He Exists," 2 n.1
"I Like a Look of Agony," 3–4
"I Like to See It Lap the Miles," 4
I'll Take My Stand, 87
"I'll Tell You How the Sun Rose," 2 n.1
Imagism, 67, 71, 75, 77–78, 79, 82
"Immortal Autumn," 90
"I'm Nobody! Who Are You?" 2 n.1

Impersonal poetry, 63, 84–85, 104
"In a Station of the Metro," 79
In Cold Blood, 53
"Indian Camp," 134
Indians, 7, 32
Indian Summer, 38–39
"In Distrust of Merits," 83
In Dubious Battle, 138
"I Never Lost as Much but Twice," 2 n.1
"I Never Saw a Moor," 5
In His Steps, 23
Initiation, 19, 31, 32, 33, 116, 131, 141
"in Just—," 92
Innocents Abroad, The, 30, 31
"Interview with President Lincoln," 7
In the Tennessee Mountains, 12
Invisible Man, 65, 142
Irony, 8, 19, 26, 33, 36, 38, 39
Irving, Washington, 12
"I Taste a Liquor Never Brewed," 3
"I've Seen a Dying Eye," 2 n.1
"I Want to Know Why," 116–117

James, Henry, 27, 28, 36, 39–44, 50, 52, 57, 58, 79, 114, 117, 119, 122, 123, 125, 128, 130, 132, 133, 146, 148, 159, 168, 199–201
James, William, 40, 139
Jarrell, Randall, 99, 100–101, 105, 230
J. B., 90
Jeffers, Robinson, 80–81, 83, 221–222
Jennie Gerhardt, 22, 51
Jewett, Sarah Orne, 18–19, 190–191
Jewish fiction, 145–146
"Jilting of Granny Weatherall, The," 121
Johnston, Richard Malcolm, 12
John Ward, Preacher, 23
"Jolly Corner, The," 43
Jones, Ernest, 165
Jones, Howard Mumford, 45, 46
Jones, LeRoi (Imamu Amiri Baraka), 64, 95, 103, 111–113, 234
Joyce, James, 44, 64, 75, 77, 121, 129, 136
Jung, C. G., 44, 98, 139, 166

Jungle, The, 22, 23
"Just Lost, When I Was Saved!" 2 n.1

Kaddish, 108–109
"Keela the Outcast Indian Maiden," 144–145
Kerouac, Jack, 99, 107, 108
Kerr, Orpheus C., 6
"Killers, The," 133
King, Clarence, 24
King, Grace, 12
King of Folly Island and Other People, The, 18 n.6
Kirkland, Joseph, 29
Krutch, Joseph Wood, 164

La Farge, John, 24
"Lady or the Tiger, The?" 29
Lanier, Sidney, 12, 23
"Last Night That She Lived, The," 2 n.1
Last Tycoon, The, 122
Lazarus Laughed, 152
Lesser, Simon O., 164
Letters from the Earth, 30
Lewis, R. W. B., 166
Lewis, Sinclair, 52, 55, 58, 59, 117–119, 141, 237–238
Life of Nancy, The, 18 n.6
Life on the Mississippi, 32–33
Light in August, 65, 129
Lincoln, Abraham, 36
Lindsay, Vachel, 72, 216
Literary Comedians, 6–9, 30, 187–188
"Livvie," 144
Local color, 10–21, 29–35, 54, 55, 58, 114–115, 188–191
Locke, David Ross, 6, 22
London, Jack, 20, 46, 50, 54, 118, 205–206
Long Day's Journey into Night, 150, 152, 154, 159
Look Homeward, Angel, 136, 137
Looking Backward, 23
"Lost Boy, The," 137
"Love Calls Us to the Things of This World," 105
Love poetry, 2, 5
"Love Song of J. Alfred Prufrock, The," 79, 84, 85–86, 93, 102

Lowell, Amy, 67, 214
Lowell, James Russell, 22
Lowell, Robert, 63, 64, 96, 101–102, 104, 109, 110, 230–231
"Luck of Roaring Camp, The," 12, 13
Lynn, Kenneth, 165

McCullers, Carson, 65, 148
MacLeish, Archibald, 63, 89–90, 163, 226
McTeague, 50–51
Maggie: A Girl of the Streets, 22, 47, 48, 49, 58
Mailer, Norman, 47, 64
Main Currents in American Thought, 165
Main Street, 118, 119
Main-Travelled Roads, 22, 56
Major, Charles, 29
Malamud, Bernard, 146
Malapropism, 6, 8
"Malcolm X," 104
"Man Against the Sky, The," 61
Manhattan Transfer, 125, 126, 127
"Man That Corrupted Hadleyburg, The," 35–36
Man Who Knew Coolidge, The, 118
Marco Millions, 151, 152
Marquand, J. P., 118, 123
Marx, Karl, 45, 46, 54, 126, 165
Masters, Edgar Lee, 55, 59, 95, 118, 208
Matthiessen, F. O., 41, 161, 165, 166
Medievalism, 24–25, 35
Melancholy, 4, 30
Melville, Herman, 41, 49, 73, 80, 81, 129, 130, 142, 150, 152, 156, 165
Mencken, H. L., 87, 141
"Mending Wall," 69
"Metaphysical Poets, The," 84
"Mill, The," 60
Millay, Edna St. Vincent, 90–91, 226
Miller, Arthur, 66, 119, 157–159, 257–258
Mills, Ralph J., Jr., 104
"Mind Is an Enchanting Thing, The," 83
Mingo and Other Sketches in Black and White, 17 n.5
Minister's Wooing, The, 11

"Miniver Cheevy," 60
Miss Lonelyhearts, 65
"Mrs. Ripley's Trip," 56
Miss Ravenel's Conversion, 23
"Miss Tempy's Watchers," 18
"Mr. Edwards and the Spider," 101–102
"Mr. Flood's Party," 60
Mr. Sammler's Planet, 145, 146
"Mr. Terrapin Shows His Strength," 16 n.3
"Mr. Wolf Makes a Failure," 16 n.3
Mitchell, S. Weir, 29
Moby-Dick, 102, 164, 167
Mock-heroic passages, 13, 32
Modern Instance, A, 37–38
Mont-Saint-Michel and Chartres, 25, 26
Moody, William Vaughn, 58–59, 208
"Moon and the Yew Tree, The," 110–111
"Moon in the Mill-Pond, The," 16 n.3
Moore, Marianne, 63, 64, 72, 77, 82–83, 222–223
More, Paul Elmer, 162
Mourning Becomes Electra, 150, 151
"Much Madness Is Divinest Sense," 2 n.1
Murder in the Cathedral, 84, 86
Murfree, Mary N., 12
Murray, Henry, 164
My Ántonia, 115
"My Life Closed Twice before Its Close," 5
Mysterious Stranger, The, 36
Myth: criticism, 166–167; drama, 151, 159; fiction, 139, 143; poetry, 75–76, 81, 84, 94; in Uncle Remus, 17
Myth-Archetype Criticism, 143, 161, 163, 166–167, 260

"Narrow Fellow in the Grass, A," 4–5
Nasby, Petroleum Vesuvius, 6, 22
Nationalism, 11
Native of Winby and Other Tales, A, 18 n.6
Native Son, 53, 141, 142
Naturalism, 35, 36, 45–46, 47–58 passim, 81, 116, 123, 201–202

Nature, 2, 3, 4, 5, 31
Necessary Angel, The, 74
Negroes, 11, 14, 34. *See also* Slavery
"Neighbor Rosicky," 115
New Criticism, 87, 88, 90, 128, 161, 162–163, 259
Newell, Robert H., 6
"New England Nun, A," 20
New England Nun and Other Stories, A, 20 nn.9 and 10
New Humanism, 161, 162, 168, 259
New Poetry, 59, 60, 63, 68
Nick Adams stories, 120, 133–134
Night of the Iguana, The, 156
Noon Wine, 120, 121
"No Place for You, My Love," 144
Norris, Frank, 22, 36, 46, 50–51, 54, 55, 203–204
"Not with a Club, the Heart Is Broken," 2 n.1
"Novel Démeublé, The," 114
Nye, Edgar W. (pseud. Bill Nye), 6

Objective correlative, 63, 84, 85, 90
"Occurrence at Owl Creek Bridge, An," 29
O'Connor, Flannery, 65, 143, 147–149, 252–253
Octopus, The, 22, 50, 51
Odets, Clifford, 158
"Of All the Souls That Stand Create," 2 n.1
"Of Modern Poetry," 74
Of Time and the River, 136
O. Henry (pseud. William Sydney Porter), 21
Old Chester Tales, 11
Old Creole Days, 14
Old Man and the Sea, The, 132, 133, 134–135
"Old Man's Winter Night, An," 69
"Old Mr. Marblehall," 144
"Old Mortality," 120
"Old Times on the Mississippi," 33
Oldtown Folks, 11
O'Neill, Eugene, 46, 62, 66, 150–154, 156, 157, 158, 165, 253–255
"Only Rose, The," 18

Onomatopoeia, 4, 17
"On the Walpole Road," 20
"Open Boat, The," 48, 49–50, 167
Opus Posthumous, 74
"Outcasts of Poker Flat, The," 13

Page, Thomas Nelson, 12, 22
"Pain—Has an Element of Blank," 2 n.1
Pale Horse, Pale Rider, 120, 121
Paradox, 26
Parrington, V. L., 165
"Passing of Sister Barsett, The," 18
"Past Is the Present, The," 82
Pastures of Heaven, The, 139, 140
Paterson, 76–77, 78
"Patterns," 67
Pearl of Orr's Island, The, 11, 18
Pembroke, 20
People, Yes, The, 71
"Performance, The," 106
Personal poetry, 64, 84, 96, 98, 99, 102, 106, 108, 109–110
Personal Recollections of Joan of Arc, 31 n.2
Personification, 4
"Peter Quince at the Clavier," 74
"Petrified Man," 144
Phoenix, John, 6
Piatt, John James, 36
Pierre, 164
Pike County Ballads, 11
Pit, The, 22, 50
"Place in Fiction," 143
"Plain Language from Truthful James," 14
Plantation tradition, 17
Plath, Sylvia, 64, 109–111, 233–234
Playing the Mischief, 24
"Plea for Romantic Fiction, A," 50
Poe, Edgar Allan, 43, 72, 164
"Poem for Black Hearts, A," 112–113
Poems of Two Friends, 36
"Poetry," 83
Poetry and the Age, 100
"Poet Turns on Himself, The," 106
Poganuc People, 11
Ponder Heart, The, 144

Point of view, 26, 34, 49, 57, 64; Faulkner, 129; in James, 40–41

Porter, Katherine Anne, 64, 119–121, 133, 238–239

Porter, William Sydney, 21

"Portrait d'une Femme," 79

Portrait of a Lady, The, 41, 57

Pound, Ezra, 59, 60, 63, 67, 68, 75, 76, 77–80, 82, 83, 89, 90, 92, 93, 94, 95, 96, 99, 101, 102, 106, 129, 142, 161, 163, 219–221

Prairie Folks, 56

"Prayers of Steel," 71

Price, The, 157, 158

Primitivism, 7, 18–19

Prince and the Pauper, The, 31 n.2

Princess Casamassima, The, 40

Prophet of the Great Smoky Mountains, The, 12

Psychoanalytical Criticism, 161, 163, 164, 259–260

Psychology, 2, 4, 5, 16, 29, 37

Pudd'nhead Wilson, 35

Puns, 5. *See also* Wordplay

"Pupil, The," 43

"Quaker Graveyard in Nantucket, The," 102

"Queen-Ann's Lace," 76

Queen's Twin and Other Stories, The, 18 n.6

Ransom, John Crowe, 63, 87–89, 101, 225–226

Realism: drama, 66, 151–153, 155, 158, 159–160; in humor, 7; later fiction, 64, 119–120, 122–123, 128, 132–133, 138, 144, 146, 148; local color, 10, 15, 16, 17, 20; Twain, Howells, and James, 27–44

"Real Thing, The," 42

Red Badge of Courage, The, 47, 48, 49

"Red Leaves," 129

Red Pony, The, 141

Red Rock, 22

"Red Wheelbarrow, The," 75

Regionalism, 56, 58, 69, 114–115; in southern fiction, 65, 120, 128–131, 143–144, 148–149. *See also* Local color

Religion, 22–23, 29

Revolt from the village, 59, 117, 118–119

"Revolt of Mother, The," 20

Rhyme, 3, 4

Rice, Elmer, 65, 154–155, 158, 255–256

"Richard Cory," 60

Richards, I. A., 163

"Rich Boy, The," 122

Riddle, 4, 5

Riley, James Whitcomb, 11, 12

Rise of Silas Lapham, The, 38

"River-Merchant's Wife: A Letter, The," 79

"Road Not Taken, The," 70

"Roan Stallion," 81

Robber Bridegroom, The, 143, 144

Robinson, Edwin Arlington, 59–61, 68, 105, 208–209

Robinson, Rowland E., 11

Roderick Hudson, 41

Rodman the Keeper, 12

Roethke, Theodore, 64, 97–99, 104, 106, 109, 110, 229

Romanticism, 10, 15; criticism, 162; drama, 152, 153; later fiction, 122–123, 132, 136, 138–140; poetry, 73, 75, 84, 91, 96–97, 98, 104, 107, 109–110; versus realism, 27–29; in Twain, Howells, 30, 33, 36–37, 38

"Romanticism and Classicism," 162

"Rose for Emily, A," 129

Roth, Philip, 64, 146

Roughing It, 31–32

"Route of Evanescence, A," 5

Roxy, 12

Russell, Irwin, 11

"Safe in Their Alabaster Chambers," 2 n.1

Sam Lawson's Oldtown Fireside Stories, 11

Sandbox, The, 159

Sandburg, Carl, 70–71, 93, 95, 126, 215–216

Santayana, George, 84

Sartoris, 129

Satire, 13, 14–15, 23–26, 29–36

Schorer, Mark, 163

Science, 24–26

Scott, (Sir) Walter, 28, 33

Scribner's Monthly, 11

"Sculptor's Funeral, The," 115

Sea of Cortez, The, 139, 140

Sea-Wolf, The, 54

Seize the Day, 146

Shapiro, Karl, 64, 93, 99–100, 101, 106, 112, 161, 229–230

Shaw, Henry Wheeler, 8–9, 188

Sheldon, Charles M., 23

Shillaber, Benjamin P., 32

"Shine, Perishing Republic," 81

Ship of Fools, 119, 120

"Short Happy Life of Francis Macomber, The," 132

Sinclair, Upton, 22, 23, 52, 55

Sister Carrie, 22, 50, 51, 52–53

Skin of Our Teeth, The, 156

"Skunk Hour," 102

Slavery, 15–17, 33–34, 35

"Sleepers, The," 63

Small town, 29. *See also* Revolt from the village

Smith, Charles Henry, 6, 22

Smith, (Captain) John, 24

Smith, Seba, 7

"Snake, The," 138

Snodgrass, W. D., 64

"Snows of Kilimanjaro, The," 132, 133

Snyder, Gary, 64

Social critics, 22–26

Social protest, discussion of: S. Anderson, 116; Cummings, 91; Dos Passos, 126–127; Garland, 56–57; Ginsberg, 107; Lewis, 118; Millay, 90–91; Steinbeck, 138–141; Wharton, 57–58; Wright, 142

"Society upon the Stanislaus, The," 13

"Some Keep the Sabbath Going to Church," 2 n.1

"somewhere i have never travelled," 92

"Song for a Dark Girl," 96

"Song of Myself," 63

Son of the Middle Border, A, 56

"Soul Selects Her Own Society, The," 4

Sound and the Fury, The, 64, 128, 129, 130, 131

Spears, M. K., 94

Spirit of the Times, The, 11

Spoon River Anthology, 59

"Spring and All," 76

Staples, Hugh B., 102

"Steeple-Jack, The," 83

Stein, Gertrude, 116, 133

Steinbeck, John, 46, 51, 55, 58, 116, 126, 138–141, 248–250

Stevens, Wallace, 63, 64, 72–74, 75, 217–218

Stevenson, Robert Louis, 40, 50, 64, 125

"Still, Citizen Sparrow," 105

"Still Moment, A," 144

Stockton, Frank, 29

Stoic, The, 53

"Stopping by Woods on a Snowy Evening," 70

Story of a Country Town, The, 29

"Story of a Novel, The," 135, 137

"Story of the Deluge, The," 16 n.3, 17

Stowe, Harriet Beecher, 11, 18

Strange Interlude, 151, 152

Street Scene, 155

Styron, William, 47, 65

Suddenly Last Summer, 156

Summer, 57

Summer and Smoke, 156

Sun Also Rises, The, 86, 131, 134

"Sunday Morning," 70, 74

"Sunflower Sutra," 108

"Sweeney Among the Nightingales," 86

Sweet Bird of Youth, 156

Sweet Thursday, 139

Symbolism: in Adams, 26; criticism, 164; fiction, 120, 123–124, 128, 133; poetry, 70, 73, 76, 78, 86, 94

Synesthesia, 4

Tales of New England, 18

Tall tale, 31, 32, 33

Tate, Allen, 87, 94, 161, 163

"Technique as Discovery," 163

Tendencies in Modern American Poetry, 67

Tender Is the Night, 122

"Tennessee's Partner," 13

"Test, The," 113

"That Evening Sun," 129

"There Came a Day at Summer's Full," 2 n.1

"There's a Certain Slant of Light," 4

"These Are the Days When Birds Come Back," 2 n.1

"Thirteen Ways of Looking at a Blackbird," 74

"This Is My Letter to the World," 4

This Side of Paradise, 121

"This Was a Poet," 2 n.1

Thoreau, Henry David, 91, 147, 151, 165

Those Extraordinary Twins, 31 n.2

"Thought Went up My Mind Today, A," 2 n.1

Three Soldiers, 125

Through the Eye of the Needle, 23, 39

Tiny Alice, 160

Titan, The, 53

"'Tite Poulette," 14

To a God Unknown, 140

"To Build a Fire," 54

"To Fight Aloud, Is Very Brave," 2 n.1

"To Hear an Oriole Sing," 2 n.1

Tolstoy, Leo, 37

"To Make a Prairie It Takes a Clover and One Bee," 2 n.1

Tom Sawyer Abroad, 31 n.2

Tom Sawyer, Detective, 31 n.2

Tortilla Flat, 138, 139

Tourgée, Albion W., 22

"Tract," 76

"Tradition and the Individual Talent," 62, 84

Tramp Abroad, A, 31 n.2, 32

Traveler from Altruria, A, 39

Travels with Charley, 138, 140

Travel writing, 31

Tricksters, 16–17, 33–34, 35

Trilling, Lionel, 161, 165

Turn of the Screw, The, 42–43, 164

Twain, Mark. *See* Clemens, Samuel Langhorne

Uncle Remus, His Songs and Sayings, 17 n.4

Uncle Remus tales, 15–17

Uncle Tom's Children, 141

"Undefeated, The," 133

Understanding Poetry, 163

Understatement, 8, 26, 30

"Under the Lion's Paw," 56–57

"Unfinished Story, An," 21

Unpromising hero, 31, 33

Unvanquished, The, 131

U. S. A., 65, 125, 126, 127, 140

Utopias, 23, 39

Varieties of Religious Experience, 139

"Village Singer, A," 20 n.10

Violent Bear It Away, The, 65, 147, 149

Virginian, The, 12

Vonnegut, Kurt, 64

"Voyages II," 94

Waggoner, Hyatt, 74

Wallace, Lew, 29

War, 23–24, 39, 49, 62, 91, 99–102, 106, 125–127, 131–134

Ward, Artemus, 7–8, 187–188

Warren, Robert Penn, 64, 65, 87, 88, 163

"Was," 129

Waste Land, The, 78, 79, 84, 85, 86, 89, 93, 94, 130, 133

"Way I Read a Letter's—This, The," 2 n.1

Web and the Rock, The, 136

Welty, Eudora, 65, 143–145, 148, 251

West, Nathanael, 65, 148

West, Ray B., 120

Wharton, Edith, 55, 57–58, 207–208

"What Are Years?" 83

What Is Man? 31 n.2

"What Soft—Cherubic Creatures," 2 n.1

When Knighthood Was in Flower, 29

White Fang, 54

"White Heron, The," 19

White Heron and Other Stories, A, 18 n.6, 19 n.7

Whitlock, Brand, 36

Whitman, Walt, 56, 59, 63, 70, 71, 72, 75,

80, 81, 83, 93, 94, 98, 99, 106, 107, 108, 109, 112, 127, 136, 138, 142, 165

Who's Afraid of Virginia Woolf? 154, 159

"Why I Live at the P. O.," 144

"Why the Alligator's Back Is Rough," 17

"Wide Net, The," 144

Wife of His Youth and Other Stories of the Color Line, The, 12

Wilbur, Richard, 101, 104–105, 232

Wilder, Thornton, 156

"Wild Nights—Wild Nights!" 2 n.1

Williams, Tennessee, 47, 66, 155–157, 158, 256–257

Williams, William Carlos, 59, 63, 68, 72, 74–77, 78, 79, 82, 83, 90, 110, 151, 218–219

Wilson, Edmund, 161, 164

Winesburg, Ohio, 59, 116, 117

Wings of the Dove, The, 41

"Winter Dreams," 122, 123–124

Winters, Yvor, 75, 94, 163

Wise Blood, 147

Wister, Owen, 12

With the Procession, 22

Wolfe, Thomas, 135–137, 246–248

"Woman at the Washington Zoo, The," 101

"Wonderful Tar-Baby Story, The," 16, 17

Woolson, Constance Fenimore, 12

Wordplay, 8

Wordsworth, William, 73, 74, 75, 97, 98, 136

"Worn Path, A," 143, 144, 145

Wright, James, 64, 95

Wright, Richard, 53, 65, 141–143, 250–251

"Yachts, The," 76

Yage Letters, The, 107

Yeats, William Butler, 78, 98

"You, Andrew Marvell," 90

You Can't Go Home Again, 136

Zola, Émile, 27–28, 29, 45, 46, 50, 52, 55, 125, 162

Zoo Story, The, 111, 159

Zury, the Meanest Man in Spring County, 29